Pa[...]

Books for cooks.

Pied à Terre - Charlotte St

quirinale , gt Peter St

Richard Corrigan - Romilly St

Inter Cuti - Randall

goring

ZAGAT®

London
Restaurants
2008

LOCAL EDITORS AND COORDINATORS
Sholto Douglas-Home and Susan Kessler
STAFF EDITOR
Troy Segal

Published and distributed by
Zagat Survey, LLC
4 Columbus Circle
New York, NY 10019
T: 212.977.6000
E: london@zagat.com
www.zagat.com

ACKNOWLEDGMENTS

We thank Deborah Bennett,
Karen Bonham, Caroline Clegg,
Claire Coleman, Ricki Conway,
Alex, Louis and Tallula Douglas-
Home, Victoria Elmacioglu,
Rosanne Johnston, Larry Kessler,
Le Cordon Bleu (London), Pamela
and Michael Lester, Leuka 2000,
Margaret Levin, Anne Semmes,
Alexandra Spezzotti, Peter Vogl,
Susan and Jeffrey Weingarten, as
well as the following members of
our staff: Chris Miragliotta
(editorial project manager),
Caitlin Eichelberger (editorial
assistant), Brian Albert, Sean
Beachell, Maryanne Bertollo,
Sandy Cheng, Reni Chin, Larry
Cohn, Alison Flick, Jeff Freier,
Caroline Hatchett, Roy Jacob,
Natalie Lebert, Mike Liao, Dave
Makulec, Rachel McConlogue,
Andre Pilette, Becky Ruthenburg,
Kilolo Strobert, Donna Marino
Wilkins, Sharon Yates
and Kyle Zolner.

Contents

Ratings & Symbols

Zagat Top Spot	Name	Symbols	Cuisine	Zagat Ratings			
				FOOD	DECOR	SERVICE	COST

Area, Address & Contact*

☒ **Tim & Nina's** ◗ *British*

	▽ 23	5	9	£9

Covent Garden | Exeter St., WC2 (Covent Garden) | 020-7123 4567 | www.zagat.com

Review, surveyor comments in quotes

Open seven days a week, 24 hours a day (some say that's "168 hours too many"), this "chaotic" Covent Garden dive serving "cheap, no-nonsense" fish 'n' chips is "ideal" for a "quick grease fix"; no one's impressed by the "tired, tatty decor" or "patchy service", but judging from its "perpetual queues", the "no-frills" food and prices are "spot-on."

Ratings

Food, Decor and **Service** are rated on a scale of 0 to 30.

0 – 9	poor to fair
10 – 15	fair to good
16 – 19	good to very good
20 – 25	very good to excellent
26 – 30	extraordinary to perfection
▽	low response	less reliable

Cost reflects our surveyors' average estimate of the price of a dinner with one drink and service and is a benchmark only. Lunch is usually 25% less.

For **newcomers** or survey **write-ins** listed without ratings, the price range is indicated as follows:

I	£20 and below
M	£21 to £35
E	£36 to £50
VE	£51 or more

Symbols

☒	Zagat Top Spot (highest ratings, popularity and importance)
◗	serves after 11 PM
⑤	closed on Sunday
Ⓜ	closed on Monday
⊄	no credit cards accepted

Maps

Index maps show restaurants with the highest Food ratings in those areas.

---

* From outside the U.K., dial international code (e.g. 011 from the U.S.) +44, then omit first zero of the listed number.

subscribe to zagat.com

About This Survey

Here are the results of our **2008 London Restaurants Survey,** covering 1,119 establishments in the city as well as favourites outside the metropolitan area. Like all our guides, it's based on the collective opinions of thousands of savvy local consumers.

WHO PARTICIPATED: Input from 5,336 avid diners forms the basis for the ratings and reviews in this guide (their comments are shown in quotation marks within the reviews). Of these surveyors, 39% are women, 61% men; the breakdown by age is 10% in their 20s; 28%, 30s; 23%, 40s; 20%, 50s; and 19%, 60s or above. Collectively they bring roughly 705,000 annual meals worth of experience to this Survey. We sincerely thank each of these participants – this book is really "theirs."

HELPFUL LISTS: Whether you're looking for a celebratory meal, a hot scene or a bargain bite, our lists can help you find exactly the right place. See Most Popular (page 7), Key Newcomers (page 9), Top Ratings (pages 10–16), Best Buys (page 17) and Set-Price Bargains (page 18). We've also provided 37 handy indexes.

OUR LOCAL TEAM: Special thanks go to our local editors and coordinators, who have been with this guide since its first edition in 1996: Susan Kessler, cookbook author and consultant for numerous lifestyle publications in the U.K. and U.S., and Sholto Douglas-Home, a London restaurant critic for over 15 years and an international marketing executive.

ABOUT ZAGAT: This marks our 28th year reporting on the shared experiences of consumers like you. What started in 1979 as a hobby involving 200 of our friends has come a long way. Today we have over 300,000 surveyors and now cover dining, entertaining, golf, hotels, movies, music, nightlife, resorts, shopping, spas, theatre and tourist attractions worldwide.

SHARE YOUR OPINION: We invite you to join any of our upcoming surveys – just register at **zagat.com,** where you can rate and review establishments year-round. Each participant will receive a free copy of the resulting guide when published.

AVAILABILITY: Zagat guides are available in all major bookstores, by subscription at **zagat.com** and for use on a wide range of mobile devices via **Zagat To Go.**

FEEDBACK: There is always room for improvement, thus we invite your comments and suggestions about any aspect of the guide's performance. Just contact us at london@zagat.com.

New York, NY
12 September, 2007

Nina and Tim Zagat

What's New

 Not only is the London restaurant scene in robust health these days – it is literally more healthy. The British government banned smoking in restaurants and other public spaces this past summer (a policy endorsed by 93% of surveyors), and close to one in three respondents say that they will now eat out more than before – understandable, as smoke fumes ranked on last year's Survey as the second greatest irritant in London eateries. Alas, no legislation seems to be pending against poor service, cited by 53% as the factor they dislike most about dining out.

ORGANIC ORIGINS: Paralleling the growth of organic sections in supermarkets, more and more restaurants are trumpeting their use of sustainably raised or hormone-free ingredients – including British newcomers like the boisterous Bumpkin and the earthy Butcher & Grill. Others, like Acorn House and Stanza, make a point of using regionally grown produce. But whilst 54% of surveyors say they're willing to pay more for organic fare, nearly one in five doubt the veracity of provenance claims – which may be why Tom's Kitchen, the latest from chef Tom Aikens, showcases its suppliers with biographical leaflets and photographs on the walls.

CHANGING OF THE GUARD: This past spring, omnipresent restaurateur Sir Terence Conran spun off his stable of eateries into a new company, D&D London, and already the firm has refreshed some ageing hipsters, like Bluebird in Chelsea, and opened new ones, such as South Bank's swank Skylon. Meanwhile, the well-manicured eyebrows of Mayfair rose at the summer announcement that Mark Birley, king of the private clubs (e.g. Annabel's, Harry's Bar), had sold his empire to Richard Caring, owner of such dining icons as The Ivy and Le Caprice.

RULE EUROPA: Although Asian fare is always hot, Londoners currently are embracing the European: nearly half of surveyors cite the latter as their cuisine of choice (the specific top two are Italian with 24%, followed by French with 18%). A variety of arrivals is responding to the call, such as St. Alban, which offers a culinary tour of the Continent from east to west, and Trinity, which paints quirky regional touches across a Modern European canvas.

THE LUSH LIFE: Other cities may be seeing an onset of less-formal dining, but – assuming money were no object – most surveyors (35%) would prefer to dine in a haute cuisine restaurant, over a bistro (26%), gastropub (7%) or other casual option (11%). That may explain why the average cost of a meal went up nearly 3% to £39 over last year, and why 74% of surveyors say they're spending more than they did back in 2005. Even so, 80% are eating out as much as or more often than they did two years ago – London's tables are too tempting to resist.

London
12 September, 2007

Sholto Douglas-Home

Most Popular

Each surveyor has been asked to name his or her five favourite places. This list reflects their choices, which are also plotted on the map at the back of the book.

1. Wagamama
2. Nobu London
3. Ivy, The
4. Gordon Ramsay/68 Royal
5. J. Sheekey
6. Wolseley, The
7. Gordon Ramsay/Claridge's
8. Le Gavroche
9. Rules
10. Zuma
11. Hakkasan
12. Square, The
13. Gaucho Grill
14. Zafferano
15. Le Caprice
16. Pétrus
17. Amaya
18. Yauatcha
19. Pizza Express
20. Tamarind
21. Locanda Locatelli
22. Asia de Cuba
23. Le Manoir/Quat Saisons
24. Savoy Grill*
25. Belgo
26. Chez Bruce
27. Capital Rest.
28. Fat Duck
29. Royal China
30. L'Atelier/Robuchon
31. River Café
32. Busaba Eathai
33. Maze
34. Cinnamon Club
35. Carluccio's
36. Nobu Berkeley St
37. Galvin Bistrot
38. Cipriani
39. Bibendum
40. St. John

It's obvious that many of the above restaurants are among the London area's most expensive, but if popularity were calibrated to price, we suspect that a number of other restaurants would join the above ranks. Given the fact that both our surveyors and readers love to discover dining bargains, we have added a list of 80 Best Buys on page 17. These are restaurants that give real quality at extremely reasonable prices.

* Indicates a tie with restaurant above

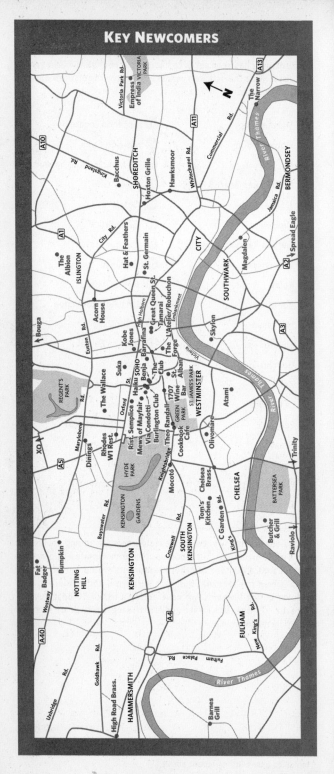

Key Newcomers

There's always a new flavour of the month on London's busy restaurant scene. Below is our take on some of the past year's most notable arrivals. (For a complete list of Additions, see page 203.)

Acorn House	Hoxton Grille
Albion, The	Kobe Jones
Atami	L'Atelier/Robuchon
Bacchus	Magdalen
Barnes Grill	Mews of Mayfair
Barrafina	Mocotó
Benja	Narrow, The
Bouga	Olivomare
Bumpkin	Raviolo
Burlington Club	Rhodes W1 Rest.
Butcher & Grill	Rist. Semplice
C Garden	1707 Wine Bar
Chelsea Brass.	Skylon
Club, The	Spread Eagle
Cookbook Cafe	St. Alban
Dinings	St. Germain
Empress of India	Suka
Fat Badger	Tamarai
Forge, The	Theo Randall
Great Queen St.	Tom's Kitchen
Haiku	Trinity
Hat & Feathers	Via Condotti
Hawksmoor	Wallace, The
High Road Brass.	XO

At publication time, several places with illustrious pedigrees were pending in Mayfair: **La Petite Maison,** a Nice import from one of Zuma's principals, and **Wild Honey,** a spin-off of super-hot Arbutus. Later on, lauded Shropshire destination **Hibiscus** is relocating to smart Mayfair digs; the Greyhound team unveils **The Rosendale,** a Dulwich gastropub; and Levant's Tony Kitous dishes up another North African experience with **Kenza** in the City. The bandwagon of Big-Name ventures rolls on: the peripatetic Gordon Ramsay is planning more pubs, along with a separate grill for his Maze in Mayfair; Tom Aikens opens seafooder **Tom's Place** in Chelsea; and Rowley Leigh debuts **Le Café des Anglais** in the Whiteleys shopping centre. There are hot happenings in hotels too: chef extraordinaire Alain Ducasse's fine-dining restaurant for The Dorchester and Richard Corrigan's eatery, earmarked for a spring 2008 arrival in the revamped Grosvenor House.

Top Food Ratings

Ratings are to the left of names. Lists exclude places with low votes.

28 Chez Bruce
   Gordon Ramsay/68 Royal
   Hunan
   Le Manoir/Quat Saisons
   Square, The
   Pétrus
   Pied à Terre

27 La Trompette
   Le Gavroche
   River Café
   Fat Duck
   Nobu London
   Capital Rest.
   Morgan M*
   Waterside Inn
   Enoteca Turi
   Defune
   Rasoi Vineet Bhatia*

26 L'Atelier/Robuchon
   Roussillon

Zuma
Theo Randall
Assaggi
Miyama
Foliage
Café Japan
Club Gascon
Mosimann's (club)
Nobu Berkeley St
Umu
Tom Aikens
Jin Kichi
Aubergine
Zafferano
Nahm

25 Gordon Ramsay/Claridge's
   Quirinale
   Clarke's
   Quilon

BY CUISINE

AMERICAN
23 Sophie's Steak
20 Lucky 7
19 Eagle Bar Diner
   Christopher's
18 Bodeans

ASIAN
23 Eight Over Eight
22 e&o
   Asia de Cuba
   Great Eastern
21 Cocoon

BRITISH (MODERN)
28 Chez Bruce
25 Clarke's
   St. John
24 Glasshouse, The
   Graveye Manor

BRITISH (TRAD.)
24 ffiona's
   Wilton's
   Dorchester/The Grill
   Bentley's
   Mark's Club (club)

CHINESE
28 Hunan
25 Yauatcha
   Kai Mayfair
24 Hakkasan
   Royal China Club

CHOPHOUSES
24 Rib Room
23 Rules
   Sophie's Steak
22 Gaucho Grill
   Guinea Grill

ECLECTIC
26 Mosimann's (club)
24 Lanes
22 Michael Moore
   Banquette
   Providores, The

EUROPEAN (MODERN)
27 La Trompette
   Fat Duck
26 Foliage
25 Gordon Ramsay/Claridge's
24 Arbutus

FISH 'N' CHIPS

24	Two Brothers Fish
	Sweetings
23	North Sea
20	Seashell
18	Livebait

FRENCH (BISTRO)

24	Galvin Bistrot
23	Le Café du Marché
22	Racine
	Bibendum Oyster
	La Poule au Pot

FRENCH (CLASSIC)

27	Le Gavroche
	Waterside Inn
24	L'Oranger
23	French Horn
22	Oslo Court

FRENCH (NEW)

28	Gordon Ramsay/68 Royal
	Le Manoir/Quat Saisons
	Square, The
	Pétrus
	Pied à Terre

INDIAN

27	Rasoi Vineet Bhatia
25	Quilon
	Amaya
	Tamarind
	Zaika

ITALIAN

27	River Café
	Enoteca Turi
26	Theo Randall
	Assaggi
	Zafferano

JAPANESE

27	Nobu London
	Defune
26	Zuma
	Miyama
	Café Japan

LEBANESE

24	Ishbilia
22	Al Waha
	Al Hamra
	Fairuz
	Al Sultan

MEDITERRANEAN

25	Moro
24	Ottolenghi
23	Fifteen
22	Pescatori
21	Eagle, The

PIZZA

24	Osteria Basilico
23	Delfino
	Il Bordello*
	Buona Sera
	Oliveto

SEAFOOD

25	J. Sheekey
24	Wilton's
	Bentley's
	Sweetings
23	Le Suquet

SPANISH

24	Cambio de Tercio
23	El Pirata
	Fino
22	Tapas Brindisa
	Salt Yard

THAI

26	Nahm
23	Patara
22	Churchill Arms
21	Busaba Eathai
	Crazy Bear

VEGETARIAN

27	Morgan M
26	Roussillon
25	Gate, The
24	Food for Thought
	Rasa

BY SPECIAL FEATURE

BREAKFAST
(other than hotels)

24	Cinnamon Club
23	Ladurée
21	Cecconi's
	Wolseley, The
20	Aubaine

BRUNCH

25	Clarke's
24	Le Caprice
22	Lundum's
	Providores, The
19	Tom's Kitchen

BUSINESS LUNCH

- 28 Square, The
- 27 Le Gavroche
- 25 Greenhouse, The
- 24 Cinnamon Club
- 21 St. Alban

CHEESE BOARDS

- 28 Chez Bruce
  Gordon Ramsay/68 Royal
  Square, The
  Pétrus
- 26 Tom Aikens

CHILD-FRIENDLY

- 27 River Café
- 26 Zuma
- 21 La Famiglia
- 20 Aubaine
  San Lorenzo

COMMUNAL TABLES

- 24 La Fromagerie
  Ottolenghi
  Food for Thought
- 22 Baker & Spice
- 21 Busaba Eathai

EXPERIMENTAL

- 27 Fat Duck
- 25 Locanda Locatelli
- 24 Books for Cooks
- 21 Sketch/Lecture Rm.
  Archipelago

GASTROPUBS

- 24 Anchor & Hope
- 23 Anglesea Arms
- 22 Churchill Arms
  Pig's Ear
- 21 Cow Dining Rm.

HOTEL DINING

- 28 Le Manoir/Quat Saisons
  Pétrus
    (The Berkeley)
- 27 Nobu London
    (Metropolitan Hotel)
  Capital, The
  Waterside Inn

IN-STORE EATING

- 24 Books for Cooks
- 20 Fifth Floor
- 19 Nicole's
- 17 Carluccio's
  202

LATE NIGHT

- 26 L'Atelier/Robuchon
- 25 Roka
- 24 Hakkasan
- 23 Ivy, The
- 21 Cecconi's

MEET FOR A DRINK

- 26 Zuma
  L'Atelier/Robuchon
  Nobu Berkeley St
- 25 Moro
- 24 Hakkasan

NEWCOMERS (RATED)

- 26 L'Atelier/Robuchon
  Theo Randall
- 22 Mews of Mayfair
- 21 St. Alban
  Bacchus

OLDE ENGLAND

- 24 Wilton's (1742)
  Savoy Grill (1889)
  Sweetings (1889)
- 23 Hind's Head (1690)
  Ritz (1906)

OUTDOOR

- 27 River Café
- 25 Ledbury, The
- 22 Santini
  La Poule au Pot
  Le Pont de la Tour

PEOPLE-WATCHING

- 27 Nobu London
- 26 Zuma
- 25 Maze
- 21 Wolseley, The
- 20 Cipriani

PRIVATE CLUBS

- 26 Mosimann's
- 24 Harry's Bar
  Morton's
  Mark's Club
- 22 Annabel's

PRIVATE ROOMS

- 28 Square, The
  Pétrus
- 26 Zafferano
- 25 Amaya
- 21 China Tang

ROOM WITH A VIEW

- 27 Waterside Inn
- 26 Foliage
- 24 Ubon
- 23 Rhodes 24
- 22 Le Pont de la Tour

SMALL PLATES

- 28 Hunan
- 26 Club Gascon
- 25 Amaya
-    Maze
- 24 Le Cercle

SUNDAY LUNCH/ COUNTRY

- 28 Le Manoir/Quat Saisons
- 27 Waterside Inn
- 24 Gravetye Manor
-    Vineyard/Stockcross
- 23 Hind's Head

SUNDAY LUNCH/ TOWN

- 28 Chez Bruce
- 27 River Café
- 25 Yauatcha
-    Orrery
- 22 Racine

TASTING MENU

- 28 Gordon Ramsay/68 Royal Square, The
- 27 Fat Duck
- 26 Zuma
-    Tom Aikens

TEA SERVICE
(other than hotels)

- 25 Yauatcha
- 24 La Fromagerie
- 23 Ladurée
- 21 Wolseley, The
- 20 Aubaine

THEATRELAND

- 26 L'Atelier/Robuchon
- 25 J. Sheekey
- 23 Richard Corrigan
-    Ivy, The
- 21 St. Alban

WINNING WINE LISTS

- 28 Gordon Ramsay/68 Royal Square, The
-    Pétrus
- 26 Tom Aikens
- 25 Greenhouse, The

BY LOCATION

BELGRAVIA

- 28 Pétrus
- 26 Mosimann's (club)
-    Zafferano
-    Nahm
- 25 Amaya

BLOOMSBURY/ FITZROVIA

- 28 Pied à Terre
- 25 Latium
-    Roka
- 24 Hakkasan
-    Rasa

CANARY WHARF

- 24 Quadrato
-    Ubon
-    Royal China
- 22 Gaucho Grill
- 20 Moshi Moshi

CHELSEA

- 28 Gordon Ramsay/68 Royal
- 27 Rasoi Vineet Bhatia
- 26 Tom Aikens
-    Aubergine
- 25 Ziani

CHISWICK

- 27 La Trompette
- 21 Gourmet Burger
- 20 Sam's Brass.
-    High Road Brass.
-    FishWorks

CITY

- 25 Haz
- 24 Sweetings
- 23 Rhodes 24
-    Vivat Bacchus
-    Café Spice Namasté

CLERKENWELL

- 25 Moro
- 21 Eagle, The
- 19 Fish Shop
-    La Porchetta
- 18 Strada

COVENT GARDEN

- 26 L'Atelier/Robuchon
- 25 J. Sheekey
- 24 Food for Thought
- Savoy Grill
- Clos Maggiore

HAMPSTEAD

- 26 Jin Kichi
- 22 Gaucho Grill
- 21 Gourmet Burger
- 20 Artigiano
- Good Earth

ISLINGTON

- 27 Morgan M
- 24 Ottolenghi
- Rasa
- 22 Upper Glas
- 20 Duke of Cambridge

KENSINGTON

- 25 Clarke's
- Zaika
- 24 ffiona's
- Locanda Ottoemezzo
- 22 Koi

KNIGHTSBRIDGE

- 27 Capital Rest.
- 26 Zuma
- Foliage
- 24 Ishbilia
- Park, The

MARYLEBONE

- 27 Defune
- 25 Locanda Locatelli
- Orrery
- 24 La Fromagerie
- Galvin Bistrot

MAYFAIR

- 28 Square, The
- 27 Le Gavroche
- Nobu London
- 26 Theo Randall
- Miyama

NOTTING HILL

- 26 Assaggi
- 25 Ledbury, The
- 24 Ottolenghi
- Notting Hill Brass.
- Books for Cooks

PICCADILLY

- 24 Yoshino
- Bentley's
- 22 Gaucho Grill
- 1707 Wine Bar
- 21 Noura

SHOREDITCH/ SPITALFIELDS/HOXTON

- 23 Fifteen
- Viet Hoa
- 22 St. John Bread/Wine
- Eyre Brothers
- Great Eastern

SMITHFIELD

- 26 Club Gascon
- 25 St. John
- 23 Le Café du Marché
- 20 Smiths/Top Floor
- Smiths/Dining Rm.

SOHO

- 25 Yauatcha
- 24 Alastair Little
- Arbutus
- 23 Red Fort
- Richard Corrigan

SOUTH KENSINGTON

- 24 L'Etranger
- Star of India
- Cambio de Tercio
- Bibendum
- 23 Patara

ST. JAMES'S

- 24 L'Oranger
- Wilton's
- Le Caprice
- 23 Ritz, The
- 22 Green's

IN THE COUNTRY

- 28 Le Manoir/Quat Saisons
- 27 Fat Duck
- Waterside Inn
- 24 Gravetye Manor
- Vineyard/Stockcross

Top Decor Ratings

Ratings are to the left of names.

__29__ Les Trois Garçons	Hakkasan
	Rules
__27__ Cliveden House	Umu
Ritz, The	Blue Elephant
Gravetye Manor	Pasha
Sketch/Lecture Rm.	
Archipelago	__24__ Gordon Ramsay/68 Royal
Le Manoir/Quat Saisons	Cocoon
Taman gang	Amaya
	L'Atelier/Robuchon
__26__ Sketch/Gallery	Lanes
Lanesborough	Savoy Grill
Mosimann's (club)	Annabel's (club)
Waterside Inn	Dorchester/The Grill
Wolseley, The	Gordon Ramsay/Claridge's
	Le Gavroche
__25__ Pétrus	George (club)
Wallace, The	Clos Maggiore
Momo	China Tang
Home House (club)	Brown's/The Grill
La Porte des Indes*	Harry's Bar (club)
Rhodes 24*	

OUTDOORS

Albion, The	La Poule au Pot
Belvedere, The	Ledbury, The
C Garden	Le Pont de la Tour
Coq d'Argent	River Café
La Famiglia	Suka

ROMANCE

Club Gascon	Lundum's
Galvin/Windows	Momo
Gordon Ramsay/Claridge's	Pétrus
La Poule au Pot	Ritz, The
Le Gavroche	Sketch/Lecture Rm.

ROOMS

China Tang	Rhodes W1 Rest.
Gilgamesh	Ritz, The
Hakkasan	Sketch/Lecture Rm.
L'Atelier/Robuchon	Wolseley, The
Les Trois Garçons	Zuma

VIEWS

Blueprint Café	Narrow, The
Foliage	Oxo Tower
Galvin/Windows	Skylon
Inn The Park	Ubon
Le Pont de la Tour	Waterside Inn

Top Service Ratings

Ratings are to the left of names.

28	Gordon Ramsay/68 Royal

27	Lanes
	Waterside Inn

26	Le Manoir/Quat Saisons
	Le Gavroche
	Square, The
	Quadrato
	Mark's Club (club)
	Pétrus
	Capital Rest.
	Foliage
	Fat Duck

25	Roussillon
	French Horn
	Chez Bruce
	Dorchester/The Grill
	Mosimann's (club)
	Quirinale
	Oslo Court

George (club)
Pied à Terre
Ritz, The
Brown's/The Grill
Park, The
Gravetye Manor
La Trompette
Cliveden House
Annabel's (club)
Harry's Bar (club)
Lanesborough*

24	Latium
	Gordon Ramsay/Claridge's
	La Genova
	Savoy Grill
	Goring Dining Rm.
	Greenhouse, The
	Launceston Place*
	Ledbury, The
	River Café

Best Buys

1. Food for Thought
2. Leon
3. Books for Cooks
4. Churchill Arms
5. Little Bay
6. Mildreds
7. Tokyo Diner
8. Jenny Lo's Tea
9. New Tayyabs
10. Gourmet Burger
11. Ed's Easy Diner
12. Lucky 7
13. Wagamama
14. Patisserie Valerie
15. Le Pain Quotidien
16. Pepper Tree
17. Chelsea Bun
18. Babes 'n' Burgers
19. La Porchetta
20. Mandalay
21. Busaba Eathai
22. Masala Zone
23. North Sea
24. Fire & Stone
25. Gallipoli
26. New Culture Rev.
27. Chowki Bar
28. Original Lahore
29. Viet Hoa
30. Ye Olde Cheshire
31. Court
32. Troubadour, The
33. Ask Pizza
34. Pizza Express
35. Alounak
36. Imli
37. Bodeans
38. Le Mercury
39. New World
40. Wong Kei

OTHER GOOD VALUES

Abeno
Arkansas Café
Baker & Spice
Barrafina
Basilico
Belgo
Bloom's
Carluccio's
Chinese Experience
Chuen Cheng Ku
Comptoir Gascon
Crazy Homies
Daquise
ECapital
Efes Kebab House
El Rincon Latino
Firezza
Four Seasons Chinese
Giraffe
Golden Dragon

Itsu
Joy King Lau
Khan's
Kulu Kulu
La Fromagerie
Meson Don Felipe
Moshi Moshi
Mr. Kong
Ottolenghi
Ping Pong
Sofra
Soho Spice
Song Que Café
Strada
Taqueria
Tas
Thai Pavilian
Tom's Deli
Two Brothers Fish
Yo! Sushi

DINNER (£35 & UNDER)

Alastair Little	30.00	11 Abingdon Road	19.50
Albannach	27.50	Fifth Floor	19.50
Al Duca	23.50	Fiore	24.00
Alloro	28.50	Glasshouse, The	35.00
Almeida	17.50	Green Cottage	18.00
Avenue, The	19.95	Greyhound, The	27.00
Bank Westminster	17.95	Imperial China	14.95
Bellamy's	24.00	Kensington Place	24.50
Bengal Clipper	10.00	La Trompette	35.00
Bertorelli	16.50	Latium	24.50
Blue Elephant	35.00	Launceston Place	18.50
Blueprint Café	22.50	Lundum's	21.50
Boisdale	17.80	Morgan M	34.00
Brasserie Roux	24.50	Motcombs	15.75
Café Fish	12.50	Ozer Restaurant & Bar	10.95
Café Japan	17.00	Plateau	25.00
Café Spice Namasté	30.00	R.S.J.	15.95
Caravaggio	19.50	Rasa*	25.00
Champor-Champor	27.90	Sam's Brasserie & Bar	12.50
Chez Gérard*	16.95	Skylon	29.50
Cipriani	35.00	Tendido Cero	25.00
Clos Maggiore	24.50	Thai Square*	21.95
Coq d'Argent	27.00	Via Condotti	24.50
Deya	27.00	Yoshino	25.00
ECapital	8.80	Zafferano	29.50

---

* Price may be lower at select branches.

subscribe to zagat.com

RESTAURANT
DIRECTORY

	FOOD	DECOR	SERVICE	COST

Abbeville, The *British/European* ▽ 15 | 13 | 11 | £24

Clapham | 67-69 Abbeville Rd., SW4 (Clapham South) | 020-8675 2201 | fax 8675 2212 | www.theabbeville.com

It's "great as a local, but not worth an expedition" to Clapham for this "incredibly noisy when full", easy-going gastropub with "solid" Modern European–Traditional British fare and "friendly staff (when they are not rushed off their feet)."

Abeno *Japanese* 21 | 12 | 18 | £24

Bloomsbury | 47 Museum St., WC1 (Holborn) | 020-7405 3211 | fax 7405 3212

Abeno Too *Japanese*

Leicester Square | 17-18 Great Newport St., WC2 (Leicester Sq.) | 020-7379 1160
www.abenoco.co.uk

For "a real taste of Japan in London", this unpretentious duo ("no money spent on decor") in Bloomsbury and Leicester Square specialise in "authentic okonomiyaki" ("basically, a Japanese pancake") that's "cooked in front of you" and other "excellent interpretations of street snacks"; they're "perfect for a quick, inexpensive and unusual" meal – and "fun for bringing friends."

Abingdon, The *European* 22 | 18 | 21 | £34

Kensington | 54 Abingdon Rd., W8 (Earl's Ct./High St. Kensington) | 020-7937 3339 | fax 7795 6388 | www.theabingdonrestaurant.com

"Essentially a gastropub, but the quality of food and lovely room feel more like a restaurant" attest admirers of this "buzzy", "cosy" "gem a stone's throw away from Kensington High Street", with an "inventive, dependable" Modern European menu that "changes regularly" and "smiling", "knowledgeable staff"; "comfy couches" and "big, red dinerlike booths add massively to the charm."

About Thyme Bar & Bistro *European* - | - | - | M

Pimlico | 82 Wilton Rd., SW1 (Victoria) | www.aboutthyme.co.uk

This "surprising find across from the new Sainsbury's in Pimlico" has "become a favourite of many, and not just locals" thanks to a "tasty, excellent value" Modern European menu that "always has variety", plus a "great welcome" from service that "goes the extra mile"; P.S. it's usually "no trouble getting a table on short notice midweek."

Academy *British* 13 | 14 | 14 | £22

Piccadilly | Royal Academy of Arts | Piccadilly, W1 (Green Park/Piccadilly Circus) | 020-7300 5608 | www.royalacademy.org.uk

"If you are visiting the Royal Academy" and "want to rest your feet" for a "quick snack", this "delightful", popular cafe has an "excellent buffet" of Modern British fare; "choose carefully, and it can be good value."

NEW Acorn House 🛇 *British* ▽ 19 | 19 | 15 | £35

King's Cross | 69 Swinton St., WC1 (King's Cross) | 020-7812 1842 | www.acornhouserestaurant.com

"The standard-bearer for ecological eateries" – with carbon-neutral paint on the walls and biodegradable takeaway packaging – this "welcome addition to King's Cross" from a co-founder of Fifteen boasts "lovely ambience in a modern setting"; whilst "the care put into the Modern British food" is appreciated, the deli-counter may be preferable, given the "slightly chaotic service."

Adam Street *British*

▽ 20 | 19 | 20 | £31

Covent Garden | 9 Adam St., WC2 (Charing Cross) | 020-7379 8000 | fax 7379 1444 | www.adamstreet.co.uk

"Hidden away in the [18th-century] vaults under Adam Street" off the Strand, this "eclectic" private club opens its doors during the day to non-members with a "warm reception greeting"; the "keen staff" serve "new British classics" that are "quite good, and quite a bargain if you order off the pre-set menu."

Addendum 🗷 *European*

– | – | – | E

Tower Bridge | Apex City of London Hotel | 1 Seething Ln., EC3 (Tower Hill) | 020-7977 9500 | fax 7977 9529 | www.addendumrestaurant.co.uk

"Good for a business lunch in an area without many great restaurants", this "chic" hotel near the Tower of London offers two options: a formal, low-ceilinged restaurant serving "inventive, capably executed" Modern European dishes, and a more "reasonably priced" brasserie with handsomely large windows; it "can be quiet, but nothing wrong with that."

Admiral Codrington, The *British/European*

18 | 17 | 17 | £33

Chelsea | 17 Mossop St., SW3 (South Kensington) | 020-7581 0005 | fax 7589 2452 | www.theadmiralcodrington.co.uk

"Walk past a smoky pub scene in front and find yourself in a contemporary dining room" with a "retractable summer roof" that "adds light and charm" to this "fish specialist gastropub" with a "straightforward" Modern British–European menu and clientele that ranges from Sloane Rangers to "braying estate agents with red socks"; P.S. "Mossop Street can be tough to find, even for cabbies."

Admiralty, The *British*

19 | 19 | 21 | £46

Covent Garden | Somerset House, The Strand, WC2 (Temple) | 020-7845 4646 | fax 7845 4658

"In former admiralty offices within Somerset House", this "stately dining room" is "a step back in time that either woos or woes": some praise the "sound Modern British food" and "service to match", whilst others pan the "overpriced, twiddly" fare and "staff who waiver between hyper-attentive and disinterested"; no doubt it "depends on whether eating in a place of historic interest" floats your boat or not.

Aglio e Olio ☻ *Italian*

21 | 14 | 16 | £25

Chelsea | 194 Fulham Rd., SW10 (South Kensington) | 020-7351 0070

"One could go every day of the week" declare devotees of this "buzzing" Chelsea trattoria where a "delightfully mixed crowd" dines on "steady", "simple Italian food" with "seasonal flavours" that's "cheap for the area"; whilst "not for a relaxed meal" (too "cramped" and "service is patchy"), it still makes a "great place for when you run out of ideas."

	FOOD	DECOR	SERVICE	COST

Alastair Little ●🅂 *British* | 24 | 15 | 21 | £49

Soho | 49 Frith St., W1 (Leicester Sq./Tottenham Court Rd.) | 020-7734 5183 | fax 7734 5206

"Despite the name, Juliet Peston does the cooking" – and most feel she "has maintained the high standard" set by this Soho stalwart in the '80s; if a few feel this Modern Brit is "resting on good will from days gone by" – the dining room definitely "needs a thorough refresh" – the "adorable service" and "intimate atmosphere" still attract an "arty crowd, especially later in the evening."

Albannach 🅂 *Scottish* | 14 | 16 | 12 | £37

Soho | 66 Trafalgar Sq., WC2 (Charing Cross/Leicester Sq.) | 020-7930 0066 | fax 7389 9800 | www.albannach.co.uk

"A useful oasis near Trafalgar Square", this "loud" Scottish-themed haunt (tartan touches and "novelty kilted waiters") is "a bar with a restaurant as an afterthought" – whilst it's "easy to get lost in the single-malts" and "amazing cocktails", the fare is "mediocre" and the "service really bad"; but if you do eat, regulars recommend you "have the haggis!"

NEW Albion, The *British* | – | – | – | M

Islington | 10 Thornhill Rd., N1 (Angel) | 020-7607 7450 | www.the-albion.co.uk

This country-style Georgian pub in the middle of Islington – feted for its impressive 450-sq.-meter garden with fruit trees and clinging wisteria – has received a sympathetic refurb after being taken over by chef Richard Turner (ex Automat); the midpriced Traditional British menu features classics such as shepherd's pie and bubble and squeak, with BBQ and spit roasts prepared outside in the summer.

Al Duca 🅂 *Italian* | 19 | 15 | 17 | £39

St. James's | 4-5 Duke of York St., SW1 (Green Park/Piccadilly Circus) | 020-7839 3090 | fax 7839 4050 | www.alduca-restaurant.co.uk

"Busy on working days, but a paradise on weekends", this "somewhat cramped" "standby" near St. James's Square is appreciated for Italian fare that "never disappoints", mainly because of the "remarkably good value set menus" (including "one of the best theatre deals in town").

Z Al Hamra ● *Lebanese* | 22 | 14 | 18 | £34

Mayfair | 31-33 Shepherd Mkt., W1 (Green Park) | 020-7493 1954 | fax 7493 1044

Brasserie Al Hamra 🅂 *Lebanese*

Mayfair | 52 Shepherd Mkt., W1 (Green Park) | 020-7493 1068 | fax 7355 3511

www.alhamrarestaurant.co.uk

"Popular with Middle Eastern plutocrats, cosmocrats" and "well-heeled" locals, this Shepherd Market Lebanese offers "delectable" fare, including a "tempting assortment of mezze"; even if service is "somewhat abrupt" and the "setting ordinary", it's often "bustling" at the "particularly nice" pavement tables; P.S. whilst it's "akin to eating in a cafeteria", the Brasserie across the street has lower prices and French charcuterie.

	FOOD	DECOR	SERVICE	COST

Alloro ☒ *Italian*
22 | 17 | 22 | £50

Mayfair | 19-20 Dover St., W1 (Green Park) | 020-7495 4768 | fax 7629 5348

"Great for business or a glam date", this "polished act" in Mayfair boasts "accomplished" Italian *cucina* that's "delicious in its simplicity", supported by "helpful, unobtrusive staff"; just be advised that the food and, especially, the "wines can be pricey."

All Star Lanes *American*
15 | 19 | 17 | £26

Bloomsbury | Victoria House | Bloomsbury Pl., WC1 (Holborn) | 020-7025 2676 | fax 7025 2677 ●
NEW Bayswater | Whiteleys Shopping Ctr. | Porchester Gdns., W2 (Paddington) | 020-7313 8360
www.allstarlanes.co.uk

Granted, the American "diner-style food" is "mainly functional", but this "plush" pair of "retro luxury bowling alleys" in Bloomsbury and Bayswater (by August 2007) still are a "cool idea for a night out", especially if you book the "private room with your own lanes and bar."

Almeida *French*
18 | 18 | 18 | £44

Islington | 30 Almeida St., N1 (Angel/Highbury & Islington) | 020-7354 4777 | fax 7354 2777 | www.almeida-restaurant.co.uk

"An oasis of informal elegance off achingly trendy Upper Street", this local "mainstay" for Almeida Theatre-goers gets a "good buzz", particularly post-curtain; however, the Classic French "*carte* is generally unchanging – a matter of reassurance to some, but disappointment to others" – and that, plus "overblown" prices and "slow service", makes it missable to many.

Alounak ● *Persian*
23 | 15 | 16 | £22

Westbourne Grove | 44 Westbourne Grove, W2 (Bayswater/Queensway) | 020-7229 4158 | fax 7792 1219
Olympia | 10 Russell Gdns., W14 (Olympia) | 020-7603 1130

The "tight quarters" and "no-frills" decor notwithstanding, patrons proclaim this a "pleasant Persian" pair, primarily on account of the "awesome", "melt-in-your-mouth" cooking at "reasonable prices"; "bring your own wine" and "expect to wait an eternity for a table", whether in Westbourne Grove or Olympia.

Al Sultan *Lebanese*
22 | 15 | 20 | £33

Mayfair | 51-52 Hertford St., W1 (Green Park) | 020-7408 1155 | fax 7408 1113 | www.alsultan.co.uk

Despite its 22 years, this "pleasant surprise" is "less well known than many other Lebanese, but is preferable" for its "attentive service" and "authentic", "consistently delicious" cooking; some connoisseurs claim it's "not cheap for Middle Eastern fare – guess you pay for the location" in Shepherd Market.

☒ Al Waha ● *Lebanese*
22 | 16 | 20 | £31

Bayswater | 75 Westbourne Grove, W2 (Bayswater/Queensway) | 020-7229 0806 | www.waha-uk.com

"Contemporary interpretations of Lebanese cuisine" that "pack a punch", along with "homely service", draw followers to this small

	FOOD	DECOR	SERVICE	COST

Westbourne Grove eatery; it's "not much to look at" and "gets tight on a busy evening", but "they also do a wonderful, nicely presented delivery service."

☑ Amaya ● *Indian* — 25 | 24 | 21 | £52

Belgravia | 15-19 Halkin Arcade, Motcomb St., SW1 (Knightsbridge) | 020-7823 1166 | fax 7259 6464 | www.realindianfood.com

"As Nobu is to Japanese, this is to Indian" gush groupies of this "gorgeous", "glitzy" Belgravia eatery – "low lighting and candles everywhere" – whose "tasty, grilled" small plates and "curries with class" make "a refreshing departure from the usual"; some pout the "pricey" "portions are small", but most of the "manicured clientele" maintain this colony of the Chutney Mary empire is "a serious find in London's high-end food stakes."

Ambassador, The *European* — ▽ 21 | 17 | 19 | £29

Clerkenwell | 55 Exmouth Mkt., EC1 (Farringdon) | 020-7837 0009 | www.theambassadorcafe.co.uk

A "great bistro atmosphere" prevails at this "much-needed" newcomer to the ranks of casual Exmouth Market eateries, which has established itself as a "friendly purveyor" of "tasty", "not-too-expensive" Modern European cuisine; open from 8:30 AM, it already has a reputation as "the perfect brunch spot."

Amici Bar & Italian Kitchen *Italian* — ▽ 15 | 16 | 17 | £34

Wandsworth | 35 Bellevue Rd., SW17 (Wandsworth Common) | 020-8672 5888 | www.amiciitaly.co.uk

"They allow groups to linger" in the "casual" setting of well-spaced tables and comfy sofas at this "friendly-family restaurant" owned by Christopher Gilmour (of Christopher's) overlooking Wandsworth Common; whilst "nothing special", the menu provides "authentic Italian" dishes from various regions.

Anchor & Hope *British* — 24 | 15 | 18 | £33

Waterloo | 36 The Cut, SE1 (Waterloo) | 020-7928 9898

"If you must go to a gastropub, then this is the one to go to" maintain mavens of this "busy" Modern Brit in Waterloo, whose "heavenly, hearty food in hefty portions" is ideal "to share family-style"; although the "no-bookings policy is a killer" ("best arrive early"), "it's worth the wait at the bar, in the street, anywhere"; N.B. they do take reservations for Sunday lunch.

Andrew Edmunds *European* — 22 | 19 | 21 | £37

Soho | 46 Lexington St., W1 (Oxford Circus/Piccadilly Circus) | 020-7437 5708

"Most would walk past and ignore" this "hidden" "Soho diehard" – pity, because they'd miss a "rustic ambience" with "lots of romantic candles" ("perfect for a second date"), a "daily changing", "great-value" Modern European menu of "simple dishes that's complemented by an extensive wine list" and "staff who know how to please"; in short, a "fantastic cubbyhole", even if it can "feel a little claustrophobic."

	FOOD	DECOR	SERVICE	COST

Anglesea Arms *British*
23 | **19** | **15** | **£29**

Shepherd's Bush | 35 Wingate Rd., W6 (Goldhawk Rd./Ravenscourt Park) | 020-8749 1291 | fax 8749 1254

"Shepherd's Bush should rejoice" that it has this "relaxed" gastro-pub, a "mainstay" for Modern British fare that's "amazing value", considering it's "cooked to perfection"; "the excellence of the food is not matched in the service" – "the waits can be eternal" – but with "big leather sofas, an open fire" and "offbeat", mismatched chairs, it's "a fantastic place to while away an afternoon."

Annabel's ●☒ *British/French*
22 | **24** | **25** | **£75**

Private club; inquiries: 020-7629 1096

The "ultimate London private club", this 45-year-old Berkeley Square landmark "is cool again", offering an "exclusive, elusive" combo of "divine people-watching", "glamourous" atmosphere and "top-notch service"; sure, it's "vvvvvery expensive" "for drinks, dancing" and decent Classic French–British cuisine, "but remember, you get what you pay for" at this "perfectly mah-velous" place.

Annex 3 ●☒ *French*
▽ **16** | **26** | **14** | **£41**

Fitzrovia | 6 Little Portland St., W1 (Oxford Circus) | 020-7631 0700 | www.annex3.co.uk

Its "just-dropped-some-acid decor lends charm" to this Oxford Circus site, where a "loud lounge" serving "lethal cocktails" dominates the adjacent dining room ("don't expect to have any meaningful conversations"); the menu is "nothing special", though a post-Survey switch to French fare may outdate that view, along with the Food score.

Annie's *British*
▽ **21** | **22** | **21** | **£29**

Barnes | 36-38 White Hart Ln., SW13 (Barnes Bridge B.R.) | 020-8878 2020 | fax 8876 8478
Chiswick | 162 Thames Rd., W4 (Kew Bridge B.R.) | 020-8994 6848

"All things to everyone – romantic for two, fun for families, lunch with the girls" – characterises these Barnes and "Chiswick treasures" where "friendly staff" serve "comforting", "commendable" Modern British meals, amidst the "cosy", mismatched furniture; small wonder that brunching locals "love to hang out here all day long."

Aperitivo ●☒ *Italian*
20 | **17** | **18** | **£26**

Soho | 41 Beak St., W1 (Oxford Circus/Piccadilly Circus) | 020-7287 2057 | www.aperitivo-restaurants.com

"Hidden on Beak Street – thousands walk past without realising it" – this "busy" tapas bar offers a "good atmosphere for catching up with friends" over "interesting Italian" nibbles; still, sceptics shrug "it's the kind of place you love when you're there – but would never go back to."

Aquasia *Asian/Mediterranean*
▽ **21** | **24** | **25** | **£50**

Chelsea | Wyndham Hotel | Chelsea Harbour, SW10 (Earl's Ct.) | 020-7823 3000 | fax 7352 8174 | www.conradlondon.com

A "stunning view of Chelsea Harbour" and the river is the main claim to fame of this modern Asian-Med bistro; it's frequented primarily by hotel guests, though all can enjoy its "alfresco dining in summer."

Arbutus *European*

24	17	18	£42

Soho | 63-64 Frith St., W1 (Leicester Sq./Tottenham Court Rd.) |
020-7734 4545 | www.arbutusrestaurant.co.uk

"If you can ignore the rather drab, noisy room" and "patchy service",
you too may "join the crowd raving about" this "welcome addition to
the Soho scene"; accolades accrue for Modern European cuisine that
"dazzles in the mouth" and is "decently priced" ("especially given the
location"), and for a "super wine list that encourages experimenta-
tion", as most "bottles are available in 250 ml carafes"; N.B. watch
for Wild Honey, a Mayfair offshoot set to open mid-July 2007.

☑ Archipelago ☒ *Eclectic*

21	27	22	£49

Fitzrovia | 110 Whitfield St., W1 (Goodge St./Warren St.) |
020-7383 3346 | fax 7383 7181

Those who "like to experiment" when they eat – think "locusts,
chocolate-covered scorpions and kangaroo" – find this "very, very
odd" Fiztrovian Eclectic with "exotic jungle decor" and "dark",
"romantic" ambience is "always an amazing experience"; but it's
"atrociously expensive" too, leading sceptics to suggest, "less
insects, more chef-ing please."

Ark ☒ *Italian*

15	13	15	£45

Notting Hill | 122 Palace Gardens Terrace, W8 (Notting Hill Gate) |
020-7229 4024 | fax 7792 8787 | www.ark-restaurant.com

"In an exclusive neighbourhood" near Notting Hill Gate, this "intimate" Italian serves "upscale food and wines" that seem "a tad
overpriced" say those who deem the menu "good, but not exceptional"; nor do the floral arrangements atone for its rather basic
digs: "you can only enhance a 'hut' so much."

Armani Caffé ☒ *Italian*

17	20	17	£32

Knightsbridge | Emporio Armani | 191 Brompton Rd., SW3
(Knightsbridge) | 020-7584-4549 | fax 7823 8854 |
www.emporioarmani.com

With "light, well-prepared" Italian dishes "served by model types"
wearing "Giorgio's stylish designs", the Emporio Armani's recently
refurbed cafe – all modern and mirrored – is as much "a place to be
seen and to watch people" as a "convenient shopping" pit stop.

Artigiano *Italian*

20	18	22	£36

Hampstead | 12A Belsize Terrace, NW3 (Belsize Park/Swiss Cottage) |
020-7794 4288 | fax 7435 2048 | www.etruscarestaurants.com

"Get the West End feel without the West End price" at this airy,
"bustly" trattoria in "cute little Belsize Village"; with "friendly, professional staff" presenting "surprisingly good modern Italian" cooking, it's perfect "for a quick pre-something meal."

Asadal *Korean*

-	-	-	M

Holborn | 229-231 High Holborn, WC1 (Holborn) | 020-7430 9006 |
www.asadal.co.uk

Sitting "on top of Holborn tube station", this "surprisingly pleasant",
"swanky Korean" (a spin-off from a New Malden eatery) makes up for

having "no daylight in the basement" premises with "bright ideas in the kitchen department"; in particular, the "at-table BBQ is a good choice."

Asakusa *Japanese*   - | - | - | M

Camden Town | 265 Eversholt St., NW1 (Morningtown Crescent St.) | 020-7388 8533

"The space is a little cramped" and "the service fast and furious, but if you want to sample some of the best sushi without paying the earth", try this "hidden gem" of a Camden Japanese; it's "always full of locals", enjoying the "delicious" fare as well as "the fine sake."

☑ Asia de Cuba ❶ *Asian/Cuban*   22 | 23 | 19 | £52

Covent Garden | St. Martin's Lane Hotel | 45 St. Martin's Ln., WC2 (Leicester Sq.) | 020-7300 5588 | fax 7300 5540 | www.chinagrillmanagement.com

Still "swank, sleek and happening several years after its opening", this Theatreland haunt serves "creative" "Cuban classics with an Oriental twist" in "jumbo portions" – "so order less than you might think"; some tut it's "tired", with "service not up to the price mark"; but the "models and mega-stars" keep it so "loud" "you can't hear yourself think – or taste"; P.S. "don't wear white, you might blend into the background."

Ask Pizza *Pizza*   16 | 13 | 15 | £18

Bloomsbury | 48 Grafton Way, W1 (Warren St.) | 020-7388 8108 | fax 7388 8112 ❶
Mayfair | 121-125 Park St., W1 (Marble Arch) | 020-7495 7760 | fax 7495 7760
Victoria | 160-162 Victoria St., SW1 (St. James's Park/Victoria) | 020-7630 8228 | fax 7630 5218
Hampstead | 216 Haverstock Hill, NW3 (Belsize Park/Chalk Farm) | 020-7433 3896 | fax 7435 6490 ❶
Chelsea | 300 King's Rd., SW3 (Sloane Sq.) | 020-7349 9123
Putney | 345 Fulham Palace Rd., SW6 (Hammersmith/Putney Bridge) | 020-7371 0392
South Kensington | Unit 23-24, Gloucester Arcade, SW7 (Gloucester Rd.) | 020-7835 0840 ❶
Chiswick | 219-221 Chiswick High Rd., W4 (Turnham Green) | 020-8742 1323 ❶
Kensington | 222 Kensington High St., W8 (High St. Kensington) | 020-7937 5540 | fax 7937 5540
Notting Hill | 145 Notting Hill Gate, W11 (Notting Hill Gate) | 020-7792 9942
www.askcentral.co.uk
Additional locations throughout London

"Lazy and formulaic" they may be, but for a "functional quick lunch" or "dinner of convenience", this "nice and casual" Italian chain furnishes "low-priced" pizzas and pastas "you can't be bothered to make at home"; P.S. "don't forget the salads, they are excellent."

☑ Assaggi ☒ *Italian*   26 | 15 | 23 | £53

Notting Hill | 39 Chepstow Pl., 1st fl., W2 (Notting Hill Gate) | 020-7792 5501 | fax 0870-0051 2923

The "mood is set by the exuberant maitre d' who explains the menu with gusto and passion" at this "exquisite Italian" in a "homely", albeit "spartan", room "above a pub" in Notting Hill; the "simple, rustic" dishes are "magnificently executed" and "beautifully served" – all of which explains why it's so "very hard to get a table."

NEW Atami Restaurant & Bar 🗷 *Japanese*

▽ 24 | 20 | 19 | £43

Westminster | 37 Monck St., SW1 (St. James's Park) | 020-7222 2218 | www.atami-restaurant.com

"In a neighbourhood where good places are sparse", this "fantastic new addition" to Westminster (hence, a few "MPs from Parliament nearby") is a "design-led Japanese" displaying "originality and class" in both the "sleek" decor and cuisine – "inventive dishes, plus your staple sushi"; the "courteous service" is "a bit slow", however.

Aubaine *French*

20 | 19 | 16 | £35

NEW **Piccadilly** | 4 Heddon St., W1 (Piccadilly Circus) | 020-7440 2510
South Kensington | 260-262 Brompton Rd., SW3 (South Kensington) | 020-7052 0100 | fax 7052 0622
www.aubaine.co.uk

"More sophisticated than the usual bistro" (and perhaps more pricey), this Brompton Cross venue is open all day for "rustic", "well-conceived French classics"; "service could be more professional", but the Provençal-style premises are "always crowded" with "Sloane Square princesses and their banker boyfriends", especially at "tremendously popular weekend brunch"; P.S. the Piccadilly premises opened in May.

Auberge du Lac 🅼 *French*

▽ 23 | 22 | 22 | £65

Welwyn | Brocket Hall | Hertfordshire | 01707 368888 | fax 01707 368898 | www.brocket-hall.co.uk

Its "picturesque setting makes this a special place" believe boosters of Brocket Hall's restaurant right on the banks of The Broadwater; but despite its "keen staff", French–Modern European menu and "wine list full of big names", sceptics say "standards have slipped since Jean-Christophe Novelli left" this "stunning location."

🗷 Aubergine 🗷 *French*

26 | 20 | 24 | £71

Chelsea | 11 Park Walk, SW10 (Gloucester Rd./South Kensington) | 020-7352 3449 | fax 7351 1770 | www.auberginerestaurant.co.uk

From its low-key "side street location" in Chelsea, this "quaint place subtly exerts its culinary clout" through chef William Drabble's "seductive" New French food – the "pièce de résistance is the degustation menu" – "executed with style" and served by "attentive, yet unobtrusive" staff; a few malcontents "expect more for this kind of cash", but most maintain this is "a model for how haute cuisine should be conducted"; P.S. the lunch prix fixe is a relative "bargain."

Aurora 🗷 *British/French*

19 | 20 | 20 | £55

City | Great Eastern Hotel | 40 Liverpool St., EC2 (Liverpool St.) | 020-7618 7000 | fax 7618 7001 | www.great-eastern-hotel.co.uk

"Full of City types having corporate lunches (so, not a romantic spot)", this handsome, high-ceilinged Hyatt Hotels–owned dining room suits the suits with "perfectly laid tables" and "decent" Modern British–Classic French cuisine ("some dishes light, some heavy"); but, given the hefty price tags, "you better hope someone else is picking up the bill."

Automat ● *American* | 17 | 19 | 15 | £33 |

Mayfair | 33 Dover St., W1 (Green Park) | 020-7499 3033 | www.automat-london.com

"Feels like New York has come to London" with this "train-carriage-styled" "clubby diner" whose seating options include "cosy booths or a light, airy greenhouse at the rear"; "sadly, the decor is better than the food" – "jazzed-up American-style" basics – and don't "expect too much of the service", but at least it's "reasonably priced for Mayfair."

Avenue, The ●🅉 *European* | 18 | 20 | 17 | £52 |

St. James's | 7-9 St. James's St., SW1 (Green Park) | 020-7321 2111 | fax 7321 2500 | www.danddlondon.com

"Chic", if somewhat "cold", this "modern, glass-fronted restaurant in the heart of St. James's" has "stood the test of time" (well, 13 years, anyway) as an "expense-account haunt" serving "simple, hearty" Modern European meals; what keeps it "heaving", however, is the "vibrant" bar – "young professionals stop in after work or the theatre."

Awana *Malaysian* | 17 | 20 | 18 | £42 |

Chelsea | 85 Sloane Ave., SW3 (South Kensington) | 020-7584 8880 | fax 7584 6188 | www.awana.co.uk

"Malaysian food is a rare treat" in London, so many salute this "slick" Chelsea site from Mango Tree owner Eddie Lim, designed to resemble a teak-lined plantation house (albeit one centred around a bar serving "spicy" satays); "even if enjoyable", it's "expensive", however – and, critics cavil, "unatmospheric" as well.

Axis 🅉 *British/Eclectic* | 20 | 21 | 20 | £46 |

Covent Garden | One Aldwych Hotel | 1 Aldwych, WC2 (Charing Cross/ Covent Garden) | 020-7300 0300 | fax 7300 0301 | www.onealdwych.com

"Usefully located under the hip One Aldwych Hotel" in Covent Garden, this "stylish" (some say "stark"), "high-ceilinged basement restaurant" makes a "sophisticated" choice "when you need to impress"; the Eclectic–Modern British menu is "a steady performer", if "not exactly value for money" warn the economical – except for the "top pre-theatre prix fixe"; P.S. beware, the "noise can be traumatic on jazz evenings."

Aziz *Moroccan* | ▽ 17 | 20 | 13 | £34 |

Fulham | 30-32 Vanston Pl., SW6 (Fulham Broadway) | 020-7386 0086 | fax 7610 1661 | www.delaziz.co.uk

Run by a husband-and-wife team, this "buzzy", "atmospheric" Fulham venue is a veritable "Moroccan wonderland", with "belly-dancing nights", hookah pipes in the lounge bar and "good food" from a "reasonably priced" North African menu.

Babes 'n' Burgers *Hamburgers*   17 | 11 | 13 | £15

Notting Hill | 275 Portobello Rd., W11 (Ladbrock Grove) |
020-7229 2704 | fax 7792 5670 | www.babesnburgers.com

"Packed with visitors to Portobello Market, families and locals
(weekends are bit of a nightmare)", this "little place" specialises in
"made-from-scratch" organic hamburgers and staff who are "great
with babies"; numerous salads and non-red meat alternatives make
it "good for veggie" or fat-avoiding friends too.

Babylon *European*   20 | 24 | 20 | £46

Kensington | The Roof Gdns. | 99 Kensington High St., W8
(High St. Kensington) | 020-7368 3993 | fax 7938 2774 |
www.roofgardens.com

In between the "fantastic gardens" and "dynamite view from the
rooftop terrace", it "feels like an oasis" at Sir Richard Branson's
"funky" Modern European high above Kensington High Street; it's a
"young person's restaurant", with diners gaining access Fridays-
Saturdays to the affiliated nightclub below, and if foes feel the "location deserves better food", it's "still good value, by London
standards" – especially for lunch.

NEW Bacchus 🗷 *Eclectic*   21 | 16 | 21 | £46

Hoxton | 177 Hoxton St., N1 (Old St.) | 020-7613 0477 | fax 7100 1704 |
www.bacchus-restaurant.co.uk

"Fine dining in a casual gastropub setting" summarises this Eclectic,
whose "bold, dashing" dishes "are more hit than miss" and staff are
"friendly without being overbearing"; the vaguely "'70s-influenced
decor can look pretty basic", and the Hoxton location downright
"frightening", but most will bacchus up when we say this novice is
"worth the effort to get to."

Baker & Spice *Mediterranean*   22 | 16 | 15 | £22

Belgravia | 54-56 Elizabeth St., SW1 (Sloane Sq./Victoria) |
020-7730 3033 | fax 7730 3188
Kilburn | 75 Salusbury Rd., NW6 (Queens Park) | 020-7604 3636 |
fax 7604 3646
NEW St. John's Wood | 20 Clifton Rd., W9 (Warwick Ave.) |
020-7266 1122 | fax 7266 3535
Chelsea | 47 Denyer St., SW3 (Knightsbridge/South Kensington) |
020-7589 4734 | fax 7823 9148
www.bakerandspice.com

Yes, the "prices are mind-boggling", but they really have some of
"the best pastries, baked goods" and Med savouries at these "brilliant" "bespoke delis" around town; if the "service seems variable"
and the communal tables "cramped", remember these are "mainly
takeaway places" – and besides, "sometimes you [just] need
a pricey cookie."

Balans ☽ *British*   16 | 15 | 17 | £26

Soho | 60 Old Compton St., W1 (Leicester Sq./Piccadilly Circus) |
020-7439 2183 | fax 7734 2665
Earl's Court | 239 Old Brompton Rd., SW5 (Earl's Ct./West Brompton) |
020-7244 8838 | fax 7244 6226

(continued)

Balans

Chiswick | 214 Chiswick High Rd., W4 (Turnham Green) |
020-8742 1435
Kensington | 187 Kensington High St., W8 (High St. Kensington) |
020-7376 0115 | fax 7938 4653

Balans Cafe ❶ *British*

Soho | 34 Old Compton St., W1 (Leicester Sq./Piccadilly Circus) |
020-7439 3309
www.balans.co.uk

Established in 1986, these "gay-friendly", "busy", "buzzy" bistros
remain "reliable fallbacks" for brunch – they open at 8 AM (60 Old
Compton Street is also "classic for a Soho night out", as it serves until
dawn); if the Modern British fare is "blessedly cheap but decidedly
mediocre", well, watching the "always-attractive young men" is "the
main event here, as is the campy, flirtatious service."

Balham Kitchen & Bar *British*　　16 | 18 | 14 | £30

Balham | 15-19 Bedford Hill, SW12 (Balham B.R.) | 020-8675 6900 |
fax 8673 3965 | www.balhamkitchen.com

This Nick Jones-owned Modern Brit is "a favourite brunch spot for
trendy Balhamites" to enjoy "long rambling meals" within a "romantic atmosphere"; many "would love to love this place", but there are
too many downsides – specifically, a bar "full of braying voices" and
"waiters who think they're too good to be serving food."

Baltic ❶ *Polish*　　21 | 21 | 19 | £39

Southwark | 74 Blackfriars Rd., SE1 (Southwark) | 020-7928 1111 |
fax 7928 8487 | www.balticrestaurant.co.uk

"Hidden away where you least expect it" in a "cavernous" 1850s
coach-builders workshop, this "boisterous" but "stylish"
"Southwark stalwart" supplies "rib-sticking" Polish fare in "generous portions", plus "killer *wodkas*" "to work through whilst waiting
for the food"; best of all, there's "no shock when the bill arrives."

Bam-Bou ⌧ *SE Asian*　　21 | 22 | 18 | £40

Fitzrovia | 1 Percy St., W1 (Tottenham Court Rd.) | 020-7323 9130 |
fax 7323 9140 | www.bam-bou.co.uk

"Reminiscent of '30s French colonial style, the decadent
atmosphere" of this "great Fitzrovian townhouse" with "various
floors for dining" "lends ambience" to the "exotic", "fragrant"
Southeast Asian cuisine; "service can be spotty", so some stick to
the "top-floor bar, which gets cool chicks" (just "watch those stairs
after two mai tais").

Bangkok ⌧ *Thai*　　▽ 19 | 12 | 18 | £25

South Kensington | 9 Bute St., SW7 (South Kensington) |
020-7584 8529

"Still chugging on after 40 years" – it claims to be the oldest Thai
in town – this South Kensington "cosy local" is a place "where
nothing changes", neither the "low-risk" "good-value" grub, nor
the nondescript decor.

Bankside 🆔 British — 19 | 16 | 17 | £28

City | 1 Angel Ct. | 30 Throgmorton St., EC2 (Bank) | 084-5226 0011 |
fax 7796 3737
Southwark | 32 Southwark Bridge Rd., SE1 (London Bridge) |
020-7633 0011 | fax 7633 0011
www.banksiderestaurants.co.uk

With a Modern British menu that ranges from steak to aubergine cannelloni, it's a "safe option to invite anyone" to this "nice, if not exceptional" pair in Southwark and the City ("hidden away, near the old Stock Exchange"); the experience, whilst "more gastropub than restaurant", at least "provides good value for money."

Bank Westminster & Zander Bar 🆔 European — 18 | 17 | 19 | £38

Victoria | 45 Buckingham Gate, SW1 (St. James's Park) |
020-7379 9797 | fax 7240 7001 | www.bankrestaurants.com

"Tucked away" in a "great atrium" overlooking a residential Victoria courtyard, these premises are a "power-dining venue for local business", serving "imaginative" Modern European cuisine with a "quick turnaround"; its "bar, the longest in the U.K., is worth seeing", "but climbing through it to get to the dining room can be a drag."

Banquette Eclectic — 22 | 21 | 20 | £47

Covent Garden | Savoy Hotel | The Strand, WC2 (Covent Garden/Embankment) | 020-7420 2392 | fax 7592 1601 |
www.gordonramsey.com

"It's the Savoy, so you can't really go wrong here" at this discreet (remember it "if you're having an affair") Eclectic eatery say those enamoured by the "comfortable ambience" and "carefully prepared" "mixed bag of a menu"; whilst it's "perfect for a quick bite", however, some are "left scratching our heads at the cost"; N.B. due to close in late 2007 during the hotel's renovation.

NEW Barnes Grill British — - | - | - | E

Barnes | 2-3 Rocks Ln., SW13 (Barnes Bridge) | 020-8878 4488 |
fax 8878 5922 | www.awtrestaurants.com

The latest in chef-entrepreneur Antony Worrall Thompson's grills galaxy (Kew Grill, Notting Grill), this Barnes Britisher specialises in – you guessed it – grilled steaks (there's also chicken and fish, but it's really "not for non-meat eaters") in a hunting-lodge setting that combines cushions of "purple, reds and pinks with brown leather and animal heads"; though "staff are very friendly", that doesn't mollify many for the "enormous bill."

Barnsbury, The British — ▽ 21 | 20 | 19 | £26

Islington | 209-211 Liverpool Rd., N1 (Angel) | 020-7607 5519 |
fax 7607 3256 | www.thebarnsbury.co.uk

Whether it's a "cosy wintery evening by the fire or a Pimms-filled summer afternoon in the garden", this "pleasing pub off the Islington beaten track" is "always busy", thanks to a "warm welcome" and Modern British fare that's "different enough to draw people"; oh, and it's "dog-friendly" too.

	FOOD	DECOR	SERVICE	COST

NEW Barrafina ⓩ *Spanish* ▽ 24 | 19 | 21 | £34

Soho | 54 Frith St., W1 (Leicester Sq./Piccadilly Circus) | 020-7813 8016 | www.barrafina.co.uk

It's just 23 stools surrounding an L-shaped bar, but "Fino's younger brother" is a "beacon of Spanish gastronomic excellence", attracting a "cool, understated crowd" with "excellent Barcelona-quality tapas" ("the highest form of snacking"), "knowledgeable staff" and a "great sherry" selection; but "you can't book", so "be prepared to queue" at this "great addition to the Soho scene."

Bar Shu ◑ *Chinese* 22 | 17 | 16 | £36

Soho | 28 Frith St., W1 (Leicester Sq./Tottenham Court Rd.) | 020-7287 8822 | fax 7287 8858 | www.bar-shu.co.uk

"Hot, hot, hot in more ways than one", this "smart" Soho site is a rare Szechuan specialist in town, preparing "authentic", "unusual dishes covered in vibrant red chilli" that makes them "fiery like a dragon, and refreshingly so"; although "surprisingly brusque service lets it down", most agree this "tongue-tingling" spot is "a cut above."

Basilico *Pizza* 17 | 7 | 15 | £16

Finchley | 515 Finchley Rd., NW3 (Finchley Rd.) | 080-0316 2656 | fax 7794 4737
Islington | 26 Penton St., N1 (Islington) | 080-0093 4224 ◑
Clapham | 175 Lavender Hill, SW11 (Clapham) | 080-0389 9770 | fax 7978 4254 ◑
Fulham | 690 Fulham Rd., SW6 (Fulham Broadway) | 080-0028 3531
Richmond | 178 Upper Richmond Rd., SW14 (Mortlake) | 080-0096 8202
www.basilico.co.uk

"Real Italian pizza, delivered in a reliable manner" – along with "carefully prepared" side dishes and gourmet salads – makes this "efficient" quintet a "neighbourhood favourite", wherever that neighbourhood may be; though "mostly for takeaway", a few have seating too.

Bedford & Strand ⓩ *British/French* ▽ 17 | 18 | 18 | £37

Covent Garden | 1A Bedford St., WC2 (Covent Garden) | 020-7836 3033 | www.bedford-strand.com

"The real draw is the wine list" at this "welcome addition to Covent Garden" – a casual, old-fashioned, bistro-like wine bar whose "good" menu (a mélange of British and French) includes an "outstanding board of English cheeses"; "knowledgeable staff" complete the picture.

Beiteddine ◑ *Lebanese* ▽ 22 | 14 | 21 | £47

Knightsbridge | 8 Harriet St., SW1 (Knightsbridge/Sloane Sq.) | 020-7235 3969 | fax 7245 6335 | www.beiteddinerestaurant.com

"In an unpretentious environment" (some say "boring"), this glass-fronted Knightsbridge eatery is "among the better places" around town for "traditional", "high-end Lebanese" victuals; but bear in mind it's "not a cheap experience."

	FOOD	DECOR	SERVICE	COST

Z Belgo *Belgian* — 19 | 16 | 17 | £24

Covent Garden | 50 Earlham St., WC2 (Covent Garden) | 020-7813 2233 | fax 7209 3212

Chalk Farm | 72 Chalk Farm Rd., NW1 (Chalk Farm) | 020-7267 0718 | fax 7284 4842

www.belgo-restaurants.com

It's "like dining in a 1980s music video" at this communal-table, "chaotic", "cavernous" Covent Garden and Chalk Farm pair where staff dressed as "Trappist monks serve hearty Belgian fare", "mainly mussels" and frites ("anything else, skip it") – along with a "mind-boggling beer list" of brews; "although a bit 'fast-food' in its feel" and "upscale frat scene" in its ambience, it's "perfect for an early dinner" from 5–6:30 PM, when the price equals the time of your order (Earlham Street only).

Bellamy's Ⓩ *French* — 18 | 18 | 21 | £55

Mayfair | 18-18A Bruton Pl., W1 (Bond St./Green Park) | 020-7491 2727 | fax 7491 9990 | www.bellamysrestaurant.co.uk

An "excellent spot for lunch with your favourite hedge fund manager", this "clubby" venue "off the main drag" in Mayfair attracts a new- and "old-money crowd" with "thoughtful service" and "ambience that lends itself to companionable conversation"; the French brasserie fare is "well prepared" – if "not an excuse not to go to Paris."

Belvedere, The *British/French* — 20 | 23 | 19 | £47

Holland Park | Holland Park, off Abbotsbury Rd., W8 (Holland Park) | 020-7602 1238 | fax 7610 4382 | www.belvedererestaurant.co.uk

"Eat in style with well-heeled locals" at this "exquisite" eatery ("seemingly in the country", actually "the middle of Holland Park") where Marco Pierre White protégé Billy Reed prepares Modern British–New French cuisine that's quite "good, if not exceptional"; staff can be "a bit slow", but why rush your stay in such "pleasant surroundings"; P.S. "Sunday brunch is fabulous."

Benares *Indian* — 23 | 23 | 20 | £53

Mayfair | 12A Berkeley Square House, Berkeley Sq., W1 (Green Park) | 020-7629 8886 | fax 7499 2430 | www.benaresrestaurant.com

Its "lush decor" – "beautifully modern with classical touches" – is the first sign there's something different about this "edgy Indian" in Berkeley Square; chef-patron Atul Kochhar's "menu seems limited at first, but every dish is outstanding", "always pushing the envelope"; a few protest the "pushy staff", but still, this "sleek" site stays "busy with business types" who can bear the "nose-bleeding prices."

Bengal Clipper ● *Indian* — 21 | 19 | 19 | £30

Tower Bridge | Cardamom Bldg. | 31 Shad Thames, SE1 (London Bridge/Tower Hill) | 020-7357 9001 | fax 7357 9002 | www.bengalclipper.co.uk

"In a city with plenty of competition", this Bengali near Tower Bridge offers "a change from ordinary curry houses", thanks to a "wide selection" of "reasonably priced" and "interestingly spiced" dishes; the staff's "laid-back attitude" and Tuesday–Saturday "piano player make up for the impersonal decor."

	FOOD	DECOR	SERVICE	COST

Benihana *Japanese*
18 | 15 | 19 | £38

Piccadilly | 37 Sackville St., W1 (Green Park/Piccadilly Circus) | 020-7494 2525 | fax 7494 1456
Swiss Cottage | 100 Avenue Rd., NW3 (Swiss Cottage) | 020-7586 9508 | fax 7586 6740
Chelsea | 77 King's Rd., SW3 (Sloane Sq.) | 020-7376 7799 | fax 7376 7377
www.benihana.com

"The food all tends to taste the same and the room's a bit bland, but the chefs' performances and the overall experience keep you coming back" to these Japanese known for "spinning knives" and "slicing and dicing" the food "in front of you"; even so, opponents opine they're "overpriced and under-imaginative" – "McDonald's with grown-up utensils."

NEW Benja *Thai*
- | - | - | E

Soho | 17 Beak St., W1 (Oxford Circus/Piccadilly Circus) | 020-7287 0555 | fax 7287 0056

Its name means 'five' and the quintet theme runs throughout this three-storey elegant Soho newcomer, from the five taste sensations (sweet, spicy, sour, bitter and salty) of its "pricey but very good" traditional Thai fare to the five colours (red, black, green, turquoise and yellow) in its "great" decor, which includes wall-mounted ceramic flying fish and carved lotus.

Ben's Thai *Thai*
∇ 15 | - | 15 | £19

St. John's Wood | 15 Clifton Rd., W9 (Maida Vale/Warwick Ave.) | 020-7266 3134 | fax 7221 8799

"Cheap and tasty eats above a pub" sums up this "reliable" Thai, which recently moved to different St. John's Wood digs; fans enjoy the "authentic" food, but "just wish they wouldn't hurry you so much" to finish it.

Bentley's *British/Seafood*
24 | 19 | 21 | £49

Piccadilly | 11-15 Swallow St., W1 (Piccadilly Circus) | 020-7734 4756 | fax 7758 4140 | www.bentleys.org

Now "under the sway of respected chef Richard Corrigan, this strictly British seafood house has enhanced its past reputation" for "fish that's sublime"; diners can go for the "lively" "outstanding oyster bar" ("one of the best options after-theatre") or "ambrosial Dover sole" in the more "intimate" upstairs; "not cheap", but amidst the "hustle and bustle of Piccadilly", it's "a real plus for the London scene."

Bertorelli *Italian*
17 | 17 | 16 | £32

NEW Covent Garden | 37 St. Martin's Ln., WC2 (Covent Garden) | 020-7836 5837 | fax 7240 8462
Covent Garden | 44A Floral St., WC2 (Covent Garden) | 020-7836 3969 | fax 7836 1868 ☻
Soho | 11-13 Frith St., W1 (Leicester Sq./Tottenham Court Rd.) | 020-7494 3491 | fax 7439 9431 ☻
Fitzrovia | 19 Charlotte St., W1 (Goodge St./Tottenham Court Rd.) | 020-7636 4174 | fax 7467 8902

(continued)

(continued)

Bertorelli
Blackfriars | 1 Plough Pl., EC4 (Chancery Ln.) | 020-7842 0510 | fax 7842 0511 Ⓢ
City | Plantation Pl. | 15 Mincing Ln., EC3 (Bank/Monument) | 020-7283 3028 | fax 7929 5987 Ⓢ
www.santeonline.co.uk

"Casual", "cheap and cheerful" characterises this chain that's "like Chez Gérard, only Italian" (the same group owns both); sure, they're "a bit basic on the decor" and "the waiters could do with a week in charm school", but "the formula" is "a favourite" for a quick meal, and the Covent Garden branches are "handy" "pre- and post-theatre."

Bevis Marks Ⓢ *British/Jewish*   – | – | – | E
City | 4 Heneage Ln., EC3 (Aldgate/Liverpool St.) | 020-7283 2220 | fax 7283 2221 | www.bevismarkstherestaurant.com

It's "hard to find" in the annex of an 18th-century Aldgate synagogue, but this "pricey" Modern Brit with "loads of character" is "worth the effort" for "surprisingly excellent", innovative kosher victuals (plus some Jewish favourites); "they go the extra mile with service" too.

Ⓩ Bibendum *French*   24 | 23 | 22 | £57
South Kensington | Michelin House | 81 Fulham Rd., SW3 (South Kensington) | 020-7581 5817 | fax 7823 7925 | www.bibendum.co.uk

21 years on, it's "still a hit" say fans of this "stylish" New French in the "whimsical Michelin building" (the tyre company's "old U.K. HQ"), where the "innovative" fare is "a feast for the eyes and palate", aided by "delightful service"; the bellicose blow a gasket at the "eye-popping prices", but most declare they could "die in bliss" here.

Bibendum Oyster Bar *French/Seafood*   22 | 21 | 19 | £39
South Kensington | Michelin House | 81 Fulham Rd., SW3 (South Kensington) | 020-7589 1480 | fax 7823 7925 | www.bibendum.co.uk

"How amusing to sit in an old garage and eat oysters" at this "lively" Brompton Cross bistro where a display of "fabulous winkles, shrimp and lobster" forms the backbone of the "good, cold" French menu; whilst "pricey", it's still a "cheaper way to visit this wonderful landmark" – the 1911 Michelin building – than the restaurant upstairs.

Bierodrome *Belgian*   17 | 14 | 14 | £23
Covent Garden | 67 Kingsway, WC2 (Charing Cross/Holborn) | 020-7242 7469 | fax 7242 7493 Ⓢ
Islington | 173-174 Upper St., N1 (Highbury & Islington) | 020-7226 5835 | fax 7704 0632
Clapham | 44-48 Clapham High St., SW4 (Clapham North) | 020-7720 1118 | fax 7720 0288 ☽
www.belgo-restaurants.co.uk

"With 1,000 heavenly beers", this "brash" Belgian brigade is "probably a better bar than restaurant" – especially given the "dingy" digs and seemingly "intentionally rude staff"; still, given the "economic" prices, it's a place for the "young crowd" to "come for a mussels fix."

	FOOD	DECOR	SERVICE	COST

Big Easy *American*
16 15 16 £27

Chelsea | 332-334 King's Rd., SW3 (Sloane Sq.) | 020-7352 4071 | fax 7352 0844 | www.bigeasy.uk.com

"Bring an appetite – you forget how big those American portions are" – to this King's Road "heaven for surf 'n' turf lovers", where the fare is "well priced" if "executed without a whole lot of flair"; the crab-shack setting is "great for kids" and groups, but "if you like blending with the younger generation, remember your earplugs – the [nightly] live music is very loud."

Bistrotheque *French*
19 18 21 £32

Bethnal Green | 23-27 Wadesdon St., E2 (Bethnal Green) | 020-8983 7900 | fax 8880 6433 | www.bistrotheque.com

Down an "unappealing side street" in Bethnal Green (like "a hilarious gangland hideaway"), this "trendy" haunt hits the mark with "simple, strong French bistro cooking", "really friendly staff" and "convivial atmosphere"; there's also a "boisterous" downstairs "bar that's worth a visit in itself" – if only for the "transvestite cabaret."

Bistrot 190 *British/Mediterranean*
▽ 19 22 19 £38

South Kensington | Gore Hotel | 190 Queen's Gate, SW7 (Gloucester Rd./South Kensington) | 020-7584 6601 | fax 7589 8127 | www.gorehotel.com

Amidst the "charming surroundings of a Victorian hotel", this eatery offers the "warm, welcoming atmosphere of a club", along with an "imaginative" Traditional British–Med menu and a "buzzy bar scene next door"; it's "handy for the Royal Albert Hall" too.

Black & Blue *Chophouse*
17 15 16 £28

Marylebone | 90-92 Wigmore St., W1 (Bond St.) | 020-7486 1912 | fax 7486 1913

Borough | Borough Mkt. | 1-2 Rochester Walk, SE1 (London Bridge) | 020-7357 9922

Hampstead | 205-207 Haverstock Hill, NW3 (Belsize Park) | 020-7443 7744 | fax 7443 7744

South Kensington | 105 Gloucester Rd., SW7 (Gloucester Rd.) | 020-7244 7666 | fax 7244 9993

Kensington | 215-217 Kensington Church St., W8 (Notting Hill Gate) | 020-7727 0004 | fax 7229 9359

www.blackandblue.biz

"Functional", if "a bit formulaic", this "casual" chophouse chain is a "good place to placate carnivorous instincts"; the "high ceilings and comfy booths" have a "retro feel", but "getting a table can be pot-luck", as, "irritatingly, they don't take bookings."

Blah! Blah! Blah! ⊠⊅ *Vegetarian*
▽ 18 11 13 £24

Shepherd's Bush | 78 Goldhawk Rd., W12 (Goldhawk Rd.) | 020-8746 1337 | fax 7328 3138

The "good, wholesome veggie fare more than amply fills a hole" at this "relaxed", recently refurbed Shepherd's Bush venue; if staff "make you feel like you owe them a favour", at least it "being a BYO keeps things reasonable."

	FOOD	DECOR	SERVICE	COST

Blakes ● *Eclectic*

| | 19 | 24 | 22 | £59 |

South Kensington | Blakes Hotel | 33 Roland Gdns., SW7 (Gloucester Rd./
South Kensington) | 020-7370 6701 | fax 7373 0442 |
www.blakeshotels.com

"Still one of the sexiest dining rooms in town", this "dark", "discreet"
South Ken hotel "hang for supermodels" is a "beautiful" backdrop
for those who "enjoy being pampered"; many just "go for the decor",
though: the Asian-Eclectic fare may provide "Phuket on a plate", but
comes at "are-you-kidding-me" prices.

Blandford Street ⊠ *British/European*

| | 18 | 18 | 20 | £44 |

Marylebone | 5-7 Blandford St., W1 (Bond St.) | 020-7486 9696 |
fax 7486 5067 | www.blandford-street.co.uk

"Suitable for both business and pleasure", this "lovely find" in
Marylebone has a "sturdy", "well-done" if "workmanlike" Modern
British–European menu and "unobtrusive servers"; there's also the
option to "bring wine for a reasonable corkage."

Bleeding Heart ⊠ *French*

| | 22 | 20 | 20 | £44 |

Holborn | 4 Bleeding Heart Yard, off Greville St., EC1 (Farringdon) |
020-7242 8238 | fax 7831 1402

Bleeding Heart Tavern ⊠ *British*

Holborn | 19 Greville St., EC1 (Farringdon) | 020-7404 0333 |
fax 7831 1402
www.bleedingheart.co.uk

"A bit off the beaten track" in a "historic" Holborn courtyard, this
venue is actually "a collection of great spots": a "cosy" bistro
with "cute Swiss log cabin decor" and a more "fancy" "atmospheric downstairs" restaurant, both serving "wholesome, satisfying" New French fare and "well-priced wines"; then there's the
informal Tavern on Greville Street, "good for Traditional British
soul food and a pint"; main complaint for all: "why don't they
open at the weekend?"

Bloom's *Deli/Jewish*

| | 19 | 8 | 14 | £23 |

Golders Green | 130 Golders Green Rd., NW11 (Golders Green) |
020-8455 1338 | fax 8455 3033 | www.bloomsrestaurant.co.uk

Dating back to 1920, "this old-fashioned, family-run kosher restaurant has decided to get with the competition" in Golders Green and
"undergone refurbishment" (not fully reflected in the Decor score);
it remains "the place to go for salt beef" and other "solid" Jewish delights, "presented in a hurry."

Bluebird *European*

| | - | - | - | E |

Chelsea | 350 King's Rd., SW3 (Sloane Sq.) | 020-7559 1000 |
fax 7559 1111 | www.bluebird-restaurant.co.uk

"Overlooking King's Road", this "sunlit, air-filled loft" has undergone a
"recent decor revamp to make it less noisy, more comfortable" and
intimate; exec chef Mark Broadbent has remodelled the menu in
Modern European mode, and the surrounding complex now includes a larger lounge/bar; the alfresco cafe remains ("what would
Chelsea be without the Bluebird for all the birds to be seen at?").

	FOOD	DECOR	SERVICE	COST

Blue Elephant ● *Thai* — `20` `25` `19` `£44`

Fulham | 4-6 Fulham Broadway, SW6 (Fulham Broadway) |
020-7385 6595 | fax 7386 7665 | www.blueelephant.com

"Koi carp, bridges", "beautiful plants and streams in the middle of
Fulham" – "the decor never ceases to surprise" at this "exotic tropi-
cal jungle"; true, the "traditional Thai food", though "nice", "would
be one-third of the price without all the razzamatazz", and the "staff
in military-style outfits" "can be slow"; still, whilst "weird and
wacky, somehow it works."

Blueprint Café *European* — `18` `21` `18` `£38`

Tower Bridge | Design Museum | Butler's Wharf, 28 Shad Thames, SE1
(London Bridge/Tower Hill) | 020-7378 7031 | fax 7357 8810 |
www.blueprintcafe.co.uk

"Not a cafe, but a full and fancy restaurant", this "modern", "minimalist" museum dining room offers a Modern European menu that's
"enjoyable" (especially the "good value lunch"); but some argue the
"real reason to go is the exquisite view of the river and Tower
Bridge" – "if you're lucky enough to get a seat on the porch."

Bodeans *BBQ* — `18` `13` `16` `£19`

Soho | 10 Poland St., W1 (Oxford Circus) | 020-7287 7575 |
fax 7287 4342
Clapham | 169 Clapham High St., SW4 (Clapham Common) |
020-7622 4248 | fax 7622 3087
Fulham | 4 Broadway Chambers, SW6 (Fulham Broadway) |
020-7610 0440 | fax 7610 1115
www.bodeansbbq.com

"Great big servings" of "cheap" vittles make this trio "a true home
for Americans dying for the finer art of ribs" and other barbecued
treats; the "physical space is nothing to write home about", but
"lonely expats" insist this is "the closest London gets to Dixie" –
"and if you're lucky, they'll be showing U.S. football too."

Boisdale ☒ *British/Scottish* — `20` `20` `19` `£48`

Victoria | 13 Eccleston St., SW1 (Victoria) | 020-7730 6922 |
fax 7730 0548 ●
City | Swedeland Ct. | 202 Bishopsgate, EC2 (Liverpool St.) |
020-7283 1763 | fax 7283 1664
www.boisdale.co.uk

"Where else would you try your first haggis" than at this "eccentric"
duo in Victoria and the City that "really do traditional Scottish very
well", complete with "tartan surroundings" and a "sterling selection
of whiskies"; the rest of the "old-time" British cuisine is "a bit heavy"
(and "expensive") for some tastes, and "service seems to be bi-
polar", but the live "jazz evenings are great."

Bombay Bicycle Club *Indian* — `18` `15` `17` `£30`

Hampstead | 3A Downshire Hill, NW3 (Hampstead) | 020-7435 3544 |
fax 7794 3367
Clapham | 95 Nightingale Ln., SW12 (Clapham South) | 020-8673 6217 |
fax 8673 9100

(continued)

(continued)

Bombay Bicycle Club

Holland Park | 128 Holland Park Ave., W11 (Holland Park) |
020-7727 7335 | fax 7727 7305
www.thebombaybicycleclub.co.uk

They're "more expensive than your average curry house, but they don't serve your average curry" at this Indian trio; despite the Indo-European decor, they "lack atmosphere" some say – hence the "unbeatable takeaway" proves "popular."

Bombay Brasserie ❶ *Indian*

22	22	19	£37

South Kensington | Courtfield Rd., SW7 (Gloucester Rd.) |
020-7370 4040 | fax 7835 1669 | www.bombaybrasserielondon.com

For a "high-end Indian fix" with "that Merchant-Ivory feeling", this slightly pricey South Ken stalwart remains "a classic" choice where diners can "dig deep into the exotic menu, or play it safe"; foes feel the "service is somewhat uptight" and the decor "tired" – but the latter at least is slated for a post-Survey refurb.

Bonds *French*

▽ 20	21	20	£52

City | Threadneedles Hotel | 5 Threadneedle St., EC2 (Bank) |
020-7657 8088 | fax 7657 8100 | www.theetoncollection.com

"In a relative wilderness of good food", this New French's "flavoursome" fare is "more interesting than most City restaurants'"; the "swanky" "converted bank" venue and staff who "just let you be" make it a "location where deals get done (or at least discussed)" – mainly during the week (it only serves breakfast Saturday–Sunday).

☒ Books for Cooks ☒☒ *Eclectic*

24	21	21	£18

Notting Hill | 4 Blenheim Cres., W11 (Ladbroke Grove/Notting Hill Gate) |
020-7221 1992 | fax 7221 1517 | www.booksforcooks.com

"An iconic destination for serious cooks", this "teeny tiny" cafe "located at the back of a unique bookshop" off Ladbroke Grove features "wildly exciting", "experimental" Eclectic meals (one choice per day), using recipes "taken from featured cookbooks"; it's "the biggest bargain in town – but don't tell anyone, it's busy enough."

NEW Bouga *Moroccan*

-	-	-	M

Muswell Hill | 1 Park Rd., N8 (Archway) | 020-8348 5609

"A fun addition to buzzy Crouch End", this newcomer dishes up all the Moroccan mainstays, plus "great cocktails" and weekend belly dancers, amidst the candlelit contours of an Old Marrakech setting.

Boxwood Café ❶ *British*

21	20	21	£59

Belgravia | The Berkeley | Wilton Pl., SW1 (Knightsbridge) |
020-7235 1010 | fax 7235 1011 | www.gordonramsay.com

Strictly speaking, this "stylish", "buzzy" Gordon Ramsay–owned eatery is "not a cafe at all" attest fans who fall for the "imaginative" takes on Modern British "comfort food" (like "the heavenly veal and foie gras burger") and "attentive-without-being-starchy service"; admittedly, whilst "cheaper than other Ramsay [venues], it's not cheap at all", and hostiles huff it "has a hotel-restaurant feel about it" too (well, it *is* in the Berkeley).

	FOOD	DECOR	SERVICE	COST

Brackenbury, The *European*
18 | 15 | 18 | £32

Hammersmith | 129-131 Brackenbury Rd., W6 (Goldhawk Rd./
Hammersmith) | 020-8748 0107 | fax 8748 6159

"Perhaps not worth a special trip, but if you're out west", this "neighbourhood haunt" in Hammersmith offers "inventive" Modern
European meals with "agreeable service"; the brown-and-green interior can be "cramped", so there's gratitude for the "outside
seating in good weather."

Bradley's 𝕄 *British/French*
▽ 15 | 14 | 16 | £39

Swiss Cottage | 25 Winchester Rd., NW3 (Swiss Cottage) |
020-7722 3457 | fax 7435 1392

Those Swiss Cottagers who claim to be "lucky to have this as a local"
cite a "consistently good" Classic French–Modern British menu with
"great deals" for the "pre-theatre crowd"; that said, others find it "hard
to understand why this rather ordinary place inspires such loyalty."

Brasserie Roux ❶ *French*
20 | 20 | 18 | £46

St. James's | Sofitel St. James London | 8 Pall Mall, SW1 (Piccadilly Circus) |
020-7968 2900 | fax 7389 7647 | www.sofitelstjames.com

Benefiting from the "grandeur" of the high-ceilinged premises, this
St. James's brasserie has its supporters for "good-quality" French fare
on an Albert Roux-inspired menu ("very worthwhile pre-theatre"),
with "tempting wine bargains"; but cynics say "you'll rue the day you
went here", citing "boring" food and a "lack of atmosphere."

Brasserie St. Quentin *French*
18 | 18 | 18 | £40

Knightsbridge | 243 Brompton Rd., SW3 (Knightsbridge/
South Kensington) | 020-7589 8005 | fax 7584 6064 |
www.brasseriestquentin.co.uk

"No matter what you're in the mood for, you can find something" on
the "solid" Classic French menu of this brasserie "in a great location
between the V&A Museum and Harrods"; a few find it "overpriced",
given the "noisy" digs and "forgetful service", but "for an ordinary
meal", it's "a great staple in your wardrobe."

Brian Turner Mayfair *British*
21 | 19 | 21 | £51

Mayfair | Millennium Hotel Mayfair | 44 Grosvenor Sq., W1 (Bond St./
Green Park) | 020-7596 3444 | fax 7596 3443 | www.millenniumhotels.com

"Perhaps a notch down from the top-list celebrity-chef dining establishments", Brian Turner's "sophisticated" Mayfair site still offers
"unobtrusive service" and "tasty Traditional British fare" fans find;
opponents opine it's "overpriced" – "can only be trading on the 'I've
seen him on the telly' factor" – though the "set-price menu makes
the bill less likely to drain the colour from your face."

Brinkley's ❶ *Eclectic*
▽ 16 | 16 | 18 | £32

Chelsea | 47 Hollywood Rd., SW10 (Earl's Ct./South Kensington) |
020-7351 1683 | fax 7376 5083 | www.brinkleys.com

A "favourite hangout for Chelsea girls and their companions", this
Eclectic "Hollywood Road venue serves good grub" at reasonable
prices – plus there's "a great wine selection if you get your bottle

from the shop" next door; "charming, if sometimes haphazard staff" and a garden that's "amazing in summer and nice in winter" (it's heated) complete the picture.

Browns *British*

16 | 17 | 17 | £31

Covent Garden | 82-84 St. Martin's Ln., WC2 (Leicester Sq.) | 020-7497 5050 | fax 7497 5005
Mayfair | 47 Maddox St., W1 (Bond St./Oxford Circus) | 020-7491 4565 | fax 7497 4564
City | 8 Old Jewry, EC2 (Bank) | 020-7606 6677 | fax 7600 5359 🖪
Canary Wharf | Hertsmere Rd., E14 (Canary Wharf/West India Quay) | 020-7987 9777 | fax 7537 1341
Tower Bridge | Shad Thames, SE1 (London Bridge) | 020-7378 1700 | fax 7378 7468
Islington | 9 Islington Green, N1 (Angel) | 020-7226 2555 | fax 7359 7306
www.browns-restaurants.com

Strategically situated around town, these "cavernous", "casual 'pubby'" haunts offer a Traditional "British–meets-brasserie" menu; "nothing says 'must go here'", but "if you want to eat without fuss or expense" for lunch, or "you're in the mood for crowds" at night, they're "reliable" (but be aware – "as it gets busier", service gets slower).

Brown's Hotel - The Grill *British*

22 | 24 | 25 | £56

Mayfair | Brown's Hotel | Albemarle St., W1 (Green Park) | 020-7518 4060 | fax 7493 9381 | www.brownshotel.com
"After the recent renovation", this newly "chic", slightly modernised Mayfair hotel grill is "as good a treat in haute cuisine as ever", with a "delicious", "classic" British bill of fare – "even the [carving] trolley" – and "professional" service; naturally nostalgists note it's "lost its old charm" and is "too much like a typical hotel" (i.e. "expensive" "for what you get"), but devotees declare it's "destined to be a classic" again; P.S. you "must book" the "ultimate English experience" – afternoon tea in the lounge.

Brunello *Italian*

▽ 20 | 20 | 19 | £67

Kensington | Baglioni | 60 Hyde Park Gate, SW7 (Gloucester Rd./High St. Kensington) | 020-7368 5900 | fax 7368 5701 | www.baglionihotellondon.com
If you like a "loud" look, you'll "love the decor" – imagine a gold-leaf, "Disney meets *Hammer House of Horror*" effect – of this hotel dining room overlooking Kensington Gardens ("perfect location"); as for the Eclectic-Italian fare, it's "good, not great" – especially given the "outrageous prices", so, better stick to the "interesting bar scene."

Buen Ayre *Argentinean*

▽ 23 | 15 | 25 | £30

Hackney | 50 Broadway Mkt., E8 (Bethnal Green) | 020-7275 9900 | fax 7900 3941
Santa Maria *Argentinean*
Battersea | 129 Queenstown Rd., SW8 (Clapham Common) | 020-7622 2088 | fax 7627 8544
www.buenayre.co.uk
It might look "extremely basic", but there's "high-quality Argentine" fare – especially "huge, astonishing steaks" – at this

Hackney grill that also specialises in "sparkling service"; N.B. the younger Battersea branch is now separately owned under the name Santa Maria.

Builders Arms *British*

| 17 | 18 | 14 | £25 |

Chelsea | 13 Britten St., SW3 (Sloane Sq./South Kensington) | 020-7349 9040 | fax 7351 3181 | www.geronimo-inns.co.uk

This "cute little pub tucked away off King's Road" attracts a "younger", "stylish Chelsea" crowd with its "awesome fireplace" and an "atmosphere so warm, you feel like you're sitting in someone's living room"; there's "decent grub" on the Traditional British menu, though it's "marred by random service."

Bull, The *European*

| ∇ 19 | 18 | 16 | £39 |

Highgate | 13 North Hill, N6 (Highgate) | 0845-456 5033 | fax 0845-456 5034 | www.inthebull.biz

"Buzzing most evenings", this gastropub is becoming a "'simple food' hit" in Highgate, as its Modern European fare features "fantastically well-sourced ingredients" (a "bit pricey – but that keeps the commoners away!"); "friendly service" can be "haphazard, but is getting better."

NEW Bumpkin ● *British*

| 21 | 20 | 20 | £37 |

Notting Hill | 209 Westbourne Park Rd., W11 (Notting Hill/Westbourne Park) | 020-7243 9818 | www.bumpkinuk.com

For a "hearty" British "country meal with a twist of London hippiness thrown in", try this triparte "newcomer to Notting Hill"; "each level has something to offer": a "lively, fresh, ground-floor" brasserie ("be ready to wait" as you can't book, except on Sunday), a more "romantic" restaurant upstairs and finally, "don't miss the [for-hire] whisky lounges on the top floor"; "the staff welcome you like they've known you for years" – and indeed, "you won't want to leave."

Buona Sera ● *Italian*

| 23 | 19 | 20 | £28 |

Battersea | 22-26 Northcote Rd., SW11 (Clapham Junction B.R.) | 020-7228 9925 | fax 7228 1114
Chelsea | 289A King's Rd., SW3 (Sloane Sq.) | 020-7352 8827 | fax 7352 8827

The "innovative" setting of bunk bed–style tables "is a brilliant way to make the most of the limited floor space (makes dropping your fork a bit of a hazard, though)" at these Chelsea and Battersea Italians; "family-friendly at weekends", but "equally good for a night out with the girls", their "excellent selection of pizza and pasta" "never disappoints" as long as you "don't expect fireworks."

NEW Burlington Club ●⊠ *Spanish*

| – | – | – | E |

Mayfair | 12 New Burlington St., W1 (Oxford Circus/Piccadilly Circus) | 020-7734 0233 | fax 3102 3071 | www.burlingtonclub.com

Mayfair mavens bask in the Basque bites, served amidst decor of coloured lights and whimsical furniture, of this new small-plates place; a few feel it's "expensive for tiny tapas – better to come later", when it becomes a bar/lounge featuring fresh juice cocktails.

	FOOD	DECOR	SERVICE	COST

☑ Busaba Eathai *Thai*
21 | 19 | 16 | £21

Bloomsbury | 22 Store St., WC1E (Goodge St.) | 020-7299 7900 | fax 7299 7909
Marylebone | 8-13 Bird St., W1 (Bond St.) | 020-7518 8080 | fax 7518 8088
Soho | 106-110 Wardour St., W1 (Piccadilly Circus/Tottenham Court Rd.) | 020-7255 8686

If you "are not put off by the queues outside" (which do "move quickly") and "don't mind the informal communal seating" ("which can either be fun or annoying"), this "funky", "fast and furious" Thai trio is "fantastic to go to alone or bring friends and share" "exotic" edibles that "won't break the bank"; "service is swift", but often "unfriendly."

Bush Bar & Grill *European*
17 | 15 | 15 | £36

Shepherd's Bush | 45A Goldhawk Rd., W12 (Goldhawk Rd./ Shepherd's Bush) | 020-8746 2111 | fax 8746 7114 | www.bushbar.co.uk

It "looks like a converted scout hut or tiny aircraft hangar" from the outside, and "feels a bit '90s" when inside, but this "Shepherd's Bush staple" has a "relaxed atmosphere that belies the sophistication" of the "reasonably priced" Modern European cooking – plus there's a "snazzy bar" with "excellent cocktails."

NEW Butcher & Grill, The *British*
▽ 15 | 15 | 16 | £36

Battersea | 39-41 Parkgate Rd., SW11 (Sloane Sq.) | 020-7924 3999 | fax 7223 7979 | www.thebutcherandgrill.com

The former Café Rouge site backing onto a tranquil Battersea dock has been transformed into a "cheerful", easy-going eatery with a "decent" Traditional British menu (though "inconsistently sized portions" can make it "a bit pricey for what you get"); staff are "well-meaning", even if some "couldn't remember what was on or off the menu"; P.S. there's also a "good in-house" butcher's shop.

Butlers Wharf Chop House *British*
20 | 21 | 20 | £43

Tower Bridge | Butlers Wharf Bldg. | 36E Shad Thames, SE1 (London Bridge/Tower Hill) | 020-7403 3403 | fax 7940 1855 | www.chophouse.co.uk

"Sit outside" and enjoy "spectacular views" of Tower Bridge and beyond on the banks of the Thames at this "buzzy" British chophouse; the "old-fashioned food" is "above average", both in quality and price – leading some to believe it tastes "better if you have an expense account" or can make use of the "excellent-value lunch."

Café Boheme ● *French*
16 | 16 | 15 | £30

Soho | 13-17 Old Compton St., W1 (Leicester Sq./Tottenham Court Rd.) | 020-7734 0623 | fax 7434 3775 | www.cafeboheme.co.uk

"Busy from dawn until dusk", this "hard to get into" cafe "hits the spot" as somewhere "cool just to hang", with "great people-watching of the Soho streets"; "atmosphere is its most redeeming trait, however" – don't expect more than "ok" eats from "rather random service", or else "stick to late-night drinks."

	FOOD	DECOR	SERVICE	COST

Café des Amis ●🅩 *French* · 19 · 17 · 18 · £35

Covent Garden | 11-14 Hanover Pl., WC2 (Covent Garden) |
020-7379 3444 | fax 7379 9124 | www.cafedesamis.co.uk
"Popular" with the "pre/post-opera hounds", this "pleasant modern
French" in a "tiny alleyway" has been a "Covent Garden standby" for
20 years – "a reasonable choice, if not a destination"; *amis* enjoy its
"ever-reliable" bistro fare "with a wine list to complement", but others find it's "more fun" to "sneak downstairs to the bar for fine
cheeses and cheeky reds."

Café Fish *British/Seafood* · 20 · 13 · 17 · £30

Soho | 36-40 Rupert St., W1 (Leicester Sq./Piccadilly Circus) |
020-7287 8989 | fax 7287 8400 | www.santeonline.co.uk
"For fresh fish, frites, fromage" and "traditionally prepared British
fare", try this "friendly" Soho seafooder in "quirky" tiled surroundings; in between the "bathroom ambience" and the pianist plugging
away nightly, it's "not for those seeking a soothing evening", but it is
"handy for Theatreland."

🆉 Café Japan 🅜 *Japanese* · 26 · 10 · 19 · £28

Golders Green | 626 Finchley Rd., NW11 (Golders Green) |
020-8455 6854 | fax 8455 6854
"What a top-flight Japanese is doing" in this "hole-in-the-wall setting" "in Golders Green is anyone's guess", but the "legend lives on"
for "spectacular sushi" and "the best grilled fish"; just remember to
"get there early, as tables go quickly" and there are no reservations;
N.B. a cash-only lunch is served weekends.

Cafe Med ● *Mediterranean* · 18 · 14 · 16 · £27

St. John's Wood | 21 Loudoun Rd., NW8 (St. John's Wood) |
020-7625 1222
"Solid Mediterranean food in a bistro setting" sums up this St. John's
Wood "standby"; area denizens deem it a "decent local if you don't
want to travel too far", given that it's "good value", the staff are "used
to dealing with kids" and there's "nice dining alfresco", come summer.

Cafe Pacifico ● *Mexican* · 18 · 15 · 16 · £26

Covent Garden | 5 Langley St., WC2 (Covent Garden) | 020-7379 7728 |
fax 7379 5933 | www.cafepacifico-laperla.com
"Don't be frightened off by the scruffy decor", "too-close tables"
and the "no-reservations chaos on weekends" – this "very lively
(sometimes too lively)" Covent Garden cantina is, converts claim,
the "only plausible Tex-Mex in town"; if some quip "that's not saying
much" – well, this is "London and not Laredo" after all.

Café Rouge *French* · 14 · 14 · 14 · £24

Covent Garden | 34 Wellington St., WC2 (Covent Garden) |
020-7836 0998 | fax 7497 0738
Knightsbridge | 27-31 Basil St., SW3 (Knightsbridge) |
020-7584 2345 | fax 7584 4253
Canary Wharf | 10 Cabot Sq., E14 (Canary Wharf) | 020-7537 9696 |
fax 7987 1232

(continued)

(continued)

Café Rouge

Highgate | 6-7 South Grove, N6 (Highgate) | 020-8342 9797
St. John's Wood | 120 St. John's Wood High St., NW8 (St. John's Wood) |
020-7722 8366 | fax 7483 1015
Clapham | 40 Abbeville Rd., SW4 (Clapham South) | 020-8673 3399 |
fax 8673 2299
Dulwich | 84 Park Hall Rd., SE21 (West Dulwich) | 020-8766 0070
Putney | 200 Putney Bridge Rd., SW15 (Putney Bridge) |
020-8788 4257
Chiswick | 227-229 Chiswick High Rd., W4 (Chiswick Park) |
020-8742 7447 | fax 8742 7557
Shepherd's Bush | 98-100 Shepherd's Bush Rd., W6 (Shepherd's Bush) |
020-7602 7732 | fax 7603 7710
www.caferouge.co.uk
Additional locations throughout London

To its *amis*, this "ubiquitous chain" is "a reliable facsimile of a simple French bistro" with a mock "Moulin Rouge-ish setting" and "affordable" fare; but antagonists see *rouge* at the "faded" decor, "predictable food and unpredictable" service that swings from "swift" to "the slowest in London."

Café Spice Namasté ⓩ *Indian*   23 | 16 | 18 | £33

City | 16 Prescot St., E1 (Aldgate/Tower Hill) | 020-7488 9242 |
fax 7488 9339 | www.cafespice.co.uk
Chef-patron "Cyrus Todiwala is a genius", and it shows in the "inventive Indian food" cooked at his colourful place "near Tower Hill" (admittedly "out-of-the-way unless you're in the City"); more controversial is the setting, a strongly hued "warehouse" that reminds one reviewer of "an '80s Mexican chain restaurant, best suited to large groups."

Caldesi ⓩ *Italian*   22 | 17 | 20 | £40

Marylebone | 15-17 Marylebone Ln., W1 (Bond St.) | 020-7935 9226 |
fax 7935 9228 | www.caldesi.com
Dining at this "intimate" trattoria is "pretty close to being back in Tuscany", thanks to cuisine that offers "a true taste of traditional" fare, an "assured welcome" ("if you're a regular") and ambience that's as "good for a celebration as for a quiet dinner for two"; if some quibble it's the "kind of place you can't find fault with until you see the price", most maintain it's "one of Marylebone's best-kept secrets."

ⓩ Cambio de Tercio ◑ *Spanish*   24 | 17 | 19 | £42

South Kensington | 163 Old Brompton Rd., SW5 (Gloucester Rd./
South Kensington) | 020-7244 8970 | fax 7373 8817 |
www.cambiodetercio.co.uk
"The crowd, the food, the pace" – it all adds up to "a truly Spanish experience" at this "absolute must-go" in South Ken with an "innovative" Iberian menu (including "the best roast baby pig in town"), "dramatic" yellow-and-red decor and "quite helpful" – if sometimes "rushed" – staff; just "don't look at what they're delivering to other tables, or you'll order too much."

			FOOD	DECOR	SERVICE	COST

Camden Brasserie *European*

▽ 21 | 17 | 22 | £30

Camden Town | 9-11 Jamestown Rd., NW1 (Camden Town) |
020-7482 2114 | fax 7482 2777 | www.camdenbrasserie.co.uk

"Still hanging in there" after 25 years, this "comfortably busy" Camden
haunt is "no more or less than a good brasserie should be", with a
"well-executed Modern European menu" ("rib of beef is the speciality"), a variety of varietals and "pleasant staff" – all "at fair prices."

Camerino 🛇 *Italian*

– | – | – | E

Fitzrovia | 16 Percy St., W1 (Tottenham Court Rd.) | 020-7637 9900 |
fax 7637 9696 | www.camerinorestaurant.com

Decked out in red, black and white, this Fitzrovian is the "sort of
place you can go to often and not get bored", thanks to "outstanding
homemade pasta" and other "authentic Italian" dishes; true, "service can be slow – but this food should not be hurried."

Canteen *British*

22 | 19 | 19 | £29

Spitalfields | 2 Crispin Pl., E1 (Liverpool St.) | 0845-686 1122 |
fax 0845-686 1144

South Bank | Royal Festival Hall | Southbank Centre Sq., Belvedere Rd.,
SE1 (Waterloo) | 0845-686 1122 🛇 Ⓜ
www.canteen.co.uk

"Just what London needs more of" cry converts to this "buzzy" Brit
set in a "modern canteen (surprise)"-style room and serving "gourmet interpretations of classic dishes" "at the right price"; "fast service" ensures the communal benches turn quickly, but "get a booth
if possible" to "watch as crowds mull past" Spitalfields Market;
P.S. those who had "fingers crossed that it expands" should rejoice:
a Royal Festival Hall offshoot opened in June 2007.

Cantina del Ponte *Italian*

17 | 15 | 13 | £36

Tower Bridge | Butlers Wharf Bldg. | 36C Shad Thames, SE1
(London Bridge/Tower Hill) | 020-7403 5403 | fax 7940 1845 |
www.cantina.co.uk

"On a sunny weekend, the buoyant mood can't be beaten" at this
"relaxed" Butlers Wharf venue; the Italian fare is "reliable", but "service is hit-and-miss", leaving some to conclude that – the "odd celeb
face" aside – its real appeal lies in the "excellent alfresco seating."

Cantina Vinopolis *Eclectic/Mediterranean*

▽ 19 | 19 | 19 | £30

South Bank | Vinopolis Museum | 1 Bank End, SE1 (London Bridge) |
020-7940 8333 | fax 7940 9339 | www.cantinavinopolis.com

"Learn about wines on a tour" of the South Bank's oenology museum
"under the arches" of a Victorian railway viaduct, and then "work your
way through the *Encyclopaedia Britannia* of a list" and a "good", wallet-
friendly Eclectic-Med menu in the airy canteen; "attentive staff" explain the "extraordinary selection" of vinos, many by the glass.

⚡ Capital Restaurant, The *French*

27 | 22 | 26 | £75

Knightsbridge | Capital Hotel | 22 Basil St., SW3 (Knightsbridge) |
020-7591 1202 | fax 7225 0011 | www.capitalhotel.co.uk

"A tiny piece of heaven in the middle of Knightsbridge" is how "dis-
cerning diners" view this "serene", "understated" hotel New French

that "gives one the impression of eating in a rich relative's dining room"; provided by near-"perfect", "pukka service", chef Eric Chavot's cuisine is "a real treat" "not to be missed" – even if it does require "a second mortgage" on the *maison*; all told, a capital experience, though perhaps "not for the young and hip."

Caraffini ●🅱 Italian

21 | 16 | 22 | £39

Chelsea | 61-63 Lower Sloane St., SW1 (Sloane Sq.) | 020-7259 0235 | fax 7259 0236 | www.caraffini.co.uk

"It's always full, so it must be good" goes the thinking about this "jolly" trattoria near Sloane Square – and indeed, the "fresh" *cucina* is quite "enjoyable", especially given the "prices that won't break the bank" and staff that exude "a genuine Italian family feeling"; the only thing not *bene* is the "unbelievable noise" in the "cramped" digs.

Caravaggio 🅱 Italian

19 | 18 | 18 | £50

City | 107-112 Leadenhall St., EC3 (Bank/Monument) | 020-7626 6206 | fax 7626 8108 | www.etruscagroup.co.uk

When seeking "a reliable spot for a business lunch in the City", diners "can do a lot worse" than this weekday-only Italian – even if the art deco-ish decor is looking "dated" and the "overworked" servers are just "ok"; "but remember, no expense account, no Caravaggio."

🆉 Carluccio's Caffe Italian

17 | 15 | 15 | £24

Bloomsbury | 8 Market Pl., W1 (Oxford Circus) | 020-7636 2228 | fax 7636 9650

Marylebone | 3-5 Barrett St., W1 (Bond St.) | 020-7935 5927 | fax 7487 5436

Marylebone | St. Christopher's Pl., W1 (Bond St.) | 020-7935 5927

Mayfair | Fenwick | 63 New Bond St., downstairs, W1 (Bond St.) | 020-7629 0699 | fax 7493 0069

Canary Wharf | Reuters Plaza | 2 Nash Ct., E14 (Canary Wharf) | 020-7719 1749 | fax 7513 1197

Smithfield | 12 West Smithfield, EC1 (Farringdon) | 020-7329 5904 | fax 7248 5981

Islington | 305-307 Upper St., N1 (Angel) | 020-7359 8167 | fax 7354 9196

Fulham | 236 Fulham Rd., SW10 (Fulham Broadway) | 020-7376 5960 | fax 7376 3698

Putney | Putney Wharf, SW15 (Putney Bridge) | 020-8789 0591 | fax 8789 8360

Hammersmith | 5-6 The Green, W5 (Ealing Broadway) | 020-8566 4458 | fax 8840 8566

www.carluccios.com

"Packed from morning to night", chef-owner Antonio "Carluccio's empire" of "casual", "comfy" cafes – "one of the foodie success stories of the new century" – offers an "affordable" experience of "quick and easy [eating], based on tried and tested" Italian recipes; it's "a great formula", the "chainy atmosphere" with "a little chaos thrown in" notwithstanding; P.S. another "big plus is the deli to pick up food for home."

	FOOD	DECOR	SERVICE	COST

Carpaccio ●☑ *Italian*
| 18 | 17 | 17 | £42 |

Chelsea | 4 Sydney St., SW3 (South Kensington) | 020-7352 3433 | www.carpaccio.uk.com

"Feeling like a neighbourhood restaurant where no one knows their neighbours" – because they're all "beautiful people" or "pretty Eurotrash" – this "crammed" Chelsea haunt is "a real scene"; whilst the dishes are "decent", it's "definitely not the place to go for great Italian food or efficient service" – or deep conversation ("you cannot talk, it's so noisy").

Casale Franco ⓜ *Italian*
| - | - | - | M |

Islington | 134-137 Upper St., N1 (Angel/Highbury & Islington) | 020-7226 8994 | fax 7359 1114

Filling the need for a "neighbourhood local" with "welcoming" staff, this "odd", theatrically themed Italian down an Islington alleyway has a "long menu ranging from pasta and pizzas to larger", more "amazing dishes."

Cay tre *Vietnamese*
| ▽ 24 | 10 | 16 | £17 |

Hoxton | 301 Old St., EC1 (Old St.) | 020-7729 8662

"Superb food rises above the surroundings" and staff ("not the most cheerful in the world") at this "true dive" in Hoxton; the Vietnamese cuisine is "reliable, quick and will fill you up" – and "astounding value" to boot.

Cecconi's ● *Italian*
| 21 | 20 | 20 | £52 |

Mayfair | 5A Burlington Gdns., W1 (Green Park/Piccadilly Circus) | 020-7434 1500 | fax 7434 2020 | www.cecconis.co.uk

"An instant success" since it was "revamped" over a year ago, this Mayfair Italian is now "as hip as London gets" – a "glitzy", "convivial" "celebrity favourite" where "friendly" staff serve "proper" Italian eats all day long; cynics sneer it's "a bit too luvvy" and "too expensive" now, but the "boisterous" brigades just "bring earplugs" and belly up to "the bar – it's hot, hot, hot on certain nights."

Cellar Gascon ●☑ *French*
| ▽ 20 | 16 | 15 | £39 |

Smithfield | 59 W. Smithfield, EC1 (Barbican/Farringdon) | 020-7796 0600 | fax 7796 0601

"The small brother of Club Gascon" a couple of doors away, this "laid-back" Smithfield site also specialises in "fantastic" "Southwest French tapas-style dishes" ("foie gras aficionados are swooning"); the nibbles are "backed up by an even better wine list", with "knowledge-able sommeliers" to guide diners through some "most attractive and unusual" varietals, "with many selections available by the glass."

NEW C Garden *Italian*
| ▽ 18 | 18 | 19 | £41 |

Chelsea | 119 Sydney St., SW3 (Sloane Sq./South Kensington) | 020-7352 2718 | www.cgarden.co.uk

After an "ownership change and refurbishment" of the site that was "formerly the Chelsea stalwart Dan's", this yellow-hued yearling, a "charming" cousin to Carpaccio, attracts a "clubby clientele" with "good Italian cooking" from a kitchen and staff that are "trying very hard"; the "outside garden is a dining treat and bonus" – when it's sunny, "the only way to pack more in it would be with olive oil."

Champor-Champor ▣ *Malaysian* | 18 | 21 | 19 | £40 |

Tower Bridge | 62-64 Weston St., SE1 (London Bridge) | 020-7403 4600 | www.champor-champor.com

"Unique" and "intimate", this London Bridge–area eatery is "eccentrically, yet brilliantly decorated" like an "Asian antiques shop", and keeps the theme going on an "adventurous" Malaysian menu; sometimes the "experimental" efforts "end up confused", but its champorions claim it's "well worth the detour."

Chancery, The ▣ *European* | ▽ 18 | 18 | 17 | £39 |

Holborn | 9 Cursitor St., EC4 (Chancery Ln.) | 020-7831 4000 | fax 7831 4002 | www.thechancery.co.uk

From the Clerkenwell Dining Room team comes this discreet "oasis in the culinary desert" of Holborn, where "attendant servers" offer a "solid, but not spectacular" Modern European menu in a modern, white-walled, wooden-floored setting that can be booked for private dinners on Saturday.

Chapter Two *European* | 24 | 15 | 22 | £38 |

Blackheath | 43-45 Montpelier Vale, SE3 (Blackheath) | 020-8333 2666 | fax 8355 8399 | www.chaptersrestaurants.co.uk

"Has never failed to delight me" gush lovers of this "reliable and reasonably priced" Blackheath haute cuisine haven whose "excellent" Modern European meals are served by staff that are "attentive, yet relaxed enough to leave you to it"; "the room lacks a bit of soul though."

Charlotte's Place *European* | - | - | - | E |

Ealing | 16 St. Matthew's Rd., W5 (Ealing Broadway/Ealing Common) | 020-8567 7541 | www.charlottes.co.uk

A "cosy" renovated Victorian home houses "excellent" Modern European fare at this bi-level Ealing Common local; "friendly service" and "enjoyable jazz" sessions on weekday evenings add to the "pleasant" ambience.

🆕 Chelsea Brasserie *French* | 16 | 15 | 15 | £40 |

Chelsea | Sloane Square Hotel | 7-12 Sloane Sq., SW1 (Sloane Sq.) | 020-7881 5999 | www.sloanesquarehotel.co.uk

"Right on Sloane Square", a revamped hotel has reopened to reveal this "Paris brasserie-esque" place, featuring a "sinful" menu that lets Francophiles get their "raclette fix"; but *hélas*, pessimists find it "pretentious in extremis", with "dull decor", "prices that must reflect their high rent and waiters you need a bullhorn to flag down"; at least "the location is great after shopping."

Chelsea Bun ● *British* | 18 | 9 | 16 | £16 |

Chelsea | Limerstone St., SW10 (Earl's Ct./Sloane Sq.) | 020-7352 3635 | fax 7376 5158 | www.chelseabun.co.uk

"Chelsea residents' idea of a working men's caff", this "terrific greasy spoon" is "the place to go to" if you "have a craving" for "that

| | FOOD | DECOR | SERVICE | COST |

perfect hung-over breakfast" and other, "so fatty good" Traditional British dishes; "but be prepared to wait for a table" at weekends.

Cheyne Walk Brasserie *French* | 23 | 22 | 20 | £49 |

Chelsea | 50 Cheyne Walk, SW3 (Sloane Sq./South Kensington) | 020-7376 8787 | fax 7376 5878 | www.cheynewalkbrasserie.com

"One of the better French brasseries – certainly one of the friendliest" is how converts characterise this Chelsea Embankment "grand, cosy local", with a huge "open fire grill adding to the splendid atmosphere" as it cooks those "classic", "simple" yet "excellent" meats; although it's on the "pricey" side, "booking's advised well in advance"; P.S. don't forget to "retire for a nightcap" to the "dream bar upstairs."

☑ Chez Bruce *British* | 28 | 21 | 25 | £57 |

Wandsworth | 2 Bellevue Rd., SW17 (Balham/Wandsworth Common B. R.) | 020-8672 0114 | fax 8767 6648 | www.chezbruce.co.uk

"Simply no restaurant can match the quality for the quid" of this "Wandsworth wonder", which has knocked off Gordon Ramsay as London's No. 1 for Food with its "reliably fantastic", "flawlessly executed" Modern British cuisine; "everything [else] about it is class" too – "knowledgeable" but "never intrusive" staff, "the extensive wine list and possibly the largest selection of cheese in town"; the "cosy" room can be "cramped", but really, "the only problem is getting a reservation" ("even for long-term customers").

Chez Gérard *French* | 18 | 17 | 17 | £37 |

Covent Garden | Opera Terrace, The Market | 45 E. Terrace, 1st fl., WC2 (Covent Garden) | 020-7379 0666 | fax 7497 9060 ◗

Holborn | 119 Chancery Ln., WC2 (Chancery Ln.) | 020-7405 0290 | fax 7242 2649 🖪

Mayfair | 31 Dover St., W1 (Green Park) | 020-7499 8171 | fax 7491 3818 🖪

Victoria | Thistle Hotel | 101 Buckingham Palace Rd., SW1 (Victoria) | 020-7868 6249 | fax 7976 6073

Fitzrovia | 8 Charlotte St., W1 (Goodge St./Tottenham Court Rd.) | 020-7636 4975 | fax 7637 4564 ◗

City | 1 Watling St., EC4 (Mansion House/St. Paul's) | 020-7213 0540 | fax 7213 0541 🖪

City | 14 Trinity Sq., EC3 (Tower Hill) | 020-7480 5500 | fax 7480 5588 🖪

City | 64 Bishopsgate, EC2 (Bank/Liverpool St.) | 020-7588 1200 | fax 7588 1122 🖪

Waterloo | 9 Belvedere Rd., SE1 (Waterloo) | 020-7202 8470 | fax 7202 8474

www.santeonline.co.uk

These "unpretentious" "Parisian brasserie–style" places in "prime locations" around town – including "a unique spot overlooking Covent Garden" – have been "reliable for years", with their "reassuringly familiar" (some say "factory"-like") menu of steak frites and such; but some suffer from "scatterbrain service", and whilst "everything seems good value, you're surprised that the bill is quite so big."

	FOOD	DECOR	SERVICE	COST

Chez Kristof ● *French*

22 | 19 | 16 | £40

Hammersmith | 111 Hammersmith Grove, W6 (Hammersmith) | 020-8741 1177 | fax 8846 3750 | www.chezkristof.co.uk

"Holding up in an odd area" in Hammersmith, this tightly packed "neighbourhood-style brasserie" is cited for Classic French fare that's "full of flavour" (pity the "staff can appear bored" serving it); all also agree the "outside tables are a treat in summer", plus there's "plenty to keep you interested" in the next-door deli, especially the "wonderful breakfast" (served until 3 PM).

NEW Chez Patrick *French* (fka Stratford's)

▽ 21 | 18 | 20 | £40

Kensington | 7 Stratford Rd., W8 (Earl's Ct./High St. Kensington) | 020-7937 6388 | www.chezpatrickinlondon.co.uk

It's now owned by Patrick Tako ("former manager at Lou Pescadou"), who gave it a bright "change of decor", but regulars are relieved the "relaxed, authentic French feel is still going strong" at this "neighbourhood place" in an old Kensington townhouse; as before, "fabulous fish" dominates the Gallic menu, which includes a "bargain set lunch."

Chiang Mai *Thai*

21 | 14 | 17 | £28

Soho | 48 Frith St., W1 (Leicester Sq./Tottenham Court Rd.) | 020-7437 7444 | fax 7287 2255

"Much better Thai food than you'd expect in the centre of Soho" is on hand at this "authentic" veteran – and at "outstanding value" too; warmed by "friendly staff", fans forgive the "frayed" decor.

China Tang ● *Chinese*

21 | 24 | 20 | £64

Mayfair | Dorchester Hotel | 53 Park Ln., W1 (Hyde Park Corner/ Marble Arch) | 020-7629 9988 | www.dorchesterhotel.com

"Enchanting art deco decor is the first thing you notice" at owner David Tang's "sophisticated" "show" in the Dorchester, where "many beautiful women and men of obvious means abound", consuming the "subtle", "smartly presented Chinese food"; but the experience is losing its tang for others, who fuss that "for all the decor", the cuisine just ranks as "very good" – hence, "vastly overpriced."

Chinese Experience *Chinese*

21 | 14 | 18 | £23

Chinatown | 118-120 Shaftesbury Ave., W1 (Leicester Sq.) | 020-7437 0377 | fax 7437 0378 | www.chineseexperience.com

With not much decor to distract you, "just close your eyes and imagine you're in Hong Kong" at this busy Chinatowner, whose "wonderful", "super-fresh dim sum" is "well worth the price"; its hours and location make it a "convenient" experience for theatre-goers too.

Chor Bizarre ● *Indian*

21 | 17 | 19 | £39

Mayfair | 16 Albemarle St., W1 (Green Park) | 020-7629 9802 | fax 7493 7756 | www.chorbizarre.com

"Authentic, family-style Indian cuisine", each dish paired with items from an "interesting wine list", makes this Mayfair subterranean subcontinental "a standout" to supporters; but reactions are less rosy to the "cluttered" antiques market–like digs: "bizarre decor indeed."

	FOOD	DECOR	SERVICE	COST

Chowki Bar & Restaurant ● *Indian*   21 | 14 | 17 | £21

Piccadilly | 2-3 Denman St., W1 (Piccadilly Circus) | 020-7439 1330 | fax 7287 5919 | www.chowki.com

"The format works every time" at this "casual" Indian whose "unusually good value" menu offers the "joy of regularly changing regional dishes", all "attractively presented"; "service can be iffy" and the "space tight", but most just "love this place"; P.S. "tucked into a tiny street near Piccadilly Circus", it's "excellent" "if you're headed to the theatre or Soho nightlife."

Christopher's   19 | 18 | 18 | £44
Covent Garden *American/Chophouse*

Covent Garden | 18 Wellington St., WC2 (Covent Garden) | 020-7240 4222 | fax 7240 3357 | www.christophersgrill.com

"Classy", "club-like surroundings" of a Covent Garden Victorian building offer an "interesting take on U.S. dining", with "reliable grills, impressive seafood" and "attentive, if not particularly knowledgeable, service"; the "pricey" bill makes some grumble it's "geared around expense-accounters", excepting the "really good" pre-theatre menus and "weekend brunch, which cures all hangover blues."

Chuen Cheng Ku ● *Chinese*   19 | 9 | 14 | £21

Chinatown | 17 Wardour St., W1 (Leicester Sq./Piccadilly Circus) | 020-7437 1398 | fax 7434 0533 | www.chuenchengku.co.uk

"Don't be misled by the exterior" (or the interior "showing its age") - this "big" Chinatown venue boasts "blooming tasty dim sum" "served from trolleys" by staff who, despite the Service score, seem "smilier than of old"; not surprisingly, it's "incredibly popular" as "a place to go before or after the theatre", especially if "there's a large group."

☑ Churchill Arms *Thai*   22 | 17 | 15 | £15

Notting Hill | 119 Kensington Church St., W8 (High St. Kensington/ Notting Hill Gate) | 020-7727 4242 | www.fullers.co.uk

It's "a bizarre mix" - "perfect" "pub with an authentic Thai restaurant attached" - but it "somehow works" at this flower-bedecked "favourite" in Notting Hill; annoyances include the need to book and "service that shoos you out the door", citing the "one-hour table rule", but the "tremendous value" makes it "worth a trip out of the way to savour."

Chutney Mary ● *Indian*   23 | 22 | 21 | £43

Chelsea | 535 King's Rd., SW10 (Fulham Broadway) | 020-7351 3113 | fax 7351 7694 | www.realindianfood.com

Whilst it's long been London's "epicentre of Indian cuisine", a recently "revamped menu (out with the Anglo-Indian, in with zesty [regional])" has blown new wind into the slightly sagging sails of this Chelsea mainstay; some snap it "strays too far from its heritage", but most salute this "ever-evolving" "slick operation"; when reserving, regulars advise "always try for the conservatory" (vs. the "dark", candlelit main room).

	FOOD	DECOR	SERVICE	COST

Chutney's *Indian*
▽ 23 | 13 | 16 | £19

Marylebone | 124 Drummond St., NW1 (Euston Sq.) | 020-7388 0604 | fax 7209 0627

For a "terrific deal", try the "fabulous lunch buffet" at this scruffy Euston haunt where the "wonderful Indian vegetarian" cooking is "still delicious after all these years" (24 and counting); "to avoid the crush, go early or on Saturday."

Cicada ⍰ *Pan-Asian*
▽ 15 | 16 | 15 | £34

Clerkenwell | 132-136 St. John St., EC1 (Farringdon) | 020-7608 1550 | fax 7608 1551 | www.cicada.nu

The first member, and "the least expensive, of the e&o" group offers a "comfortable combo" of "spicy Pan-Asian nibbles" and "lively bar" scene; so fans forgive "funky staff" (who "can be very slow") and "slightly shabby" Clerkenwell digs.

Cigala *Spanish*
22 | 17 | 19 | £35

Bloomsbury | 54 Lamb's Conduit St., WC1 (Holborn/Russell Sq.) | 020-7405 1717 | fax 7242 9949 | www.cigala.co.uk

"A real find in the neighbourhood" near the British Museum, this often "overlooked" "Iberian eatery" offers up "delicious peasant food", along with an "amazing selection of sherries" and "ports to accompany" the meal; "friendly staff" provide a "relaxing atmosphere."

☑ Cinnamon Club ⍰ *Indian*
24 | 24 | 22 | £49

Westminster | The Old Westminster Library | 30-32 Great Smith St., SW1 (Westminster) | 020-7222 2555 | fax 7222 1333 | www.cinnamonclub.com

"Enter and you believe the British still rule India" at this "upmarket" Westminster venue, whose "magnificent library setting serves as counterpoint to the unusual Indian cuisine" ("East meets West in a sensible kind of way"); the "zinging" fare is "not for the faint-walleted", and service ranges from "responsive" to "intermittently indifferent", but it's still packed with the "political 'in' crowd" from breakfast to dinner.

☑ Cipriani ◑ *Italian*
20 | 21 | 19 | £69

Mayfair | 25 Davies St., W1 (Bond St.) | 020-7399 0500 | fax 7399 0501 | www.cipriani.com

"A people-watching place if ever there was one", this "lively" "London edition" of the Cipriani chain sees "celebs, socialites and wannabes congregate" ("more plastic than in Legoland") to enjoy "fresh food true to its Italian roots"; this is "not a place to be adventurous with your palate", and it may be "the worst value for money in Mayfair", but for "entertainment" appeal alone, many think "the experience is worth it."

Circus ◑⍰ *French*
▽ 14 | 16 | 14 | £36

Soho | 1 Upper James St., W1 (Piccadilly Circus) | 020-7534 4000 | fax 7534 4010

Surrounded by "great big windows looking out onto Soho", this French bistro tempts theatre-goers with a "well-priced menu", whilst the "lively" bar below is home to a "young, hip crowd" (and "walks a tightrope between bustling and deafening"); but many mutter the food's "mediocre", and "how long should one wait for a main course – not 45 minutes", surely?

Ciro's Pizza Pomodoro ● *Pizza* 17 | 15 | 16 | £24

Knightsbridge | 51 Beauchamp Pl., SW3 (Knightsbridge) | 020-7589 1278 | fax 7589 8719
City | 7-8 Bishopsgate Churchyard, EC2 (Liverpool St.) | 020-7920 9207 | fax 7920 9206 🗷
www.pomodoro.co.uk

"If you like live music and pizza", with "lots of dancing" thrown in, this "cheap and cheerful" Italian duo in Knightsbridge and the City are "frolicking spots" indeed – that is, "if you can put up with the small space and slow service."

Citrus *Mediterranean* 20 | 19 | 21 | £33

Piccadilly | Park Lane Hotel | 112 Piccadilly, W1 (Green Park) | 020-7290 7364 | fax 7499 1965 | www.sheraton.com/parklane

"Like the name, it's fresh and refreshing" ("unexpected for a Sheraton") at this "simple, small restaurant in a cheery setting within the Park Lane Hotel"; whilst "not a destination in itself", the Med menu is "creative", and coupled with "a view of Green Park" to boot.

City Café Westminster ● *European* ▽ 19 | 19 | 18 | £25

Westminster | City Inn | 30 John Islip St., SW1 (Pimlico) | 020-7932 4600 | fax 7932 7575 | www.cityinn.com

"The food's better than you might expect – in fact, it's exceedingly good" at this "peaceful", dark-wooded Modern European "near the Tate Britain"; its £10 prix fixe is "a wonderful value for lunch", and the Sunday brunch buffet isn't bad either.

City·Miyama 🗷 *Japanese* ▽ 25 | 5 | 17 | £35

City | 17 Godliman St., EC4 (St. Paul's) | 020-7489 1937 | fax 7236 0325

Whilst the "chrome-meets-fake-wood decor might not be the freshest, the sashimi thankfully is" at this "hidden gem" of a Japanese on the "edge of the City"; the "great teppanyaki" is worth a trip too, but regulars recommend you "go at the weekend to avoid expense-account types and enjoy excellent deals."

☑ Clarke's 🗷 *British* 25 | 18 | 24 | £58

Kensington | 124 Kensington Church St., W8 (Notting Hill Gate) | 020-7221 9225 | fax 7229 4564 | www.sallyclarke.com

After almost a quarter-century, Sally Clarke's Kensington corner continues to be "consistently classy" "without the fuss often associated with high-end" places; her Modern British menus – now "with a choice of entrees" – are "still fresh" and "fabulous", the "service exceptional" and the "atmosphere pleasant" (if you "sit upstairs"); the "limited" number of offerings "aren't for everybody", but overall, this is possibly "the most reliable restaurant in London."

	FOOD	DECOR	SERVICE	COST

Clerkenwell
Dining Room & Bar ⓏEuropean
▽ 23 | 19 | 21 | £43

Clerkenwell | 69-73 St. John St., EC1 (Farringdon) | 020-7253 9000 | fax 7253 3322 | www.theclerkenwell.com

"They care whether you are pleased and whether you return" to this "understated Clerkenwell" Modern European, an "all-round solid" choice for a "pleasant, intimate" meal; perhaps the decor "lacks distinctive character", but the place "will not disappoint."

Ⓩ Cliveden House   French/Mediterranean
24 | 27 | 25 | £82

Taplow | Cliveden House Hotel | Berkshire | 01628 668561 | fax 01628 661837 | www.clivedenhouse.co.uk

Live in the "grand manner in a grand manor" at this "gorgeous" Berkshire hotel – "part of history" as the Astor family's former country house; there is "fantastic" Med cuisine in the subterranean Waldo's, whilst the upstairs "Terrace has a view" "that never ends", "decor right out of *Pride and Prejudice*" and "good, if not great" New French fare; although it's all "so expensive", most say the "atmosphere and setting are worth it" – oh, and being "treated like royalty"; N.B. Waldo's is closed Sunday–Monday.

Clos Maggiore ⓏFrench
24 | 24 | 23 | £45

Covent Garden | 33 King St., WC2 (Covent Garden/Leicester Sq.) | 020-7379 9696 | fax 7379 6767 | www.maggiores.uk.com

"Escape into a small world of intimate perfection" at this "romantic Theatreland" address, "almost Eden-like" with its "beautiful inner courtyard" ("a cloistered garden" with fireplace); the "exquisite" New French cuisine, "enormous wine list" and "superb service" mean that "reservations can take a Herculean effort" (the savvy suggest going in the early evening as a "respite from the crowds").

NEW Club Bar & Dining, The ⓏEclectic
– | – | – | E

Soho | 21-22 Warwick St., W1 (Oxford Circus/Piccadilly Circus) | 020-7734 1002 | www.theclubbaranddining.co.uk

Exposed brickwork and Gothic touches (candelabras, mirrors, etc.) set the tone at this new Soho venue in The Sugar Club's former premises; the quirky Eclectic menu stretches from toasted sandwiches and burgers to caviar and whole roast piglets, served from a narrow open kitchen; downstairs, there's a dark, sultry lounge.

Ⓩ Club Gascon ⓏFrench
26 | 21 | 22 | £62

Smithfield | 57 W. Smithfield, EC1 (Barbican/Farringdon) | 020-7796 0600 | fax 7796 0601 | www.clubgascon.com

"Never has the phrase 'quality over quantity' been more true" than with the "well-constructed", "exquisitely presented" small plates offered at this "charming Gallic experience" in an old Smithfield tea house; featuring "foie gras more ways than most people have had hot dinners", backed by an "excellent Gascon wine list", it's "perfect for a business or a romantic dinner (no small feat)"; "the bill piles up quickly", but "you won't remember what it cost, only how nice it was to be there."

	FOOD	DECOR	SERVICE	COST

Coach & Horses *British/Mediterranean*   ▽ 19 | 15 | 17 | £31

Clerkenwell | 26-28 Ray St., EC1 (Farringdon) | 020-7278 8990 |
fax 7278 1478 | www.thecoachandhorses.com

"If you can get past the less-than-grand atmosphere, you will be re-
warded with a simple, short menu" of Traditional British–Med
dishes at this "wonderful" pub "next door to the *Guardian*" in
Clerkenwell; however, you hungry types should hold your horses –
"the food's a little slow to arrive."

Cocoon ●🕾 *Pan-Asian*   21 | 24 | 17 | £55

Piccadilly | 65 Regent St., W1 (Piccadilly Circus) | 020-7494 7600 |
www.cocoon-restaurants.com

"The cocoon theme is carried throughout" this "seriously cool"
Piccadilly Pan-Asian, and whilst the "great bar scene" dominates
the "*Stingray*-like retro surroundings", there's "surprisingly good
(given its trendiness)" fusion fare to be had, especially at the "funky
sushi" bar; on the downside, the "bill leaves something to be desired" and the staff seem "gorgeously disinterested."

Collection, The ●🕾 *Eclectic*   13 | 20 | 14 | £42

South Kensington | 264 Brompton Rd., SW3 (South Kensington) |
020-7225 1212 | fax 7225 1050 | www.the-collection.co.uk

A dramatic entrance hallway and "bar so long it looks as if it's trying to
prove something" score higher than the "overpriced" Eclectic fare at
this "buzzy" Brompton Cross warehouse haunted by "celebs and social climbers alike"; the savvy stick to the "sensual drinks."

Como Lario ●🕾 *Italian*   18 | 16 | 22 | £38

Pimlico | 18-22 Holbein Pl., SW1 (Sloane Sq.) | 020-7730 2954 |
fax 7730 9046 | www.comolario.uk.com

"Slightly hidden" behind Sloane Square, this "super-welcoming"
Italian veteran (some 35 years) makes its mark "more for the singing, jovial waiters" than its "small" menu; still, it's "reasonable food
at a fair price"; "take out a few tables and it would be ideal."

Comptoir Gascon 🕾Ⓜ *French*   ▽ 21 | 16 | 15 | £29

Smithfield | 61-63 Charterhouse St., EC1 (Barbican/Farringdon) |
020-7608 0851 | fax 7608 0871 | www.clubgascon.com

For "a taste of the French *terroir* without having to fly there", *amis* appreciate this "atmospheric" bistro "in the shadow of Smithfield
Market"; since it's also a full-scale food hall, dining here is sort of
"like sitting in a shop with not many tables", but it's "a much cheaper
alternative to others in the Gascon chain."

🆕 Cookbook Cafe *European*   - | - | - | M

Mayfair | InterContinental Park Ln. | 1 Hamilton Pl., W1 (Hyde Park Corner) |
020-7409 3131 | fax 7493 3476 | www.cookbookcafe.co.uk

Following the major revamp of the InterContinental Park Lane, the new
everyday dining room (separate from Theo Randall's upscale eatery)
lives up to its name with recipe tastings, cookery classes and
bookshelf-lined decor; the Modern European menu includes four daily
specials prepared to order at an open station in the middle of the floor.

| | FOOD | DECOR | SERVICE | COST |

Coq d'Argent *French*
18 | 21 | 16 | £50

City | No. 1 Poultry, EC2 (Bank) | 020-7395 5000 | fax 7395 5050 | www.coqdargent.co.uk

Given the "killer view" from an "amazing roof garden" and a "stunning wine list almost a foot thick", it's no surprise this "competent" Classic French is "a perennial favourite" with the "City boys and girls" – hence, "rather overpriced"; cranky coqs crow this 10-year-old also "needs to refresh" the cuisine ("do they ever change the menu?") and "perennially slow service."

Costas Grill 🅱 *Greek*
▽ 18 | 11 | 18 | £19

Notting Hill | 12-14 Hillgate St., W8 (Notting Hill Gate) | 020-7229 3794 | www.costasgrill.co.uk

"My neighbourhood taverna!" hail Notting Hill nabobs of this "comfy" Greek with "nostalgic decor"; dating back to the '50s, it's an "old haunt", but the fare's "fresh", especially in the "bountiful lamb dishes", and there's also a cosy garden out back.

Cottons *Caribbean*
▽ 19 | 21 | 19 | £36

Camden Town | 55 Chalk Farm Rd., NW1 (Chalk Farm) | 020-7485 8388
Islington | 70 Exmouth Mkt., EC1 (Angel) | 020-7833 3332
www.cottons-restaurant.co.uk

With art-decked, "sunny surroundings", Camden's "old favourite is still fun after all these years"; though the "slightly pricey" Caribbean food is "delicious", it's secondary to the "great atmosphere" around the "brilliant bar" ("a visit is incomplete without a rum punch"); N.B. the Exmouth Market offshoot is much younger.

Court Restaurant *Eclectic*
16 | 21 | 14 | £21

Bloomsbury | The British Museum | Great Russell St., WC1 (Russell Sq.) | 020-7323 8990

You can't beat the "spectacular surroundings" – "mummies to the right of you, books to the left" – at the British Museum's "chic", "pleasant cafe" serving "unexpectedly upscale offerings" of an Eclectic nature; "service is not so hot" though; P.S. there's also a "low-scale snack bar" which requires "fewer pounds."

Cow Dining Room, The *British*
21 | 16 | 17 | £35

Notting Hill | 89 Westbourne Park Rd., W2 (Westbourne Park) | 020-7221 0021 | fax 7727 8687 | www.thecowlondon.co.uk

"Holy cow" cry converts to this Notting Hill eatery, which despite its name "serves such fresh seafood" "you'll eat yourself silly" ("portions aren't stingy", either); the bar specialises in "lovely oysters" and "old authentic pubby atmosphere" but is "crowded all the time", whilst "dining upstairs" in the Modern Brit restaurant "is more civilised, albeit a bit boring"; expect "iffy service" at each.

Crazy Bear, The 🅱 *Thai*
21 | 23 | 18 | £43

Fitzrovia | 26-28 Whitfield St., W1 (Goodge St.) | 020-7631 0088 | fax 7631 1188 | www.crazybeargroup.co.uk

"Funky", "fantastic", "fabulous" – all the F-words flood forth for this Fitzrovian "full of folks proud of themselves for finding it" and its interior of leather, wood and steel, including *"Alice in Wonderland* washrooms" whose "mirrored walls can confuse the unsteady"; the "high quality" of the Thai fare, "with its modern take on all the classics", is "a shocker, considering you're usually paying for atmosphere at places like this."

Crazy Homies *Mexican*   20 16 13 £23

Notting Hill | 125 Westbourne Park Rd., W2 (Royal Oak/ Westbourne Park) | 020-7727 6771 | fax 7727 6798 | www.crazyhomieslondon.co.uk

"Mexican is hard to find in London, but they do a decent job" at Tom Conran's "chill little" cantina in Notting Hill, whose eats "for the burrito-starved" are among "the best in town"; "service can be stroppy" and you "might have to wait a while to sit", but at least there are "awesome" margaritas to pass the time.

Cross Keys ● *French*   14 16 15 £29

Chelsea | 1 Lawrence St., SW3 (Sloane Sq.) | 020-7349 9111 | www.thexkeys.co.uk

"Always busy with locals", this Chelsea gastropub is "great for a group dinner" in one of its private rooms or the airy rear conservatory with a tree growing in the middle; but it makes critics cross, because the French fare, whilst "reasonable", is "not innovative" and the staff "not interested in serving, but in looking beautiful."

Cru Ⓜ *Mediterranean*   ▽ 15 18 15 £36

Hoxton | 2-4 Rufus St., N1 (Old St.) | 020-7729 5252 | fax 7729 1070 | www.cru.uk.com

"Great to have in the neighbourhood" – especially when "visiting the galleries" nearby – this converted warehouse's "competent" Mediterranean menu "complements a lengthy wine list" that veers towards smaller vineyards; but "spotty service" and "weekend invasions by wannabe Hoxtonites" means it's "maybe too popular for its own good."

Cuckoo Club Ⓢ Ⓜ *European*   15 20 17 £50

Piccadilly | Swallow St., W1 (Piccadilly Circus) | 020-7287 4300 | www.thecuckooclub.com

"In between the sophisticated ambience" and "impressive drinks", "we go cuckoo for the club" coo clients of this "hot, happening", purple-hued Piccadilly premises with a dance lounge below and a dining room above; however, some say "you should go for the party, not the food", as the "Modern European fare is mediocre" and the service somewhat attitudinal.

Da Mario ● *Italian*   22 16 19 £27

Kensington | 15 Gloucester Rd., SW7 (Gloucester Rd.) | 020-7584 9078 | fax 7823 9026 | www.damario.co.uk

"Reported to have been Princess Diana's favourite pizzeria", this "casual place in an upscale area" of Kensington attracts a "regular clientele who appreciate the homestyle atmosphere" and "strong vibrant flavours" of the "crisp, thin-crust pizzas" and other dishes on the meat-free Italian menu.

	FOOD	DECOR	SERVICE	COST

Dans Le Noir ⊠ *French*
▽ 13 | 17 | 19 | £44

Clerkenwell | 30-31 Clerkenwell Green, EC1 (Chancery Ln./ Farringdon) | 020-7253 1100 | www.danslenoir.com

The "amazing experience" of "dining in the dark" – literally – is "great for experiencing food in a whole new way" say fans of this Clerkenwell outpost of a Parisian concept; "exceptional blind servers" ("who understand your trepidation at having your sight removed") present a 'surprise menu' of New French–Eclectic fare; take the Decor score with a grain of salt, though – "how can I rate what I can't see?"

Daphne's ● *Italian*
21 | 20 | 21 | £48

Chelsea | 112 Draycott Ave., SW3 (South Kensington) | 020-7589 4257 | fax 7581 2232 | www.daphnes-restaurant.co.uk

"Busy, yet private at the same time", this "comfortable", "chic" "Chelsea institution" offers "a delightful wealth of choice on its Italian menu, backed up by a solid wine list" and "accommodating service"; if trendsetters titter it's more a "place to bring your parents", to devotees it's "always divine" – plus "you never know which celeb you'll see."

Daquise *Polish*
20 | 12 | 15 | £20

South Kensington | 20 Thurloe St., SW7 (South Kensington) | 020-7589 6117

"You step into another world" at this "old-fashioned" South Ken stalwart where the "decor is beyond kitsch (even my granny's is furnished more modern)", but the "Polish home cooking" comes in "huge portions"; it's "a great place to stuff yourself and walk away with change in your pocket"; P.S. "try not to let them sit you in the basement."

☒ Defune *Japanese*
27 | 16 | 20 | £63

Marylebone | 34 George St., W1 (Baker St./Bond St.) | 020-7935 8311 | fax 7487 3762

There are those who "refuse to have sushi anywhere else" than this "serene", "friendly" Marylebone Japanese, maintaining its "marvellous, freshest" victuals are "perfect in size and consistency"; "you'll be shocked how much you're spending", especially since the "decor's nothing fancy", but "if you have an expense account, give it a try."

Delfina ⊠ *Eclectic*
- | - | - | M

Borough | 50 Bermondsey St., SE1 (London Bridge) | 020-7357 0244 | www.delfina.org.uk

A "trendy art gallery atmosphere" pervades this "gem of a find" in an airy, 19th-century Bermondsey Street chocolate factory; and whilst some feel the "interesting" Eclectic cuisine is "not as good as the surroundings", it still attracts "office types during the week."

☒ Delfino ⊠ *Italian*
23 | 16 | 19 | £26

Mayfair | 121A Mount St., W1 (Bond St.) | 020-7499 1256 | www.finos.co.uk

A "well-priced" Italian "menu for everyone" with "probably the best pizza in London", "quick service" and "buzzy atmosphere" – "what more can one ask for from a Mayfair local?" – well, perhaps a little legroom ("tables cramped").

	FOOD	DECOR	SERVICE	COST

Deya 🗷 *Indian* | 23 | 21 | 22 | £44 |

Marylebone | 34 Portman Sq., W1 (Marble Arch) | 020-7224 0028 |
fax 7224 0411 | www.deya-restaurant.co.uk

"In a gorgeous building with beautiful windows and high ceilings",
this Portman Square Punjab "takes it up a notch" with "delicious"
Indian cuisine in meat, fish and vegetarian tasting menus; yet the
"elegant" experience "doesn't excite" some enemies, who deem it
"bland in both venue and food."

dim t *Chinese* | 16 | 14 | 14 | £23 |

Fitzrovia | 32 Charlotte St., W1 (Goodge St.) | 020-7637 1122 |
fax 7580 1574
Hampstead | 3 Heath St., NW3 (Hampstead) | 020-7435 0024 |
fax 7435 8060
Highgate | 1A Hampstead Ln., N6 (Highgate) | 020-8340 8800 |
fax 8348 1671
NEW **South Kensington** | 154-157 Gloucester Rd., SW7
(Gloucester Rd.) | 020-7370-0070
www.dimt.co.uk

"You never seem to need to book, but it's never empty either" at this
noodles, "dim sum and tasty tea" quartet where "you can order as
much or as little as you want" from a Chinese menu that's "not entirely
authentic, but good value"; although "service is inconsistent" ("orders
mixed up on occasion"), they make "a great place to meet friends."

Diner, The ❶ *American* | – | – | – | I |

Soho | 18 Ganton St., W1 (Oxford Circus) | 020-7287 8962 |
www.thedinersoho.com
Shoreditch | 128-130 Curtain Rd., EC2 (Old St.) | 020-7729 4452 |
www.thedinershoreditch.com

"Americans living in London are so excited to find a place that makes
blueberry pancakes, Mexican breakfasts and strong coffee" until
4 PM, plus multi-topped burgers and the "closest thing to a milkshake"; "sadly, the service is not up to New York snuff" at this
Shoreditch and Soho duo.

NEW **Dinings** 🗷 *Japanese* | – | – | – | M |

Marylebone | 22 Harcourt St., W1 (Edgware Rd.) | 020-7723 0666 |
fax 7723 3222

Behind a demure terrace facade in Marylebone, this tiny Japanese
offers a setting as simple as they come, with a grey stone floor and
basic wooden partitions and furniture; what distinguishes the place
(run by chef-patron Tomonari Chiba, who made his name at Nobu) is
a competitively priced menu that majors on sushi and sashimi and
varied tapas-style plates, helpfully split into hot and cold choices.

Dish Dash *Lebanese/Persian* | ▽ 18 | 20 | 18 | £28 |

NEW **Chelsea** | 9 Park Walk, SW10 (South Kensington) | 020-7352 1330
Balham | 11-13 Bedford Hill, SW12 (Balham B.R.) | 020-8673 5555 |
fax 8673 7711
www.dish-dash.com

A "wonderful variety" of Persian-Lebanese "tapas-style small
plates" and "lush cocktails" "means every visit turns up something

new" at this "pretty" pair in Balham and now Chelsea; both boast a "Middle Eastern atmosphere, with belly dancers" once a month and hookah pipes on hand.

Diverso ● *Italian*   21 | 18 | 23 | £41

Piccadilly | 85 Piccadilly, W1 (Green Park) | 020-7491 2222 | fax 7495 1977
A "haven in hectic Piccadilly", this "secret" eatery opposite Green Park provides a "comfortable" Tuscan villa-like "place for people-watching" whilst enjoying "delicious" Italian eats; the service has "a nice touch" too.

Don, The ⊠ *European*   22 | 20 | 21 | £48

City | The Courtyard | 20 St. Swithins Ln., EC4 (Bank/Cannon St.) | 020-7626 2606 | fax 7626 2616 | www.thedonrestaurant.co.uk
"Consistently packed with the great and the good from the City" – it's "one of the better places open for dinner *and* lunch – this Modern European is "hard to find, but easy to like", with "consistently high" but "not overpriced" cuisine, "unstuffy, atmospheric" premises and "staff that are a credit to the place"; there's a "good bistro downstairs" in the vaulted cellar too; P.S. the wine list includes an "interesting selection of sherries" and ports – in homage to the 1798 building's past as Sandeman's warehouse.

⊠ Dorchester Hotel - The Grill *British*   24 | 24 | 25 | £67

Mayfair | Dorchester Hotel | 53 Park Ln., W1 (Hyde Park Corner/ Marble Arch) | 020-7629 8888 | fax 7317 6464 | www.dorchesterhotel.com
"Feel like a Lord" in the "aristocratic surroundings" of the Dorchester's "timeless" dining room with its dramatic Scottish-themed mural and decor; new chef Aiden Byrne's "refined" fare is "superb" "for classic English roast beef, salmon", etc., backed up by "marvellous staff" and a "great wine expert"; ok, it's "old-fashioned, but who cares" – this is a "special-occasion place you won't regret opening your wallet for."

Dover Street Restaurant & Jazz Bar ⊠ *European*   17 | 15 | 17 | £47

Mayfair | 8-10 Dover St., W1 (Green Park) | 020-7491 7509 | www.doverst.co.uk
If "you like eating in nightclubs", "splash out and take your partner" to this "crowded" Mayfair veteran with a "Continental atmosphere" and "terrific" live jazz nightly; whilst the Modern European cooking is "not exactly high cuisine, it's not terrible either" – though, as befits a "dancing and socialising venue", the "noise level can inhibit conversation."

Dragon Castle *Chinese*   - | - | - | M

Kennington | 114 Walworth Rd., SE17 (Elephant & Castle) | 020-7277 3388
"It may not be the best location" – the "up-and-coming" if still "dubious" Elephant & Castle area – but the food's "absolutely top-drawer" at this "improbably grand dim sum parlour"; the menu features "classical Cantonese cooking" at night, whilst the daytime dim sum includes "items unavailable elsewhere"; "friendly service" too.

	FOOD	DECOR	SERVICE	COST

Draper's Arms, The *European*
▽ 18 | 16 | 18 | £27

Islington | 44 Barnsbury St., N1 (Highbury & Islington) | 020-7619 0348 | fax 7619 0413 | www.thedrapersarms.co.uk

"Jam-packed full of yummy mummies and posh dads at weekends", this Islington Modern European is "a bit pricey for elevated pub food"; but "booking is essential", which confirms that many "enjoy a thoroughly happy experience" here – plus, it's got a "garden in the back: what more could one ask for?"

Drones *European*
18 | 19 | 19 | £55

Belgravia | 1 Pont St., SW1 (Sloane Sq.) | 020-7235 9555 | fax 7235 9566 | www.whitestarline.org.uk

"An interesting place with interesting people" who give it a "clubby" feel, this Marco Pierre White-owned Modern European delivers "consistently good standards", if "no surprises"; but nonbelievers bemoan this Belgravian's "so-so service" and "pretentious" prices.

Duke of Cambridge *British*
20 | 18 | 15 | £27

Islington | 30 St. Peter's St., N1 (Angel) | 020-7359 3066 | fax 7359 1877 | www.sloeberry.co.uk

It "doesn't matter what you order, everything is equally fantastic" at this "homely" but spacious Islington Modern Brit that offers an "all-organic" "extravaganza" of food and wine – which explains why the bill can be "a mild shock" by gastropub standards; even so, "just try to get in."

Eagle, The *Mediterranean*
21 | 13 | 16 | £23

Clerkenwell | 159 Farringdon Rd., EC1 (Farringdon) | 020-7837 1353 | fax 7689 5882

"A small selection of daily dishes from a chalkboard – always fresh", "ingenious" and "cheap" Med fare – is what causes this Clerkenwell "classic" "to fill up fast" with "young, sometimes funky people"; it's "not a safe bet for the fussy", given the "limited menu", "cramped seating" and "rough 'n' ready" service, "but it's as good as it gets when it comes to gastropub food."

Eagle Bar Diner *American*
▽ 19 | 16 | 13 | £16

Fitzrovia | 3-5 Rathbone Pl., W1 (Tottenham Court Rd.) | 020-7637 1418 | www.eaglebardiner.com

"Very reasonable, considering the location" just off Oxford Street, this brown-hued venue offers a full-bore American diner menu, from carb-laden breakfasts to bourbon-laced drinks and "fantastic shakes"; but "this really is the place for burgers", both beef and "alternative" versions like kangaroo, ostrich and "the best veggie"; pity about the "inhospitable" staff.

e&o *Pan-Asian*
22 | 20 | 18 | £43

Notting Hill | 14 Blenheim Cres., W11 (Ladbroke Grove) | 020-7229 5454 | fax 7229 5522 | www.eando.nu

"You are bound to see someone from [the pages of] *Hello!* or *OK* walk in the door" of this Notting Hill hipster, still a scene after seven years thanks to its "lively" vibe and "creative", "though pricey" Pan-

Asian dishes; if cynics say the cuisine's "excellent&original no more" (been "overtaken by more adventurous players"), the majority maintain if the place "weren't so cramped and overflowing with customers, it'd be flawless."

Eat & Two Veg *Vegetarian*   17 | 15 | 18 | £21

Marylebone | 50 Marylebone High St., W1 (Baker St.) | 020-7258 8595 | fax 7258 8596 | www.eatandtwoveg.com

For "guilt-free eating", this Marylebone "vegetarian's paradise" provides an all-day array of "meatless meals", including the "perfect recovery brunch"; but the "diner"-style "decor doesn't blend with the menu", and some still "can't get excited" about the "bland, boring" edibles (though "when it's bad, they take it back with a smile").

Ebury Dining   20 | 20 | 16 | £31
Room & Brasserie *European*

Pimlico | 11 Pimlico Rd., SW1 (Sloane Sq./Victoria) | 020-7730 6784 | fax 7730 6149 | www.theebury.co.uk

A "happening bar scene with a beautiful crowd" beckons at this place near Pimlico Green, with "relaxed dining downstairs and more formal area upstairs"; both offer Modern European fare that's quite "decent", if "a bit challenging" (spiced pork belly, anyone?); also, it "tends to be busy – but that's probably because people like it here."

Ebury Wine Bar & Restaurant *Eclectic*   19 | 17 | 20 | £33

Belgravia | 139 Ebury St., SW1 (Sloane Sq./Victoria) | 020-7730 5447 | fax 7823 6053 | www.eburywinebar.co.uk

"An old reliable that wears well", this Belgravia wine bar/French bistro (fast approaching its 50th) is "loaded with neighbourhood regulars" who appreciate the "personable" service and "good Eclectic menu at reasonable prices"; on the downside, the "whimsical decor is a bit stale" and it can get "boisterous in the evenings."

ECapital ● *Chinese*   ▽ 22 | 12 | 21 | £26

Chinatown | 8 Gerrard St., W1 (Leicester Sq./Piccadilly Circus) | 020-7434 3838 | fax 7434 9991

It might have a "strange name, but there's nothing strange about the food" at this haunt that's "a little more expensive than other Chinatown places, but offers a different menu" of Shanghainese and Szechuan specialities (making a "nice change from the usual Cantonese fare"); the pink-hued premises are pretty plain, but "who needs atmosphere?" "adventurous" advocates ask.

Ed's Easy Diner *Hamburgers*   15 | 15 | 16 | £16

Covent Garden | 15 Great Newport St., WC2 (Covent Garden) | 020-7836 0271 | fax 7836 3230
Piccadilly | London Trocadero Ctr. | 19 Rupert St., W1 (Piccadilly Circus) | 020-7287 1951 | fax 7287 6998
Soho | 12 Moor St., W1 (Leicester Sq./Tottenham Court Rd.) | 020-7439 1955 | fax 7494 0173
www.edseasydiner.co.uk

"If you want the feeling of a great ol' American diner" with "juicy", "old-fashioned burgers" and "legendary milkshakes" that are "easy on the wallet, if not the waist", try this retro trio around town (the Chelsea branch is gone); but the uneasy tremble it's "getting tired", comparing the hamburgers to "thin hockey pucks on a bun."

Efes Kebab House ● *Turkish*

∇ | 18 | 12 | 15 | £20

Bloomsbury | 175-177 Great Portland St., W1 (Great Portland St.) | 020-7436 0600 | fax 7636 6293

Efes Restaurant ●◩ *Turkish*

Bloomsbury | 80-82 Great Titchfield St., W1 (Oxford Circus) | 020-7636 1953 | fax 7323 5082 | www.efesrestaurant.co.uk

"Really decent kebabs, not the usual greasy rubbish" keep regulars returning to these two "quirky" Turks (under separate ownership) in Bloomsbury; whilst "decor and ambience are nothing to write home about", the "moderate prices" and "service with a smile" compensate.

1880 ◩Ⓜ *European/French*

∇ | 21 | 23 | 23 | £71

South Kensington | Bentley Hotel | 27-33 Harrington Gdns., SW7 (Gloucester Rd.) | 020-7244 5361 | fax 7259 2121 | www.thebentley-hotel.com

"Furnished as if in your great-aunt's dreams", with "lavish" lashings of gold and marble, this "classy" act in South Ken offers "attentive ser-vice, excellent wines" and, some say, a "superb" series of Modern European–New French tasting menus; but the lachrymose lament it "lost a lot when chef Andrew Turner departed" last autumn – now the "expensive" "food tries to be cutting-edge, but misses."

1802 *British*

∇ | 16 | 18 | 16 | £30

Canary Wharf | Museum of Docklands | No. 1 Warehouse, West India Quay, Hertsmere Rd., E14 (Canary Wharf) | 087-0444 3886 | fax 7537 1149 | www.searcys.co.uk

"For a museum junky", this "cavernous" old Canary Wharf tea-sorting house next to the Museum of Docklands is "well worth a visit", serving "wholesome" if "average" Modern British "nibbles" from caterers Searcy's; but beware, it becomes home to an "after-work drinking frenzy in the early evening", when it limits the menu and forbids kids.

Eight Over Eight *Pan-Asian*

23 | 20 | 19 | £43

Chelsea | 392 King's Rd., SW3 (Sloane Sq.) | 020-7349 9934 | fax 7351 5157 | www.rickerrestaurants.com

This "sister of e&o" is "one of the best picks on King's Road" – a "fabulous hot spot" with "great people-watching" and "creative" Pan-Asian cuisine in which "flavours, colours and delightful sur-prises abound"; a few feel the minimalist Asian "decor doesn't score", but "young professionals" hail it as a "hip" option "for a date, drink or dinner with friends."

El Blason ◩ *Spanish*

∇ | 18 | 16 | 21 | £37

Chelsea | 8-9 Blacklands Terrace, SW3 (Sloane Sq.) | 020-7823 7383 | fax 7589 6313

"You are greeted like a long-lost friend even if you have never been" to this "pleasant"-looking Iberian just off King's Road; it's "much loved by local residents and those at the Spanish Consulate around the corner" for its paella, a standout on a "solid, albeit unspectacular" Spanish menu.

Electric Brasserie, The ● *Eclectic* | 19 | 18 | 15 | £33 |

Notting Hill | 191 Portobello Rd., W11 (Ladbroke Grove/Notting Hill Gate) | 020-7908 9696 | fax 7908 9595 | www.the-electric.co.uk

"Jammed with hipsters and moviegoers" "catching a flick next door", this Notting Hill hot spot "buzzes with energy" – from the "perpetually busy" bar in front to the more "intimate" brasserie behind; though the eats "take a backseat" to the scene, the Eclectic "comfort/nursery food [offers] something for everyone" – unlike the staff, which "need to go to hospitality school."

Elena's l'Etoile ⊠ *French/Italian* | 20 | 16 | 20 | £43 |

Fitzrovia | 30 Charlotte St., W1 (Goodge St.) | 020-7636 1496 | fax 7637 0122 | www.elenasletoile.co.uk

An "old show-biz hangout, still run – or at least supervised – by Elena" Salvoni, this "Classic French–Italian bistro has been in Fitzrovia forever and hopefully will stay forever" profess fans; "whilst the menu stays the same" (as does the Parisian decor with old "photographs on the walls"), it comes courtesy of "friendly, attentive service"; in short, "not exciting" – but it "never disappoints."

11 Abingdon Road *European* | 18 | 15 | 16 | £40 |

Kensington | 11 Abingdon Rd., W8 (High St. Kensington) | 020-7937 0120 | fax 7937 3049

Despite "slightly clinical decor" ("feels like a Conran shop") and "service that leaves a bit to be desired", this Sonny's sibling "provides for an enjoyable dinner" or lunch with "decent" Modern European fare; of course, it helps that it's a "not-too-pricey" "neighbourhood place", a breed that's "thin on the ground around Kensington High Street."

El Gaucho *Argentinean/Chophouse* | 21 | 15 | 19 | £30 |

Chelsea | Chelsea Farmers Mkt. | 125 Sydney St., SW3 (Sloane Sq./South Kensington) | 020-7376 8514 | fax 7589 7324
South Kensington | 30 Old Brompton Rd., SW7 (South Kensington) | 020-7584 8999 | fax 7589 7324 ●
www.elgaucho.co.uk

"Big fat steaks surrounded by beautiful people" sums up the scene at these "informal" Chelsea and "South Ken Argentinean grills" decked out like South American ranches; some gauchos grumble about the "meagre wine list", "disappointing side dishes" and "service that's casual at best", but if you want "a budget option with bags of character", they will do.

Elistano *Italian* | 18 | 13 | 17 | £32 |

Chelsea | 25-27 Elystan St., SW3 (South Kensington) | 020-7584 5248 | fax 7584 8965

On a "quiet street not far from the King's Road madness", this "small, simple" trattoria is good for "a quick bite" at "reasonable prices"; "the volume is a little loud for some tastes" "and there can be too many bambinos running around", "but with the fresh Italian fare and beautiful [Chelsea] crowd, there's plenty to shout about."

☑ El Pirata ●⊠ *Spanish*   23 | 17 | 20 | £32

Mayfair | 5-6 Down St., W1 (Green Park/Hyde Park Corner) |
020-7491 3810 | fax 7491 0853 | www.elpirata.co.uk

"Hidden in a restaurant-free part of Mayfair", this "swinging"
Spaniard "fills up quickly", as "everyone loves" "some of the tastiest
tapas around", a "fantastic wine list" and "warm, friendly" servers;
"not too pricey", it's "great for large groups", even if "the number of
people crammed in can make the place hot."

El Rincon Latino ●Ⓜ *S American/Spanish*   – | – | – | M

Clapham | 148 Clapham Manor St., SW4 (Clapham North) |
020-7622 0599

It's "always packed, so book ahead" if you want to enjoy the "wonderful tapas" and other Spanish–South American comestibles at this
"chaotic, cramped" Clapham premises; confusion aside, it's "run by
the nicest people."

Embassy ●⊠Ⓜ *European*   ▽ 13 | 14 | 9 | £41

Mayfair | 29 Old Burlington St., W1 (Green Park/Piccadilly Circus) |
020-7851 0956 | fax 7734 3224 | www.embassylondon.com

Filled with "wags, Page 3 girls and *Big Brother* rejects", this Mayfair
Modern European presents its credentials in the shape of a menu
from respected chef Garry Hollihead and alfresco tables with a
12 AM license; still, some say its "sole purpose" is to allow diners
"to queue-jump into the club", normally members-only, below.

NEW Empress of India *British*   – | – | – | M

Hackney | 130 Lauriston Rd., E9 (Bethnal Green) | 020-8533 5123 |
www.theempressofindia.com

With "stunning decor" that includes a "wonderful antique mirror",
huge shell chandeliers and wallpaper scenes of the Raj, this Victoria
Park gastropub comes from the team behind The Gun; whilst the
scene evokes colonial India, the all-day Modern Brit menu takes a
more gamey tone, with signatures such as haunch of venison and
mallard carved tableside.

Engineer, The *British*   19 | 15 | 15 | £29

Primrose Hill | 65 Gloucester Ave., NW1 (Chalk Farm) | 020-7722 0950 |
fax 7483 0592 | www.the-engineer.com

"Even though it's in la-di-da-di Primrose Hill", there's surprisingly
nice atmosphere" (with "the walled garden a bonus") to this
decade-old "see-and-be-seen" "gastropub serving consistently
good, not great food" and "wines perfectly chosen for quaff-ability";
some pout it's "overpriced", but then the Modern Brit meals come
with "cachet attached."

☑ Enoteca Turi ⊠ *Italian*   27 | 19 | 23 | £47

Putney | 28 Putney High St., SW15 (Putney Bridge) | 020-8785 4449 |
fax 8780 5409 | www.enotecaturi.com

"We have to keep reminding ourselves this is just across the
Thames, not in the hills in Tuscany" say fans of this rustic ristorante
that's "just about the best Italian in London" (and "the best in

Putney by far"); the fare "never fails to impress" and there's "a phenomenal wine list too"; "tables are too close", but "personal attention from the owner and his wife ensures" a "pleasant evening."

Enterprise, The *Eclectic*   20 | 18 | 19 | £36
Chelsea | 35 Walton St., SW3 (Knightsbridge/South Kensington) | 020-7584 3148 | fax 7584 2516
"A civilised crowd" of "oldies, 20-year-olds' groups and couples on dates" pile into this gastropub with "no pretences or attitude"; armed with "all the comfort classics", the Eclectic menu's a bit "expensive, but then again, it *is* on Walton Street"; "watch out for long waits as they do not take reservations."

Entrecote Café de Paris ● *French*   18 | 13 | 16 | £32
Marylebone | 3A-3B Baker St., W1 (Bond St./Marble Arch) | 020-7935 3030 | fax 7935 3044 | www.entrecote.co.uk
"Great for a simple steak with no fuss" (plus fries and salad), this single-recipe French in Baker Street is "loved by many"; still, sceptical surveyors shrug it's "nothing special" and "not worth any travel."

Esarn Kheaw *Thai*   - | - | - | I
Shepherd's Bush | 314 Uxbridge Rd., W12 (Shepherd's Bush) | 020-8743 8930 | fax 7243 1250 | www.esarnkheaw.co.uk
"As authentic a Thai as you are likely to find", this family-owned venue "in an incredibly tight space" near Shepherd's Bush is all about the "fantastic" menu with all "the usual suspects", plus some "regional specialities"; just bear in mind "they can be a bit heavy" on the sauce.

Essenza ● *Italian*   ∇ 18 | 13 | 17 | £34
Notting Hill | 210 Kensington Park Rd., W11 (Ladbroke Grove) | 020-7792 1066 | fax 7792 2088 | www.essenza.co.uk
Though "not up to par with sisters Osteria Basilico" or Mediterraneo "up the road", this venue is nonetheless considered "a real find" for those seeking a "nice" neighbourhood trattoria in Notting Hill, with multiregional, "modern Italian fare" and "warm staff."

Eyre Brothers ⊠ *Portuguese/Spanish*   22 | 19 | 21 | £40
Shoreditch | 70 Leonard St., EC2 (Old St.) | 020-7613 5346 | fax 7739 8199 | www.eyrebrothers.co.uk
There's "always a warm welcome and a kitchen that can produce some fine Spanish-Portuguese food" at this "sleek yet comfortable" Shoreditch eatery from the eponymous Eyres; it's a "good choice if you want something slightly different", though it "can get pricey."

Fairuz *Lebanese*   22 | 16 | 19 | £31
Marylebone | 3 Blandford St., W1 (Baker St./Bond St.) | 020-7486 8108 | fax 7935 8581
Bayswater | 27 Westbourne Grove, W2 (Bayswater/Queensway) | 020-7243 8444 | fax 7243 8777 ●
www.fairuz.uk.com
Those lusting for Lebanese find it "easy to pop into" this "casual" yellow-hued duo (separately owned) in Marylebone and Bayswater for "enormous portions" of "well-executed basics", served by "fun" staff.

	FOOD	DECOR	SERVICE	COST

Fakhreldine ● *Lebanese*
21 | 18 | 20 | £43

Piccadilly | 85 Piccadilly, 1st fl., W1 (Green Park) | 020-7493 3424 | fax 7495 1977 | www.fakhreldine.co.uk

It has "been around for ages" (actually, three decades) but there's a "contemporary" feel to this "classy" Lebanese "with fabulous views of Green Park", "accommodating service" and a menu showing a "modern twist" from a "chef with a light hand"; "high prices" deter some, who suggest "stick to the appetisers" and "interesting cocktails" ("the bar has inviting low seating").

Farm, The *French*
- | - | - | M

Fulham | 18 Farm Ln., SW6 (Fulham Broadway) | 020-7381 3331 | fax 7386 3761 | www.thefarmfulham.co.uk

"If you don't fancy cooking, this lively local" "always seems to hit the spot" for Fulham fans; whilst the Classic French fare sets off "no fireworks", the "fantastic staff are never ruffled."

NEW Fat Badger, The *British*
∇ 15 | 17 | 14 | £23

Notting Hill | 310 Portobello Rd., W10 (Ladbroke Grove/ Westbourne Park) | 020-8969 4500 | www.thefatbadger.com

It's early days for this Portobello Road newcomer that offers a "relaxed atmosphere, with comfy couches and big windows to see the world passing"; the Modern Brit menu offers some "surprisingly good" pub grub (and the "edgy neighbourhood crowd makes the food cooler"); pity the "pretty staff" seem "utterly uninterested in serving."

☑ Fat Duck, The Ⓜ *European*
27 | 22 | 26 | £118

Bray | High St., Berkshire | 01628 580333 | www.fatduck.co.uk

Chef-owner Heston Blumenthal allows his "imagination to run wild" on the "sensational, sensual" and "sublime" Modern European menu at this "now classic" Bray cottage; even "the waiters seem to enjoy working" here and serving such mainstays of "molecular gastronomy" as snail porridge and Douglas fir purée; it may be "too complicated for more than once a year", "you need a fat wallet to pay for it" and the one-hour "drive from London is a drag", but "for the brave" it's "a culinary journey" worth taking.

Feng Sushi *Japanese*
17 | 10 | 14 | £26

Borough | 13 Stoney St., SE1 (London Bridge) | 020-7407 8744 | fax 7407 8777 🔊

Chalk Farm | 1 Adelaide Rd., NW3 (Chalk Farm) | 020-7483 2929 | fax 7449 9893

Fulham | 218 Fulham Rd., SW10 (Fulham Rd.) | 020-7795 1900 | fax 7352 8262

Kensington | 21 Kensington Church St., W8 (Notting Hill Gate) | 020-7937 7927 | fax 7376 9191

Notting Hill | 101 Notting Hill Gate, W11 (Notting Hill Gate) | 020-7727 1123 | fax 7727 1125

www.fengsushi.co.uk

Whilst "expensive for what it is", this "casual" chain offers "a solid option for a sushi craving"; given the "sulking staff" and "not-much decor", though, it's "best for takeaway" or the "efficient" delivery service; N.B. in summer 2007, a branch was due to open in the revamped Royal Festival Hall.

⚡ ffiona's Ⓜ *British*

24	20	22	£36

Kensington | 51 Kensington Church St., W8 (High St. Kensington/ Notting Hill Gate) | 020-7937 4152 | www.ffionas.com
Owner Ffiona Reid-Owen "continues to be the star of the show" – "chatting to you at the table" – at this "rustic", "romantic", "candlelit" Kensingtonian that "feels like someone's home"; the "simple, yet tasty", Traditional British "comfort food" is pretty "ffabulous" too; N.B. dinner only.

Fifteen *Mediterranean*

23	18	21	£54

Hoxton | 15 Westland Pl., N1 (Old St.) | 0871-330 1515 | fax 020-7251 2749 | www.fifteenrestaurant.com
"Six years on, the fuss around Jamie Oliver's charity-program restaurant still hasn't died down" – and why not, as it remains a "refreshing" option in Hoxton, provided you "put yourself in the hands of the chefs-in-training and enjoy the ride"; they'll offer you "innovative" Med cuisine that's "awesome" (even if it's "not a bargain") in either the "casual trattoria" or the "trendy, but relaxing" dining room; service is a bit "spotty", but "charming" overall.

Fifth Floor *European*

20	17	18	£42

Knightsbridge | Harvey Nichols | 109-125 Knightsbridge, SW1 (Knightsbridge) | 020-7235 5250 | fax 0191 6019 | www.harveynichols.com
Atop "glitzy" Harvey Nic's, this dining room with colour-changing lighting "often surprises" with its "consistently good" Modern European menu that offers a "fantastic deal – unlimited house wine" on the set dinners; of course, "it's never going to be a first-rate gastronomic destination" and the "servers sometimes show a bit of attitude (why?)", but it's a "happening place" – with a "hopping bar every night of the week."

Fifth Floor Cafe *British/Mediterranean*

18	15	15	£31

Knightsbridge | Harvey Nichols | 109-125 Knightsbridge, SW1 (Knightsbridge) | 020-7823 1839 | fax 7823 2207 | www.harveynichols.com
Using the "same kitchen as the [adjacent] restaurant, but with a lighter menu" of Modern British–Med fare, Harvey Nic's "hectic", "casual" cafe is "packed with yummy mummies and shoppers" seeking "to recharge"; whilst "service varies from professional to abject indifference", it remains "relatively fast."

Fig Ⓜ *European*

-	-	-	M

Islington | 169 Hemingford Rd., N1 (Barnesbury/Caledonian Rd.) | 020-7609 3009 | www.fig-restaurant.co.uk
In a "pleasant residential street" in Islington, this low-profile eatery is "not the hippest place, but a local-crowd favourite" for Modern European cooking with "good, fresh ingredients"; what's more, the "co-owner/manager is incredibly helpful": "provenance, cooking method and even etymology of dish names are all discussed."

	FOOD	DECOR	SERVICE	COST

Ⓩ Fino Ⓢ Spanish — 23 | 19 | 20 | £47

Fitzrovia | 33 Charlotte St., W1 (Goodge St./Tottenham Court Rd.) |
020-7813 8010 | fax 7813 8011 | www.finorestaurant.com

"Truly excellent tapas" take you on a "culinary trip through Spain" at
this "hip", "high-quality" and "highly priced" Fitzrovian; if the basement digs are "disappointing", the staff are "knowledgeable" and
there's a "great" all-Iberian wine list – though "with such good house
wine, why run your finger any lower" down?

Fiore Ⓢ Italian — 21 | 19 | 23 | £46

St. James's | 33 St. James's St., SW1 (Green Park) | 020-7930 7100 |
fax 7930 4070 | www.fiore-restaurant.co.uk

"Just a great little Italian place" is how most sum up this St. James's
eatery in a "long, narrow" art-clad room; "friendly staff" make it "a
favourite for business lunches", though those not on expenses cry
"not worth the price."

Fire & Stone ◐ Pizza — 18 | 16 | 15 | £19

Covent Garden | 31-32 Maiden Ln., WC2 (Covent Garden/Leicester Sq.) |
0845-330 0139 | fax 020-7395 1969 | www.fireandstone.com

"If you want your pizzas unusual" – would you believe, a version
"with black pudding"? – then this "big", "buzzing" Covent Garden
haunt is worth a try; most clients can cope with the "canteen-style
tables and chairs", though "tardy service" lets the side down.

Firezza Pizza — 18 | 8 | 13 | £16

Islington | 276 St. Paul's Rd., N1 (Highbury & Islington) | 020-7359 7400
Battersea | 40 Lavender Hill, SW11 (Clapham Junction) | 020-7223 5535
Herne Hill | 4 Hardess St., SE24 (Lasborough Junction) | 020-7737 8000 |
fax 7737 8000
Chelsea | 116 Finborough Rd., SW10 (Earl's Court) | 020-7370 2255
Wandsworth | 205 Garratt Ln., SW18 (East Putney) | 020-8870 7070
Chiswick | 48 Chiswick High Rd., W4 (Turnham Green) | 020-8994 9494
Notting Hill | 12 All Saints Rd., W11 (Notting Hill Gate) | 020-7221 0020
www.firezza.com

Surveyors "love ordering by the metre" at this "gourmet pizza" chain,
which also offers "interesting salads"; whilst they boast "the best delivery around, eating-in is less special"; N.B. no seating at Herne Hill.

fish! Seafood — 19 | 14 | 15 | £31

South Bank | Cathedral St., Borough Mkt., SE1 (London Bridge) |
020-7407 3803 | fax 7357 8636 | www.fishdiner.co.uk

"If you love fish, you'll love fish!" quip followers of this glass-roofed
seafooder that offers "a not-creative, but good formula" – your pick
of "fresh fish, cooked as you like it with your choice of sauce"; however, the "hectic", "antiseptic" setting makes it like "eating in a fishmonger's" "in the middle of Borough Market."

Fish Hook Seafood — ▽ 24 | 16 | 22 | £39

Chiswick | 6-8 Elliott Rd., W4 (Turnham Green) | 020-8742 0766 |
fax 8742 3374 | www.fishhook.co.uk

Given the cries of "excellent" and "exceptional", surveyors seem
hooked on the fish at this "small" seafooder in Chiswick; considering

the quality, "it's probably one of the best deals in London", sweet-
ened by the way chef-patron Michael Nadra "comes out of the
kitchen" to greet diners.

Fish Shop on St. John St. Ⓜ Seafood   19 | 18 | 16 | £37

Clerkenwell | 360-362 St. John St., EC1 (Angel) | 020-7837 1199 |
fax 7837 3399 | www.thefishshop.net

"An oasis in a culinary dry spot" in Clerkenwell, this "airy" "stylish"
seafooder offers a "wide range of fish (surprise!)" with "clean, crisp
flavours"; there's an "imaginative pre-theatre prix fixe for those
heading to nearby Sadler's Wells"; service is "ok, friendly at least."

FishWorks Seafood   20 | 13 | 15 | £36

Marylebone | 89 Marylebone High St., W1 (Baker St.) | 020-7935 9796 |
fax 7935 8796

Primrose Hill | 57 Regents Park Rd., NW1 (Chalk Farm) | 020-7586 9760

Islington | 134 Upper St., N1 (Angel/Highbury & Islington) |
020-7354 1279 | fax 7226 8269

Battersea | 54 Northcote Rd., SW11 (Clapham Junction) | 020-7228 7893

NEW **Chelsea** | 212 Fulham Rd., SW10 (South Kensington) |
020-7823 3033

Fulham | 177 New King's Rd., SW6 (Parsons Green) | 020-7384 1009

Richmond | 13-19 The Square, TW9 (Richmond) | 020-8948 5965

Chiswick | 6 Turnham Green Terrace, W4 (Turnham Green) |
020-8994 0086 | fax 8994 0778

NEW **Notting Hill** | 188 Westbourne Grove, W11 (Notting Hill Gate) |
020-7229 3366
www.fishworks.co.uk

Your dinner "can be ordered off the fishmonger's counter and be
cooked to specification" at these fast-spawning fish houses; but
even friends feel the food's "freshness is really the only reason for
dining here, as the uncomfortable surroundings and disinterested
staff create an 'off' whiff"; P.S. tip: "order the specials as they out-
shine some of the standards on the menu."

Flaneur European   22 | 20 | 15 | £31

Farringdon | 41 Farringdon Rd., EC1 (Farringdon) | 020-7404 4422 |
fax 7831 4532 | www.flaneur.com

"Sitting among the aisles of a posh supermarket and eating exceptional food is an experience" at this "surprising find in an otherwise
dull part of Farringdon Road"; "using ingredients from the shop", the
"healthy" Modern European menu changes daily, but "be prepared
for laissez-faire service"; P.S. naturally, it's "a great place to pick up
some treats after the meal."

Floridita ❶Ⓧ Cuban   16 | 21 | 15 | £48

Soho | 100 Wardour St., W1 (Tottenham Court Rd.) | 020-7314 4000 |
fax 7314 4040 | www.floridita.co.uk

Although it's "more *Footballers' Wives* than Havana", this large,
"loud"-with-live-music Latino in Soho "remains reliable" for a "fun,
funky" chance to dance; the "overpriced" food gives "just a nod to
real Cuban cooking", and "takes an age to arrive", but it's just "a
sidelight to the rum drinks and encounters" anyway.

	FOOD	DECOR	SERVICE	COST

☑ Foliage *European/French* · 26 | 23 | 26 | £71

Knightsbridge | Mandarin Oriental Hyde Park | 66 Knightsbridge, SW1 (Knightsbridge) | 020-7201 3723 | fax 7235 2001 | www.mandarinoriental.com

"Beautiful in every respect" maintain admirers of the Mandarin Oriental's dining room where "culinary wizard Chris Staines" produces Classic French–Modern European cuisine "with vision, zest and skill", served by "gracious staff" in Adam Tihany–designed premises ("light, with big windows"); though the "cost is equal to trans-Atlantic airfare", "it's worth every posh penny"; P.S. "ask for a window table" to savour the "splendid view of Hyde Park."

☑ Food for Thought 🖘 *Vegetarian* · 24 | 10 | 16 | £10

Covent Garden | 31 Neal St., WC2 (Covent Garden) | 020-7836 9072

"Get to know your neighbours over enormous portions" of "hearty vegetarian fare" at this Covent Garden "cramped cellar where table-sharing is compulsory at peak times"; the "innovative recipes are nowhere near the traditional view of veggie" – and "so good you wouldn't know they're healthy", for both body and bank account (this is London's Top Best Buy).

Food Room, The 🆂🅼 *French/Mediterranean* · - | - | - | M

Battersea | 123 Queenstown Rd., SW8 (Queenstown Rd.) | 020-7622 0555 | fax 7622 9543

A rather "charmless space" belies the "delectable", "amazingly good value" Med–New French fare in "substantial portions (and definitely not nouvelle!)" at this "unexpected gem in the backstreets of Battersea"; "the food's accompanied, almost literally", by a "young team anxious to please."

🆕 Forge, The ☯ *European* · - | - | - | E

Covent Garden | 14 Garrick St., WC2 (Covent Garden/ Leicester Sq.) | 020-7379 1432 | fax 020-7379-1530 | www.theforgerestaurant.co.uk

Sibling of stalwarts Le Café du Jardin and Le Deuxième, this "welcome" Covent Garden novice takes over the erstwhile L'Estaminet space to offer seafood-centric Modern European fare in an uncluttered, exposed-brick setting; pluses include a lengthy wine list (more than 500 labels!) and a cosy basement bar serving an edited menu; though "reactive rather than proactive", staff offer "attention when needed."

Fortnum's Fountain 🆂 *British* · 20 | - | 19 | £29

St. James's | Fortnum & Mason | 181 Piccadilly, W1 (Green Park/ Piccadilly Circus) | 020-7973 4140 | fax 7437 3278 | www.fortnumandmason.co.uk

As part of the "Fortnum & Mason's refit", this "favourite lunchtime haunt" of "fur-clad ladies" is getting a face-lift, by architect David Collins (who did Nobu and The Wolseley) no less; slated to have reopened in August 2007, it'll still serve Traditional British fare, but later into the night.

		FOOD	DECOR	SERVICE	COST

Four Seasons Chinese ● *Chinese* | 22 | 7 | 11 | £23 |

Bayswater | 84 Queensway, W2 (Bayswater) | 020-7229 4320 | fax 7229 4320

"Everyone orders the justly famous roast duck" at this "hugely popular" Queensway Chinese, which "offers some of the most authentic food in London" – and at "low prices" to boot; just "be prepared for substandard service" and to "get there before 6 PM or you'll wait" as "they don't take reservations."

1492 ● *S American* | ▽ 21 | 17 | 21 | £29 |

Fulham | 404 North End Rd., SW6 (Fulham Broadway) | 020-7381 3810 | fax 7381 1402 | www.1492restaurant.com

The "delicious" "mix of dishes from different South American countries" and "attentive, ready-to-help staff" are guaranteed to "put you in the Latin mood" at this casual North End Road haunt; "loud music" and indigenous decorative artefacts add to the "great atmosphere."

Foxtrot Oscar *British* | 15 | 14 | 16 | £27 |

Chelsea | 79 Royal Hospital Rd., SW3 (Sloane Sq.) | 020-7352 7179 | fax 7351 1667 | www.foxtrotoscarchelsea.com

"A real local joint, hidden from tourists" with its own "loyal following" ("ageing Sloanies" and even "Prince William have hung out here"), this "small", Chelsea "insiders' club" serves "decent British nursery food"; it's "fun, so long as you don't expect too much from the kitchen."

Franco's ⊠ *Italian/Mediterranean* | 15 | 14 | 17 | £43 |

St. James's | 61 Jermyn St., SW1 (Green Park) | 020-7499 2211 | fax 7495 1375 | www.francoslondon.com

Dating back to the '40s, this low-profile St. James's Italian-Med is "good for a quiet business lunch" as it "never seems too busy"; but it was taken over by Wilton's a while back, and foes frankly feel the change "has ruined a classic."

Frankie's Italian Bar & Grill *Italian* | 15 | 17 | 15 | £34 |

Knightsbridge | 3 Yeoman's Row, downstairs, SW3 (Knightsbridge) | 020-7590 9999 | fax 7590 9900

NEW Marylebone | Selfridges | 400 Oxford St., lower ground fl., W1 (Bond St.) | 020-7318 3981

Piccadilly | The Criterion | 224 Piccadilly, W1 (Picadilly Circus) | 020-7930 0488 | fax 7930 8380 ●

Putney | 263 Putney Bridge Rd., SW15 (Putney Bridge) | 020-8780 3366

Chiswick | 68 Chiswick High Rd., W4 (Stafford) | 020-8987 9988 | fax 8987 9911

www.frankiesitalianbarandgrill.com

Developed in partnership with top jockey Frankie Dettori, this quintet in the Marco Pierre White stable is "popular with families" for "quick" Italian-American eats served amidst a "vast array of shiny material (including supersize glitter balls" and mosaics); alas, naysayers are "not inspired", suggesting "Frankie should stick to riding."

	FOOD	DECOR	SERVICE	COST

Franklins *British*
▽ 19 | 17 | 19 | £32

Kennington | 205-209 Kennington Ln., SE11 (Kennington) 🗑 Ⓜ
Dulwich | 157 Lordship Ln., SE22 (East Dulwich) | 020-8299 9598
Devotees dub this "buzzing" "little local" "East Dulwich's best" for its
"quality" Modern British fare in "a cosy pub setting"; in contrast, con-
trarians charge it's "popular but strikingly overrated" – the "food
combinations are more interesting on paper than in the mouth";
N.B. the Kennington sib replaces a branch of The Painted Heron.

Frederick's 🗑 *British/European*
20 | 19 | 19 | £45

Islington | 106 Camden Passage, N1 (Angel) | 020-7359 2888 |
fax 7359 5173 | www.fredericks.co.uk
For "a family celebration, romantic interlude or just spur-of-the-
moment" meal, this "perennial favourite of the Islington set" offers
an "elegant setting" and "lovely deck and garden"; but whilst disciples declare the Modern British–European menu "always delivers",
sceptics sneer this "standby can be counted on not to surprise", except on the "expensive" bill.

French Horn *French*
23 | 21 | 25 | £61

Sonning | French Horn Hotel | Berkshire | 01189 692204 |
fax 01189 442210 | www.thefrenchhorn.co.uk
In a "dreamy location by the river" Thames, this Sonning family-run
19th-century inn an hour outside London is "worth the trip" for
"lovely" Classic French cuisine (including "duck roasted right in
front of you over an open fire"), an "excellent wine cellar" and "comforting" service; even if it "just falls short" of its "fancy prices", it's
"great for impressing."

French House, The 🗑 *French*
▽ 17 | 15 | 15 | £28

Soho | 49 Dean St., W1 (Piccadilly Circus/Tottenham Court Rd.) |
020-7437 2477 | fax 7287 9109
Walking up to this "Soho classic" (as De Gaulle did during World
War II) situated above a "cosy" pub is like climbing "a culinary stair-
way to heaven" – if your idea of bliss is an "old-fashioned, authentic
French bistro"; it "serves nothing but standards, like confit de ca-
nard, but does it so well."

Friends ❶ *Italian*
▽ 18 | 14 | 19 | £28

Chelsea | 6 Hollywood Rd., SW10 (Fulham Broadway/South Kensington) |
020-7376 3890 | fax 7352 6368
Whether or not it's "the friendliest place in town", this just-off-
Fulham-Road "local" is lauded as the "ultimate casual dining destination" "for children and larger groups"; the "always fresh" Italian
cuisine concentrates on pizza – "ask for them thin and crispy" – and
there are some "good, comparatively inexpensive wines" too.

Frontline *British*
13 | 19 | 14 | £33

Paddington | 13 Norfolk Pl., W2 (Paddington) | 020-7479 8960 |
fax 7479 8961 | www.thefrontlineclub.com
"Sleek, yet still comfortable", this clubby-looking Traditional Brit is
co-owned by a TV cameraman – hence, the decor featuring "stark

pictures of frontline moments that provide a talking point"; but whilst "it stands out in a restaurant-starved area" (Paddington), the "food is not really memorable", and "haphazard service" hardly helps the cause.

Fung Shing ● *Chinese* | 22 | 13 | 18 | £31 |

Chinatown | 15 Lisle St., WC2 (Leicester Sq.) | 020-7437 1539 | fax 7743 0284 | www.fungshing.co.uk

"Divine seasonal specials", "unusual foods like eel done well" and "authentic" Cantonese standards served by "smiling waiters" have made this Chinatown veteran a "family favourite" for decades; it's also "great for pre- or post-theatre dining" even if the "tired" setting "looks like the set from a bad Peter Sellers movie."

Gaby's ⊘ *Jewish/Mideastern* | - | - | - | I |

Covent Garden | 30 Charing Cross Rd., WC2 (Leicester Sq.) | 020-7836 4233

"When there isn't time for a more swept-up place", theatre-goers trek to this small late-night veteran in a "handy location" in Leicester Square; it's "reliable" for Middle Eastern and "down-home" delicatessen, "but there's no atmosphere except for the staff's mood."

Galicia ●M *Spanish* | ∇ 22 | 9 | 20 | £29 |

Notting Hill | 323 Portobello Rd., W10 (Ladbroke Grove) | 020-8969 3539

"Locally orientated, and not at all pretentious", this "wonderful leftover from old Portobello" Road days offers "good", "down-home Spanish cooking", with "fantastic geriatric waiters"; it's "not sophisticated at all, but for the price point, it's fine" – and there are so "few other places to find old men with crazy moustaches sitting at the bar."

Gallipoli *Turkish* | 18 | 17 | 16 | £20 |

Islington | 102 Upper St., N1 (Angel) | 020-7359 0630 | fax 7704 0496
Islington | 107 Upper St., N1 (Angel) | 020-7226 5333 | M
Islington | 120 Upper St., N1 (Angel) | 020-7359 1578 | fax 7704 0496
www.gallipolibazaar.com

It's "like walking into Istanbul" at this "atmospheric" Turkish with "three locations in Upper Street" – each "a favourite with locals, and understandably so", thanks to "plentiful portions" of "easy-going food" at a "bargain" price; if "service can be hit-and-miss", it's not surprising given they're often "overcrowded" with "lively" groups.

Galvin at Windows
Restaurant & Bar *French* | 22 | 23 | 21 | £65 |

Mayfair | London Hilton on Park Ln. | 22 Park Ln., W1 (Hyde Park Corner) | 020-7208 4021 | www.hilton.co.uk

"Bag a table by the window for the most amazing views" (like "the Queen's garden") at this "sleek, minimalist" venue atop the Hilton on Park Lane; but if the weather is obstructive, "not to worry as the food will more than make up for it" – "subtle" New French dishes, "superbly executed"; perhaps cousin Galvin Bistrot de Luxe has "better food at better value", but this one remains "a place for the power wallets to impress."

	FOOD	DECOR	SERVICE	COST

✦ Galvin Bistrot de Luxe *French*

| 24 | 20 | 20 | £44 |

Marylebone | 66 Baker St., W1 (Baker St.) | 020-7935 4007 |
fax 7486 1735 | www.galvinbistrotdeluxe.co.uk

"On otherwise bleak Baker Street, there's "a real bistro in London"
at last – the Galvin brothers' highly hyped "gem" with its "superb atmosphere", "robust" "French food as it used to be" and a "fine wine
list"; if the "knowledgeable" service can be "painfully slow", it
fails to deter the "good mix of people" – from a "mature crowd"
to the more "boisterous" – who have "nothing but superlatives
for this place."

Garbo's *Swedish*

| ▽ 15 | 12 | 17 | £28 |

Marylebone | 42 Crawford St., W1 (Baker St./Marylebone) |
020-7262 6582 | fax 7262 6582

"If you are into Scandinavian cuisine", this "quiet" Marylebone veteran is "worth a visit" for "old-fashioned food" "just like in
Stockholm"; as for the decor, it's "as though you have stepped into
grandma Svensson's house", highlighted by the elk's head staring
down from the wall.

✦ Gate, The ⊠ *Vegetarian*

| 25 | 16 | 22 | £30 |

Hammersmith | 51 Queen Caroline St., W6 (Hammersmith) |
020-8748 6932 | www.thegate.tv

"In an atmosphere that will bring you back to days spent in student
cafes" (i.e. "not posh"), this "magnificent vegetarian" "behind the
Apollo Theatre" has an "inventive" menu that "proves that food
without meat isn't bland or boring" – and could "make even the biggest carnivore think" about converting.

✦ Gaucho Grill *Argentinean/Chophouse*

| 22 | 18 | 18 | £41 |

Holborn | 125-126 Chancery Ln., WC2 (Chancery Ln.) | 020-7242 7727 |
fax 7242 7723 ⊠
Piccadilly | 25 Swallow St., W1 (Piccadilly Circus) | 020-7734 4040 |
fax 7734 1076 ●
Broadgate | 5 Finsbury Ave., EC2 (Liverpool St.) | 020-7256 6877 |
fax 7795 2075
City | 1 Bell Inn Yard, EC3 (Bank/Monument) | 020-7626 5180 |
fax 7626 5181
Canary Wharf | 29 Westferry Circus, E14 (Canary Wharf) |
020-7987 9494 | fax 7987 9292
Hampstead | 64 Heath St., NW3 (Hampstead) | 020-7431 8222 |
fax 7431 3714 ●
Chelsea | 89 Sloane Ave., SW3 (South Kensington) | 020-7584 9901 |
fax 7584 0045
Richmond | The Towpath | Riverside, near Richmond Bridge,
Richmond (Richmond) | 020-8948 4030 | fax 8948 2945
www.gaucho-grill.com

"Feel like a cowboy in the Pampas" amidst the "masculine atmosphere" of these "loud" Latin Americans with "cheeky waitresses"
and trademark cow-hide chairs ("uncomfortable if wearing sheer
hosiery"); a few find it "formulaic", advising "enter only with a fat
wallet", but "if you're a lover of divine bovine", you'll "get your fill of
Argentinean beef" you "can cut with a butter knife" here.

Gay Hussar ⓩ *Hungarian*

	FOOD	DECOR	SERVICE	COST
	16	16	18	£36

Soho | 2 Greek St., W1 (Tottenham Court Rd.) | 020-7437 0973 | fax 7437 4631 | www.gayhussar.co.uk

"Soho restaurants come and go", but this "crowded" stalwart has "stayed on" (and on and on), offering "Hungarian comfort food" that's "good, if a little much" and "service that's as genially haphazard as ever"; the "time-machine" setting is dominated by "striking cartoons" of "eminent politicos past and present."

Geales Fish Restaurant *Seafood*

	FOOD	DECOR	SERVICE	COST
	-	-	-	M

Notting Hill | 2 Farmer St., W8 (Notting Hill Gate) | 020-7727 7528 | fax 7229 8632

"One of the original old-time fish houses in Notting Hill" (established 1939) has reopened post-Survey after a revamp by new owners, the team behind Embassy; the decor retains a rustic look (e.g. gingham-check tablecloths), and the menu of "simple dishes done heartily" now features new options from chef Garry Hollihead.

George ⓩ *European*

	FOOD	DECOR	SERVICE	COST
	22	24	25	£68

Private club; inquiries: 020-7491 4433

With a "perfect combination of sophistication and casual style", this "exclusive", "glamourous dining club" in Mayfair attracts a "swish crowd" with an "unfussy" Modern European menu that "suits all tastes" and "willing service"; it's "expensive, but worth every pence"; P.S. don't forget the "fantastic bar downstairs."

Getti *Italian*

	FOOD	DECOR	SERVICE	COST
	17	16	16	£33

Marylebone | 42 Marylebone High St., W1 (Baker St./Bond St.) | 020-7486 3753 | fax 7486 7084
St. James's | 16-17 Jermyn St., SW1 (Piccadilly Circus) | 020-7734 7334 | fax 7734 7924 ⓩ
www.getti.com

"Not a destination for foodies, but not bad neighbourhood eateries either" sums up this "simple" low-profile pair of Italians in St. James's and an "upmarket area of Marylebone"; "so-so service" lets the side down, but Jermyn Street's prix fixes are "great deals pre-theatre."

Giardinetto ⓩ *Italian*

	FOOD	DECOR	SERVICE	COST
	▽ 19	13	20	£63

Mayfair | 39-40 Albemarle St., W1 (Green Park) | 020-7493 7091 | fax 7493 7096 | www.giardinetto.co.uk

Some "impressive" Italian dishes and a "huge selection of wines" are the main appeal of this "expensive" Mayfair eatery; but foes find the glass-and-metal "minimalist" surrounds are "too trendy by far (and not even that attractive)", and overall, "something seems missing."

Gilgamesh ☻ *Pan-Asian*

	FOOD	DECOR	SERVICE	COST
	20	21	14	£49

Camden Town | The Stables, Camden Mkt. | Chalk Farm Rd., NW1 (Camden Town/Chalk Farm) | 020-7482 5757 | www.gilgameshbar.com

"Excellent news for [style-challenged] Camden": the advent of this "cavernous" yearling with "spectacular" surrounds – "think Inca temple" or *Raiders of the Last Ark* theme park" – and Pan-Asian fare that's "surprisingly good for a 'scene' restaurant"; some skewer the "spotty" staff – if "decor is over the top, service is under the table" –

but then "what do you expect from a place this size"?; P.S. "heavy pickup scene" in the "lovely bar."

Ginger *Bangladeshi*

▽ 17 | 14 | 15 | £25

Bayswater | 115 Westbourne Grove, W2 (Notting Hill Gate) | 020-7908 1990 | fax 7908 1991

"Trendy" "takes on Indian food" at prices offering "so much bang for the buffeted buck" make many believe in this Bangladeshi, but "painfully slow, albeit charming, staff let the place down"; overall, it's "fine for Westbourne Grove locals, but that's it."

Giovanni's ● ⊠ *Italian*

21 | 20 | 20 | £32

Covent Garden | 10 Goodwin's Ct., WC2 (Covent Garden) | 020-7240 2877

"Tucked away off a Jack the Ripper-esque alleyway" in Covent Garden, this "hideaway" offers an "atmospheric" outlet for "quality" "traditional Italian fare" from "friendly host and staff"; it gets "crowded, but you're able to hear one another."

Giraffe *Eclectic*

17 | 15 | 17 | £20

Marylebone | 6-8 Blandford St., W1 (Baker St./Bond St.) | 020-7935 2333 | fax 7935 2334

Spitalfields | Spitalfields Mkt. | Unit 1, Crispin Pl., E1 (Liverpool St.) | 020-3116 2000 | fax 3116 2001

Waterloo | Royal Festival Hall | Unit 1 & 2, Riverside Level 1, SE1 (Waterloo) | 020-7928 2004 | fax 7620 1952

Hampstead | 46 Rosslyn Hill, NW3 (Hampstead) | 020-7435 0343 | fax 7431 1317

Muswell Hill | 348 Muswell Hill Broadway, N10 (Highgate) | 020-8883 4463 | fax 8883 1224

Islington | 29-31 Essex Rd., N1 (Angel) | 020-7359 5999 | fax 7359 6158

Battersea | 27 Battersea Rise, SW11 (Clapham Common/ Clapham Junction) | 020-7223 0933 | fax 7223 1037

Richmond | 30 Hill St., TW9 (Richmond) | 020-8332 2646 | fax 8332 9171

Chiswick | 270 Chiswick High Rd., W4 (Turnham Green) | 020-8995 2100 | fax 8995 5697

Kensington | 7 Kensington High St., W8 (High St. Kensington) | 020-7938 1221 | fax 7938 3330

www.giraffe.net

Additional locations throughout London

With an "organic, ethically led philosophy to both food and the environment" – and "worldly music" as a backdrop – this "child-friendly" chain offers "healthy portions" from a "diverse" Eclectic menu; as they get "full of yummy mummies and their rug rats", "you must like noise to eat here", but still, it's an "interesting concept" that "caters for all ages" ("kids get a balloon", "you get a cocktail") – and is "cheap" to boot.

Glasshouse, The *British*

24 | 20 | 23 | £55

Richmond | 14 Station Parade, Kew (Kew Gdns.) | 020-8940 6777 | fax 8940 3833 | www.glasshouserestaurant.co.uk

In an area "known almost exclusively for its wonderful botanical garden", this Kew "jewel" provides a "virtual tour de force of gastronomic delights" on its seasonally oriented Modern British menu, served in a "light, airy" room by "courteous" staff; it suffers from "strange acoustics" – all that namesake glass – but basically is "another winner from the Chez Bruce family."

Golden Dragon ● *Chinese*

20	12	16	£23

Chinatown | 28-29 Gerrard St., W1 (Leicester Sq./Piccadilly Circus) | 020-7734 2763 | fax 7734 1073

"Hong Kong through and through", this Chinatown behemoth "gets extremely crowded" on account of "some seriously good food" and "lots of dim sum"; if "the service goes erratically from rush to snail's pace", you "can't get more authentic than this" cuisinewise – and it's "great value" too.

Golden Hind *Seafood*

-	-	-	M

Marylebone | 73 Marylebone Ln., W1 (Bond St.) | 020-7486 3644

"Attracting tourists and locals alike" – who are "spoilt for choice" with the selection of "light, flaky, fresh fish" plus "the best chips and mushy peas" – this "humble, yet delightful establishment" is "not to be missed"; even though "portions can be small, the quality is incredible"; P.S. now run by a "charming" Greek family, it's been frying "just off the Marylebone High Street" since 1914.

Good Earth, The *Chinese*

20	16	18	£34

Knightsbridge | 233 Brompton Rd., SW3 (Knightsbridge/South Kensington) | 020-7584 3658 | fax 7823 8769
Hampstead | 143-145 The Broadway, NW7 (Mill Hill B.R.) | 020-8959 7011 | fax 8959 1464

"Gorge yourself as if you haven't eaten in a week" at this Mandarin pair in Knightsbridge and Hampstead, which have "been reliable for eons" (well, decades) for "big portions" of "quality food" in "better-than-average" Asian digs; but a few grouse this "good earth needs some nurturing", especially the "hit-or-miss service."

Gopal's of Soho ●☒ *Indian*

▽			
22	11	17	£30

Soho | 12 Bateman St., W1 (Leicester Sq./Tottenham Court Rd.) | 020-7434 1621 | fax 7434 0840

"Memories of the British Raj are alive" at this "old standby" in Soho, where the "Indian fare" includes "good veggies"; "there are more distinctive places now", but it still comes "recommended."

☑ Gordon Ramsay at Claridge's *European*

25	24	24	£89

Mayfair | Claridge's Hotel | 45 Brook St., W1 (Bond St.) | 020-7499 0099 | fax 7499 3099 | www.gordonramsay.com

"His kitchen might be hell, but the food is heavenly" at TV star/chef Gordon Ramsay's "art deco fantasy" ("red drapes, swirly light fixtures") in Claridge's, where the team led by exec toque Mark Sargeant is "inspired to deliver" "ever-so-imaginative" Modern European "refined classics" with "old-world charm"; sure, it's a "budget-buster" and, some believe, "a bit of a let-down lately", but most hail it as a "heady wonderland experience"; P.S. "lunch provides 80 percent of the experience at 20 percent of the cost."

	FOOD	DECOR	SERVICE	COST

☑ Gordon Ramsay
at 68 Royal Hospital Rd. ⑧ *French* — 28 | 24 | 28 | £107

Chelsea | 68 Royal Hospital Rd., SW3 (Sloane Sq.) |
020-7352 4441 | fax 7352 3334 | www.gordonramsay.com

"Dine at the altar of the master", Gordon Ramsay – a "superlative experience" for "serious foodies" in "crisp, chic" Chelsea quarters; the "rich and complex", "hellishly good" New French cuisine is ferried by "suave staff", who deliver "royal treatment" that remains London's No. 1 for Service (manager Jean-Claude Breton "deserves to be as famous as Gordon"); it's "eye-wateringly expensive" – perhaps one reason why it was edged out as No. 1 for Food this year – but all in all, Ramsay's "flagship is sailing high."

Goring Dining Room *British* — 23 | 23 | 24 | £57

Victoria | Goring Hotel | 15 Beeston Pl., SW1 (Victoria) | 020-7396 9000 |
fax 7834 4393 | www.goringhotel.co.uk

Exuding an "old-world elegance with a touch of modern humour" (e.g. the whimsical crystal chandeliers), this "peaceful" Goring Hotel dining room offers "no glitz – just fabulous" "Traditional hearty British food" matched by "courteous service"; although it attracts a "mature clientele", it's "not fuddy-duddy", particularly the "plentiful, delicious tea."

Gourmet Burger Kitchen *Hamburgers*
(aka GBK) — 21 | 12 | 14 | £15

NEW **Covent Garden** | 13-14 Maiden Ln., WC2 (Covent Garden) |
020-7240 9617 | fax 7240 3908

Hampstead | 200 Haverstock Hill, Belsize Park, NW3 (Belsize Park) |
020-7443 5335 | fax 7443 5339

Hampstead | 331 West End Ln., NW6 (West Hampstead) |
020-7794 5455 | fax 7794 4401

Battersea | 44 Northcote Rd., SW11 (Clapham Junction B.R.) |
020-7228 3309 | fax 7223 3561

Fulham | 49 Fulham Broadway, SW6 (Fulham Broadway) |
020-7381 4242 | fax 7381 3222

Putney | 333 Putney Bridge Rd., SW15 (Putney Bridge) | 020-8789 1199 |
fax 8780 1953

Richmond | 15-17 Hill Rise, TW10 (Richmond) | 020-8940 5440 |
fax 8940 5772

Wimbledon | 88 The Broadway, SW19 (Wimbledon) | 020-8540 3300 |
fax 8543 1947

Bayswater | 50 Westbourne Grove, W2 (Bayswater/Royal Oak) |
020-7243 4344 | fax 7243 4234

Chiswick | 131 Chiswick High Rd., W4 (Turnham Green) |
020-8995 4548 | fax 8995 4572

www.gbkinfo.com

Additional locations throughout London

"Gargantuan burgers" ("your mouth hurts from having to open so wide") with "adventurous" toppings are what make these fast-fooders such "favourites"; whilst "staff could be a little more proactive", this "happening" chain is "excellent value" and "great for families", especially as "they'll make adjustments to suit" dietary demands.

	FOOD	DECOR	SERVICE	COST

Goya ● *Spanish* — 16 | 13 | 18 | £30

Belgravia | 2 Eccleston Pl., SW1 (Victoria) | 020-7730 4299
Pimlico | 34 Lupus St., SW1 (Pimlico) | 020-7976 5309
www.goyarestaurants.co.uk

"Easy on the wallet and tasty on the belly", these two tapas bars in Pimlico and Belgravia are "fun for a quick snack and hello to chums"; even if the Spanish menu and decor are not much better than "basic", "all the waiters are friendly."

☑ Gravetye Manor *British* — 24 | 27 | 25 | £66

East Grinstead | Gravetye Manor | Vowels Ln., West Sussex | 01342 810567 | fax 01342 810080 | www.gravetyemanor.co.uk

"Oozing charm and graciousness" in the Elizabethan style, this "marvellous country hotel" in Sussex ("close to Gatwick") is "perfectly set up for a weekend getaway" of being "comforted and cosseted"; an "inventive" Modern British menu uses "ingredients raised on the estate" – even the "water from their deep well is delicious" – and is "worth the journey" (but "do stay overnight").

Great Eastern Dining Room ☒ *Asian* — 22 | 18 | 19 | £41

Shoreditch | 54-56 Great Eastern St., EC2 (Liverpool St./Old St.) | 020-7613 4545 | fax 7613 4137 | www.greateasterndining.co.uk

"Cool", "stylish" and "lively", this 10-year-old "sister of e&o" is a "Shoreditch standard"; a new chef has edged the Asian fare up a "delicious" notch, and the "friendly bar staff" are "competent in all the best cocktails"; it's "reasonably priced for the location" too.

NEW Great Queen Street *British* — - | - | - | E

Covent Garden | 32 Great Queen St., WC2 (Covent Garden/Holborn) | fax 7404 9582

Just off Drury Lane, this bohemian newcomer comes courtesy of "people who know their business" (indeed, they're the Anchor & Hope team); it mixes a "nice" rustic setting – abundant wood and blood-red walls – with "imaginative, seasonal Modern British food" and old-world wine served in glass tumblers; but some scold an "inability to cope with the volumes, which they surely were expecting by now?"

Green & Red Bar & Cantina *Mexican* ▽ 20 | 15 | 18 | £32

Bethnal Green | 51 Bethnal Green Rd., E1 (Liverpool St./Shoreditch) | 020-7749 9670 | fax 7749 9671 | www.greenred.co.uk

"Even if the surroundings don't feel very Mexican" (they're "*sans* sombreros and moustaches"), the regional Jaliscan *cucina* comes across as "chillingly authentic" at this "lively" Bethnal Green cantina; of course, for some amigos it's all about alcohol here ("no better tequila list in town!"); P.S. *senoras*, beware: part of the ceiling "above the bar is glass and everyone gets a view" into the tables above.

Green Cottage *Chinese* — - | - | - | I

Finchley | 9 New College Parade, Finchley Rd., NW3 (Finchley Rd./Swiss Cottage) | 020-7722 5305

"Reopened after a long closure due to fire", this "plain", down-to-earth Finchley Chinese is once again "packed with happy customers waiting patiently for tables"; the "reliably good" cuisine ("try the crispy duck" or other Cantonese-style BBQ) is "pretty basic", but also "fantastically low-priced."

Greenhouse, The Ⓢ French   25 | 23 | 24 | £78

Mayfair | 27A Hay's Mews, W1 (Green Park) | 020-7499 3331 | fax 7499 5368 | www.greenhouserestaurant.co.uk
In the "secluded setting" of a "hidden Mayfair mews", this "enchanting" eatery from restaurateur Marlon Abela (Umu, Morton's) is lauded for a "gorgeously prepared" New French menu that "mixes slightly quirky flavours with standard ones", "presented with flair" by service that's "excellent without being stifling"; true, it can be "difficult to get past the price tag", but you could economise with the wine, as the "simply stunning" list contains "both full and half-bottles."

Green Olive, The Italian   20 | 18 | 21 | £36

St. John's Wood | 5 Warwick Pl., W9 (Warwick Ave.) | 020-7289 2469 | fax 7289 2463
It's "like dining in someone's house" to visit this "little-known" "sister to Red Pepper", "tucked away" in St. John's Wood; the "reliable" Italian fare is cooked with "flair", and the staff's "caring attitude is appreciated."

Green's British/Seafood   22 | 20 | 21 | £55

St. James's | 36 Duke St., SW1 (Green Park/Piccadilly Circus) | 020-7930 4566 | fax 7930 2958 | www.greens.org.uk
Within "hushed" St. James's premises "redolent of a gentlemen's club" ("expect lots of old school ties"), this Traditional Brit is a "trusted standby" for "succulent" seafood; a few flinch at the "pretentious atmosphere", advising "dress well if you want to feel at home" here.

Greig's ❶ British/Chophouse   21 | 19 | 19 | £44

Mayfair | 26 Bruton Pl., W1 (Bond St.) | 020-7629 5613 | fax 7495 0411 | www.greigs-restaurant.com
"If meat is for you", so may be this Mayfair chophouse, which for nearly 60 years has set "a good standard for British food and service" within clubby digs (oak panelling and stained-glass window provide "early evening atmosphere"); still, some shrug it off as "expensive, but nothing special."

Grenadier, The British   16 | 20 | 17 | £31

Belgravia | 18 Wilton Row, SW1 (Hyde Park Corner) | 020-7235 3074
"Oozing history", this "old guards officers' mess" – "good enough for the Duke of Wellington" back in the day, and "one or two ghosts" now – "remains a standby" in Belgravia; foes "feel the legend is more interesting than the Traditional British food", but there's "no better place for a pint" or the "best Bloody Mary in town."

Greyhound, The Ⓜ British/European   ▽ 19 | 18 | 16 | £40

Battersea | 136 Battersea High St., SW11 (Clapham Junction) | 020-7978 7021 | fax 7978 0599 | www.thegreyhoundatbattersea.co.uk
"Whether it's a gastropub or a restaurant with a bar is questionable", but why debate when this "buzzy" Battersea haunt offers

"imaginative" Modern British–European fare (including "rather macho" dishes like smoked eels and horseradish ice cream) and "interesting wines"; but the belligerent bark that "customers take second place" to staff attitude.

Groucho Club, The ☒ British 19 | 21 | 18 | £42
Private club; inquiries: 020-7439 4685

An "'in' place for the media elite" and "great for star-spotting", this colourful (literally and figuratively) Soho private club is open all day, serving Modern British fare that gets "an A for effort" from friends, a D for "disappointing" from foes; "but you don't go for the food" here – "the action takes place at the two funky bars."

Grumbles British/French ▽ 17 | 15 | 16 | £27
Pimlico | 35 Churton St., SW1 (Pimlico/Victoria) | 020-7834 0149 | fax 7834 0298 | www.grumblesrestaurant.co.uk

This "sweetly cosy local" in Pimlico makes a "great winter-warmer eatery", with a "varied menu" of French bistro and Traditional British "comfort dishes"; P.S. tip: "upstairs is less cramped" than down.

Guinea Grill ☒ British/Chophouse 22 | 17 | 20 | £47
Mayfair | 30 Bruton Pl., W1 (Bond St.) | 020-7499 1210 | fax 7491 1442 | www.theguinea.co.uk

"Just the place for a clubby, macho" meal, this "intimate" "quintessential British establishment" in Mayfair "provides safe harbour" for "well-prepared" chophouse fare – "heavy on steaks" and "amazing steak and kidney pie"; but it's getting "tattered around the edges" and many bemoan the menu prices ("a guinea will buy you nothing here").

Gun, The British 19 | 21 | 16 | £33
Canary Wharf | 27 Coldharbour, E14 (Canary Wharf) | 020-7515 5222 | www.thegundocklands.com

Offering "history by the bucketload" (it was once a trysting place for Lord Nelson), this "true pub oasis" in Canary Wharf has an "imaginative" Modern British menu, along with "great Portuguese-style BBQ" outside in summer; it's "let down by slack service" – but that "provides time to absorb the pleasant surroundings" and "spectacular view across the river" to the Dome.

Gung-Ho ☺ Chinese ▽ 21 | 15 | 18 | £33
Hampstead | 328-332 West End Ln., NW6 (West Hampstead) | 020-7794 1444 | fax 7794 5522

In Hampstead, this "lively Chinese full of local families" is a moderate option for "high-quality" fare (which "can be spicy, so watch out"); even if it "could do with a face-lift", regulars revel in its reliability: "you know exactly what you'll get, and they never disappoint."

NEW Haiku ☒ Pan-Asian - | - | - | E
Mayfair | 15 New Burlington Pl., W1 (Oxford Circus) | 020-7494 4777 | www.haikurestaurant.com

This hip new Pan-Asian sits in a cul-de-sac "just off Regent Street, hidden" behind huge wood blinds; it's spread over three dark floors, each with a single-technique kitchen that produces raw, steamed or sizzling fare; there's also a "bar area for the 'been-shopping-on-Bond-Street-and-my-Choos-are-killing-me' crowd."

☑ Hakkasan ● Chinese
24 | 25 | 19 | £57

Bloomsbury | 8 Hanway Pl., W1 (Tottenham Court Rd.) | 020-7927 7000 | fax 7907 1889

So "legendary" that "reservations are traded on the futures market", this "sophisticated" seven-year-old is a "standard-setter" for "sumptuous boudoir decor" (carved out of "a converted underground car park" in Bloomsbury), "equally seductive cocktails" and "inventive, delectable" Chinese fusion fare; despite being "abuzz with noise", "outrageous prices" and "staff that think they're too sexy for their jobs", there "couldn't be a cooler" place "to chill out."

Halepi ● Greek
24 | 11 | 18 | £29

Bayswater | 18 Leinster Terrace, W2 (Lancaster Gate/Queensway) | 020-7262 1070 | fax 7262 2630

The space may be the "closest thing to a Greek fishing boat this side of the Channel", but this "old-fashioned, family-run" Hellenic makes a "wonderfully hospitable" haven; Bayswater boosters say bring an appetite, as the "consistently high-standard" fare "just keeps coming."

Hand & Flowers, The British/French
- | - | - | E

Marlow | 126 West St., Buckinghamshire | 01628 482277

If breezing through Buckinghamshire, you might find it handy to stop at this small pub/eatery, a medieval cottage with "great ambience" (exposed beams, etc.); the New French–British menu "with lots of tempting choices" is "great for Sunday lunch"; N.B. as we write, plans were afoot to open an inn next door.

Harbour City ● Chinese
20 | 15 | 16 | £25

Chinatown | 46 Gerrard St., W1 (Leicester Sq./Piccadilly Circus) | 020-7439 7859 | fax 7734 7745

There are "lots of Chinese eating here, so you know it's authentic" claim converts to this Chinatown Cantonese; they've got "some of the best dim sum around" at "a fairly reasonable price", but staff "tend to serve very quickly (so don't order everything at once)."

Hard Rock Cafe ● American
13 | 19 | 15 | £24

Piccadilly | 150 Old Park Ln., W1 (Green Park/Hyde Park Corner) | 020-7629 0382 | fax 7629 8702 | www.hardrock.com

"Everything you'd expect from a Hard Rock Cafe" is at the Hyde Park Corner branch – "the original, with the coolest decor of them all" ("see Lennon's handwritten songs"); cuisinewise, you also "know what you're getting" – "run-of-the-mill American staples" served by "bored staff" with a side of "unbearable noise"; but if you don't mind "tourist-trap" prices, "get your T-shirt, have the burger and move on."

Harlem ● American
16 | 18 | 15 | £25

Westbourne Grove | 78 Westbourne Grove, W2 (Bayswater/Queensway) | 020-7985 0900 | fax 7985 0901 | www.harlemsoulfood.com

This "atmospheric", all-day eatery in Westbourne Grove is "the place to go for a fix of fried chicken", "dependable burgers" and other American "soul food, Brit-style"; but even expats admit there's "nothing about this place that reminds one of Harlem" except for the "great downstairs bar" where "DJs spin hip-hop."

Harry Morgan's *Deli/Jewish* | 16 | 9 | 12 | £23 |

Knightsbridge | Harrod's | 87-135 Brompton Rd., SW1 (Knightsbridge) | 020-7730 1234
Fitzrovia | 6 Market Pl., W1 (Oxford Circus) | 020-7580 4849 ⑤
St. John's Wood | 29-31 St. John's Wood High St., NW8 (St. John's Wood) | 020-7722 1869
www.harryms.co.uk

If you're "hankering for an authentic salt beef sandwich", chicken soup and other Jewish classics, this 60-year-old "decent deli" in St. John's Wood (with two young offshoots) serves food "just like mother used to, only mother did it much cheaper" – and faster ("I'm still waiting to be served").

Harry's Bar ●⑤ *Italian* | 24 | 24 | 25 | £73 |

Private club; inquiries: 020-7408 0844

"The 'in' spot if you want to see anyone of importance", this "lively" private dining club in Mayfair exudes the "luxury of a past era", with a rich Northern Italian "menu that always surprises", "brilliant staff" dressed "like indulgent matrons" and "lots of space nearby for your car and driver"; in short, "a special treat" "worth every ridiculous cost."

Hartwell House *British* | ▽ 19 | 21 | 21 | £72 |

Aylesbury | Hartwell House | Oxford Rd., Buckinghamshire | 01296 747444 | fax 01296 747450 | www.hartwell-house.com

"So romantic", this "country house hotel" makes a "spectacular place for afternoon tea" or "formal dining" in a lemon-coloured salon; staff are "well-trained", and the Modern British fare is "good for the area" – a "blissful" bit of Buckinghamshire.

NEW Hat & Feathers ⑤ *European* | – | – | – | M |

Clerkenwell | 2 Clerkenwell Rd., EC1 (Barbican) | 020-7490 2244

"Love the lively bar, love the quiet and elegant upstairs, love the food" gush fans of this new Clerkenwell Modern European, a characterful 1870 boozer revamped with Victorian faux gas lights, large mirrors and gold-leaf cornicing; a "spartan wine list is the only complaint."

NEW Hawksmoor ⑤ *Chophouse* | ▽ 28 | 16 | 24 | £44 |

Shoreditch | 157 Commercial St., E1 (Liverpool St./Shoreditch) | 020-7247 7392 | www.thehawksmoor.com

First have some "delightful cocktails, then onto the real reason for the visit – the steaks, simply the best you can get in London" rave reviewers about this eclectically furnished grill; the grub's "accompanied by delicious sides" and "divine" sundaes, and "friendly, helpful" staff further ensure it's "worth the walk from Liverpool Street tube."

Haz ● *Turkish* | 25 | 16 | 20 | £27 |

City | 9 Cutler St., E1 (Liverpool St.) | 020-7929 7923 | fax 7623 5132

"The best Turkish food in London" – "satisfying", "healthy" and "cooked to order on the open" grill hail habitués of this "popular" haunt; whilst it would "benefit from fewer tables to feel less like a canteen", "the dining experience is much improved in the evening or weekend when the [lunchtime] City folk have departed."

NEW High Road Brasserie European   20 | 24 | 19 | £41

Chiswick | High Road House | 162-166 Chiswick High Rd., W4 (Turnham Green) | 020-8742 7474 | www.highroadbrasserie.co.uk

"Once again, Nick Jones [Soho House] has worked his magic", creating a "chic" scene at this "buzzy" blue and brown–toned Chiswick brasserie; there are "fabulous cocktails" and a Modern European "menu that covers a bit of something for everyone" ("better on the grilled meats than more complex dishes" perhaps); stung by "snippy" servers, some wonder "will this star last?", but for now, it's "hard to get a walk-in table."

Hind's Head British   23 | 18 | 20 | £41

Bray | High St., Berkshire | 01628 626151 | fax 01628 6223394 | www.hindsheadhotel.co.uk

Now "under the co-direction of Heston Blumenthal of The Fat Duck" nearby, this "oldie worldly" Traditional Brit in Bray is worth a heads-up – and in fact "the place to be Sunday lunchtime"; "don't be tricked into thinking it's pub grub – it's Heston's twist on home-cooked treats" (e.g. "to-die-for triple-cooked chips"); "food can be slow coming out of the kitchen", but otherwise, "this vision of a gastropub really works."

Z Home House ☯ British/European   20 | 25 | 21 | £59

Private club; inquiries: 020-7670 2100

The "elegant surroundings of this posh private club" – all high ceilings, crystal chandeliers and silk-padded walls – attract an "über-cool media crowd" to its Portman Square premises; "attentive service" boosts the "expensive" but "surprisingly good" Modern European–British fare, and for that "decadent dining" feeling, "have dessert in a cosy corner of one of the sitting rooms."

Hoxton Apprentice Eclectic   ∇ 18 | 20 | 17 | £32

Hoxton | 16 Hoxton Sq., N1 (Old St.) | 020-7749 2828 | fax 7749 2829 | www.hoxtonapprentice.com

"Run as a charity to train unemployed young people" in restaurant pursuits, this "useful concept" in a landmarked "former schoolhouse" in Hoxton "performs very well" with its "simply executed" Eclectic menu; it's also "good value, so you can't lose supporting a cause like this."

NEW Hoxton Grille, The Eclectic   - | - | - | M

Shoreditch | Hoxton Hotel | 81 Great Eastern St., EC2 (Old St.) | 020-7739 9111 | www.grillerestaurants.com

A "pretty interior courtyard" is the key feature to this low-profile but hip Hoxton Hotel venue serving "hearty helpings" of "solid" "basic British"-Eclectic eats; pioneering surveyors say it's "good value by London standards", however – as at many novices – "staff are still finding their feet."

	FOOD	DECOR	SERVICE	COST

Z Hunan Ⓢ Chinese
Pimlico | 51 Pimlico Rd., SW1 (Sloane Sq.) | 020-7730 5712 |
fax 7730 8265

`28 | 14 | 22 | £44`

The trick is to let chef-owner Mr. Peng "know what you like and
it will keep coming" at this "fine choice for the Chinese connois-
seur" in Pimlico; admirers call it "incomparable" for its
Hunanese dishes "dependant on the day's market" and delivered
in "tasty little bites"; just be prepared to "ignore the cold surroundings" and "remember to say when you are full – otherwise
they will keep feeding you!"

Hush Ⓢ British/French
Mayfair | 8 Lancashire Ct., W1 (Bond St.) | 020-7659 1500 |
fax 7659 1501 | www.hush.co.uk

`17 | 19 | 16 | £45`

"In a beautiful cobblestone courtyard" "off Bond Street" lies this triparte venue: a Modern British brasserie, an "upstairs restaurant"
doing Classic French fare and a lounge "packed with after-work gals
looking for action"; food- and servicewise, "it could do better", and
(belying its name) it's "almost always too loud", so the savvy "try to
wait for the warm weather, when dining outside is a pleasure."

Ikeda Ⓢ Japanese
Mayfair | 30 Brook St., W1 (Bond St.) | 020-7629 2730 |
fax 7490 5992

`▽ 21 | 11 | 18 | £51`

"Forget the decor – the reason you come" to this "plain", pint-size
Mayfair Japanese is for "awesome food", including "unbeatably
fresh", "fantastic sushi and sashimi" as well as cooked fare; just bear
in mind it is "very expensive."

Ikkyu Japanese
Bloomsbury | 67A Tottenham Court Rd., W1 (Goodge St.) |
020-7636 9280

`▽ 19 | 9 | 13 | £19`

Though it's "hidden" in Tottenham Court Road, it seems "so Tokyo-
like" at this "absolute gem" of a Japanese, given the "authentic"
fare, "obvious skill of the chefs" and, alas, "quite rushed" staff; it's
also "high value for money."

Z Il Bordello Italian
Wapping | 81 Wapping High St., E1 (Wapping) | 020-7481 9950

`23 | 16 | 20 | £33`

An "excellent find in Wapping", this "lively" local trattoria is
"always busy", doling out "huge portions" of "pizza, pasta or
classic meat dishes" "at a great price"; "friendly Italian waiters
enhance the experience."

Il Convivio Ⓢ Italian
Belgravia | 143 Ebury St., SW1 (Sloane Sq./Victoria) | 020-7730 4099 |
fax 7730 4103 | www.etruscarestaurants.com

`23 | 20 | 22 | £43`

"Airy" and "mercifully uncrowded", this "cosmopolitan" Italian
"never disappoints" disciples with its "generally delicious, varied
menu" served by "attentive, but never intrusive" staff and a "really
good sommelier"; "one of the best" of The Boot in Belgravia – but
one of the "most expensive" too.

| | FOOD | DECOR | SERVICE | COST |

Il Falconiere ◗🅕 *Italian* ▽ 15 13 13 £30

South Kensington | 84 Old Brompton Rd., SW7 (Gloucester Rd./ South Kensington) | 020-7589 2401 | fax 7589 9158 | www.ilfalconiere.co.uk

Owned and run by the Mosquera family for 25 years, this "well-maintained, friendly" South Ken trattoria packs in the tables tight with a "serviceable" Italian menu featuring "very good value" prix fixe options (like a "decent £12.50 lunch") that "may not be expensive, but is a case of getting what you pay for."

Il Portico ◗🅕 *Italian* 22 15 23 £35

Kensington | 277 Kensington High St., W8 (High St. Kensington) | 020-7602 6262

"A neighbourhood favourite", "this family-run restaurant makes you feel right at home" cry Kensingtonians who crave its "classic" "savoury, satisfying" Italian dishes and "heartfelt service"; best of all, "the bill still leaves some change for the homemade desserts."

Imli *Indian* 20 16 18 £22

Soho | 167-169 Wardour St., W1 (Tottenham Court Rd.) | 020-7287 4243 | fax 7287 4245 | www.imli.co.uk

It's an "excellent concept": "Indian-style tapas" with "interesting twists" at outstanding prices" proclaim proponents of this "trendy cool" Tamarind offshoot; staff are "relaxed and helpful", and whilst some find the "extremely orange decor" "odd", most salute this "spicy, not stodgy" Soho subcontinental.

Imperial China ◗ *Chinese* 21 18 16 £26

Chinatown | 25A Lisle St., WC2 (Leicester Sq./Piccadilly Circus) | 020-7734 3388 | fax 7734 3833 | www.imperial-china.co.uk

"An attempt to upgrade the Chinatown experience that works" declare devotees of this venue with "modern" earth-toned decor, "out-of-this-world dim sum" and "better-than-average Cantonese" cuisine; "it's huge, so you can always get a seat", though that means "superstore-style service" as well; but "if you hire one of the private rooms, you can also indulge in a little karaoke."

Imperial City 🅕 *Chinese* ▽ 17 17 16 £38

City | Royal Exchange, Cornhill, EC3 (Bank) | 020-7626 3437 | fax 7338 0125 | www.orientalrestaurantgroup.co.uk

"The wonderful red-brick vaulted ceilings" below the Royal Exchange create "great surroundings" for this "good business lunch place in the City" – even if the "reliable" Chinese "food should be better for the cost"; N.B. the Decor score doesn't reflect a recent refurb.

Inaho 🅕 *Japanese* ▽ 21 10 16 £32

Bayswater | 4 Hereford Rd., W2 (Bayswater/Queensway) | 020-7221 8495

"Old-fashioned, excellent fare" from sushi to teriyaki is on hand at this Bayswater Asian; it's "as authentic as you'll get, but authentic Japanese is often not luxurious" lament those who've experienced its "tiny, basic" digs.

	FOOD	DECOR	SERVICE	COST

Incognico ⊠ French
21 | 18 | 18 | £41

Soho | 117 Shaftesbury Ave., WC2 (Leicester Sq./Tottenham Court Rd.) | 020-7836 8866 | fax 7240 9525 | www.incognico.com

Just by Cambridge Circus, this "clubby feel"-ing, often-"overlooked" venue is "wonderfully convenient for the theatre", offering "terrific Classic and New French" brasserie fare; still, some find it "shockingly expensive" now that there are "no more prix fixe" options.

Indian Zing Indian
- | - | - | M

Hammersmith | 236 King St., W6 (Ravenscourt Park) | 020-8748 5959

Aiming to be "a dining rather than just a feeding experience", this "upmarket Indian" in Hammersmith is "recommended" for its "imaginative" cuisine (e.g. monkfish tikka) and the "amazing ambience" of its contemporary, bright decor; however, a few cynics suggest it's "not as different as the hype would suggest."

Indigo ● European
22 | 22 | 23 | £45

Covent Garden | One Aldwych Hotel | 1 Aldwych, WC2 (Charing Cross/Covent Garden) | 020-7300 0400 | fax 7300 1001 | www.onealdwych.com

"Get a table next to the railing and enjoy an unimpaired view of the lobby bar below" at the One Aldwych Hotel's "cool" mezzanine Modern European, serving "substantial" meals "with international flavour to business travellers"; "the decor and setting help justify the price tag", as does "smart, friendly" staff.

Inn The Park British
17 | 18 | 14 | £33

St. James's | St. James's Park, SW1 (St. James's Park) | 020-7451 9999 | fax 7451 9998 | www.innthepark.com

"Overlooking the lake and trees" "in the heart of St. James's Park", this biparte Oliver Peyton-owned pavilion sees "tourists mingling with government officials"; but it's a "strange concept" – those "in the restaurant section are a table away from [cafeteria] tray-wielding patrons", the Traditional British "food's mediocre" and the service "chaotic"; "an idyllic setting", "but that's about it."

Inside ⓜ European
▽ 24 | 16 | 18 | £32

Greenwich | 19 Greenwich South St., SE10 (Greenwich) | 020-8265 5060 | www.insiderestaurant.co.uk

"Close to Greenwich station, this small, unobtrusive restaurant" delights locals with its "fresh", "unfussy" Modern European fare and "reasonable service" in "simple, clean" premises; although the bare floors make it "a bit noisy", boosters believe it "the best in this part of London."

Isarn Thai
▽ 22 | 20 | 18 | £28

Islington | 119 Upper St., N1 (Angel) | 020-7424 5153

Owned by the sister of Hakkasan restaurateur Alan Yau, this "sleek" Islington eatery is "easy-to-miss but worth seeking out" for "amazing Thai food" at "remarkably good value"; "friendly service" goes down well too.

	FOOD	DECOR	SERVICE	COST

☑ Ishbilia *Lebanese*
24 | 12 | 18 | £36

Belgravia | 9 William St., SW1 (Knightsbridge) | 020-7235 7788 |
fax 7235 7771 ❶

Knightsbridge | Harrods | 87-135 Brompton Rd., 2nd fl., SW1
(Knightsbridge) | 020-7893 8598

The "sublime" Lebanese cuisine is "as good as anything in Beirut" at
this "wonderful, warm, whimsical" Belgravia "local" (with a Harrods
sib), "usually packed" with "tables full of families"; "uninspiring decor" doesn't seem to deter from the "convivial atmosphere" created
by "engaging staff."

Ishtar ❶ *Turkish*
▽ 22 | 21 | 21 | £25

Marylebone | 10-12 Crawford St., W1 (Baker St.) | 020-7224 2446 |
www.ishtarrestaurant.com

"Feel as if you're dining on the Bosporus" at this "truly excellent
Turk" in Marylebone; the food's "authentic" if "a touch different
from the norm", "the ambience is nice, with low lighting and [open]
kitchen activity to keep one entertained", and "service is friendly";
add in music on weekends, and it's "just a great place all round."

Island Restaurant & Bar *Eclectic*
- | - | - | M

Bayswater | Royal Lancaster Hotel | Lancaster Terrace, W2
(Lancaster Gate) | 020-7551 6070 | fax 7551 6071 |
www.islandrestaurant.co.uk

A "much needed 'real' restaurant in the Paddington culinary
desert", this hotel eatery with subtle hues and big windows on the
edge of Hyde Park has a new chef and new Eclectic menu that, whilst
"generally quite good", "can be a bit uneven."

itsu *Japanese*
18 | 15 | 15 | £24

Soho | 103 Wardour St., W1 (Oxford Circus/Piccadilly Circus) |
020-7479 4794 | fax 7479 4795

Canary Wharf | Cabot Pl. E., 2nd fl., E14 (Canary Wharf) | 020-7512 5790 |
fax 7512 5791 🅂

Chelsea | 118 Draycott Ave., SW3 (South Kensington) | 020-7590 2400 |
fax 7590 2403
www.itsu.co.uk

It's "a miracle you can eat fresh raw fish so casually at such reasonable prices" say fans of this "hustling", "competent" chain where a
"conveyor belt delivers" hot and cold Japanese fare within a '60s-
mod setting; it's "not the greatest", but "kids love it" and it's "quick"
("service can't be better when you serve yourself").

☑ Ivy, The ❶ *British/European*
23 | 21 | 23 | £55

Covent Garden | 1 West St., WC2 (Leicester Sq.) | 020-7836 4751 |
fax 7240 9333 | www.the-ivy.co.uk

Sprinkled with "stars of stage and screen" – "beware the paparazzi
when you leave" – "this Theatreland diva is still getting rave reviews
and standing-room crowds" thanks to her "energised atmosphere",
Modern British-Euro "home-cooked-style food" ("simple", yet "terrific") and "polished service"; critics may cavil "it's become something of a cliché", but even they admit they'd "lie, cheat and steal to
get into" this "beyond-trendy cafeteria for celebrities."

Jaan *French*

FOOD	DECOR	SERVICE	COST
–	–	–	E

Covent Garden | Swissôtel London - The Howard | 12 Temple Pl., WC2 (Temple) | 020-7300 1700 | fax 7240 7186

"An oasis in an area not blessed with good restaurants", this "elegant" Embankment venue offers "delicious", "slightly Asian-inspired" French fare supplied by "charming service"; the decor features floor-to-ceiling glass doors opening onto a garden terrace (hence, "late spring to autumn is the time to visit").

Jade Garden ● *Chinese*

FOOD	DECOR	SERVICE	COST
19	14	16	£25

Chinatown | 15 Wardour St., W1 (Leicester Sq./Piccadilly Circus) | 020-7437 5065 | fax 7429 7851 | www.londonjadegarden.co.uk

"It hums, it sings, it's noisy – it's like Hong Kong" at this "crowded" Chinatown stalwart, with "pretty decent" dim sum and "inexpensive" Mandarin mains; disregard staff that are "even rude to native speakers (that's telling you something)"; oh, and "don't forget to pretend you know what you're ordering."

Jenny Lo's Tea House ⊠⇆ *Chinese*

FOOD	DECOR	SERVICE	COST
20	9	17	£15

Belgravia | 14 Eccleston St., SW1 (Victoria) | 020-7259 0399

Some say "it's more like a takeaway place", but "for people who are comfortable with basic decor and communal tables", this "real jewel" in Belgravia from Ken Lo's daughter, Jenny, offers a "solid experience" of "fresh, quick, healthy" Chinese fare at "great value."

Jim Thompson's *Thai*

FOOD	DECOR	SERVICE	COST
15	20	16	£29

Finchley | 889 Green Lns., N21 (Southgate/Wood Green) | 020-8360 0005 | fax 8364 3006

Fulham | 617 King's Rd., SW6 (Fulham Broadway) | 020-7731 0999 | fax 7731 2835

Putney | 408 Upper Richmond Rd., SW15 (East Putney) | 020-8788 3737 | fax 8788 3738

"Fun in a tacky, touristy way", this Thai trio comes laden with Asian artefacts for sale; the "quirky" "decor is the best thing going" for it protest purists – "go for a pint by all means, but get your curry elsewhere."

⊉ Jin Kichi Ⓜ *Japanese*

FOOD	DECOR	SERVICE	COST
26	10	17	£34

Hampstead | 73 Heath St., NW3 (Hampstead) | 020-7794 6158 | fax 7794 6158 | www.jinkichi.com

Almost every critic calls it "cramped", but "what it lacks in space, it makes up for in quality" at this Hampstead "survivor", an "outstanding" option for a "range of choices" of Japanese cuisine ("the yakitori grill bar is the true star here"); "be sure to book in advance" as it is, unsurprisingly, "hard to get into."

Joe Allen ● *American*

FOOD	DECOR	SERVICE	COST
17	16	17	£35

Covent Garden | 13 Exeter St., WC2 (Covent Garden) | 020-7836 0651 | fax 7497 2148 | www.joeallenrestaurant.com

A is for Joe Allen, adored by "A-listers treading the boards", even though the old Theatrelander is all "about the atmosphere", rather than the "average" if "always reliable" "authentic American" eats, or poster-adorned decor "in need of a spruce-up"; P.S. ask for the "off-the-menu burger."

	FOOD	DECOR	SERVICE	COST

Joe's *British*
∇ 19 | 17 | 16 | £36

South Kensington | 126 Draycott Ave., SW3 (South Kensington) |
020-7225 2217 | fax 7584 1133

"Ladies who lunch" are a regular fixture at this casual Brompton
Cross bistro, set opposite its owner, the Joseph store; whilst the
Modern British meals are merely "reliable", "no one expects any
wow in their food" – though some oomph might be appreciated in
staff that are "good-looking, but not trained."

Joe's Restaurant Bar *British*
21 | 17 | 17 | £36

Knightsbridge | Joseph | 16 Sloane St., SW1 (Knightsbridge) |
020-7235 9869 | fax 7235 3218

A "multicultural melting pot of rich Londonites, topped off with
fresh food and polite service" summarises the "upscale" scene at
this "healthy" Modern Brit basement cafe; as its locale in the Joseph
store suggests, it's also "quite an expensive place" where the "portions are sized for models, not men."

Joy King Lau ◐ *Chinese*
20 | 9 | 12 | £21

Chinatown | 3 Leicester St., WC2 (Leicester Sq./Piccadilly Circus) |
020-7437 1133 | fax 7437 2629

This "crowded" Chinatown veteran "may not look like much" – it's
"rather glum" in truth – but it "just sticks to doing good, old-fashioned
dim sum well", along with "inexpensive" Cantonese mains; "service
is efficient, if a little off-hand" (even so, "expect to queue").

☒ J. Sheekey ◐ *Seafood*
25 | 21 | 23 | £55

Covent Garden | 28-32 St. Martin's Ct., WC2 (Leicester Sq.) |
020-7240 2565 | fax 7497 0891 | www.j-sheekey.co.uk

The "peerless seafood has barely stopped breathing" at this "discreet" Theatreland "bastion" where "the warmly lit, woody interior
complements the conviviality"; throw in "unerring service" and a
"chance to celeb-spot" amongst all "the thespians after a show",
and this "slick outfit" "is "rightly revered", "like her sister, The Ivy."

Julie's ◐ *British*
18 | 22 | 19 | £41

Notting Hill | 135 Portland Rd., W11 (Holland Park) | 020-7229 8331 |
fax 7229 4050 | www.juliesrestaurant.com

Like "a grandfather clock in the corner, Julie's keeps on ticking", let-
ting Notting Hill lovebirds bill and coo in its "maze of differently
themed rooms" with "cute nooks" as it's done since 1970; the
"homely, comforting" Modern British "food is fine if not mind-
blowing", and it's all "so romantic, you ignore the bill" at the end.

Just St. James's ☒ *British*
16 | 19 | 15 | £46

St. James's | 12 St. James's St., SW1 (Green Park) | 020-7976 2222 |
fax 7976 2020 | www.juststjames.com

"Beautiful, with marble columns", "the decor overshadows the
food" at this Modern Brit in a converted St. James's bank; despite a
"brash" bar crowd, the "cavernous" space can offer a "relaxing"
evening, though the "expense-account" bills cause some to "prefer
Just Oriental", its sibling with separate bar and DJ downstairs.

	FOOD	DECOR	SERVICE	COST

❷ Kai Mayfair *Chinese*
25 | 21 | 22 | £56

Mayfair | 65 S. Audley St., W1 (Bond St./Marble Arch) | 020-7493 8988 | fax 7493 1456 | www.kaimayfair.co.uk

Embark on a "dining adventure" at this "delightful spot in quiet Mayfair", whose "Chinese food for grown-ups" takes "the concept of originality to extremes"; the setting – "beautiful", "if a bit corporate" – proves Asian eateries "can be posh", and staff pay "meticulous attention to detail"; sure, it's "crazy expensive", but many maintain it's "the best of its kind."

Kandoo ❶ *Persian*
- | - | - | I

Marylebone | 458 Edgware Rd., W2 (Edgware Rd.) | 020-7724 2428 | fax 7724 6769

Family-run, traditionally decorated and low-profile, this "solid neighbourhood restaurant" on Edgware Road serves "reliable Persian" fare with some "tasty specialities", and "the fact it's BYO helps keeps the cost down."

Kastoori *Indian*
- | - | - | I

Balham | 188 Upper Tooting Rd., SW17 (Tooting Bec/Tooting Broadway) | 020-8767 7027

The few who know it fawn over this family-run, "inventive" "veg-only" veteran in Tooting, deemed "interesting" for its "unusual" East African–Indian menu in digs decorated with stone temple dancers.

Kensington Place ❶ *British*
20 | 16 | 18 | £43

Kensington | 201-209 Kensington Church St., W8 (Notting Hill Gate) | 020-7727 3184 | fax 7229 2025 | www.dandlondon.com

"Bask in the happy atmosphere" and enjoy "a blissful foodie experience" at this "boisterous" Modern Brit in Kensington; for 20 years, this "old favourite never failed to please" – but longtime chef-owner Rowley Leigh recently departed and whilst few changes are planned, this may not appease those who hate the "harried service" and "far too noisy room."

Kettners ❶ *Eclectic*
15 | 20 | 17 | £30

Soho | 29 Romilly St., W1 (Leicester Sq.) | 020-7734 6112 | fax 7287 6499 | www.pizzaexpress.com/kettners

"Opulent dining rooms and tinkling piano" "kind of mask the average food" at this historic townhouse, a "true Soho icon" now owned by Pizza Express; still, it's "always buzzing" with punters chomping on "posh pizza" and other Eclectic eats; plus the "cosy champagne bar" makes "a great place to meet."

Kew Grill *British*
18 | 16 | 15 | £45

Richmond | 10B Kew Green, TW9 (Kew Gdns.) | 020-8948 4433 | fax 8605 3532 | www.awtrestaurants.com

In "comfortable surroundings that match the area perfectly", this rustic Kew venue – run by celebrity chef Antony Worrall Thompson and wife Jay – is "great for meat eaters", but "dull if you don't want beef"; some also believe this Modern Brit could offer "more welcoming service."

	FOOD	DECOR	SERVICE	COST

Khan's ◐ *Indian*
20 | 10 | 14 | £19

Bayswater | 13-15 Westbourne Grove, W2 (Bayswater/Queensway) |
020-7727 5420 | fax 7229 1835 | www.khansrestaurant.com

Since 1977, this "Indian food factory" has been a halal haven for
"tried-and-true", "inexpensive" eats; whilst critics khan no longer
stand certain aspects – "tired" decor, "curt staff" (maybe "rudeness
is part of the allure"?) and "worst of all – no alcohol served", "locals
and tourists alike flock" to this "cavernous" Bayswater "stalwart."

Khan's of Kensington ◐ *Indian*
22 | 13 | 16 | £26

South Kensington | 3 Harrington Rd., SW7 (South Kensington) |
020-7584 4114 | fax 7581 2900

"Inspired food" at a "reasonable price" keeps this South Ken Indian
going; but several say it's a "great place to pick up takeaway – then
you don't have to deal with the lazy service" and "boring" decor.

Kiku *Japanese*
24 | 17 | 21 | £44

Mayfair | 17 Half Moon St., W1 (Green Park) | 020-7499 4208 |
fax 7409 3359 | www.kikurestaurant.co.uk

"Superb sashimi and sushi" and other "excellent", "traditional" dishes
set the scene at this "serene", "proper" "Mayfair Japanese"; aside
from the "great-value" set lunches, though, it's "quite expensive."

NEW Kobe Jones *Japanese*
18 | 16 | 13 | £43

Bloomsbury | St. Giles Hotel | 111A Great Russell St., WC1
(Tottenham Court Rd.) | 020-7300 3250 | fax 7300 3254 |
www.kobejones.com.au

"In surroundings that take you East" (lots of red-and-black lacquer
and dark wood), this large Bloomsbury neophyte offers "Japanese
fusion dishes" (e.g. green-tea salmon, sake-infused trifle) that seem
"strange" to some, "interesting" to others; overall, the "food's not as
excellent as the prices might suggest" – and "staff don't look like
they know the place."

Koi *Japanese*
22 | 18 | 19 | £48

Kensington | 1E Palace Gate, W8 (Gloucester Rd./High St. Kensington) |
020-7581 8778 | fax 7589 2788

For "fantastic teppanyaki" and "decent sushi in Kensington", locals
rely on this "pleasant" Japanese adorned with traditional low tables
and floor mats; if the "speedy service" is maybe *too* speedy", at
least that makes it ideal "for a quick bite on the way home."

NEW Konstam
at the Prince Albert ⑤ *British*
- | - | - | M

King's Cross | 2 Acton St., WC1 (King's Cross) | 020-7833 5040 |
www.konstam.co.uk

"All credit to Ollie Rowe", the celebrity chef behind this King's Cross
yearling, which exclusively uses "London's varied produce" to
support local farmers; but some scoff there's "no point using ingredients sourced within the M25 if they don't taste nice", and the
"highly designed" interior, dominated by dangly chain fixtures, "is
not much to my taste."

Kulu Kulu Sushi 🅢 *Japanese*

FOOD	DECOR	SERVICE	COST
20	9	15	£23

Covent Garden | 51-53 Shelton St., WC2 (Covent Garden) |
020-7240 5687 | fax 7240 5687
Soho | 76 Brewer St., W1 (Piccadilly Circus) | 020-7734 7316 |
fax 7734 6507
South Kensington | 39 Thurloe Pl., SW7 (South Kensington) |
020-7589 2225 | fax 7589 2225

"A conveyor belt covered in delectable bites of sushi", along with
cooked "Japanese standards", is the simple formula at this "excellent value" trio; the decor's "very "no-frills", but the "service is brisk
and the chefs will prepare on demand" too.

La Bouchée *French*

FOOD	DECOR	SERVICE	COST
20	17	18	£33

South Kensington | 56 Old Brompton Rd., SW7 (South Kensington) |
020-7589 1929 | fax 7584 8625

Cited as a "good place for a low-key date" – if you don't mind being
"crammed in tightly" – this "candlelit" South Ken site serves "tasty
bistro" fare "without pretension" ("even the French find it French");
"enthusiastic" staff "make up for the ho-hum decor."

La Brasserie *French*

FOOD	DECOR	SERVICE	COST
16	15	13	£32

South Kensington | 272 Brompton Rd., SW3 (South Kensington) |
020-7581 3089 | fax 7581 1435

This "crowded" Brompton Cross veteran comes bearing all "the
charm and defects of many a Parisian brasserie": the former includes "traditional, no-nonsense" fare ("predictable, but sometimes that is just what one wants"); the latter, "worn ambience" and
waiters who veer from "indifferent to rude."

L'Accento Italiano 🅢 *Italian*

FOOD	DECOR	SERVICE	COST
-	-	-	E

Bayswater | 16 Garway Rd., W2 (Bayswater/Queensway) |
020-7243 2201 | fax 7243 2201

"A neighbourhood staple for those in-the-know" confide the cog-
noscenti about this "quaint" "little" Italian that's "great in the summer when the doors open" onto its quiet Bayswater street; the "daily
prix fixe menu is the way to go" to avoid otherwise upscale prices.

La Collina *Italian*

FOOD	DECOR	SERVICE	COST
-	-	-	M

Primrose Hill | 17 Princess Rd., NW1 (Chalk Farm) |
020-7483 0192

"The most recent incarnation at this delightful Primrose Hill spot" is
a "wonderful neighbourhood" eatery "serving interesting Italian
food" in "homelike, generous portions"; "the room is tiny (understandable given the rents charged today)", but come summer,
there's a "lovely garden."

Ladbroke Arms *European*

FOOD	DECOR	SERVICE	COST
20	16	14	£30

Notting Hill | 54 Ladbroke Rd., W11 (Holland Park/Notting Hill Gate) |
020-7727 6648 | fax 7727 2127 | www.ladbrokearms.com

With "well-cooked" Modern European fare, a "cosy environment"
and a hip local "Euro crowd", this Notting Hill gastropub is "always
a pleasure", with the added perk of a front patio for "eating outside
on a nice day"; shame that "service is a little rude at times."

	FOOD	DECOR	SERVICE	COST

Ladurée *French*

23 | 21 | 18 | £33

Knightsbridge | Harrods | 87-135 Brompton Rd., ground fl., SW1 (Knightsbridge) | 020-7893 8293 | fax 3155 0112 | www.laduree.com
"Already an institution", this "totally *femme, frivolous*" Harrods outpost of the famed "Parisian patisserie" "gives a feeling of being caught between *Alice in Wonderland*'s dream and Marie Antoinette's boudoir"; alongside the "decadent" display of "inventive macaroons" and other "sinful" delights, the Classic French menu includes "interesting salads and other fare", making it "perfect for a shopping break" – just "leave the diet at home."

La Famiglia ● *Italian*

21 | 16 | 22 | £41

Chelsea | 7 Langton St., SW10 (Fulham Broadway/Sloane Sq.) | 020-7351 0761 | fax 7351 2409 | www.lafamiglialondon.com
"It's all in the name: a family feeling from the moment you enter" this "humming" World's End 40-year-old that "never seems to lose its hearty enthusiasm" (the room could use "a face-lift", though); the "rustic" Tuscan cuisine is "well executed", even if the menu seems "suspiciously long"; P.S. the "glassed-in back area is fantastic."

La Figa *Italian*

- | - | - | M

Canary Wharf | The Mosaic | 45 Narrow St., E14 (Limehouse) | 020-7790 0077
"Limehouse is lucky to have such quality so close" say fans of this "lively" trattoria, sister to Il Bordello, with a "friendly neighbourhood ambience" and Italian menu of "good-value" staples ("humongous pizza and all the pasta classics"); "staff really care" too.

La Fromagerie Café *European*

24 | 17 | 15 | £24

Marylebone | 2-4 Moxon St., W1 (Baker St.) | 020-7935 0341 | fax 7935 0341 | www.lafromagerie.co.uk
"Amazingly fresh", "adventurous" and "artery-clogging" Modern European dishes "hit just the right note" at this "crowded eatery at the back" of a "frantic" but "fantastic" *fromagerie* in Marylebone; some snarl "the service is always slow" – unless it's just that the "smell of wonderful cheese wafting through the air makes you so hungry!"

La Genova 🅱 *Italian*

23 | 19 | 24 | £52

Mayfair | 32 N. Audley St., W1 (Bond St.) | 020-7629 5916 | fax 7629 5916 | www.lagenovarestaurant.com
An "old-style, elegant Italian with the owner still very much in charge", "making you feel at home", characterises this "cosy" Mayfair haunt; "the food's always fresh, with a wide variety of options" on the Ligurian-oriented menu; P.S. "walk-ups welcome."

Lamberts 🅼 *British*

▽ 25 | 18 | 23 | £36

Balham | 2 Station Parade, Balham High Rd., SW12 (Balham) | 020-8675 2233 | www.lambertsrestaurant.com
"Relaxed" and "intimate", this Balham Modern Brit "tries hard to please" (and largely succeeds) with an "ambitious" menu of "cooked-to-order" "classics with a twist" (e.g. "excellent mutton dish"); it's "perhaps a touch overpriced", even for an "upper-bracket local."

	FOOD	DECOR	SERVICE	COST

Z Lanes *Eclectic*   24 24 27 £63

Mayfair | Four Seasons Hotel | Hamilton Pl., W1 (Green Park/ Hyde Park Corner) | 020-7499 0888 | fax 7493 6629 | www.fourseasons.com/london

From its "full English breakfasts" to the "rib roast carved at tableside" at dinner, this all-day Eclectic restaurant on the first floor of the Four Seasons Hotel is a "superb" "sure bet" for "travellers and locals alike"; surveyors smile on service that manages to be both "exemplary" and "down-to-earth for [such] a high-end place", and the marbled, stained-glass room offers "nice views" up Park Lane.

Z Lanesborough Conservatory *Eclectic*   21 26 25 £59

Belgravia | The Lanesborough | 1 Lanesborough Pl., SW1 (Hyde Park Corner) | 020-7259 5599 | fax 7259 5606 | www.lanesborough.co.uk

"As picturesque a dining room you'll see" – with "delicate colours, whimsical palms and a hint of the Orient" – the Lanesborough's "bright" conservatory "is still a top-flight place" for a "splendid tea-time fantasy" or "romantic dinner dance"; the "refined" Eclectic fare is "quite good", if "underwhelming at hotel prices", but most praise the "prompt, attentive service."

Langan's Bistro Z *British/French*   19 19 22 £47

Marylebone | 26 Devonshire St., W1 (Baker St.) | 020-7935 4531 | fax 7493 8309 | www.langansrestaurants.co.uk

"A classical bistro that never fails to bring enjoyment", this Marylebone veteran prepares "plentiful", "reliable" Traditional British–French fare; despite the "original art and photography of [founder] Langan's friends, such as David Hockney", the place is "getting a little shabby around the edges", but it still appeals as "a safe haven from the overly hip."

Langan's Brasserie ◑Z *British/French*   18 19 17 £48

Mayfair | Stratton House | Stratton St., W1 (Green Park) | 020-7491 8822 | fax 7493 8309 | www.langansrestaurants.co.uk

Maybe it's "living on past glories" – "most of the celebrities have moved on" – but for the "old faithful", this Mayfair "fixture" remains a supreme "place to unwind"; the menu's "a strange mix of French and English" "comfort food at uncomfortable prices", and staff range from "charming" to cold, but "be honest – you go for the atmosphere, with a buzz that would get a dead man high."

Langan's Coq d'Or   ▽ 22 21 22 £38
Bar & Grill *British/French*

Earl's Court | 254-260 Old Brompton Rd., SW5 (Earl's Ct.) | 020-7259 2599 | fax 7370 7735 | www.langansrestaurant.co.uk

"Nice and laid-back", this little-known Earl's Court outpost of the Langan's group, comprising a formal restaurant and enclosed terrace grill/bar, makes a "real classic venue" to "sit and watch the world pass" by; the kitchen is "comfort-food central", churning out "consistent" British–French bistro classics.

	FOOD	DECOR	SERVICE	COST

NEW Langtry's British
– – – E

Knightsbridge | Cadogan Hotel | 21 Pont St., SW1 (Knightsbridge/
Sloane Sq.) | 020-7201 6619 | www.langtrysrestaurant.com

This handsome, high-ceilinged dining room in the **Cadogan Hotel**
has recently received an elegant revamp that blends modern design
touches with the statuesque details (e.g. a Carrera marble
fireplace) that you'd expect in actress Lillie Langtry's lavish 19th-
century home; the Modern British menu showcases regional
produce, and "Sunday lunch, with its never-empty glass of Perrier-
Jouët, is a treat."

La Noisette 🗷 French
21 17 21 £75

Belgravia | Jumeirah Carlton Tower Hotel | 164 Sloane St., SW1
(Knightsbridge) | 020-7750 5000 | fax 7750 5001 |
www.gordonramsay.com

"Good teaming of an experimental chef and master of the London
culinary scene" sums up the partnership of Bjorn van der Horst and
Gordon Ramsay at this "classy restaurant overlooking Sloane
Street"; served in "small portions", the New French fare is "very accomplished", "but nothing is a 'wow'"; at least the "warm, polished
service" humanises the "tailored, masculine decor."

Lansdowne, The European
20 14 12 £26

Primrose Hill | 90 Gloucester Ave., NW1 (Chalk Farm) | 020-7483 0409 |
fax 7586 1723

"A class above your average gastropub", this Primrose Hill
"hangout" – bar downstairs, more "comfortable surroundings
upstairs" – has "everything you want for a light-hearted meal out
with friends": "crowded scene", "good star-spotting" and a "wide
menu" of Modern Euro fare; just don't be surprised by "surly staff":
"had to wave my arms to get attention."

La Perla Bar & Grill Mexican
15 14 16 £26

Covent Garden | 28 Maiden Ln., WC2 (Charing Cross/Covent Garden) |
020-7240 7400 | fax 7836 5088
Fitzrovia | 11 Charlotte St., W1 (Tottenham Court Rd.) | 020-7436 1744 |
fax 7436 1911
www.cafepacifico-laperla.com

"Six thousand miles from Mexico" they may be, but this "casual"
duo in Covent Garden and Fitzrovia "draw the crowds" with "authentic Baja-style food" ("the spicy salsa is totally tantalising"); some insist, though, they're "not really a place to eat – just keep bringing
those jugs of cocktails!"

La Piragua S American
∇ 15 9 13 £23

Islington | 176 Upper St., N1 (Highbury & Islington) | 020-7354 2843 |
fax 7354 2843 | www.lapiragua.co.uk

"Packed with students and men who want a rib-sticking meal", this
"decent Latin American" in Islington specialises in "huge steaks"
from Argentina, "without the fussy, pricey trimmings"; "don't expect finesse" from the surroundings or service either, as "staff
are run ragged.

	FOOD	DECOR	SERVICE	COST

La Porchetta Pizzeria *Pizza*   19 | 13 | 17 | £18

Holborn | 33 Boswell St., WC1 (Holborn) | 020-7242 2434 **⊠**
Clerkenwell | 84-86 Rosebury Ave., EC1 (Angel) | 020-7837-6060 |
fax 7837 6200
Muswell Hill | 265 Muswell Hill Broadway, N10 (Highgate) |
020-8883 1500 **●**
Islington | 141-142 Upper St., N1 (Angel/Highbury & Islington) |
020-7288 2488 **●**
Stoke Newington | 147 Stroud Green Rd., N4 (Finsbury Park) |
020-7281 2892 | fax 7837 6200 **●**

Possibly "the clangiest, bangiest restaurants on earth" ("could do
with improved acoustics"), this chain is "heaving every night" with
"young professionals, families and groups celebrating birthdays"
over "amazingly cheap" Italian fare, primarily "pizzas bigger
than toilet seats."

⊠ La Porte des Indes **●** *Indian*   21 | 25 | 19 | £43

Marylebone | 32 Bryanston St., W1 (Marble Arch) | 020-7224 0055 |
fax 7224 1144 | www.laportedesindes.com

"Decorated in colonial Raj style, complete with palms and a water-
fall", this "splendid"-looking eatery ("from the folks who brought
you Blue Elephant") serves "unusual", "upscale", "French-style
Indian food"; and even if the "erratic service" "doesn't keep up" all
the time, most concede this mammoth near Marble Arch is "perhaps a bit OTT, but it works."

La Poule au Pot *French*   22 | 23 | 20 | £44

Pimlico | 231 Ebury St., SW1 (Sloane Sq.) | 020-7730 7763 |
fax 7259 9651

It's "hard to beat the seductive atmosphere" at this Pimlico veteran
where "calorifically amazing" "cooking as it used to be in rural France"
is served with a traditionally "Gallic approach to customer care";
even if "the bill can crank up", it's "worth the splurge", plus there's
"perfect summer dining by candlelight on the outside pavement."

L'Artiste Muscle *French*   ∇ 19 | 12 | 18 | £26

Mayfair | 1 Shepherd Mkt., W1 (Green Park) | 020-7493 6150

"A genuinely bohemian bar/restaurant" that "could easily be in
Paris", this "tiny" Shepherd Market "hole-in-the-wall" offers "solid"
bistro fare that's "unchallenging" but "excellent value"; P.S. "try for
an outside table in good weather."

La Rueda **●** *Spanish*   14 | 13 | 14 | £27

Marylebone | 102 Wigmore St., W1 (Bond St.) | 020-7486 1718 |
fax 7486 1718
Clapham | 66-68 Clapham High St., SW4 (Clapham Common/
Clapham North) | 020-7627 2173 | fax 7627 2173
Fulham | 642 King's Rd., SW6 (Fulham Broadway) | 020-7384 2684 |
fax 7384 2684
www.larueda.co.uk

"Don't be surprised to find only Spanish being spoken at the next
table" of this Iberian trio, "excellent for chilling out over" "solid, if
uninspiring tapas" and mains; "service ranges from appalling to

	FOOD	DECOR	SERVICE	COST

acceptable depending on how busy they are", but there's "authentic" "atmosphere at weekends when dancing and merry-making are encouraged."

Z NEW L'Atelier de Joël Robuchon ● French

26 | 24 | 24 | £85

Covent Garden | 13-15 West St., WC2 (Leicester Sq.) | 020-7010 8600

NEW La Cuisine French

Covent Garden | L'Atelier de Joël Robuchon | 13-15 West St., WC2 (Leicester Sq.) | 020-7010 8600

Super-chef Joël Robuchon has "hit town with his fantastic creativity" at this "thrilling" Theatreland yearling; there's a "chic" red/black eatery with a "wall of green plants" and counter seating, and up above, a "black and white kitchen"–themed restaurant, La Cuisine, both offering different iterations of "divine *nouvelle cuisine française*"; given the "minuscule mains", it's all too "pricey" and "pretentious" pessimists protest, but "if you really want to impress, this is where to come"; P.S. there's also a "boudoirlike bar" on the top floor.

Latium ⓩ Italian

25 | 19 | 24 | £44

Fitzrovia | 21 Berners St., W1 (Goodge St.) | 020-7323 9123 | fax 7323 3205 | www.latiumrestaurant.com

"They pack them in" to this "real find" in Fitzrovia, where diners are "welcomed professionally", then fed "impeccable Italian dishes", including "various types of ravioli"; though the "tempting wine list can rack up the bill", a "reasonable" meal "can be had with study."

Z La Trompette European/French

27 | 21 | 25 | £51

Chiswick | 5-7 Devonshire Rd., W4 (Turnham Green) | 020-8747 1836 | fax 8995 8097 | www.latrompette.co.uk

Surveyors "sound the trumpets" for this "hidden" "blessing for Chiswick locals" (sister of Chez Bruce), an "elegant" venue with "expertly prepared" Modern European–New French cooking, a "wine list to dive into" and "attentive, but not cloying service"; whilst the "fixed-price menus make for excellent cost control", it's "great to impress for business or that second date (may be a bit flashy for a first)."

La Trouvaille ⓩ French

20 | 17 | 20 | £39

Soho | 12A Newburgh St., W1 (Oxford Circus) | 020-7287 8488 | fax 7434 4170 | www.latrouvaille.co.uk

"No trendy themes or pompous fusion" here at this "sweet" Soho spot – "just really good, fresh French fare" (both Classic and New), served amidst somewhat "formal decor" by "fun staff" – all "without breaking the bank" as well.

Launceston Place British

21 | 21 | 24 | £52

Kensington | 1A Launceston Pl., W8 (Gloucester Rd.) | 020-7937 6912 | fax 7938 2412 | www.danddlondon.com

"Genteel dining" in a "wonderful warren of a restaurant" is what to expect at this "tranquil" townhouse in Kensington, where "consistently good" Modern British cuisine is "complemented by" "caring, knowledgeable staff"; if a few fret this twentysomething seems "tired", it's still "the best place for a meal with the parents."

L'Aventure 🗷 French

22 | 20 | 20 | £45

St. John's Wood | 3 Blenheim Terrace, NW8 (St. John's Wood) | 020-7624 6232 | fax 7625 5548

This "secluded" St. John's Wood bistro is "like stepping into another, French world" where the classic "fare is cooked to a high standard"; and even if the service swings from "friendly" to "eccentric" , all appreciate the "outdoor area for those global-warming nights."

Le Boudin Blanc French

22 | 17 | 20 | £43

Mayfair | Shepherd's Mkt. | 5 Trebeck St., W1 (Green Park) | 020-7499 3292 | fax 7495 6973 | www.boudinblanc.co.uk

"You forget that it isn't Paris" at this "*vrai français* in Shepherd Market", an "authentic bistro" in everything from the "country-style" cuisine to the "crowded" scene; "staff are helpful", but "rushed."

Le Café du Jardin ❶ European

19 | 17 | 18 | £40

Covent Garden | 28 Wellington St., WC2 (Covent Garden) | 020-7836 8769 | fax 7836 4123 | www.lecafedujardin.com

"Conveniently located in Covent Garden", this stalwart serves a "solid", "midrange" Modern European menu; even if "seating is close enough to rub elbows" and "service is variable", all concede its "bargain" prix fixe is "perfect before a show" (or after).

🗷 Le Café du Marché 🗷 French

23 | 20 | 19 | £43

Smithfield | 22 Charterhouse Sq., EC1 (Barbican) | 020-7608 1609 | fax 7251 8575

"Those in-the-know" about this "secluded" Smithfield site applaud its "romantic" atmosphere – "wooden beams" and "soft live music" – as well as its "lovely comfort food" *à la française,* which includes a "cheese trolley that virtually wheels itself to your table", so "if you are dieting, go some place else."

🗷 Le Caprice ❶ British/European

24 | 21 | 23 | £56

St. James's | Arlington House | Arlington St., SW1 (Green Park) | 020-7629 2239 | fax 7493 9040 | www.le-caprice.co.uk

"Still a thrill after all these years" (25, to be exact), this "stellar, star-studded" St. James's "institution" has its "high standards upheld by [director] Jesus Adorno", who oversees the "slick" service and the "never-failing", "fresh Modern British–European" fare; if "tables are squeezed-in" and "dark art deco setting" could be "jazzed up a little", this remains "an exciting address."

Le Cercle 🗷🗷 French

24 | 22 | 19 | £48

Chelsea | 1 Wilbraham Pl., SW1 (Sloane Sq.) | 020-7901 9999 | fax 7901 9111 | www.clubgascon.com

"Minimalist on decor, maximalist on the taste buds", this "discreet" ("black dress, dahling") Sloane Square site stars an "unusual" New French menu of "shareable tapas" with a "strong Southwest emphasis"; those "little plates can get expensive", but the prix fixe "lunch is a breathtaking bargain"; P.S. "beg or bribe for a corner booth."

	FOOD	DECOR	SERVICE	COST

Le Colombier *French*
20 | 17 | 21 | £48

Chelsea | 145 Dovehouse St., SW3 (South Kensington) | 020-7351 1155 | fax 7351 5124

"Filled with regulars", this Chelsea bistro beckons with a "classic" French "menu that never changes – but that's the attraction", especially when supported by "efficient service"; it's "more for older couples than young groups", but there's "always a good atmosphere", especially on the large front terrace.

Ledbury, The *French*
25 | 23 | 24 | £65

Notting Hill | 127 Ledbury Rd., W11 (Westbourne Park) | 020-7792 9090 | fax 7792 9191 | www.theledbury.com

After "a stunning debut" in 2005, this "elegant" Notting Hill sister of The Square "continues to please" with "inventive" New French cuisine that, whilst occasionally "over-the-top", hits "orgasmic" levels; "nicely spaced" tables that "strike the perfect balance between buzzy and so loud you can't have a conversation" and "gracious service" add to the appeal; it's even "not as expensive as you think it's going to be", given how "wonderful" it is.

Le Deuxième ● *European*
20 | 17 | 19 | £37

Covent Garden | 65A Long Acre, WC2 (Covent Garden) | 020-7379 0033 | fax 7379 0066 | www.ledeuxieme.com

"Simple and chic", this Covent Garden sibling of Le Café du Jardin "reliably delivers Modern European cuisine – nice, if not very adventurous"; it gets "a little cramped before curtain time", but that's not surprising given the "unbeatable pre-theatre menu."

Lee Ho Fook ● *Chinese*
17 | 10 | 11 | £23

Chinatown | 15-16 Gerrard St., W1 (Leicester Sq./Piccadilly Circus) | 020-7494 1200 | fax 7494 1700

A "stalwart in Chinatown" since 1960, this "Hong Kong–style cafe" still delivers "decent dim sum" and Mandarin mains; just know "the waiters are antagonistic", imparting "an implied pressure to order" from every cart, and the "hole-in-the-wall" decor is "not looking good."

☑ Le Gavroche ☒ *French*
27 | 24 | 26 | £95

Mayfair | 43 Upper Brook St., W1 (Marble Arch) | 020-7408 0881 | fax 7491 4387 | www.le-gavroche.co.uk

"As expensive as it gets, but as fabulous as it can be" sums up Michel Roux Jr.'s "magnificent" Mayfair "bastion" of haute cuisine in a "sumptuous" "snug basement setting with a real sense of exclusivity"; the "*superbe*" kitchen doesn't "miss a beat" and "every detail is attended to" by "exemplary" staff; modernists may mutter "this 1950s rendition of fancy French" "needs updating", but the overwhelming opinion is "the old style still works."

☑ Le Manoir aux Quat'Saisons *French*
28 | 27 | 26 | £97

Great Milton | Le Manoir aux Quat'Saisons Hotel | Church Rd., Oxfordshire | 01844 278881 | fax 01844 278847 | www.manoir.com

"Spectacular in all respects", chef-owner Raymond Blanc's "ethereal" 15th-century manor house in the Cotswolds "never fails to impress", from its "magical setting" – "stunning gardens" in summer, "welcoming fires" in winter – to its "genius" New French cuisine "lovingly prepared" "from perfect ingredients" grown on-site, and complemented by "solicitous, polite service"; so "sell the family silver and book a table" – better yet, book a "wonderful" bedroom and "stay overnight."

Le Mercury ● French | 18 | 17 | 19 | £22 |

Islington | 140A Upper St., N1 (Angel/Highbury & Islington) | 020-7354 4088 | fax 7359 7186

For "a romantic local dinner" lit by "flattering candles", this "charming", "elbow-to-elbow establishment" is "indispensable" to Islingtonians, and whilst the "decent" New French menu "never seems to change", it comes at "an unbeatable price"; accompanied by service that "tries very hard."

Lemonia ● Greek | 20 | 15 | 18 | £30 |

Primrose Hill | 89 Regent's Park Rd., NW1 (Chalk Farm) | 020-7586 7454 | fax 7483 2630

"Always a hustling, bustling place" ("be sure to make reservations"), this "cheerful" "Primrose Hill institution" "treats you like family", rustling up "reliable", "great-value" Greek fare that covers "all the favourites"; there's also a "lovely place to sit in the sun" (perhaps preferable to the "noisy" interior).

Leon Mediterranean | 19 | 15 | 16 | £13 |

NEW Covent Garden | 73-746 The Strand, WC2 (Covent Garden) | 020-7240 3070 | fax 7240 9988
Knightsbridge | 136 Brompton Rd., SW3 (Knightsbridge) | 020-7589 7330 | fax 7589 7346
NEW Marylebone | 275 Regent St., W1 (Oxford Circus) | 020-7495 1514 🛇
Soho | 35 Great Marlborough St., W1 (Oxford Circus) | 020-7437 5280
City | 12 Ludgate Circus, EC4 (Blackfriars) | 020-7489 1580 🛇
Spitalfields | 3 Crispin Pl., E1 (Liverpool St.) | 020-7247 4369 | fax 7377 1653
www.leonrestaurants.co.uk

"Who knew healthy food could taste so good?" – those patronising this fast-growing fast-food chain, that's who, with its "natural", "ethical" offerings that include "hearty" Med fare, "super salads" and "wraps that fill the gap", all "in funky atmosphere"; "portions are small" – but isn't that better for you, anyway?

Le Pain Quotidien Bakery/Belgian | 19 | 17 | 15 | £18 |

Marylebone | 72-75 Marylebone High St., W1 (Baker St./Regent's Park) | 020-7486 6154
Soho | 18 Great Marlborough St., W1 (Oxford Circus/Piccadilly Circus) | 020-7486 6154 | fax 7486 6164
South Bank | Royal Festival Hall | 12-13 Festival Walk, Belvedere Rd., SE1 (Waterloo) | 020-7486 6154
Kensington | 9 Young St., W8 (Notting Hill Gate) | 020-7486 6154
www.lepainquotidien.com

"You'll never know who you'll meet at the communal tables" of these "rustic" Belgian bakeries that, as "long queues" attest, "make eating bread trendy again"; the "artfully displayed sandwiches" and "amazing pastries" are "enjoyable", the "confused service" "rather annoying."

Le Palais Du Jardin ◑ *French* | 18 | 16 | 16 | £40 |

Covent Garden | 136 Long Acre, WC2 (Covent Garden/Leicester Sq.) | 020-7379 5353 | fax 7379 1846 | www.lpdj.co.uk

"Dazzlingly bright inside" and offering a "good people-watching terrace" outside, this "big, bustling" brasserie specialises in "fresh fish" and New French fare; if some claim this *"jardin* is feeling overgrown and a little seedy", theatre-goers give it a thumbs-up for its "convenient" Covent Garden location.

Le Pont de la Tour ◑ *French/Seafood* | 22 | 23 | 20 | £63 |

Tower Bridge | Butlers Wharf Bldg. | 36D Shad Thames, SE1 (London Bridge/Tower Hill) | 020-7403 8403 | fax 7940 1835 | www.lepontdelatour.co.uk

Its "spectacular setting on the Thames", basking "in the reflected light of Tower Bridge", makes this Classic French a "solid choice for quality dining"; if pessimists posit the *pont* "feels a little passé", especially given the "sky-high prices", its "wide choice of seafood" and "deep, varied wine list" remain "reliable for an all-round special occasion."

Le Relais de Venise l'entrecôte *French* | 18 | 15 | 15 | £31 |

Marylebone | 120 Marylebone Ln., W1 (Bond St./Marylebone) | 020-7486 0878 | fax 7486 0879 | www.relaisdevenise.com

"A chip off the old Parisian block", this Marylebone import serves a single-item, "straightforward menu" of "simple but fine steak frites" with a secret "magnificent sauce"; it's "the "perfect place to take anyone slow" to order – "you only decide" which dessert you want.

L'Escargot ◑⊠ *French* | 22 | 21 | 20 | £48 |

Soho | 48 Greek St., W1 (Leicester Sq./Tottenham Court Rd.) | 020-7437 6828 | fax 7437 0790 | www.whitestarline.org.uk

"One of Soho's longest-established restaurants" (born 1927), this "old-school" Classic French remains a "favourite" "for a business dinner" or "pre-theatre option", especially if you sit upstairs in the art-filled Picasso Room; "cheap it's not", though, and the not-impressed snap "a snail would beat me in a race to my next visit here."

⊠ Les Trois Garçons ◑⊠ *French* | 19 | 29 | 21 | £54 |

Shoreditch | 1 Club Row, E1 (Liverpool St.) | 020-7613 1924 | fax 7012 1236 | www.lestroisgarcons.com

Its "great kitsch look" of "taxidermy, antiques" and handbags hung from the ceiling "never fails to amaze guests" at this Shoreditch site, who've voted it No. 1 for Decor; the "relatively traditional" French food is "good", but "should be better given how expensive it is" snap cynics – both kitchen and staff "have delusions of grandeur."

Le Suquet ◑ *French/Seafood* | 23 | 17 | 20 | £46 |

Chelsea | 104 Draycott Ave., SW3 (South Kensington) | 020-7581 1785 | fax 7225 0838

With a "1960s French Riviera feel about it" and a "seafood platter that could feed Napoleon's army", this "raffish bistro" in Brompton

Cross is "always bustling", not least because "they take care of regulars, of which there are many"; it "may be a tad overpriced", but it's "still a lot of fun."

⚡ L'Etranger French

| | 24 | 18 | 21 | £53 |

South Kensington | 36 Gloucester Rd., SW7 (Gloucester Rd.) |
020-7584 1118 | fax 7584 8886 | www.etranger.co.uk

"Wonderfully inventive" and "stylishly presented", "the cooking is an unusual blend of French sophistication with an Asian twist" at this "best-kept secret" on Gloucester Road; those who aren't strangers to it "love the wine list and helpful staff"; however, they advise "avoid the back room, as it vibrates from the disco downstairs."

Le Vacherin French

| | ▽ 23 | 16 | 21 | £41 |

Chiswick | 76-77 South Parade, W4 (Chiswick Park) | 020-8742 2121 |
fax 8742 0799 | www.levacherin.co.uk

Boasting "good, robust French cooking" – in season, the namesake dish is "divine" – this low-profile Chiswick eatery is "praised" for "working hard and doing well", even if the "bistro-style surroundings" are just "so-so."

Levant ● Lebanese

| | 19 | 23 | 15 | £41 |

Marylebone | Jason Ct. | 76 Wigmore St., W1 (Bond St.) |
020-7224 1111 | fax 7486 1216 | www.levant.co.uk

This "loud" Marylebone Lebanese offers a "fantastic setting – authentic down to the shisha pipes, belly dancers" and "low sofas and tons of cushions to sit on"; a "variety of well-prepared" fare comes in "great set meals if you go in a group", but since it's "almost more nightclub than restaurant", this is "not the place for romance."

Levantine ● Lebanese

| | ▽ 20 | 21 | 19 | £33 |

Paddington | 26 London St., W2 (Paddington) | 020-7262 1111 |
fax 7402 4039 | www.levant.co.uk

"More peaceful and friendly than older sister" Levant (though it also has a belly dancer nightly), this "cosy" "Paddington location makes a great date place for close conversation mixed with delicious mezzes" and other "authentic Middle Eastern food with a twist of Europe" amidst flowers, floating candles and Lebanese antiques.

Light House Eclectic

| | ▽ 17 | 17 | 17 | £40 |

Wimbledon | 75-77 Ridgeway, SW19 (Wimbledon) | 020-8944 6338 |
fax 8946 4440 | www.lighthousewimbledon.com

An "innovative" Eclectic menu and "friendly staff" make this "well-managed outfit" "a light at the end of the tunnel of SW19 chain restaurants" that dominate Wimbledon; "given this, they get away with prices that are slightly over the mark" for "nothing really exciting" foes fume.

L'Incontro ● Italian

| | 20 | 18 | 19 | £63 |

Pimlico | 87 Pimlico Rd., SW1 (Sloane Sq.) | 020-7730 3663 |
fax 7730 5062 | www.lincontro-restaurant.com

"Genuine" Italian cuisine, along with a "first-rate wine list with good-value labels", is the focus of this "pleasant place" in Pimlico, which "now has more buzz, and better service"; nevertheless, an "inconsistent" kitchen causes naysayers to snap it's "not worth the cost."

Little Bay ❶ *European/Mediterranean* | 21 | 17 | 20 | £17

Farringdon | 171 Farringdon Rd., EC1 (Farringdon) | 020-7278 1234 | fax 7278 5368
Kilburn | 228 Belsize Rd., NW6 (Kilburn Park) | 020-7372 4699 | fax 7223 6131 ⊟
Battersea | 228 York Rd., SW11 (Clapham Junction/Wandsworth Town) | 020-7223 4080 | fax 7223 6131
Fulham | 140 Wandsworth Bridge Rd., SW6 (Parsons Green) | 020-7751 3133 | fax 7223 6131
www.little-bay.co.uk

"You have to come very early or very late" to this quartet, which "have been discovered" for their "smiling staff" and uniquely "cheerful" ambience (Kilburn boasts "fantastic balcony tables", like a theatre, and Battersea offers "live opera singers"); "diners almost sit on top of each other, but no one complains" because the "super-cheap" Modern European–Med menu with its "constantly changing specials makes cooking at home pointless."

Little Italy ❶ *Italian* | 16 | 12 | 17 | £32

Soho | 21 Frith St., W1 (Leicester Sq./Tottenham Court Rd.) | 020-7734 4737 | fax 7734 1777

By day, this "divine dive" in Soho is a "typical Italian" serving up "big portions" of "acceptable, if unimaginative food" with a "warm, friendly smile"; but after dark, "it's a nightclub" with a "late kitchen closing" (3 AM) and an atmosphere where "no one can resist dancing."

Livebait *Seafood* | 18 | 13 | 16 | £32

Covent Garden | 21 Wellington St., WC2 (Covent Garden) | 020-7836 7161 | fax 7836 7141 ⊠
Waterloo | 43 The Cut, SE1 (Waterloo) | 020-7928 7211 | fax 7928 2279
www.santeonline.co.uk

"Unquestionably fresh fish" ("could have swum up the Thames that morning") at this "noisy" seafood duo in Waterloo and Covent Garden; whilst it "looks stark with all the tiles" and service can be "slapdash", "it does what it says on the tin", and for "fair prices" too.

Living Room, The ❶ *European* | 19 | 20 | 16 | £42

Piccadilly | 3-9 Heddon St., W1 (Oxford Circus/Piccadilly Circus) | 087-0166 2225 | fax 0166 2226 | www.thelivingroomw1.co.uk

There is indeed a "relaxed living-room style" to this "funky" Piccadilly bar/brasserie in a converted post office; the Modern European offers "nothing to complain about, but nothing special" either – and is "actually a bit expensive"; so some suggest "sticking to bar snacks" and listening to the bands playing nightly.

☑ Locanda Locatelli *Italian* | 25 | 22 | 22 | £64

Marylebone | Hyatt Regency London - The Churchill | 8 Seymour St., W1 (Marble Arch) | 020-7935 9088 | fax 7935 1149 | www.locandalocatelli.com

"Leave the family-style for another day – this is the place" for a "posh" experience attest *amici* of Italian "icon Giorgio Locatelli's" "outstanding, inventive" Northern Italian *cucina* in a Portman Square hotel; it's "popular with the glitterati", causing some to sigh "I'm not famous enough to get much service", but nearly everyone else would "eat here often – if it weren't so horrifically expensive."

Locanda Ottoemezzo ⍰ *Italian*

24 | 20 | 24 | £42

Kensington | 2-4 Thackeray St., W8 (High St. Kensington) | 020-7937 2200 | fax 7937 9871 | www.locandaottoemezzo.co.uk

"A terrific find off High Street Kensington", this "tiny, somewhat cramped" spot with "deep purple and red decor (refreshingly anti-beige!)" and "lots of silver screen" memorabilia on the walls features a "hearty", "exemplary Italian" menu that "never disappoints", even though it's "quite pricey"; "accommodating service" also gets the thumbs-up.

Loch Fyne *Seafood*

18 | 15 | 16 | £30

Covent Garden | 2-4 Catherine St., WC2 (Covent Garden) | 020-7240 4999 | fax 7240 4499 | www.lochfyne.com

"More a brasserie than a loch", this "solid seafooder in the heart of Theatreland" is "a bright, loud" place for a "quick meal" at "reasonable prices"; if the "hurry-up" service and "formulaic" fare give it "the feel of a chain" – well, it *is* one, with 30 branches throughout the UK.

Lonsdale, The *European*

▽ 15 | 21 | 13 | £33

Notting Hill | 48 Lonsdale Rd., W11 (Ladbroke Grove/Notting Hill Gate) | 020-7727 4080 | fax 7727 6030 | www.thelonsdale.co.uk

"Girls just wanna have fun, so this is where they come": a "hip", designer-y Notting Hill haunt for "a fashionable crowd" ("the later the night, the busier it gets"); most "go for the cocktails but skip the food", though the menu's recently taken on a Modern European cast.

L'Oranger ⍰ *French*

24 | 22 | 24 | £66

St. James's | 5 St. James's St., SW1 (Green Park) | 020-7839 3774 | fax 7839 4330 | www.loranger.co.uk

"Excelling in the traditional ways without being pretentious", this "discreet" "place for high-powered bankers" in St. James's has "comfortable" "banquettes rather than hard modern edges", and shows "undoubted artistry" on its "high-end" (if "not cutting-edge") Classic French menu and "intelligent wine list"; "incredibly pleasant management and service" ensure "a wonderful experience overall."

Lou Pescadou ●⍰Ⓜ *French/Seafood*

20 | 12 | 18 | £34

Earl's Court | 241 Old Brompton Rd., SW5 (Earl's Ct.) | 020-7370 1057 | fax 7244 7545

"Everyone goes for the fish, which is tops" – though there's some "excellent French food" too – at this quirky Earl's Court eatery where "friendly owners" cater to a clientele of "mostly regulars."

L-Restaurant & Bar *Spanish*

- | - | - | M

Kensington | 2 Abingdon Rd., W8 (High St. Kensington) | 020-7795 6969 | fax 7795 6968 | www.l-restaurant.co.uk

Those "impressed by this little"-known venue just off Kensington High Street cite "delightful Spanish-inspired fare" made from "simple, quality ingredients"; other pluses include "friendly staff" and "elegant decor", which features an impressive, retractable glass roof and stone flooring.

Luciano ⊠ *Italian* 20 | 18 | 17 | £54

St. James's | 72-73 St. James's St., SW1 (Green Park) | 020-7408 1440 | fax 7493 6670 | www.lucianorestaurant.co.uk

With a mix of "beautiful people" and "business suits", Marco Pierre White's "sophisticated" St. James's venue is an "all-round winner" to fans who fawn over its "fabulous bar", "varied" Italian menu and "deep wine list"; but critics claim this "overpriced", "chaotic" *cucina* "misses the mark" ("not sure if it's a restaurant or drinks place").

Lucio *Italian* 21 | 19 | 20 | £47

Chelsea | 257-259 Fulham Rd., SW3 (South Kensington) | 020-7823 3007 | fax 7823 3009

The "courteous" eponymous patron is "always at hand to guide you through a menu" of "seasonal" "contemporary Italian" dishes at this "favourite" in Fulham Road; however, sinking scores suggest now that it's "beginning to attract the A- (and B-) list crowd", service and food "seem less important than the cut of the clothes or hair."

☑ Lucky 7 *American* 20 | 17 | 14 | £18

Notting Hill | 127 Westbourne Park Rd., W2 (Royal Oak/ Westbourne Park) | 020-7727 6771 | fax 7727 6798 | www.lucky7london.co.uk

It "feels like you're stepping into a small American diner" at Tom Conran's "vintage-y" Notting Hill spot, which gets "a bit chaotic" (notably "at weekends, given the horrific queues"), but is "great for a burger" and a "filling milkshake"; "you cannot beat it for price" either.

Lundum's *Danish* 22 | 24 | 24 | £49

South Kensington | 117-119 Old Brompton Rd., SW7 (Gloucester Rd./ South Kensington) | 020-7373 7774 | fax 7373 4472 | www.lundums.com

When you need "a change from the standard gastropub", this "family-run" South Ken Scandinavian is "always reliable" for "delicious Danish" cuisine, especially on the "wacky Sunday smorgasbord lunch", "served with flair in congenial surroundings"; small wonder supporters say this "well-kept secret should get out."

Made in Italy ❶ *Italian* 21 | 12 | 13 | £27

Chelsea | 249 King's Rd., SW3 (Sloane Sq./South Kensington) | 020-7352 1880

"Bring your sense of humour" to this "frenetic" Chelsea trattoria; "tables are scarce (with nowhere to wait)" and "service is poor", but the "great atmosphere" and "rustic" Italian staples (starring *delizioso* pizza") make it a "perennial favourite", and "good value" to boot.

NEW Magdalen ⊠ *European* - | - | - | E

Borough | 152 Tooley St., SE1 (London Bridge) | 020-7403 1342 | fax 7403 9950 | www.magdalenerestaurant.co.uk

"Pure breeding shows through" - the chef-owner's pedigree includes Anchor & Hope and The Fat Duck - at this "excellent newcomer" near London Bridge; with an "imaginative, well-planned" Modern European menu and elegant cream-and-aubergine decor, it will satisfy either as a "chilled-out, after-work affair or casual weekend venue."

Maggie Jones's *British* `21 | 21 | 20 | £36`
Kensington | 6 Old Court Pl., W8 (High St. Kensington) | 020-7937 6462 | fax 7376 0510

"If you're jonesing for Traditional British" food, this Kensington old-timer is "the perfect place", with "hearty meals" to satisfy "Jurassic appetites" ("order chicken and get the whole bird, almost"); its "quirky" "country-kitchen decor" makes a "great gathering place for friends" or with "a date (first or 300th)."

Ma Goa *Indian* `23 | 14 | 22 | £31`
Fulham | 194 Wandsworth Bridge Rd., SW6 (Parsons Green) | 020-7384 2122 Ⓜ
Putney | 242-244 Upper Richmond Rd., SW15 (East Putney) | 020-8780 1767
www.ma-goa.com

The "innovative" Goan "food's always full of flavour" at these "family-run, with a welcoming feel" Fulham and Putney Indians; "good with children", "courteous staff" compensate for "cramped" environs.

Malabar ◗ *Indian* `20 | 13 | 18 | £27`
Notting Hill | 27 Uxbridge St., W8 (Notting Hill Gate) | 020-7727 8800 | www.malabar-restaurant.co.uk

"Indian as it should be – not your usual heavy curries, but light, spicy" cuisine is on the cards at this "neighbourhood place" in a Notting Hill backstreet; some blanch at the "bright", "barren" digs, but it's "perfect before the cinema next door" anyway.

Malabar Junction *Indian* `23 | 18 | 19 | £25`
Bloomsbury | 107 Great Russell St., WC1 (Tottenham Court Rd.) | 020-7580 5230 | fax 7436 9942 | www.malabarjunction.com

This "unusual" Indian is one of the "best places to eat around the British Museum", thanks to its "excellent Keralan" menu and "keen service"; the glass-roofed "gazebo setting" with "plants and paintings all around" manages to seem "spacey and cosy at the same time."

Mamounia Lounge ◗ *Lebanese/Moroccan* `▽ 17 | 20 | 18 | £48`
Mayfair | 37A Curzon St., W1 (Green Park) | 020-7629 2211 | fax 7629 6611 | www.mamounialounge.com

"Smoke a hookah whilst you sip a drink", surrounded by a "fabulous crowd" of "flashy women in pursuit of men with Maseratis", at this "loud" Mayfair lounge ("music earplugs a must"); "then indulge in Lebanese-Moroccan food" in the "classy", colourful downstairs restaurant where "all that's missing are belly dancers."

Mandalay 🅢 *Burmese* `23 | 7 | 21 | £19`
Marylebone | 444 Edgware Rd., W2 (Edgware Rd.) | 020-7258 3696 | fax 7258 3696

"You'll fill your belly and not empty your wallet" at this "low-budget" "basic" Burmese; despite being in a "dodgy" stretch of Edgware Road, it "attracts regulars from all over London" with an "amazing variety" of "delicately prepared dishes, served with genuine friendliness."

Mandarin Kitchen ◑ *Chinese*   23 | 10 | 14 | £33

Bayswater | 14-16 Queensway, W2 (Bayswater/Queensway) | 020-7727 9012 | fax 7727 9468

A "huge menu" with "some of the most unusual seafood outside Hong Kong" ("the lobster noodles are fantastic") makes this "crowded" Queensway Chinese a "must-go place", but there "isn't much decor to speak of" and "surly service" "lets this place down big time."

Mango Tree *Thai*   20 | 20 | 18 | £40

Victoria | 46 Grosvenor Pl., SW1 (Hyde Park/Victoria) | 020-7823 1888 | fax 7838 9275 | www.mangotree.org.uk

"Snazzy Thailand comes to London" in the form of this "trendy" Victoria Station venue (i.e. "hip"-looking, but in "need of some soundproofing"); the "extensive menu" includes "interesting dishes alongside staple standards", and is overseen by staff that, whilst "always polite", get "too busy for their own good."

Manicomio *Italian*   18 | 16 | 16 | £37

Chelsea | 85 Duke of York Sq., SW3 (Sloane Sq.) | 020-7730 3366 | fax 7730 3377 | www.manicomio.co.uk

With "crisp, contemporary surroundings" and a "wonderful" terrace, this "busy" Italian in the old Duke of York Barracks near Sloane Square makes a "useful" stop "whilst shopping"; otherwise, some would avoid the "above-standard" but "uneven" fare and "generally rather frantic" service; P.S. "check out the small food market next door" for takeaway.

Mao Tai ◑ *Chinese*   22 | 17 | 16 | £36

Fulham | 58 New King's Rd., SW6 (Parsons Green) | 020-7731 2520 | fax 7471 8992 | www.maotai.co.uk

"Even on a bad day, it's still good" at this "classy Chinese in Parsons Green" that also serves "respectable", "healthy-looking" Southeast Asian dishes; scores for the "comfortable" decor may not fully reflect a "recent refurb" after a fire in early 2007.

Mark's Club ☒ *British/French*   24 | 23 | 26 | £85

Private club; inquiries: 020-7499 2936

"The height of refinement", this "most formal of clubs" in Mayfair is "like dining at a rich friend's house (with lots of staff)"; "superb" Classic French–British "comfort food" and an "impeccable wine list" are supported by "superior" service, and whilst it's "a bit stuffy, that's part of the charm"; "at least you can have a conversation here."

Maroush ◑ *Lebanese*   20 | 13 | 16 | £27

Knightsbridge | 38 Beauchamp Pl., SW3 (Knightsbridge) | 020-7581 5434 | fax 7723 3161
Marylebone | 1-3 Connaught St., W2 (Marble Arch) | 020-7262 0222
Marylebone | 21 Edgware Rd., W2 (Marble Arch) | 020-7723 0773 | fax 7723 3161
Marylebone | 4 Vere St., W1 (Bond St.) | 020-7493 5050 | fax 7723 3161
(continued)

(continued)

Maroush

Marylebone | 62 Seymour St., W1 (Marble Arch) | 020-7724 5024 | fax 7723 3161

Marylebone | 68 Edgware Rd., W2 (Marble Arch) | 020-7224 9339 | fax 7723 3161

www.maroush.com

This longtime Lebanese chain "can always be counted on" for a "veritable feast" of "classic cuisine" at "relatively inexpensive" rates; "open very late", they're a "3 AM staple for a schwarma" – indeed, many "go for the longer hours rather than the food."

Marquess Tavern, The British

-	-	-	M

Islington | 32 Canonbury St., N1 (Highbury & Islington) | 020-7354 2975 | www.themarquesstavern.co.uk

"The quality of the ingredients shines through" the Traditional British cuisine at this "casual" Islington pub dating back to the 1850s; an airy "glass-ceiling dining room", "knowledgeable servers and a great beer list" add to its appeal as an "awesome place to meet up with friends for a chill evening."

Masala Zone Indian

19	16	16	£19

Mayfair | 9 Marshall St., W1 (Oxford Circus/Piccadilly Circus) | 020-7287 9966 | fax 7287 8555

Islington | 80 Upper St., N1 (Angel) | 020-7359 3399 | fax 7359 6560

Earl's Court | 147 Earl's Court Rd., SW5 (Earl's Ct.) | 020-7373 0220 | fax 7373 0990

www.realindianfood.com

"Sure, it feels a bit like a cafeteria and the mains arrive suspiciously quickly", but that doesn't stop "a diverse crowd of students, musicians, businesspeople and tourists" from sampling the "array of Indian street food" at this trio, 'cos their Thalis make "a treat when you are almost skint."

Mash ⓩ British

▽ 12	13	12	£30

Bloomsbury | 19-21 Great Portland St., W1 (Oxford Circus) | 020-7637 5555 | fax 7637 7333 | www.mash-bar.co.uk

It's "hard to tell where the restaurant begins and the bar ends" at this haunt just off Oxford Street that's "great if you like a crowd"; but even fans acknowledge its '70s-style, once-"cool look is getting tired" and the Modern British eats "fairly basic."

Matsuri Japanese

21	16	19	£43

Holborn | 71 High Holborn, WC1 (Holborn) | 020-7430 1970 | fax 7430 1971 ⓩ

St. James's | 15 Bury St., SW1 (Green Park) | 020-7839 1101 | fax 7930 7010

www.matsuri-restaurant.com

With tableside-prepared teppanyaki and sushi that garner "high marks for style and even higher marks for substance", these "authentic" Japanese in St. James's ("a bit sterile") and younger Holborn sib (more "elegant") come "highly recommended" as "places to entertain", especially "on the company credit card."

	FOOD	DECOR	SERVICE	COST

Maxwell's ● *American* — 17 | 14 | 15 | £29

Covent Garden | 8 James St., WC2 (Covent Garden) | 020-7836 0303 | fax 7240 3562 | www.maxwells.co.uk

"Packed with tourists and locals looking for a good time", this "cuddly" Covent Garden stalwart serves "solid" "American chain–like" food – "nothing too fancy, which is fine if that's what you want"; those who don't, mutter it's "mainstream blah."

☑ Maze *French* — 25 | 21 | 23 | £66

Mayfair | 10-13 Grosvenor Sq., W1 (Bond St.) | 020-7107 0000 | fax 7107 0001 | www.gordonramsay.com

"The great man goes tapas" at this highly hyped two-year-old in "Gordon Ramsay's stable" in Grosvenor Square, where "creative" Asian-inflected New French small plates make a "fantastic way to sample different flavours without popping buttons"; cynics snap the yellow-beige "decor lacks character" and the "knowledgeable" "service is uneven", but most are "enthusiastic" about this "exciting concept" (just "be prepared to be a-mazed at the cost").

Medcalf *British* — ∇ 23 | 17 | 18 | £31

Clerkenwell | 40 Exmouth Mkt., EC1 (Angel/Farringdon) | 020-7833 3533 | fax 7833 1321 | www.medcalfbar.co.uk

Set in an old butcher's shop, this "trendy" Exmouth Market haunt is "not for the fussy", but does feature a "Modern British menu of robust, interesting" fare; if you want to "just relax and enjoy the food", though, better "get in early before the nighttime-scene crowds" kick in.

Mediterraneo ● *Italian* — 22 | 16 | 19 | £35

Notting Hill | 37 Kensington Park Rd., W11 (Ladbroke Grove) | 020-7792 3131 | fax 7243 3630 | www.mediterraneo-restaurant.co.uk

"The neighbourhood Italian if you live in heaven" gush Notting Hill *amici* of this "crowded" "classic that never changes" its "homely dishes" ("wonderful sea bass") or "accessible service"; "cramped conditions" aside, it's "a good alternative when [nearby sister] Osteria Basilico is booked."

Mela ● *Indian* — 23 | 16 | 19 | £28

Covent Garden | 152-156 Shaftesbury Ave., WC2 (Leicester Sq.) | 020-7836 8635 | fax 7379 0527 | www.melarestaurant.co.uk

Take "a tour of India" via the "mélange of regional dishes" offered by this "delectable" subcontinental; "attentive but not pushy" service, a "remarkable value" prix fixe and its location 'twixt Covent Garden and Soho make it perfect "for the pre-theatre set."

Memories of China *Chinese* — 21 | 16 | 18 | £43

Belgravia | 65-69 Ebury St., SW1 (Victoria) | 020-7730 7734 | fax 7730 2992
Kensington | 353 Kensington High St., W8 (High St. Kensington) | 020-7603 6951 | fax 7603 0848

After 28 years this "dependable" Belgravia "favourite" (with a younger Kensington offshoot) is "still serving decent Chinese grub for Western palates" in a scene that's "more neighbourly than hip";

naysayers note that it's "not memorable", except for its "bracing prices", to which regulars respond the "set menus are the way to go."

Menier Chocolate Factory Ⓜ British   14 | 16 | 17 | £24

Southwark | 51-53 Southwark St., SE1 (Borough) | 020-7407 4411 | fax 7378 1713 | www.menierchocolatefactory.com

"No dining worries before or after" a Southwark show if you patronise this "lively" cafe attached to a "fantastic theatre and gallery", formerly a chocolate factory; the Modern British fare is "reliable, if undistinguished" – and "limited" pre-curtain, when only the set menu is served.

Meson Don Felipe Ⓩ Spanish   18 | 14 | 13 | £27

Waterloo | 53 The Cut, SE1 (Southwark/Waterloo) | 020-7928 3237 | fax 7736 9857

It's "difficult to understand why anyone wouldn't enjoy a night" at this "seat-of-the-pants tapas bar" in "hot", "tiny" digs near Waterloo, "always packed to the gills" thanks to its "simple Spanish fare" at "fantastic value" and "bargain wines too"; service is "slow", but you can always watch as the "guitarist strums precariously on top of a cupboard."

Mestizo ◗ Mexican   ▽ 19 | 14 | 17 | £29

Camden Town | 103 Hampstead Rd., NW1 (Warren St.) | 020-7387 4064 | www.mestizomx.com

"A Mexican gem in a town still trying to understand where guacamole comes from", this eatery in "out-of-the-way" Camden Town boasts "original" eats, "nachos piled high and fabulous margaritas"; if the simply attired "dining room can be cold, the downstairs bar is vibrant and sexy."

Metrogusto Italian   ▽ 21 | 17 | 20 | £39

Islington | 11-13 Theberton St., N1 (Angel/Highbury & Islington) | 020-7226 9400 | fax 7226 9400 | www.metrogusto.co.uk

"Inventive" Italian cooking ("almost flawless at the price") with "lively if eccentric service" makes this "intimate" Islingtonian "just as a neighbourhood restaurant should be" – and "the best thing is the owner, who knows everybody."

Met Su Yan Pan-Asian   ▽ 16 | 15 | 16 | £36

Golders Green | 134 Golders Green Rd., NW11 (Golders Green) | 020-8458 8088 | www.metsuyan.co.uk

"Filling a kosher Asian food niche" for "the Golders Green crowd", this venue "keeps its Jewish customer base coming back for more", even if it's "costly for what you get"; but lachrymose linguists lament "'metsuyan' means excellent in Hebrew – what's Hebrew for 'passable'?"

NEW Mews of Mayfair British   22 | 21 | 21 | £50

Mayfair | 10-11 Lancashire Ct., New Bond St., W1 (Bond St./ Oxford Circus) | 020-7518 9388 | fax 7518 9389 | www.mewsofmayfair.com

"The combination of club, bar and restaurant in one place works" at this "groovy townhouse" "hidden" in a Mayfair mews; the "slinky", "feminine" upstairs dining room ("looks like an upscale department store") has an "innovative" Modern British menu that's "worth the high price" and "slick service"; the casual "scene downstairs" – reminiscent of a "cosy, ephemeral nymphs' abode" – serves "good snacks", "perfect for both clients and a date."

Meza ◗🈂 Spanish | 17 | 17 | 12 | £36 |

Soho | 100 Wardour St., W1 (Tottenham Court Rd.) | 020-7314 4002 | fax 7314 4040 | www.mezabar.co.uk

"The kind of place you'd expect someone to begin the flamenco half way through the night", this "fantastically buzzy" Soho tapas spot "traverses between eatery and noisy bar" depending on the time of day; as the "fair" Spanish fare and service is "not up there with the best", many prefer to "come for the scene and music" at the weekend, when there's a DJ.

Michael Moore ◗🈂 Eclectic | 22 | 17 | 22 | £45 |

Marylebone | 19 Blandford St., W1 (Baker St./Bond St.) | 020-7224 1898 | fax 7224 0970 | www.michaelmoorerestaurant.com

"Informative chef"-owner Michael Moore "swans around making sure everything is delicious" and "served with justified confidence" at this Marylebone Eclectic that's "cosy", despite being "bare of decoration"; still, a few feel it's "not worth the price", given the "tiny portions (I thought my starter was the amuse-bouche)."

Mildreds 🈂🍴 Vegetarian | 22 | 16 | 18 | £18 |

Soho | 45 Lexington St., W1 (Oxford Circus/Piccadilly Circus) | 020-7494 1634 | fax 7439 2392 | www.mildreds.co.uk

"Even omnivores will salivate" at this "funky", "homely" Soho vegetarian specialist whose "creative" cuisine "captures a variety of tastes", and whilst cynics cavil that "the quarters are tighter than pressed tofu" – "you may have to share tables on busy nights" – the "inexpensive" cost compensates.

Mimmo d'Ischia ◗🈂 Italian | 21 | 18 | 21 | £50 |

Belgravia | 61 Elizabeth St., SW1 (Sloane Sq./Victoria) | 020-7730 5406 | fax 7730 9439 | www.mimmodischia.co.uk

"It hasn't changed since the '70s", but this Belgravia haunt has "stood the test of time" for "good old-fashioned Italian food served with gusto"; true, the Mediterranean-style interior is looking "tired" whilst the bill is all too robust, but folks still "love it."

NEW Mimosa
Bar & Restaurant Mediterranean | - | - | - | E |

Belgravia | Jumeirah Lowndes Hotel | 21 Lowndes St., SW1 (Knightsbridge) | 020-7823 1234 | www.jumeirahlowndeshotel.com

The Dubai-based Jumeirah group has spent a tidy fortune on this boutique-y Belgravia hotel, which now features a yellow-hued dining room flooded with light from a wall of folding glass doors; the short Med menu is far from a bargain but runs from the simple to the sophisticated, whilst the small bar is open 24 hours for hotel guests.

	FOOD	DECOR	SERVICE	COST

Mint Leaf *Indian* — 20 | 22 | 17 | £46

St. James's | corner of Haymarket & Suffolk Pl., SW1 (Piccadilly Circus) | 020-7930 9020 | fax 7930 6205 | www.mintleafrestaurant.com

With dramatic lighting and "dark woods", this Haymarket haunt is "trying to be trendy – but it does look good" as it offers "tongue-tingling" "fancy Indian fusion food that actually works"; critics complain the "club atmosphere" makes it too "noisy, with couples kissing", but overall it's "one of the better posh curry houses."

Mirabelle ● *French* — 22 | 21 | 22 | £63

Mayfair | 56 Curzon St., W1 (Green Park) | 020-7499 4636 | fax 7499 5449 | www.whitestarline.org.uk

Restaurateur Marco Pierre White's re-creation of Mayfair's "legendary place from the 1950s" remains an "unashamedly escapist" venue, with a "classy clubbiness" and "sumptuous" "old-school French" fare; but dissenters declare cuisine and staff "quite variable – some nights excellent, others ordinary" – whilst the "dated decor" and "stratospheric prices" are all too constant.

Mitsukoshi *Japanese* — 19 | 15 | 20 | £37

Piccadilly | Mitsukoshi Department Store | 14-20 Lower Regent St., SW1 (Piccadilly Circus) | 020-7930 0317 | fax 7839 1167 | www.mitsukoshi-restaurant.co.uk

In a basement setting that "perfectly reproduces the typical Japanese department store restaurant look (rather bleak)", this low-key Piccadilly Asian boasts "charmingly well-mannered" staff to serve "authentic, distinctive" dishes with "very reasonable" set menus.

☑ Miyama *Japanese* — 26 | 12 | 20 | £40

Mayfair | 38 Clarges St., W1 (Green Park) | 020-7499 2443 | fax 7491 1569 | www.miyama.co.uk

This "simple little place on a side street" in Mayfair is "a favourite of the Japanese expat community", serving "exquisite", "excellent sushi and sashimi the size of which will break your chopsticks"; attentive staff" make amends for "decor that could use some work."

Mju *European* — 20 | 19 | 20 | £54

Knightsbridge | Millennium Knightsbridge Hotel | 17 Sloane St., 1st fl., SW1 (Knightsbridge) | 020-7201 6330 | fax 7201 6353 | www.mju-restaurant.co.uk

Deemed "a nice surprise for a hotel restaurant", this "pricey" Knightsbridge dining room offers "experimentally good" Modern European fare with some "funky" combinations (e.g. foie gras with raspberry sorbet), backed by a new-world wine list; but malcontents mutter it's "missing something – vibe?"

NEW Mocotó ☒ *Brazilian* — 22 | 22 | 19 | £52

Knightsbridge | 145 Knightsbridge, SW1 (Knightsbridge) | 020-7225 2300 | fax 7225 4460 | www.mocoto.co.uk

A "sexy newcomer" to Knightsbridge, this "buzzy" Brazilian is off with a bang, with "big portions" of "robust" dishes and rustic decor of wooden floors and a ceiling composed of tree trunks ("thought I was going to spot some tumbleweed"); even if the "service still has opening pains", the venue already boasts "the feel of someplace that could get too popular."

☑ Momo ● *African*   19 | 25 | 18 | £44

Piccadilly | 25 Heddon St., W1 (Piccadilly Circus) | 020-7434 4040 | fax 7287 0404 | www.momoresto.com

The "spicy smells" and "sexy, lavish" "decor transform you and set the mood" at this "intoxicating" Piccadilly North African; whilst the menu may "not rank with the heavy hitters in Arabic cuisine", it's still "a little taste of Morocco that's nearer than Marrakech"; P.S. the bar below is "worth a visit, with lively music and hookah den interior."

Mon Plaisir ●⑤ *French*   18 | 17 | 17 | £36

Covent Garden | 21 Monmouth St., WC2 (Covent Garden/Leicester Sq.) | 020-7836 7243 | fax 7240 4774 | www.monplaisir.co.uk

For "the genuine feel of France in Covent Garden", theatre-goers trek to this old-timer, a "solid" choice for "bourgeois cuisine" with "heavy flavours" and "no surprises" ("exactly as we like it"); there's also "speedy service" for the pre-curtain crowd.

Montpeliano ● *Italian*   18 | 15 | 19 | £48

Knightsbridge | 13 Montpelier St., SW7 (Knightsbridge) | 020-7589 0032 | fax 7838 0268

With a "conservatory-type room" and "quirky decor" dominated by "beautiful pictures of Hollywood stars", this "1970s Italian" in Knightsbridge "never disappoints" fans of its "simple" *cucina*; but modernists moan this "old standby" "seems a bit tired in all aspects."

Monza *Italian*   ▽ 20 | 11 | 16 | £43

Knightsbridge | 6 Yeoman's Row, SW3 (Knightsbridge/South Kensington) | 020-7591 0210 | fax 7591 0210 | www.monza-restaurant.co.uk

"A good local spot for tasty Italian treats" in "enormous, if somewhat overpriced portions" say the few who've found this Knightsbridge backstreet venue; though the Formula One design theme is "fun", it "needs a face-lift."

Morel *French/Mediterranean*   - | - | - | E

Clapham | 14 Clapham Park Rd., SW4 (Clapham Common) | 020-7627 2468 | fax 7627 2424 | www.morelrestaurant.co.uk

Offering "a good reason to visit Clapham", this cream-and-red-coloured bistro offers a "decent", Med-influenced Classic French menu amidst a modern art-adorned setting; the clientele includes "a clutch of actors, artists and writers" taking advantage of the midweek prix fixe.

☑ Morgan M Ⓜ *French*   27 | 17 | 22 | £60

Islington | 489 Liverpool Rd., N7 (Highbury & Islington) | 020-7609 3560 | fax 8292 5699 | www.morganm.com

"A real mecca for food lovers", "dedicated chef"-owner Morgan Meunier's "hidden gem" offers Islingtonians "the rare pleasure of an eponymous restaurant with the namesake firmly in control"; the experience involves "delectable" New French fare (including an "outstanding vegetarian" tasting menu), "quirky amuse-bouches and entremets", plus "staff who are trained to please"; P.S. the "refurbishment provides a better", more formal setting.

☑ Moro ⓢ *Mediterranean* | 25 | 18 | 20 | £40 |

Clerkenwell | 34-36 Exmouth Mkt., EC1 (Angel/Farringdon) | 020-7833 8336 | fax 7833 9338 | www.moro.co.uk

"The oohs and ahhs of eating" the "exotic" Med cuisine – "bursting with flavour" and "true to the Moorish spirit" – add to the "deafening noise" at this Exmouth Market eatery ("the harsh interior" doesn't help); even if staff are "not always able to keep up with the crowds", the place is "great for a gaggle of girls or a fun night with clients."

Morton's ⓢ *French* | 24 | 22 | 22 | £65 |

Private club; inquiries: 020-7518 2982

There's "something a bit special" about this "discreet, private" club with a "wonderful view over Berkeley Square"; a "quiet, elegant" dining room serves "delectable" New French food with multitudes of "waiters at your beck and call", whilst the downstairs bar features a "stunning" wall that changes colour; small wonder that some "would kill for a membership" here.

Mosaico ⓢ *Italian* ▽ | 21 | 17 | 21 | £44 |

Mayfair | 13 Albemarle St., W1 (Green Park/Piccadilly Circus) | 020-7409 1011 | fax 7493 0081 | www.mosaico-restaurant.co.uk

"Neither too fussy or too informal", this low-profile, "classy Italian in classy Mayfair" makes a "solid business-lunch type of place" with "impressive" fare (including a "good-value set meal") and "great service."

Moshi Moshi Sushi *Japanese* | 20 | 14 | 16 | £23 |

City | 24 Upper Level, Liverpool St. Station, Broadgate, EC2 (Liverpool St.) | 020-7247 3227 | fax 7247 3227 ⓢ
Canary Wharf | Canary Wharf Waitrose | Canada Pl., E14 (Canary Wharf) | 020-7512 9201 | fax 7512 9685
www.moshimoshi.co.uk

If the "locations are off-putting" – a Canary Wharf supermarket and Liverpool Street train station – the "conveyor belt is entertaining" at this "steadfast sushi" duo that "satisfies the lunch crowd" with "quality" fish, "plus a variety of Japanese dishes", all "at a reasonable price."

☑ Mosimann's ⓢ *Eclectic* | 26 | 26 | 25 | £78 |

Private club; inquiries: 020-7235 9625

"Civilised beyond civilisation as it is today", this Belgravia club offers "a supreme dining experience from start to finish"; within the "dazzling", "dramatic space" (a 19th-century former church) with "many enchanting [private] rooms", guests experience "masterful" Eclectic cooking, "world-class wines" and "interactive but not intrusive waiters"; the "only downside is you need to have a member take you."

Motcombs *Eclectic* | 17 | 16 | 18 | £43 |

Belgravia | 26 Motcomb St., SW1 (Knightsbridge/Sloane Sq.) | 020-7235 6382 | fax 7245 6351 | www.motcombs.co.uk

"Considered a safe bet by locals" and a "solid choice for business", this "clubby" (some say "cliquish") Belgravia eatery is "worth a visit,

	FOOD	DECOR	SERVICE	COST

but don't expect to be knocked out" by the "solid" Eclectic fare; it's "fun people-watching upstairs, but downstairs is a little more formal."

Moti Mahal 🖪 *Indian* ▽ 19 | 16 | 15 | £52

Covent Garden | 45 Great Queen St., WC2 (Covent Garden/Holborn) | 020-7240 9329 | fax 7836 0790 | www.motimahal-uk.com

Reopened after a "nice", contemporising makeover, this bi-level Covent Garden outpost of a Delhi-based chain offers "modern-style Indian cooking"; enthusiasts say it's "expensive, but worth it", whilst the "not-impressed" feel "prices aren't justified, given the standard of the food."

Mr. Chow ◑ *Chinese* 21 | 20 | 20 | £56

Knightsbridge | 151 Knightsbridge, SW1 (Knightsbridge) | 020-7589 7347 | fax 7584 5780 | www.mrchow.com

Exuding "the glam late-'80s in a divine way", this Knightsbridge "classic" – "the original that keeps on spawning around the world" – still attracts a "hip crowd" even though the "dark, glitzy decor" "could use some updating" and the "competent service" is "too quick"; the "haute Chinese" cuisine is "decadent" but "very expensive" ("don't let them pick the menu if you want to afford a cab home").

Mr. Kong ◑ *Chinese* 21 | 8 | 16 | £25

Chinatown | 21 Lisle St., WC2 (Leicester Sq.) | 020-7437 7341

"Mr. Kong may be no king" – he's certainly let his Chinatown palace get "shabby" – but he does offer "probably the best food available at 2 AM"; the comparatively "cheap" Cantonese cuisine, "including some dishes less common in London", is brought by "servers with wit."

🖪 Nahm *Thai* 26 | 20 | 23 | £59

Belgravia | Halkin Hotel | 5 Halkin St., SW1 (Hyde Park Corner) | 020-7333 1234 | fax 7333 1100 | www.nahm.como.bz

"If you are a fan of Thai cuisine" – and "your bank account is sufficient" – you'll find the "intricate" menu at this Belgravia hotel eatery "extraordinarily interesting" and even "inspiring"; some call the marble-floored, "minimalist" "decor cold, but warm, pleasant servers" make this a "good special-occasion restaurant."

Nam Long-Le Shaker ◑🖪 *Vietnamese* ▽ 14 | 13 | 13 | £35

South Kensington | 159 Old Brompton Rd., SW5 (Gloucester Rd./ South Kensington) | 020-7373 1926 | fax 7373 6043

"An old friend" to many for its "lively late-night [bar] scene" ("love those Flaming Ferrari cocktails"), this "funky" South Kensingtonian also offers Vietnamese vittles that are "good (enough)."

Nancy Lam's Enak Enak 🖪Ⓜ *Indonesian* – | – | – | M

Battersea | 56 Lavender Hill, SW11 (Clapham Junction) | 020-7924 3148 | fax 8241 6710 | www.nancylam.com

"Ever-entertaining" TV chef-owner Nancy Lam is "more in the background" now, but she still oversees this "wonderful Indonesian" in Battersea; if a space-doubling revamp a while back makes longtimers lament "it lacks the atmosphere of old", no one argues that the food's still *enak enak* ('yum yum').

	FOOD	DECOR	SERVICE	COST

NEW Narrow, The *British* — | — | — | M

Limehouse | 44 Narrow St., E14 (Limehouse) | 020-7592 7950 |
www.gordonramsay.com

Gordon Ramsay's first foray into "reasonably priced" pub dining debuts after a revamp of a characterful old dockmaster's house, set
dramatically "by the river" in Limehouse; it's already "packed" with
people praising the punchy Traditional British fare ("fork-tender, flavoursome pig cheeks", "heavenly egg custard") served in a simply
appointed dining room; "service is friendly, but a bit slow."

National Dining Rooms, The *British*   18 | 20 | 17 | £29

Soho | The National Gallery | Sainsbury Wing, WC2 (Charing Cross) |
020-7747 2525 | fax 7747 2496 | www.thenationalcafe.com

"When you've overdosed on art" in the National Gallery, take a
break at its "airy" dining room with a "delightful" view of Trafalgar
Square and "well-sourced, interestingly cooked" Modern British fare
"that any museum would be proud of"; even if staff "don't move
faster than the portraits on the wall", most agree it's a "fine choice"
"for a quiet, grown-up lunch" (dinner on Wednesday only).

Nautilus Fish ⊠ *Seafood*   ∇ 21 | 8 | 19 | £18

Hampstead | 27-29 Fortune Green Rd., NW6 (Kilburn/West Hampstead) |
020-7435 2532

A cross between a "sit-down restaurant" and "a chippy", this West
Hampstead seafooder "is not posh", but it is "one of those rare food
bargains in London", serving "fresh, light" fish 'n' chips, alongside a
"fine choice" of other "fried or grilled" options.

New Culture Revolution *Chinese*   17 | 11 | 15 | £17

Islington | 42 Duncan St., N1 (Angel) | 020-7833 9083
Chelsea | 305 King's Rd., SW3 (Sloane Sq.) | 020-7352 9281
Notting Hill | 157-159 Notting Hill Gate, W11 (Holland Park/
Notting Hill Gate) | 020-7313 9688
www.newculturerevolution.co.uk

This trio of "neighbourhood drop-ins" "definitely does the trick if
you're starving and craving Chinese" food in the form of "steaming
bowls of noodles" and other "wholesome, healthy" fare ("no sticky
sauces"); but whilst "cheap", they "could be more cheerful."

New Tayyabs ● *Pakistani*   24 | 12 | 14 | £16

Whitechapel | 83-89 Fieldgate St., E1 (Aldgate East/Whitechapel) |
020-7247 6400 | fax 7377 1257 | www.tayyabs.co.uk

"The length of the queues is testimony" to the "true-to-tradition
Pakistani" cooking at this "anarchic restaurant" in "edgy"
Whitechapel; given the "grubby decor" and "ultrafast" service, it's
"not the place for a quiet, intimate meal", but you can't beat the "un-
believably cheap" bill (boosted by "BYO booze").

New World ● *Chinese*   19 | 13 | 14 | £19

Chinatown | 1 Gerrard Pl., W1 (Leicester Sq.) | 020-7434 2508 |
fax 7287 8994

This huge Cantonese "stands out from the crowd" of Chinatowners
for its "super-consistent dim sum" in daytime; it's a "great place to

120

	FOOD	DECOR	SERVICE	COST

take visitors who'll be bemused by the airline-style trolleys", piloted by servers who may be "rude", but are "always quick."

Nicole's 🗷 *European/Mediterranean*   19 | 19 | 18 | £36

Mayfair | Nicole Farhi | 158 New Bond St., W1 (Bond St./Green Park) | 020-7499 8408 | fax 7409 0381 | www.nicolefarhi.com

"For a quick bite amongst the fashionable crowd", this "lively" eatery "in the basement of Nicole Fahri" has a "simple", "reasonably priced" Modern European–Med menu that's "better than you might expect" – even if a few feel the store should "stick to clothes."

🗷 Nobu Berkeley St *Japanese/Peruvian*   26 | 21 | 20 | £68

Mayfair | 15 Berkeley St., W1 (Green Park) | 020-7290 9222 | fax 7290 9223 | www.noburestaurants.com

There's always "quite a scene going on" at the Nobu empire's number-two Mayfair outpost – "hipper than the one at the Met" – where celebrities and "hedge-fund zillionaires come to play", whether it be in the "brilliant bar" or "bright dining room upstairs"; supporters still swoon over "sushi like you've never tasted before" and the Japanese-Peruvian cuisine that's "divine", if "extremely expensive"; however, the "rush 'em in, rush 'em out policy is not appreciated."

🗷 Nobu London *Japanese/Peruvian*   27 | 20 | 21 | £70

Mayfair | Metropolitan Hotel | 19 Old Park Ln., W1 (Hyde Park Corner) | 020-7447 4747 | fax 7447 4749 | www.noburestaurants.com

Even after 10 years, Nobu Matsuhisa's "sizzling" Old Park Lane "flagship is firing on all cylinders", with an "exotically marvellous" Japanese-Peruvian menu ("sushi-lovers' heaven") that "exceeds expectations"; ok, the "stark" decor "could do with a splash of paint", the "efficient service sometimes looks harassed" and "booking a table takes creativity"; but few deny this "celestial" spot – rammed with "A- through C-list celebs" – is "definitely a treat, especially if someone else drops the credit card."

Noor Jahan ● *Indian*   22 | 14 | 19 | £28

South Kensington | 2A Bina Gdns., SW5 (Gloucester Rd./South Kensington) | 020-7373 6522
Paddington | 26 Sussex Pl., W2 (Lancaster Gate) | 020-7402 2332 | fax 7402 5885

Though lacking "the glitz of new places", this fortysomething, "frenetic" duo in South Kensington and Paddington offer "properly cooked", "reliable and affordable" Indian fare and service that, "despite being busy, doesn't rush you when you're done."

🗷 North Sea 🗷 *Seafood*   23 | 11 | 19 | £20

Bloomsbury | 7-8 Leigh St., WC1 (King's Cross/Russell Sq.) | 020-7387 5892 | fax 7388 9770

With "decor to laugh at" and "local clientele to add colour", this "wonderfully old-fashioned, sit-down fish 'n' chips" shop is "worth finding" because – despite its "off-the-beaten-path" Bloomsbury address – it offers some of the "best-priced", "delectable" seafood in town.

	FOOD	DECOR	SERVICE	COST

Notting Grill *British/Chophouse*   21 | 18 | 17 | £44

Notting Hill | 123A Clarendon Rd., W11 (Holland Park/Ladbroke Grove) | 020-7229 1500 | fax 7229 8889 | www.awtrestaurants.com

Despite having "a celebrity chef as owner" ("the unassuming Antony Worrall Thompson"), this "shabby-chic" Notting Hill chophouse "retains the feel of a neighbourhood place" – one that specialises in steaks "from pedigreed beasts"; shame that "service is a bit uninterested sometimes."

Notting Hill Brasserie *European*   24 | 23 | 21 | £51

Notting Hill | 92 Kensington Park Rd., W11 (Notting Hill Gate) | 020-7229 4481 | fax 7221 1246

In a "gem of a location" in Notting Hill, this "relaxing", "romantic" eatery ("nicely spaced tables", "sophisticated decor" with "piano player [for] an added touch") fans the flames with an "inventive Modern European menu and inspired wine list", "all delivered at modest prices" given its "special-occasion" status; "professional service" completes the picture at this "well-kept secret."

Noura ● *Lebanese*   21 | 17 | 18 | £40

Mayfair | 16 Curzon St., W1 (Green Park) | 020-7495 1050 | fax 7495 1055
Piccadilly | 122 Jermyn St., SW1 (Piccadilly Circus) | 020-7839 2020 | fax 7839 7700
Victoria | 16 Hobart Pl., SW1 (Victoria) | 020-7235 9444 | fax 7235 9244
www.noura.co.uk

"Full of locals, media people and Arabian princesses", these "buzzy" Lebanese have a "vast menu" of "delicious" dishes, proffered by staff who are "attentive without being unctuous"; however, pessimists point out that "portions are big, but so are the prices."

Nozomi ● *Japanese*   19 | 18 | 16 | £55

Knightsbridge | 15 Beauchamp Pl., SW3 (Knightsbridge) | 020-7838 1500 | www.nozomi.co.uk

"Scantily dressed women and young men" "gather through the evening to clink and wink" at this "see-and-be-seen" Knightsbridge haunt; the "good Japanese fare is imaginatively served", but "big-boom speakers" blaring house music make the place "poundingly loud" as patrons "wait interminably for booked tables"; P.S. "lunch is not as crowded" (nor as noisy).

Nyonya *Malaysian*   ▽ 24 | 14 | 17 | £23

Notting Hill | 2A Kensington Park Rd., W11 (Notting Hill Gate) | 020-7243 1800 | fax 7243 2006 | www.nyonya.co.uk

Ok, it's "not the most comfortable", "but the food is delicious and cheapish" at this Notting Hill Malaysian; consisting of "cramped" counters and stools to sit on, it works "best for a quick bite pre-going out."

Odette's Ⓜ *European*   20 | 15 | 19 | £44

Primrose Hill | 130 Regent's Park Rd., NW1 (Chalk Farm) | 020-7586 8569 | fax 7586 8362

Fans feel "new management" have made a "great success" of this Primrose Hill veteran, introducing a "creative" Modern European menu and yellow-hued decor; but some advise "forget the upstairs silver service and head downstairs to the wine cellar for an intimate setting" and an additional tapas-bar menu.

Odin's ⊠ *British/French*

FOOD	DECOR	SERVICE	COST
20	22	22	£51

Marylebone | 27 Devonshire St., W1 (Baker St.) | 020-7935 7296 | fax 7493 8309 | www.langansrestaurants.co.uk

This Marylebone stalwart "with wonderful art" on the walls makes a "welcome throwback to London places" of yore, with highly "reliable" Classic French–British cuisine and "kind service"; some jeer it's "an old favourite – emphasis on the old", but "when you don't want to overwhelm a client, it's the home of the low-key business meal."

Old Bull & Bush, The *European*

FOOD	DECOR	SERVICE	COST
14	21	15	£30

Hampstead | North End Way, NW3 (Golders Green/Hampstead) | 020-8905 5456

"Now more of a restaurant than a pub" after a "fantastic renovation", this historic Hampstead Heath venue has become "a haven for yummy mummies" and the "flashy rich"; some are bullish on the Modern European eats, but those who don't beat around the bush find the fare "formulaic" and the "service patchy."

Oliveto *Italian*

FOOD	DECOR	SERVICE	COST
23	14	18	£32

Belgravia | 49 Elizabeth St., SW1 (Sloane Sq./Victoria) | 020-7730 0074 | fax 7823 5377

"Huge thin-crust pizzas with creative toppings" and other "dependably delicious", "authentic Sardinian" dishes, "served with warmth and knowledge", pull "the posh set" to this "convivial" if "cramped" and "noisy" Belgravia Italian.

Olivo *Italian*

FOOD	DECOR	SERVICE	COST
21	15	20	£37

Victoria | 21 Eccleston St., SW1 (Victoria) | 020-7730 2505

The "owner's pride shows through at this charming Sardinian" near Victoria Station; "staff that have plenty of charm" compensate for the "shabbyish digs."

NEW Olivomare ⊠ *Italian/Seafood*

FOOD	DECOR	SERVICE	COST
-	-	-	E

Belgravia | 10 Lower Belgrave St., SW1 (Victoria) | 020-7730 9022

This new Belgravia offshoot from the Olivo/Oliveto team is set in bright, gleaming premises where, apart from one wall bedecked with fishy modern artwork, everywhere is pristine white, including a quirky fishnet over one of the windows; the sophisticated Sardinian seafood menu is not long, but offers a wide selection of species.

1 Lombard Street ⊠ *French*

FOOD	DECOR	SERVICE	COST
22	20	21	£55

City | 1 Lombard St., EC3 (Bank) | 020-7929 6611 | fax 7929 6622 | www.1lombardstreet.com

"Check out the who's who in finance" at this "civilised" City dweller that boasts "the Bank of England as a neighbour" (is that why they "feel they can charge a lot"?) and a New French menu with "plenty of choice", presented by staff who "love to serve", albeit at a "snail-like" pace; if it's "not as much fun as the Brasserie" up front, its "central location is in its favour."

	FOOD	DECOR	SERVICE	COST

1 Lombard Street Brasserie 🅱 *European*   20 | 22 | 21 | £42

City | 1 Lombard St., EC3 (Bank) | 020-7929 6611 | fax 7929 6622 |
www.1lombardstreet.com

"More casual than the restaurant" at the rear – certainly more
"noisy" – this "City base for City boys" makes a "decent bet" for
"solid, if spectacular" Modern European meals (especially breakfast) in "a pleasant, airy space – the large skylight really makes the
room"; "efficient service" ensures you can "bank on it" as a "safe
venue for clients" and "for people-watching."

One-O-One *French/Seafood*   23 | - | 20 | £65

Knightsbridge | Sheraton Park Tower | 101 William St., SW1
(Knightsbridge) | 020-7290 7101 | fax 7201 7884 | www.onemansfish.com

"Delectable" fish with "a fresh twist", served by "accomplished staff",
is "the hallmark" of this "oh-so-pricey" New French in Knightsbridge;
after a "three-month overhaul" post-Survey, it was slated to unveil an
opulent new look and a selection of small plates in mid-summer 2007.

Oratory, The *British*   ∇ 18 | 18 | 14 | £34

Knightsbridge | 2332-236 Brompton Rd., SW3 (South Kensington) |
020-7584 3493 | fax 7376 5083 | www.brinkleys.com

"The real draw is the well-chosen wine list at shop prices" at this
Knightsbridge bistro; "bohemian atmosphere" and "reliable"
Modern British menu ("can't ask for too much considering the pric-
ing") make it a "really good find to take friends in town."

Oriel *European*   15 | 18 | 13 | £29

Chelsea | 50-51 Sloane Sq., SW1 (Sloane Sq.) | 020-7730 2804 |
fax 7730 7966

"Try to land a window table to watch the action on Sloane Square" at
this "usually crowded" "brasserie-cum-bar"; "if you can take the
decibels, cheek-by-jowl" seating and "slow service", the "plain"
Modern European fare will do for a "pit stop after shopping."

Original Lahore   24 | 6 | 15 | £17
Kebab House ● *Pakistani*

Whitechapel | 2-10 Umberston St., E1 (Aldgate East/Whitechapel) |
020-7481 9737 | fax 7488 1300

Highgate | 148-150 Brent St., NW4 (Hendon Central) | 020-8203 6904

"Crowded unlike everywhere else in the neighbourhood", this
Whitechapel "curry caff" "with creaky stairs and well-trodden car-
pet" is a "fail safe for scrumptious tandoori grub" (like "legendary
lamb chops") and other "amazing Pakistani" edibles; "value is guaranteed" as there's "no corkage charge for drinks" (both it and its
smaller Hendon Central sibling are BYO).

Original Tagine 🅱 *Moroccan*   20 | 14 | 18 | £27

Marylebone | 7A Dorset St., W1 (Baker St.) | 020-7935 1545

For "spicy, not pricey" fare, this Marylebone Moroccan is a "pre-
ferred choice" of many; despite somewhat "down-to-earth" digs,
the "welcoming" atmosphere makes it a "favourite before a screen-
ing at the Baker Street" cinema close by.

	FOOD	DECOR	SERVICE	COST

Orrery *French*

Marylebone | 55 Marylebone High St., W1 (Baker St./Regent's Park) | 020-7616 8000 | fax 7616 8080 | www.orreryrestaurant.co.uk

25 | 23 | 23 | £65

Flooded in natural light, this "spacious" Marylebone New French offers a "serene setting" for "understated, yet refined" and "tantalising" tasting menus – culminating in a "divine cheese tray" – "served by professional", if slightly "stiff" staff; ornery souls may sniff it's "not life-changing", and you definitely "feel the money flying from your wallet", but it's "worth every penny" for most.

Orso ● *Italian*

Covent Garden | 27 Wellington St., WC2 (Covent Garden) | 020-7240 5269 | fax 7497 2148

20 | 17 | 19 | £39

"A gathering place for the theatre crowd" (but "avoiding thundering hordes of tourists"), this '80s Theatreland eatery gets you to the show on time with "respectable", "unpretentious Italian food" and "cheerful" servers; if the place seems "a bit passé", the plus side is there's "no 'sorry we're booked' b.s."

Oscar *Eclectic*

Fitzrovia | Charlotte Street Hotel | 15 Charlotte St., W1 (Goodge St.) | 020-7806 2007 | www.charlottestreethotel.com

- | - | - | E

With a "connected bar providing great buzz", this "see-and-be-seen" all-day muralled dining room is a "solid standby" for "earthy" Eclectic cooking, even though it's "limited in choice"; P.S. the Fitzrovian hotel also houses a 60-seat cinema for weekend "film afternoons with set menus."

Oslo Court Ⓩ *French*

St. John's Wood | Charlbert St., off Prince Albert Rd., NW8 (St. John's Wood) | 020-7722 8795 | fax 7586 7695

22 | 15 | 25 | £49

"Whatever you desire, they can serve" at this St. John's Wood "'70s time warp" where they "welcome you into their family" with "massive portions" of "uncomplicated" Classic French dishes; sure, some "can't figure out why it's always packed" as it's "comforting, not exciting (like kissing your grandmother)", but the pleased plead "please God, it never changes"; P.S. there's "no chance of refusing a pudding."

Osteria Antica Bologna *Italian*

Battersea | 23 Northcote Rd., SW11 (Clapham Junction B.R.) | 020-7978 4771 | fax 7978 4771 | www.osteria.co.uk

- | - | - | M

This "small", "busy" Battersea trattoria offers a "warm welcome", "squashed tables" and "Italian [fare] so authentic, even Italians love it"; others of indeterminate origin, however, have been "disappointed" of late – "hope it's not on the wane."

Ⓩ Osteria Basilico ● *Italian*

Notting Hill | 29 Kensington Park Rd., W11 (Ladbroke Grove/ Notting Hill Gate) | 020-7727 9957 | fax 7229 7980 | www.osteriabasilico.co.uk

24 | 18 | 18 | £34

"Don't even think about just turning up" at this "Notting Hill classic" as it's "impossible to get a table" thanks to Italian cuisine (like "perfect pizzas") that "has stayed consistently great through the years"; even the "brusque" staff and "occasional chaotic moment just adds to the atmosphere"; P.S. the summer terrace "makes for great people-watching."

Osteria dell'Arancio *Italian* ▽ 20 | 18 | 20 | £41

Chelsea | 383 King's Rd., SW10 (Sloane Sq./South Kensington) | 020-7349 8111 | fax 7349 8123 | www.osteriadellarancio.co.uk
"Funky in a good way", this World's End Italian in a colourful townhouse regales with its pastiche artwork – e.g. the Queen sporting a salami crown – and "authentic regional" food and wine from the Marche; "nice staff" offset the "expensive for what you get" bill.

☑ Ottolenghi *Mediterranean* 24 | 17 | 16 | £24

Islington | 287 Upper St., N1 (Angel) | 020-7288 1454 | fax 7704 1456
Notting Hill | 63 Ledbury Rd., W11 (Notting Hill Gate) | 020-7727 1121
www.ottolenghi.co.uk
"Just walking past the window makes the mouth water" at these Med deli/cafes in Notting Hill and Islington whose "original", "sensational food and cakes" can be eaten at "one big round table" or "easily taken home"; they're "quite pricey though", and some wonder "do you have to be grumpy to work here?"

Oxo Tower *European* 20 | 24 | 19 | £58

South Bank | Oxo Tower Wharf | Barge House St., SE1 (Blackfriars/Waterloo) | 020-7803 3888 | fax 7803 3838 | www.harveynichols.com
The "breathtaking" skyline "view is the most stunning aspect of dining" at this "starkly" "elegant" eatery atop a South Bank landmark; though "good", the Modern European food "isn't the best available" ("bring a small appetite"), and service is "efficient" at best; given the "absolutely punishing prices", it's the sort of place "best done on expense account" – unless you're splurging "for a first date or anniversary."

Oxo Tower Brasserie *Asian/Mediterranean* 20 | 22 | 18 | £42

South Bank | Oxo Tower Wharf | Barge House St., SE1 (Blackfriars/Waterloo) | 020-7803 3888 | fax 7803 3838 |
www.harveynichols.com
"Floor-to-ceiling windows afford an amazing view of the city across the Thames" from this "modern" "rooftop brasserie" on the South Bank; although the Asian-Med "food can be just 'ok'" and the service "strained", "the bill is more palatable" than at the next-door restaurant, and there's the added perk of a "crowded" but "great piano bar" with live jazz; P.S. "good pre-theatre if you're going to the National."

Ozer Restaurant & Bar ➊ *Turkish* 19 | 17 | 16 | £31

Marylebone | 5 Langham Pl., W1 (Oxford Circus) | 020-7323 0505 | fax 7323 0111 | www.sofra.co.uk
"Tasty, tender Turkish fare" "with a Western twist" is the reason why mezze mavens "always come back to" this "accommodating" Sofra group-owned site just off Regent Street; but the Ottoman-style decor is "a bit over the top" for some tastes.

	FOOD	DECOR	SERVICE	COST

Painted Heron, The *Indian*
22 **19** **21** **£42**

Chelsea | 112 Cheyne Walk, SW10 (Sloane Sq.) | 020-7351 5232 | fax 7351 5213 | www.thepaintedheron.com

The "strange name belies" the "imaginative dishes" "suitable for an educated palate" at this "upmarket" "modern" Indian on Chelsea Embankment ("hard to find"); add in "friendly service" and it's clear why it's "not to be missed" – just "better be sure you can stand those spices."

Palmerston, The *British*
– **–** **–** **M**

Dulwich | 91 Lordship Ln., SE22 (East Dulwich B.R.) | 020-8693 1629 | fax 8693 9662

"A shining example of the sensitively converted gastropub", this wood-panelled East Dulwich haunt beckons with an "excellent" Modern British menu that makes use of "locally sourced, seasonal food"; a few feel "prices are steep for what you get" – especially if you go digging into the "decent wine list for a pub."

Papillon ❶ *French*
23 **22** **22** **£52**

South Kensington | 96 Draycott Ave., SW3 (South Kensington) | 020-7225 2555 | www.papillonchelsea.co.uk

"Classy and formal, but still with a neighbourhood feel", this "addition to the Brompton Cross restaurant scene" has made a "superb start" say supporters of Soren Jessen's "plush" bistro where an "inventive" "Classic French menu is presented and served well" by "non-snooty servers"; "whilst expensive", it leaves you "without feeling ripped off when you receive the bill."

Pappagallo *Italian*
▽ **21** **20** **19** **£44**

Mayfair | 54-55 Curzon St., W1 (Green Park) | 020-7629 2742 | fax 7493 4387

"A wonderful place to while away a winter evening", this "pretty" green/grey-toned Mayfair "local" offers a "good selection of Italian cuisine", including "some unusual, if expensive selections"; "warm" service augments the "inviting" ambience.

ⓩ Park, The *Pan-Asian*
24 **24** **25** **£57**

Knightsbridge | Mandarin Oriental Hyde Park | 66 Knightsbridge, SW1 (Knightsbridge) | 020-7201 3722 | fax 7235 2001 | www.mandarinoriental.com/london

There's "a brilliant view of Hyde Park" at this "little gem hidden in an impersonal room" in the Mandarin Oriental; fans fall for the "fabulous service" and the "excellent new menu" of Pan-Asian shared plates that "deliver good food at an acceptable price for the neighbourhood" – and it's "even better when the wine is included", as on the weekday prix fixe lunch.

Pasha *Moroccan*
20 **16** **17** **£34**

Islington | 301 Upper St., N1 (Angel/Highbury & Islington) | 020-7226 1454 | fax 7226 1617

Despite "bare-bones service and decor" (the latter was being revamped post-Survey), diners "come out having enjoyed a relaxing" time at this "calming" Upper Street Turk with "well-spaced tables" and "carefully prepared dishes, notable for their lightness."

Pasha ◐ *Moroccan* | 18 | 25 | 17 | £43 |

South Kensington | 1 Gloucester Rd., SW7 (Gloucester Rd.) | 020-7589 7969 | fax 7581 9996 | www.pasha-restaurant.co.uk

"In a neighbourhood lacking ambience restaurants", the "romantic" "Aladdin's cave atmosphere" of this South Ken Moroccan is like a "jump to Marrakech"; "don't expect to be bowled over by the food – it's average, and so's the service – but the tastefully beautiful belly dancers and lovely setting just about make up for it."

Passione ⊠ *Italian* | 23 | 15 | 20 | £48 |

Fitzrovia | 10 Charlotte St., W1 (Goodge St.) | 020-7636 2833 | fax 7636 2889 | www.passione.co.uk

"Eating here is always a pleasure" proclaim patrons passionate about this "Italian with a big heart" (despite "tight quarters") "in the middle of Fitzrovia"; some are "surprised at how expensive everything is", but the "fantastic food" and "willing-to-go-the-extra-mile service" "are worth it"; P.S. tip: "upstairs is more private and rarely full."

⊠ Patara *Thai* | 23 | 19 | 20 | £38 |

Knightsbridge | 9 Beauchamp Pl., SW3 (Knightsbridge/South Kensington) | 020-7581 8820 | fax 7581 2155

Mayfair | 3-7 Maddox St., W1 (Oxford Circus) | 020-7499 6008 | fax 7499 6007

Soho | 15 Greek St., W1 (Leicester Sq./Tottenham Court Rd.) | 020-7437 1071 | fax 7437 1089

South Kensington | 181 Fulham Rd., SW3 (South Kensington) | 020-7351 5692 | fax 7351 5692

www.patarathailand.com

The menu offers "a myriad of spices to greet the palate" at this "busy, buzzy" quartet with "modern yet charming ambience"; true, they're "not cheap, but they're worth the money since the food has an edge and taste that ordinary Thais don't have" – and "gracious" service to boot.

Paternoster Chop House *British/Chophouse* | 18 | 16 | 16 | £43 |

City | Warwick Ct., Paternoster Sq., EC4 (St. Paul's) | 020-7029 9400 | fax 7029 9409 | www.paternosterchophouse.com

"Good steaks" and other items from a "middle of the road" chophouse menu "pack them in" to this "spartan", "barnlike" Brit a stone's throw from St. Paul's Cathedral; "the major thing that puts you off is the noise" – "ear-splitting!" – and service that "tries, but not hard enough."

Patisserie Valerie *French* | 20 | 14 | 15 | £17 |

Belgravia | 17 Motcomb St., SW1 (Knightsbridge) | 020-7245 6161 | fax 7245 6161

Covent Garden | 8 Russell St., WC2 (Covent Garden) | 020-7240 0064 | fax 7240 0064

Knightsbridge | 215 Brompton Rd., SW3 (Knightsbridge) | 020-7823 9971 | fax 7589 4993

Knightsbridge | 32-44 Hans Cres., SW1 (Knightsbridge) | 020-7590 0905

| | FOOD | DECOR | SERVICE | COST |

(continued)

Patisserie Valerie

Marylebone | 105 Marylebone High St., W1 (Baker St./Bond St.) | 020-7935 6240 | fax 7935 6543
Piccadilly | 162 Piccadilly, W1 (Green Park) | 020-7491 1717
Soho | 44 Old Compton St., W1 (Leicester Sq.) | 020-7437 3466 | fax 7734 6133
City | The Pavillion Bldg. | Bishops Sq., 37 Brushfield St., E1 (Liverpool St.) | 020-7247 4906
Chelsea | 81 Duke of York Sq., King's Rd., SW3 (Sloane Sq.) | 020-7730 7094 | fax 7730 7094
Kensington | 27 Kensington Church St., W8 (High St. Kensington) | 020-7937 9574 | fax 7937 9574
www.patisserie-valerie.co.uk
"Humming with contented customers", this "time-honoured" chain is "a treat any time of day" for "homemade goodies in a classic French bistro manner" – though some "skip the food and go straight for" the counter-displayed confections ("calories and cholesterol, but oh so good!"); despite "crowded" digs and "service that could use an energy infusion", it's still a "sweet stop."

Patterson's 🗷 *European* | 22 | 20 | 21 | £53 |

Mayfair | 4 Mill St., W1 (Oxford Circus) | 020-7499 1308 | fax 7491 2122 | www.pattersonsrestaurant.co.uk
This "delightful" Mayfair Modern European offers a "good, all-round" package of "well-executed" fare (the "deceptively small portions do fill you up"), "efficient service" and ambience that "can get noisy but not bothersome"; on the flip side, "it's not particularly good value", aside from the "exceptional specials" and prix fixes.

Pearl *French* | 24 | 22 | 23 | £56 |

Holborn | Renaissance Chancery Court Hotel | 252 High Holborn, WC1 (Holborn) | 020-7829 7000 | fax 7829 9889 | www.pearl-restaurant.com
The "plush, seriously well-designed" interior of this "white marbled" Holborn hotel dining room is the canvas for chef Jun Tanaka's "original, carefully crafted" New French menu, served by "exceptional staff"; cynics claim it's "just not that memorable", given that "the price is high", but supporters insist it's "great for splashing out."

Pellicano *Italian* | 20 | 17 | 19 | £37 |

Chelsea | 19-21 Elystan St., SW3 (South Kensington) | 020-7589 3718 | fax 7584 1789 | www.pellicanorestaurant.co.uk
"With a loyal following amongst the locals", this "bright" eatery in a "quiet street" near Chelsea Green makes a "decent neighbourhood Italian", with "enough space between tables to allow for conversation over tasty seafood"; plus, "the prices aren't too bad" either.

Pepper Tree *Thai* | 19 | 11 | 14 | £16 |

Clapham | 19 Clapham Common South Side, SW4 (Clapham Common) | 020-7622 1758 | fax 7720 7531 | www.thepeppertree.co.uk
"You may need to recalibrate the idea of cheap and cheerful" after checking out this Clapham Common Thai, with its combination of "really tasty" "decent portions" and little prices; however, the

"noisy" digs and communal tables make it a "great stop to get the evening going", "rather than a romantic meal for two."

Pescatori ☒ Mediterranean
22 | 16 | 21 | £44

Mayfair | 11 Dover St., W1 (Green Park) | 020-7493 2652 | fax 7499 3180
Fitzrovia | 57 Charlotte St., W1 (Goodge St.) | 020-7580 3289 | fax 7580 0539
www.pescatori.co.uk

"Innovatively, expertly prepared fish" is the mainstay of the Med menu at this Mayfair and Fitzrovia pair, a family-run "reliable house of fins"; habitués also hail the "homely feel" and "lovely service."

Petersham, The European
▽ 23 | 21 | 24 | £61

Richmond | Petersham Hotel | Nightingale Ln., Richmond (Richmond) | 020-8940 7471 | fax 8939 1002 | www.petershamhotel.co.uk

"Stunning Thames views", "delicate but balanced" Modern European cuisine and "lovely service" combine to make this Richmond hotel dining room "a most excellent experience", even if its "old-world charm" strikes cynics as just "old-fashioned."

Petersham Nurseries Café Ⓜ European
▽ 25 | 21 | 18 | £38

Richmond | Petersham Nurseries | Church Ln., off Petersham Rd., Richmond (Richmond) | 020-8605 3627 | www.petershamnurseries.com

The "refreshingly unique" experience of being "surrounded by flowering plants" ("felt we were having a picnic!") makes this "charming" greenhouse cafe in "a functioning nursery" in Richmond "a delight for lunch" (the only meal offered); the daily changing "fresh and earthy" Modern European menu, whilst "expensive", reminds you "what real food tastes like."

☑ Pétrus ☒ French
28 | 25 | 26 | £95

Belgravia | The Berkeley | Wilton Pl., SW1 (Hyde Park Corner) | 020-7235 1200 | fax 7235 1266 | www.gordonramsay.com

"Luxuriate in Marcus Wareing's sublime creations" – the epitome of New French "cooking at its most cutting edge", backed by "wines that live up to the name" – at this "beautiful" Belgravia venue where "utterly professional" staff "provide tip-top service" perhaps it's un peu "pretentious", with "eye-popping prices", but it's also "everything a modern fine dining institution should be" – "so pick a special occasion, forget the cost and book it."

Phoenix Palace ◑ Chinese
23 | 17 | 15 | £27

Marylebone | 3-5 Glentworth St., NW1 (Baker St.) | 020-7486 3515

For "upmarket, relaxed Chinese dining away from the hustle and bustle of Chinatown", this Marylebone Cantonese offers "a place to experiment with confidence" from a "comprehensive menu"; "reasonable prices" compensate for "hit-and-miss service."

☑ Pied à Terre ☒ French
28 | 22 | 25 | £82

Fitzrovia | 34 Charlotte St., W1 (Goodge St.) | 020-7636 1178 | www.pied-a-terre.co.uk

"Hats off to chef Shane Osborne for the culinary masterpieces" he creates at this "small" but "stunning" New French in Fitzrovia; from the "star wine list" to the "extremely knowledgeable servers", it has "everything you could possibly want in a restaurant" (except perhaps the decor – "chic, but nothing eye-grabbing"), and so it's "worth the prices" – "you'll pay for the *pied,* but you'll leave *la terre* for *le ciel!*"

Pigalle Club, The 🗷 *European/French*   ▽ 14 | 21 | 16 | £54

Piccadilly | 215 Piccadilly, W1 (Piccadilly Circus) | 020-7734 8142 | fax 7494 2022 | www.thepigalleclub.com

Not many surveyors have found their way to this low-lit Piccadilly supper club (named and styled after a famed '40s venue); those who have, however, say "it makes a great night out – but don't just come for the Classic French–Modern European food"; the main event is the nightly cabaret, and DJ-spun tunes thereafter.

Pig's Ear *British/French*   22 | 19 | 19 | £33

Chelsea | 35 Old Church St., SW3 (Sloane Sq.) | 020-7352 2908 | fax 7352 9321 | www.thepigsear.co.uk

"Well, maybe you *can* make a silk purse from a pig's ear" quip those enamoured by this "fabulous little gastropub" in Chelsea; diners can either go to the bar with "trendy crowds" and "adult beverages aflowin'" or "upstairs, with high ceilings and tables spaced apart", for "correctly priced" New French–Traditional British cuisine; "the biggest problem is its success: it's impossible to get a table at a normal time."

Ping Pong *Chinese*   18 | 18 | 14 | £25

Marylebone | 10 Paddington St., W1 (Baker St.) | 020-7009 9600 ◑
NEW **Marylebone** | 29A James St., W1 (Bond St.) | 020-7034 3100 ◑
Soho | 45 Great Marlborough St., W1 (Oxford Circus) | 020-7851 6969 ◑
NEW **Fitzrovia** | 48 Eastcastle St., W1 (Oxford Circus) |
020-7070 0550 ◑
NEW **Fitzrovia** | 48 Newman St., W1 (Goodge St.) |
020-7291 3080
NEW **Waterloo** | Festival Terrace | Southbank Ctr., Belvedere Rd.,
SE1 (Waterloo) | 020-7960 4160 ◑
Notting Hill | 74-76 Westbourne Grove, W2 (Notting Hill Gate) |
020-7313 9832 | fax 7313 9849 ◑
www.pingpongdimsum.com

There's "great energy" within the lattice-patterned digs of this "designer dim sum" chain, which only offers "little parcels of deliciousness – perfect for a quick" meal; but "they tend to be understaffed", and, "irritatingly, no bookings" are taken (except groups); P.S. "try the jasmine tea, which blossoms in your cup."

🗷 Pizza Express *Pizza*   17 | 13 | 15 | £18

Covent Garden | 9-12 Bow St., WC2 (Covent Garden) | 020-7240 3443 |
fax 7497 0131 ◑
Knightsbridge | 7 Beauchamp Pl., SW3 (Knightsbridge) | 020-7589 2355 |
fax 7589 5159 ◑
Soho | 29 Wardour St., W1 (Leicester Sq./Piccadilly Circus) |
020-7437 7215 | fax 7494 2582
Blackfriars | 125 Alban Gate, London Wall, EC2 (Moorgate/St. Paul's) |
020-7600 8880 | fax 7600 8128

(continued)

(continued)

Pizza Express

Battersea | 46-54 Battersea Bridge Rd., SW11 (Earl's Ct./Sloane Sq.) | 020-7924 2774

Chelsea | The Pheasantry | 152-154 King's Rd., SW3 (Sloane Sq.) | 020-7351 5031 | fax 7349 9844

Fulham | 363 Fulham Rd., SW10 (Fulham Broadway/South Kensington) | 020-7352 5300 ●

Fulham | 895-896 Fulham Rd., SW6 (Parsons Green) | 020-7731 3117 | fax 7371 7884 ●

Kensington | 35 Earl's Court Rd., W8 (Earl's Ct.) | 020-7937 0761 ●

Notting Hill | 137 Notting Hill Gate, W11 (Notting Hill Gate) | 020-7229 6000 ●

www.pizzaexpress.com

Additional locations throughout London

"Perfect for a casual bite" of "decent pizza" and other Italian staples served "without fuss", this "good value" chain around town "sets the standard for reliability"; aside from the "huge variety of their premises", they offer "no surprises – but that's a good thing."

Pizza Metro Ⓜ *Pizza*

– | – | – | M

Battersea | 64 Battersea Rise, SW11 (Clapham Common/Clapham Junction B.R.) | 020-7228 3812 | fax 7738 0987 | www.pizzametropizza.com

This "big" Battersea Italian gets "extremely noisy" with the constant crowds chomping "fantastic pizza", baked in a traditional wood-burning oven and offered on a "great" 'served-by-the-metre' system.

Pizza on the Park *Pizza*

14 | 13 | 14 | £25

Belgravia | 11 Knightsbridge, SW1 (Hyde Park Corner) | 020-7235 7825 | fax 7235 6853 | www.pizzaonthepark.co.uk

"The pizzas are not bad" (after all, they're made by a certain famed chain), but "you come for the jazz", performed "loud and lively" each night at this "dated"-looking Italian-American on Hyde Park Corner; still, the "not impressed" wail "why do I have to pay extra to eat Pizza Express pizza near the park?"

PJ's Bar & Grill ● *American*

16 | 17 | 15 | £31

Covent Garden | 30 Wellington St., WC2 (Covent Garden) | 020-7240 7529 | fax 7836 3426 | www.pjsgrill.net

Chelsea | 52 Fulham Rd., SW3 (South Kensington) | 020-7581 0025 | fax 7584 0820

"Expect the usual pub fare, American-style" at these "noisy" "neighbourhood" hangouts in Chelsea ("perfect for Sunday brunch") and Covent Garden ("perfect before a performance"); though separately owned, both "can be crowded" and the "skills of the staff do not match their beauty."

Planet Hollywood ● *American*

11 | 17 | 14 | £24

Piccadilly | 13 Coventry St., W1 (Leicester Sq./Piccadilly Circus) | 020-7437 7639 | fax 7734 0835 | www.planethollywoodlondon.com

Jammed with "movie memorabilia and junk you can buy", this famous Piccadilly "theme restaurant" "provides an interesting decor" even though "it's getting a little dated now"; the "average" American burger fare is fine "if you're 15, or not from the U.K." and "need a fix of back-home food"; otherwise, "why bother?"

Plateau French

| 19 | 21 | 18 | £50 |

Canary Wharf | Canada Pl., 4th fl., E14 (Canary Wharf) | 020-7715 7100 | fax 7715 7110 | www.plateaurestaurant.co.uk

"In an interesting setting overlooking Canary Wharf", this "bright", "double-height room delivers both dramatic impact and intimate corners" for a clientele "full of the suited and booted"; both the "superb business" dining room and "better-value brasserie" offer New French cuisine that's "fine", though hostiles quip "what it lacks in quality, it compensates for in expense."

Poissonnerie
de L'Avenue ● 🗷 French/Seafood

| 21 | 18 | 20 | £52 |

Chelsea | 82 Sloane Ave., SW3 (South Kensington) | 020-7589 2457 | fax 7581 3360 | www.poissonneriedelavenue.com

"If you're looking for 'trendy', this isn't the place to come", but for a "genteel", "gentle atmosphere", this "gorgeous old-fashioned fish restaurant" at Brompton Cross fits the bill, from the Classic French preparations to the "refined service"; some sigh it seems "oh-so-tired", but the kind-hearted claim it "continues to remain a classic."

Popeseye 🗷🗷 Chophouse

| - | - | - | M |

Putney | 277 Upper Richmond Rd., SW15 (East Putney) | 020-8788 7733

Olympia | 108 Blythe Rd., W14 (Olympia) | 020-7610 4578 | fax 7376 7210 www.popeseye.com

"Don't let the decor or locations put you off" – this "mini-chain serving nothing but steak" in Olympia and East Putney is a "carnivore heaven" (all the beef comes from an old family butcher north of the border); staff offer "great hospitality" and a "bottom-less list of good clarets"; "beware though, it's cash only, with not many cashpoints nearby."

Portal 🗷 Portuguese

| - | - | - | E |

Clerkenwell | 88 St. John St., EC1 (Barbican/Farringdon) | 020-7253 6950 | fax 7490 5836 | www.portalrestaurant.com

Strikingly designed, with a covered courtyard, this Clerkenwell eatery is a portal indeed into "innovative, upscale Portuguese" and other Med fare ("the house special, 20-hour cooked pork, is a sensation"); whilst "excellent in every respect", it can be "relatively quiet, thus ensuring privacy" for those who want it.

Porters ● British

| 20 | 16 | 19 | £25 |

Covent Garden | 17 Henrietta St., WC2 (Covent Garden) | 020-7836 6466 | fax 7379 4296 | www.porters-restaurant.com

Have "fun sampling the interesting-sounding dishes", from bubble and squeak to spotted dick, at Lord Bradford's "safe", "solid" and "cheap" Covent Garden Traditional British; it's "justifiably popular with tourists" – and, admittedly, a few natives craving "food just like we got in school."

Portrait *British*

FOOD | DECOR | SERVICE | COST
| ▽ 22 | 24 | 15 | £30 |

Soho | The National Portrait Gallery | 2 St. Martin's Pl., 3rd fl., WC2 (Charing Cross/Leicester Sq.) | 020-7312 2490 | fax 7925 0244 | www.searcys.co.uk

"Bring a map to help you identify all the landmarks you'll see" from the "marvellous view" of this "eatery atop the National Portrait Gallery"; the Modern British "food is surprisingly good, and surprisingly good value", making it "worth dealing with" "rather snooty service."

Potemkin ●⊠ *Russian*

| - | - | - | E |

Tufnell Park | 144 Clerkenwell Rd., EC1 (Farringdon/Chancery Ln.) | 020-7278 6661 | fax 7278 5551 | www.potemkin.co.uk

From the borscht to the blini, "the food is indeed very good" at this Clerkenwell purple-and-red-hued Russian, one of London's few specialists in Soviet cuisine; however, not even the vodka bar's many varieties can erase the sting of service that cynics call "the worst this side of Moscow."

Potting Shed, The *British*

| - | - | - | E |

Marylebone | Dorset Square Hotel | 39 Dorset Sq., NW1 (Baker St./Marylebone) | 020-7535 0709 | fax 7724 3328 | www.dorsetsquare.co.uk

A "cosy", "very English"-garden setting (complete with terra-cotta pots and wicker chairs) characterises this "delightful" dining room where "efficient staff" serve "memorable" Modern British meals; being in a "quiet" Marylebone hotel, it's "not the place for a lively night out", but is "very nice for lunch."

Princess Garden ● *Chinese*

| 21 | 18 | 19 | £41 |

Mayfair | 8-10 N. Audley St., W1 (Bond St./Marble Arch) | 020-7493 3223 | fax 7629 3130 | www.princessgardenofmayfair.com

"Favoured by the business-lunch crowd", this "Chinese with style" "near the U.S. embassy" is "a bit pricey, but worth it" for "standard dishes, reinvented and superbly executed"; the main debating point is the service – "efficient" and "polite" vs. "slow and ungracious."

Prism ⊠ *British*

| 18 | 23 | 18 | £47 |

City | 147 Leadenhall St., EC3 (Bank/Monument) | 020-7256 3888 | fax 7191 6025 | www.harveynichols.com

Its "superb setting" – a "high-ceilinged, old banking hall" with "room between the tables" – makes this City dweller the "perfect venue for a business lunch" or "classy after-work drinks"; "clean, light Modern British dishes" and "extensive wine list" are all overseen by "efficient service"; main gripe: "the acoustics make it so noisy, you can't hear yourself chew."

Providores, The/Tapa Room *Eclectic*

| 22 | 16 | 17 | £39 |

Marylebone | 109 Marylebone High St., W1 (Baker St./Bond St.) | 020-7935 6175 | fax 7935 6877 | www.theprovidores.co.uk

"Wacky, highly imaginative" Eclectic edibles, matched with "extremely nice New Zealand wines", make for a merry time at this Marylebone fusion specialist ("Austral-Asian?") that offers "two dining options": the "always busy", "tight" Tapa Room where you "stand in line to get a table", and Providores, the "serene upstairs" ("more lonely", but you can book); "too bad" about the "frankly bland" decor and "slow staff."

Quadrato *Italian* | 24 | 22 | 26 | £51 |

Canary Wharf | Four Seasons Hotel Canary Wharf | 46 Westferry Circus, E14 (Canary Wharf) | 020-7510 1857 | fax 7510 1998 | www.fourseasons.com

"Customers are treated like kings and queens" – typical "Four Seasons-quality" treatment – at this smart, airy eatery where an "open kitchen provides a stage to watch" the creation of "superb" "regional Italian specials"; whilst some sigh about the slightly "soulless" "setting just off the lobby", few deny it's the "best bet for a high-end lunch in Canary Wharf."

Quaglino's ❷ *European* | 18 | 20 | 17 | £50 |

St. James's | 16 Bury St., SW1 (Green Park) | 020-7930 6767 | fax 7839 2866 | www.quaglinos.co.uk

Be "transformed into a '50s movie star on the grand sweeping staircase" of this "bustling, bold" behemoth, a St. James's fixture for 15 years; whilst the Modern European menu is "pretty consistent", it's "not the main attraction", and as for "service – well, they tolerate you"; in short, "a place more for the eye than a meal" – though drinks in the "fantastic bar" above are an option too.

Quality Chop House ❷ *British/Chophouse* | 20 | 16 | 19 | £39 |

Farringdon | 92-94 Farringdon Rd., EC1 (Farringdon) | 020-7837 5093 | fax 7833 8748 | www.qualitychophouse.co.uk

True to its name, this Traditional Brit serves "quality" chophouse fare in a former Farringdon workingman's canteen, complete with the original Victorian furniture in one room ("sitting on those oak benches is hard!"); whilst some claim it's "worth a visit for atmosphere", a Decor score drop suggests "the place is lacking in va-va-voom."

☑ Quilon *Indian* | 25 | 19 | 21 | £41 |

Victoria | Crowne Plaza London St. James Hotel | 41 Buckingham Gate, SW1 (St. James's Park/Victoria) | 020-7821 1899 | fax 7828 5802 | www.quilon.co.uk

"In its own way, great" say those familiar with this "modern"-looking Indian in a "corporate" hotel south of St. James's Park; it's applauded for "amazing" Keralan cooking that's "true to the region" – though "quite pricey" compared to more standard subcontinental sites.

☑ Quirinale ☒ *Italian* | 25 | 20 | 25 | £47 |

Westminster | 1 Great Peter St., SW1 (Westminster) | 020-7222 7080 | fax 7233 3080 | www.quirinale.co.uk

"Combining an elegant simplicity with high-quality service", this "Westminster favourite gets the vote" – as well as attracts "the occasional MP" – for "divine" Italian cooking "plus the best selection of cheeses"; although the "comfortable" cream-coloured setting can be "a bit quiet", the "intimate" basement makes it feel "like a club."

	FOOD	DECOR	SERVICE	COST

Quo Vadis 🅂 *Italian* | 18 | 16 | 16 | £46 |

Soho | 26-29 Dean St., W1 (Leicester Sq./Tottenham Court Rd.) |
020-7437 9585 | fax 7736 7593 | www.whitestarline.org.uk

Offering "a quiet contrast to the hustle and bustle of Soho on the
other side of the window", this "old-timer" still "delivers decent Italian
dishes" amidst Damien Hirst artwork advocates argue; but critics
contend (and sagging scores suggest) it has "seen better days."

🆉 Racine *French* | 22 | 18 | 21 | £46 |

Knightsbridge | 239 Brompton Rd., SW3 (Knightsbridge/
South Kensington) | 020-7584 4477 | fax 7584 4900

"A haute-bistro that never fails" say *amis* of this "busy" Knightsbridge
haunt where "the ambience is authentic", down to the "tables close
together"; the "hearty" French fare is "a joy" and staff "have the formula for making one feel at home", despite "prices that seem high."

Rainforest Cafe *American* | 11 | 21 | 13 | £27 |

Piccadilly | 20-24 Shaftesbury Ave., W1 (Piccadilly Circus) |
020-7434 3111 | fax 7434 3222 | www.therainforestcafe.co.uk

Although "not quite what a true rainforest is like", this "hectic"
Piccadilly "playground" "keeps the little ones interested" with "fantasy" decor "full of automated animals"; adults may find it "a tough
place to take", though, since the American "food is nothing to hoot
about", and "they have to wait long hours to get served."

Randall & Aubin *British/European* | 19 | 17 | 17 | £33 |

Soho | 14-16 Brewer St., W1 (Piccadilly Circus) | 020-7287 4447 |
fax 7287 4488

Chelsea | 329-331 Fulham Rd., SW10 (Fulham Broadway/
South Kensington) | 020-7823 3515 | fax 7823 3991
www.randallandaubin.co.uk

"Fast and flamboyant", this Soho ex-butcher's shop ("white-tiled
walls" et al.) is a "fun, frantic place to grab some good [fish] and staple British grills"; just bear in mind it "can be clubby and loud" at
night, and the "casual service" "erratic"; the calmer Chelsea sib offers
"steady-as-she-goes seafood" with a Modern European flavour.

Ransome's Dock *British/Eclectic* | ▽ 20 | 13 | 19 | £44 |

Battersea | 35-37 Park Gate Rd., SW11 (Sloane Sq./South Kensington) |
020-7223 1611 | fax 7924 2614 | www.ransomesdock.co.uk

Chef-owner "Martin Lam excels himself" at this unassuming
Battersea dockside eatery, preparing "hearty" Modern British–
Eclectic "fare with flair" – though oenophiles opine the global "wine
list is the star of the show"; all's served in an "efficient" manner.

Raoul's *Mediterranean* | 16 | 14 | 13 | £26 |

St. John's Wood | 13 Clifton Rd., W9 (Warwick Ave.) | 020-7289 7313 |
fax 7266 4752

Notting Hill | 105-107 Talbot Rd., W11 (Westbourne Park) |
020-7229 2400 | fax 7243 8070
www.raoulsgourmet.com

"More of a hangout than a real restaurant", this St. John's Wood
Med cafe and younger Notting Hill offshoot (with "retro '60s de-

cor") are "heaving at the weekend for brunch", which stars "strange-coloured but good-tasting Italian eggs"; they're much quieter on weekdays, but expect "appallingly slow service" whenever you go.

Rasa *Indian* | 24 | 17 | 20 | £31 |

Mayfair | 6 Dering St., W1 (Bond St./Oxford Circus) | 020-7629 1346 | fax 7637 0224 🖫

Fitzrovia | 5 Charlotte St., W1 (Tottenham Court Rd.) | 020-7637 0222 | fax 7637 0224

Islington | Holiday Inn King's Cross | 1 King's Cross Rd., WC1 (Farringdon/Kings Cross) | 020-7833 9787 🖫

Stoke Newington | 55 Stoke Newington Church St., N16 (Stoke Newington B.R.) | 020-7249 0344 | fax 7637 0224 ◗
www.rasarestaurants.com

"Complex, perfumed" Keralan dishes "will change how you see Indian food" at this "expanding chain"; whilst their menus differ, all offer "superb vegetarian specialities" – some venues are completely veggie – at "reasonable prices", in digs that are "a cross between a handmade hippie joint and upscale" subcontinental.

☑ Rasoi Vineet Bhatia 🖫 *Indian* | 27 | 19 | 23 | £65 |

Chelsea | 10 Lincoln St., SW3 (Sloane Sq.) | 020-7225 1881 | fax 7581 0220 | www.vineetbhatia.com

With an "exquisite Indian" menu of "dishes that tempt and surprise", chef-owner Vineet Bhatia's "charming" Chelsea townhouse (recently given a light refurb) is "always a pleasure", smoothed along by "superb service"; if a few flinch at the "high-end prices", even they are "entertained" by this "epicurean delight."

NEW Raviolo *Italian* | - | - | - | M |

Balham | 1 Balham Station Rd., SW12 (Balham) | 020-8772 0433 | fax 8675 6167 | www.raviolo.co.uk

"Well-located" opposite Balham Station, this "excellent newcomer" offers low-priced "Italian tucker" emphasising the eponymous "ravioli, and lots of it!"; communal tables with bench seating and menus that double as place mats complete the picture of this "cheerful" neighbourhood trattoria.

Real Greek Mezedopolio, The 🖫 *Greek* | 16 | 14 | 14 | £26 |

Hoxton | 14-15 Hoxton Mkt., N1 (Old St.) | 020-7739 8212 | fax 7739 4910

Real Greek Souvlaki & Bar, The *Greek*

NEW Covent Garden | 60-62 Long Acre, WC2 (Covent Garden) | 020-7240-2292

Marylebone | 56 Paddington St., W1 (Baker St.) | 020-7486 0466

Clerkenwell | 140-142 St. John St., EC1 (Farringdon) | 020-7253 7234 | fax 7253 7235 🖫

Borough | Riverside House | 2A Southwark Bridge Rd., SE1 (London Bridge/Southwark) | 020-7620 0162

Putney | 31-33 Putney High St., SW15 (Putney Bridge) | 020-8788 3270
www.therealgreek.com

"Rediscover Greek food" ("true Greek, not Cypriot!") at this chain that's "a planet away from the stereotypical taverna"; the "honest"

Hellenic fare is "reasonably priced", "but it's not much for your money" mutter malcontents, and it's brought "by people who don't want to be waiters"; P.S. in late 2006, the Hoxton original vanished into Mezedopolio, a mezze-serving wine bar.

Rebato's ⊠ *Spanish* | - | - | - | M |

Waterloo | 169 S. Lambeth Rd., SW8 (Stockwell) | 020-7735 6388 | www.rebatos.com

For "a genuine Spanish" experience near Stockwell, surveyors commend this unpretentious 24-year-old, with a bar serving "excellent tapas" and airy, skylit restaurant at the rear for the "best", bargain-priced Iberian fare, all attended to by "lovely" staff.

Red Fort *Indian* | 23 | 21 | 20 | £42 |

Soho | 77 Dean St., W1 (Oxford Circus/Tottenham Court Rd.) | 020-7437 2525 | fax 7434 0721 | www.redfort.co.uk

This "sophisticated", "swish" Soho subcontinental satisfies supporters – including Tony Blair – with regional cuisine "with interesting twists", red-toned "modern decor" and "service with a smile"; some grumble about being "rushed out for the next sitting", but even "people who swear they'd never eat Indian food beg to go back."

Red Pepper *Italian* | 19 | 12 | 14 | £27 |

St. John's Wood | 8 Formosa St., W9 (Warwick Ave.) | 020-7266 2708 | fax 7266 5522

"A true local" "for the Maida Vale area", this place is "always packed", thanks to "brilliant" pizzas and other "casual" Italian eats; but the "narrowly spaced tables mean it's noisy and cramped" ("particularly downstairs"), and "service is too swift" for some tastes.

Refettorio ⊠ *Italian* | ▽ 20 | 16 | 18 | £46 |

Blackfriars | Crowne Plaza | 19 New Bridge St., EC4 (Blackfriars) | 020-7438 8052 | fax 7438 8088 | www.london-city.crowneplaza.com

"In a section of town" with limited culinary options, the Crowne Plaza's "inviting" dining room by Blackfriars Bridge makes a "trustworthy" spot for "unusual Italian concoctions", plus a "range of delicious cold meats" and cheese on display; pity that the "City location means City prices."

Refuel *European* | ▽ 12 | 20 | 18 | £45 |

Soho | Soho Hotel | 4 Richmond Mews, W1 (Tottenham Court Rd.) | 020-7559 3000 | fax 7559 3003 | www.sohohotel.com

"Excellent for people-watching", "with occasional celeb-spotting" thrown in for good measure, this "buzzy" Soho Modern European offers "original decor" (dig the wall of potted plants) but also "unexceptional" eats; hence many opt for the "great bar and lounge" – notwithstanding having to "get past the throng" there.

Reubens *Deli/Jewish* | 20 | 12 | 13 | £25 |

Marylebone | 79 Baker St., W1 (Baker St.) | 020-7486 0035 | fax 7486 7079 | www.reubensrestaurant.co.uk

"Go when you're starving – you'll leave stuffed" from this casual deli-cum–dining room in Marylebone; the "real-deal kosher", "wholesome Jewish-European food" offers "lots for the price, and lots of chatter too"; N.B. closing times vary on Fridays.

🆕 Rhodes Bar-B-Q Ⓜ *BBQ*

Docklands | 61 Wapping Wall, E1 (Wapping) | 020-7474 4289 | www.rhodesbbq.com

No, it's not another Gary Rhodes venue – instead, this tiny yearling is bringing a bit of America's Deep South to the Docklands, with various barbecued meats and the usual sides; patrons are encouraged to write on the white walls.

☑ Rhodes Twenty Four Ⓢ *British* | 23 | 25 | 23 | £59 |

City | Tower 42 | 25 Old Broad St., 24th fl., EC2 (Bank/Liverpool St.) | 020-7877 7703 | fax 7877 7725 | www.rhodes24.co.uk

For "power eating at its best" – with a "spectacular" Pan-London "view thrown in" – chef Gary "Rhodes can always be counted on" at this "airport lounge"-like aerie in a City skyscraper ("security at the building entrance reminds you of a visit to MI5"); the "blessedly short menu" offers a "nouvelle take on Traditional British food", and "service is attentive" – though "mainly to those dining on expenses" some say; it's "not in the same class" as other "expensive" venues, but "the location is the saving grace."

Rhodes W1 Brasserie *British*

Marylebone | Cumberland Hotel | Great Cumberland Pl., W1 (Marble Arch) | 020-7479 3838 | fax 7479 3888 | www.garyrhodes.com

Alongside celebrity chef Gary Rhodes' more rarefied Restaurant in the Cumberland Hotel lies this brasserie/bar behemoth with a nightclub vibe (a DJ spins on weekends) and "trendy" lounge areas; whilst the Modern British fare is "well cooked, it's just not terribly interesting."

🆕 Rhodes W1 Restaurant Ⓢ Ⓜ *British*

Marylebone | Cumberland Hotel | Great Cumberland Place, W1 (Marble Arch) | 020-7479-3737 | fax 7479 3888 | www.rhodesw1.com

The combination of chef Gary Rhodes' sophisticated Modern British menu (including a small-plates offering) and designer Kelly Hoppen's glammed-up decor (dominated by weeping willow–like beaded chandeliers) creates a dramatic setting for this swanky new venue that sits alongside the toque's eponymous Brasserie in the Cumberland Hotel (though it has its own entrance on Bryanston Street).

☑ Rib Room, The *British/Chophouse*

Belgravia | Jumeirah Carlton Tower Hotel | 2 Cadogan Pl., SW1 (Knightsbridge/Sloane Sq.) | 020-7858 7053 | fax 7823 1708 | www.jumeirahcarltontower.com

A "private-club atmosphere" (all "dark wood, brass and leather") "makes a great business destination" out of this Traditional Brit in Belgravia; it might cost "an arm and a leg, but is worth it" for "some of the best beef dishes in London"; "service is excellent if they know you."

	FOOD	DECOR	SERVICE	COST

Riccardo's *Italian*
18 | 11 | 18 | £36

Chelsea | 126 Fulham Rd., SW3 (Gloucester Rd./South Kensington) | 020-7370 6656 | fax 7373 0604

"Bring a crowd, order a bunch, and munch" the "very constant" Tuscan tapas at this "buzzy" Chelsea Italian; some lament the lack of creature comforts ("paper napkins, no tablecloths"), given that "prices have risen" lately; but there's a "great patio for dining" year-round (it's covered).

Richard Corrigan at Lindsay House 🗷 *British/Irish*
23 | 19 | 20 | £71

Soho | 21 Romilly St., W1 (Leicester Sq./Piccadilly Circus) | 020-7439 0450 | fax 7437 7349 | www.lindsayhouse.co.uk

Far "from the maddening crowds of Soho", this "quirky", "cosy" townhouse sets the scene for Richard Corrigan's "Irish-inspired dishes", plus some "amazing" Modern British ones; the experience can be "variable" – "as the restaurant fills, the kitchen is overwhelmed, and service suffers" – but most smile on this "serendipitous find."

Richoux *British*
15 | 15 | 15 | £25

Knightsbridge | 86 Brompton Rd., SW3 (Knightsbridge) | 020-7584 8300 | fax 7589 8547

Mayfair | 41A S. Audley St., W1 (Bond St.) | 020-7629 5228 | fax 7493 4329

Piccadilly | 172 Piccadilly, W1 (Green Park/Piccadilly Circus) | 020-7493 2204 | fax 7495 6658

St. John's Wood | 3 Circus Rd., NW8 (St. John's Wood) | 020-7483 4001 | fax 7483 3810

www.richoux.co.uk

"In a setting right out of Edwardian times" (e.g. "old-fashioned"), this "classic, cutesy" chain of tearooms is a "solid standby" for Traditional British "comfort food" all day (cream tea or "breakfast is best"); if staff move at a "slow pace", that's "perfect" "after a hectic day of shopping."

NEW Ristorante Semplice 🗷 *Italian*
– | – | – | E

Mayfair | 10 Blenheim St., W1 (Bond St.) | 020-7495 1509

With its luxe but "tasteful" decor of polished ebony and gold walls, leather seats and a Murano chandelier, it's hard to believe this Mayfair space used to house a fish 'n' chip shop; now a Northern Italian calls it home, with rich and richly priced dishes "of great promise."

🗷 Ritz, The *British/French*
23 | 27 | 25 | £71

St. James's | Ritz Hotel | 150 Piccadilly, W1 (Green Park) | 020-7300 2370 | fax 7300 2375 | www.theritzlondon.com

"Formality at its finest" reigns at the Ritz Hotel dining room, a "romantic", "regal reminder of a bygone era", complete with a "high level of white-tie service" and highly "enjoyable" Traditional British–Classic French cuisine; a few whisper the "food quality doesn't match the price and fuss", but who else offers the "vintage experience of dinner dances" at weekends – or "the tea of all teas" in the adjacent Palm Court?

| | FOOD | DECOR | SERVICE | COST |

Riva *Italian* ▽ 20 | 13 | 20 | £52

Barnes | 169 Church Rd., SW13 (Hammersmith) | 020-8748 0434 | fax 8748 0434

"Sophisticated", "authentic" Northern Italian *cucina* and an "amazing wine list" have won "a wide following" for this "limited space"; locals love it, even if those outside Barnes bark it's "not brilliant."

Z River Café *Italian* 27 | 22 | 24 | £63

Hammersmith | Thames Wharf | Rainville Rd., W6 (Hammersmith) | 020-7386 4200 | fax 7386 4201 | www.rivercafe.co.uk

Boasting "joyful" "unfussy dishes that showcase exquisite ingredients to beautiful effect", this Italian "evergreen" "never fails to delight", even after 20-plus years; "decor and ambience display a similar lack of pretension, and the informally clad staff clearly enjoy working here"; yes, the Thames-side Hammersmith "location is a problem", but it's "so worth the trip" – especially if you can "sit on the terrace (the view's as good as the food)."

Rivington Grill Bar Deli *British* 20 | 18 | 18 | £36

Greenwich | Greenwich Picturehouse Cinema | 178 Greenwich High Rd., SE10 (Greenwich) | 020-8293 9270 **M**

Shoreditch | 28-30 Rivington St., EC2 (Old St.) | 020-7729 7053 | fax 7729 7086

www.rivingtongrill.co.uk

An "energetic atmosphere" pervades this "popular" duo in "bright, cavernous" Shoreditch premises and within the Greenwich Picturehouse complex; despite its pedigree – same owners as The Ivy and Le Caprice – reviewers report "uneven" experiences with both the "hearty" Traditional British cooking and "friendly" but "slapdash service."

Roast *British* 19 | 23 | 17 | £44

Borough | Borough Mkt. | The Floral Hall, Stoney St., SE1 (London Bridge) | 020-7940 1300 | fax 7940 1301 | www.roast-restaurant.com

This "wonderful-looking", "modern, glass sky box sitting above" "picturesque old" Borough Market is open all day for "adventurous" Modern British grub derived from the grocers below; but sceptics say it "seemed stronger when it first opened" in 2005, citing "so-so food" and "service so slow, it leaves you hanging longer than their meat."

Rocket *Mediterranean* 17 | 17 | 16 | £30

Mayfair | 4 Lancashire Ct., W1 (Bond St.) | 020-7629 2889 | fax 7629 2881 **S**

NEW **City** | 6 Adams Ct., EC2 (Bank/Liverpool St.) | 020-7628 0808 | fax 7628 0809 **S**

Putney | Putney Wharf | Brewhouse St., SW15 (East Putney) | 020-8789 7875 | fax 8789 7876

www.rocketrestaurants.co.uk

The Med menu is "nothing too fancy" – "huge salads", "über-sized pizzas" – but it "hits the spot" at this "casual", good-value" trio in Putney (which "takes advantage of the river views"), in a Mayfair courtyard and in a new, "modern" City locale; staff are "good, but there's never enough of them."

	FOOD	DECOR	SERVICE	COST

Rodizio Rico ● *Brazilian*
15 | 12 | 15 | £27

Islington | 77-78 Upper St., N1 (Angel) | 020-7354 1076 | fax 7359 8952
Bayswater | 111 Westbourne Grove, W2 (Bayswater) | 020-7792 4035 | fax 7243 1401
www.rodizio.co.uk

"Passed 'round on skewers", "the meat just keeps coming" ("vegans need not apply") at these "all-you-can-eat" Brazilian churrascaria joints in Islington and Westbourne Grove; whilst a "decent" option "if you're on a tight budget", it's "a gimmick" growl grouches – the grub's "merely passable."

Roka ● *Japanese*
25 | 20 | 19 | £54

Fitzrovia | 37 Charlotte St., W1 (Goodge St./Tottenham Court Rd.) | 020-7580 6464 | fax 7580 0220 | www.rokarestaurant.com

"Zuma's little sister" in Charlotte Street – a "sexy", "sophisticated room of pale wood and glass" – is "notable in its own right", with a "fantastic robata grill" ("see the chefs at work") and "positively sublime" Japanese dishes at "high prices when everything is so tempting"; "haphazard service" irks some, but all "love lounging in the Shochu" bar downstairs with its "deceptively dangerous cocktails."

Rosmarino *Italian*
17 | 16 | 18 | £44

St. John's Wood | 1 Blenheim Terrace, NW8 (St. John's Wood) | 020-7328 5014 | fax 7625 2779 | www.rosmarino.co.uk

A Food score slide supports the sentiment that this St. John's Wood Italian, cuisinewise, is "not as entertaining as it was", especially given its "steep prices"; but a "comprehensive wine list, including great obscure bottles" mollifies many, and overall, it's "still a nice place", especially on the "lovely summer patio."

☑ Roussillon ⓢ *French*
26 | 23 | 25 | £72

Pimlico | 16 St. Barnabas St., SW1 (Sloane Sq./Victoria) | 020-7730 5550 | fax 7824 8617 | www.roussillon.co.uk

"Deserves to be better known than it is" say fans of this "quiet" Pimlico place with a pleasantly "informal" feel ("like walking into someone's lounge"); but there's nothing casual about chef/co-owner Alexis Gauthier's "high-end, creative" New French cooking that "emphasises vegetables"; with perks like "pampering" service and a "fabulous wine list with one of the smartest sommeliers", it's "worth going on a special occasion – or just to treat yourself."

Rowley's *British*
19 | 19 | 17 | £36

St. James's | 113 Jermyn St., SW1 (Piccadilly Circus) | 020-7930 2707 | fax 7839 4240 | www.rowleys.co.uk

It's "not haute cuisine", but the "speciality beef served with herby butter and a mountain of fries" is why many "become a fan" of this "unchanging" Traditional Brit in St. James's; the "old-world" setting dating back to 1790 offers an "intimate", slightly "formal" environment "ideal for business diners or a romantic evening."

☑ Royal China *Chinese*
24 | 16 | 16 | £30

Marylebone | 24-26 Baker St., W1 (Baker St.) | 020-7487 4688 | fax 7935 7893

(continued)

Royal China

Canary Wharf | 30 Westferry Circus, E14 (Canary Wharf) | 020-7719 0888 | fax 7719 0889

St. John's Wood | 68 Queen's Grove, NW8 (St. John's Wood) | 020-7586 4280 | fax 7722 4750

NEW Fulham | 805 Fulham Rd., SW6 (Parsons Green) | 020-7731 0081 | fax 7384 2998

Bayswater | 13 Queensway, W2 (Queensway) | 020-7221 2535 | fax 7792 5752

www.royalchinagroup.co.uk

"Dim sum as it's meant to be – fast, fabulous" and "freshly prepared" – makes this "crowded" quintet a "real nosher's paradise"; there are also "excellent Cantonese" mains, and "all for a reasonable price", so it's "worth putting up with surly service", "slightly Joan Collins–style black and gold decor" and "about a million other people."

Royal China Club *Chinese*

24 | 18 | 20 | £44

Marylebone | 40-42 Baker St., W1 (Baker St.) | 020-7486 3898 | fax 7486 6977 | www.royalchinaclub.co.uk

"A more refined sister to the Royal China venues", this Chinese "a little off the beaten path on Baker Street" offers "unusual dim sum" "without the queue" and "sparkling" seafood dishes (diners can pick their fish from the tanks on display); "polite service" is appreciated.

Royal Exchange
Grand Café & Bar 🅢 *European*

16 | 22 | 17 | £32

City | The Royal Exchange, The Courtyard, EC3 (Bank) | 020-7618 2480 | fax 7618 2490 | www.royalexchangegrandcafeandbar.com

In the "stunning setting" of the old Royal Exchange's interior central courtyard, this Modern European cafe is "good for a high-class snack" of cold (mainly crustacean) dishes – even if its large atrium makes it a "bit like eating in a fishbowl"; it's also "interesting for happy-hour drinks."

R.S.J. 🅢 *British*

21 | 15 | 20 | £39

Waterloo | 33 Coin St., SE1 (Waterloo) | 020-7928 4554 | fax 7401 2455 | www.rsj.uk.com

"A solid choice when in eye-distance of the National Theatre", this "nifty spot" is most "famous for its wines" ("the Loires are the real attraction"); but "staff are warm", the Modern British fare is "reliably good" and the "pre- and post-theatre menus offer excellent value."

🖻 Rules ● *British/Chophouse*

23 | 25 | 22 | £51

Covent Garden | 35 Maiden Ln., WC2 (Covent Garden) | 020-7836 5314 | fax 7497 1081 | www.rules.co.uk

"Britannia rules" at this 1798 "classic" in Covent Garden, where "classic gentlemen's club decor, with fireplaces and a stags head on the wall" (imagine "Watson and Holmes sitting at the next table") create a "warm, gracious setting" for "delightfully no-nonsense" Traditional British fare ("focused on game") that's "a bit pricey", but "always a treat"; yes, it's "a tourist mecca", and "service can be slow, but we don't care", 'cos there's "nothing like it anywhere in London."

	FOOD	DECOR	SERVICE	COST

Sabor ● *S American*
▽ 22 | 17 | 23 | £30

Islington | 108 Essex Rd., N1 (Angel) | 020-7226 5551 | fax 7288 0880 | www.sabor.co.uk

An "A for effort" is awarded this "lively" Islingtonian – an "odd-shaped room" peppered with "cool" carnival masks and other Amazonian knickknacks, serving "satisfying" South American fare from a "reasonably priced" menu of "iconic dishes"; a "great wine list and friendly service" add to its appeal.

Saki Bar & Food Emporium ⊠ *Japanese*
- | - | - | E

Smithfield | 4 W. Smithfield, EC1 (Barbican/Farringdon) | 020-7489 7033 | www.saki-food.com

Whether it be the modern, black-and-red-hued basement restaurant, or the street-level deli/noodle bar, there's a "good assortment of Japanese specialities and the biggest sake list ever seen" at this Smithfield venue; surveyors also "have to comment on the toilets" that spray water from below – an "interesting" experience to say the least.

Sakura *Japanese*
23 | 9 | 12 | £27

Mayfair | 9 Hanover St., W1 (Oxford Circus) | 020-7629 2961

"It can be very busy and pretty noisy, but the sushi is fresh, good" and "unbeatable for the price" at this "shabby" "authentic Japanese dive" near Oxford Circus; "you have to wait too long to get in, but service is lightning fast once you get seated."

Sale e Pepe ●⊠ *Italian*
20 | 16 | 22 | £44

Knightsbridge | 9-15 Pavilion Rd., SW1 (Knightsbridge) | 020-7235 0098 | fax 7225 1210 | www.saleepepe.co.uk

"After all these years" (34 to be precise), this "crowded, clubby trattoria" in a Knightsbridge backstreet is a "real favourite" thanks to "entertaining", "singing waiters" (some seeming to "have been around since Pompeii got levelled") who serve "consistently good" "traditional Italian food" with "a smile and irreverence."

Salisbury, The *British*
- | - | - | M

Fulham | 21 Sherbrooke Rd., SW6 (Fulham Broadway/Parsons Green) | 020-7381 4005 | fax 7381 1002 | www.thesalisbury.co.uk

This "classic pub" in Fulham was revamped recently, and now a whimsically modern dining area is paired with a "sound, simple" Traditional British menu; whilst "service is a bit spotty", and there's "more braying than in a farmyard", many will "still go back."

Salloos ●⊠ *Pakistani*
23 | 16 | 20 | £45

Belgravia | 62-64 Kinnerton St., SW1 (Hyde Park Corner/Knightsbridge) | 020-7235 4444

For over 30 years, this "terrific, upscale Pakistani on an easy-to-miss side street" in Belgravia has been known for "spicy" "northwestern frontier cuisine at its best"; though this family-run venue's "no bargain", the "passionate service" makes it feel "like eating at your grandmother's."

	FOOD	DECOR	SERVICE	COST

Salt Yard ⊠ European
22 | 15 | 19 | £35

Fitzrovia | 54 Goodge St., W1 (Goodge St.) | 020-7637 0657 |
fax 7580 7435 | www.saltyard.co.uk

"Not for the faint-of-hearing", this Fitzrovian spread over two "very busy" floors places "an emphasis on tapas" ("oh, those courgette flowers!") that "elevates the concept to a new level"; there are also "reasonably priced" Modern Euro mains served by "accommodating staff."

Salusbury Pub & Dining Room *Italian/Mediterranean*
▽ 18 | 13 | 13 | £29

Kilburn | 50-52 Salusbury Rd., NW6 (Queen's Park) | 020-7328 3286

"Well-thought-out", "homemade"-tasting Italian-Med "gastropub grub" "compensates for the noise and folksy decor" that's looking "rather jaded" at this "popular" (some say "too popular") Queen's Park haunt; N.B. their deli next door sells mainly organic fare.

Sam's Brasserie & Bar ● European
20 | 20 | 20 | £38

Chiswick | Barley Mow Ctr. | 11 Barley Mow Passage, W4 (Chiswick Park) | 020-8987 0555 | fax 8987 7389 | www.samsbrasserie.co.uk

It's "still a bit of a secret in Chiswick", but those who know the "omnipresent" Sam Harrison's "bright" brasserie – where "anyone from grandma to trendsetters" feels at home – appreciate its "imaginative" Modern Euro menu; but foes fret about "appalling acoustics" ("none of our party could hear each other") and find it "overpriced."

San Lorenzo ●⊠⇴ *Italian*
20 | 17 | 18 | £58

Knightsbridge | 22 Beauchamp Pl., SW3 (Knightsbridge) | 020-7584 1074 | fax 7584 1142

San Lorenzo Fuoriporta *Italian*

Wimbledon | 38 Wimbledon Hill Rd., SW19 (Wimbledon) | 020-8946 8463 | fax 8947 9810
www.sanlorenzo.com

"Some people love it, some people don't get it", but Mara and Lorenzo Berni's Knightsbridge "institution" "still packs them in", offering "the occasional celebrity sighting"; "behind the hype and hoopla is some very good Italian food" and "gracious" service, although it's "annoying" they "still do not accept credit cards"; P.S. the branch run by the Bernis' boys remains "a staple" during Wimbledon.

Santa Lucia ● *Italian*
▽ 22 | 16 | 19 | £32

Chelsea | 2 Hollywood Rd., SW10 (South Kensington) | 020-7352 8484 | fax 7351 2390

"An Italian neighbourhood place", this "cosy" Chelsea venue serves up pizza and other staples that are "surprisingly good" "and certainly reasonably priced"; but sometimes it becomes "too crowded", and decorators dis the Neapolitan farmhouse look as "tired."

Santini *Italian*
22 | 18 | 21 | £52

Belgravia | 29 Ebury St., SW1 (Victoria) | 020-7730 4094 | fax 7730 0544 | www.santini-restaurant.com

In the "foodie desert that is Victoria", this "long-time neighbourhood Italian" a stone's throw away delights disciples with its "good, not faddish food" and "beautiful patio" (especially "now the traffic flow has been changed"); but cynics find it an "overpriced, overhectic" venue, with "service that's efficient, but could be more amiable."

Sarastro ● *Mediterranean* 12 | 21 | 13 | £37

Covent Garden | 126 Drury Ln., WC2 (Covent Garden) | 020-7836 0101 | fax 7379 4666 | www.sarastro-restaurant.com

For "offbeat", "kitschy decor", "operatic interludes" and a "joyful, dotty theatrical ambience", this "unusual" Drury Lane venue "needs to be seen to be believed", but if you are looking for "gastronomy – no", the Mediterranean "food remains disappointing", not helped by "seriously poor" service.

Sardo 🎇 *Italian* 23 | 15 | 20 | £45

Fitzrovia | 45 Grafton Way, W1 (Warren St.) | 020-7387 2521 | fax 7387 2559 | www.sardo-restaurant.com

"Luscious Sardinian cuisine", "authentic and imaginative", sets apart this "lively" "neighbourhood Italian" in Fitzrovia; the "small" surroundings can be "claustrophobic", but all appreciate "polite staff" and a "wine list full of affordable choices" from The Boot.

Sardo Canale *Italian* 20 | 19 | 16 | £42

Primrose Hill | 42 Gloucester Ave., NW1 (Camden Town/Chalk Farm) | 020-7722 2800 | www.sardocanale.com

This Sardo sib in a "lovely setting" – a "romantic" courtyard with an ancient olive tree beside Regent's Park canal – offers a "hearty" Sardinian menu (with "some uncommon dishes") that "doesn't disappoint", even if "the prices seem high"; "service can be uneven, but is always anxious to please."

Sarkhel's Ⓜ *Indian* 22 | 12 | 20 | £29

Wimbledon | 197-199 Replingham Rd., SW18 (Southfields) | 020-8870 1483 | fax 8871 0808 | www.sarkhels.com

"Tantalising Indian dishes", "closely supervised by star chef Udit Sarkhel", "drown out the shoddy" decor at this Southfields site; given the area's culinary limits, it retains its "legendary" status, even as nostalgists sigh it's "not what it was" – or perhaps the problem's that it *is* what it was ("the menu hasn't changed for years").

Sartoria 🎇 *Italian* 20 | 20 | 19 | £49

Mayfair | 20 Savile Row, W1 (Oxford Circus/Piccadilly Circus) | 020-7534 7000 | fax 7534 7070 | www.sartoriabar.co.uk

This "large, airy dining room plus bar" has a "sophisticated", if "subdued" ambience as it serves "consistent" Italian fare and wines; whilst "not a destination", it's "ideal for business or treating elderly relatives", as all leave "feeling as good as any of the bespoke suits made next door on Savile Row."

Satsuma *Japanese* 20 | 14 | 16 | £24

Soho | 56 Wardour St., W1 (Leicester Sq./Piccadilly Circus) | 020-7437 8338 | fax 7437 3389

The "communal seating invites camaraderie" at this "convivial" canteen in Soho, where a "young, hip crowd" congregate for "easy-on-the-wallet" Japanese fare, including "killer bento boxes" and now noodles; the "no-nonsense" service is "handy in a hurry."

Sauterelle 🅱 *French*

— | — | — | E

City | The Royal Exchange | The Courtyard, EC3 (Bank) | 020-7618 2483 | fax 7618 2490 | www.restaurantsauterelle.co.uk

A "great setting in the Royal Exchange", overlooking the historic courtyard, makes an "unusual" backdrop for the "fresh", fish-oriented cuisine at this Classic French; if a handful find it "slightly disappointing given the grand" surrounds, most agree it's "a good experience overall" (even if the "toilets are far away").

🛛 Savoy Grill *British*

24 | 24 | 24 | £61

Covent Garden | Savoy Hotel | The Strand, WC2 (Covent Garden/Embankment) | 020-7592 1600 | fax 7592 1601 | www.gordonramsay.com

Whilst the Savoy's closure for renovation in late 2007 looms large, there's still time to sample its "sumptuous", art deco-styled dining room where Marcus Wareing's "top-drawer" Modern British fare and "silky smooth", "savvy service" "make one want to fight for Queen and country"; if a few rebels baulk at the "stuffy undercurrent" and "über-expensive" prices, patriots are pleased with this power brokers' haunt.

Scalini ◗ *Italian*

23 | 16 | 20 | £45

Chelsea | 1-3 Walton St., SW3 (Knightsbridge/South Kensington) | 020-7225 2301 | fax 7581 4224

Aged 20, this trattoria "around the corner from Harrods" remains one of "the buzzing-est Italians" around, with "great celebrity-spotting" and "plenty of eye-candy" squeezed "sardine-style" into seats; the "old-style" food's "as good as ever", if "a bit overpriced"; but what irks most are the "acoustically appalling" digs that "badly need an update."

Scott's *Seafood*

22 | 23 | 19 | £63

Mayfair | 20 Mount St., W1 (Bond St.) | 020-7495 7309 | fax 7629 5457 | www.scotts-restaurant.com

It's "fabulous to have this veteran back, and oh, so much better" after the "striking refurb" given it by "the same ownership" as The Ivy; the Mayfair premises now boast a "chic" oak-panelled look and "flavoursome" fish and game, plus a "magnificent oyster bar"; only, staff are "not yet up to scratch for the prices."

Seashell 🅱 *Seafood*

20 | 9 | 14 | £24

Marylebone | 49-51 Lisson Grove, NW1 (Marylebone) | 020-7224 9000 | fax 7724 9071 | www.seashellrestaurant.co.uk

It looks "nothing fancy" ("shabby" in truth) and "service is painfully slow", but this Marylebone veteran offers the "quintessential London" experience of "perfectly fried fish accompanied by the typical" trimmings, like "top-notch chips" or "delicious mushy peas."

🆕 1707 Wine Bar *British*

22 | 21 | 22 | £30

Piccadilly | Fortnum & Mason | 181 Piccadilly, W1 (Green Park/Piccadilly Circus) | 020-7734 8040 | fax 7437 3278

"Well done, Fortnum's, for entering the 21st century with such style" – in the shape of this "classy" new David Collins–designed wine bar (named for F&M's year of birth), which makes the most of the retailer's "wonderful wine selection"; it's supported by Traditional British snacks prepared in the Piccadilly premises' adjacent Food Halls – so "where can you go wrong?"

Shanghai Blues ● *Chinese* | 21 | 22 | 21 | £36 |

Holborn | 193-197 High Holborn, WC1 (Holborn) | 020-7404 1668 | fax 7404 1448 | www.shanghaiblues.co.uk

"Tucked away in Holborn", this "warming" restaurant/bar is "appealing for both business and pleasure"; "although slightly pricier than Chinatown" venues nearby, the "innovative dim sum" (noon–5 PM) and "succulent" Chinese mains are "beautifully presented"; P.S. it gets "busy on Friday and Saturday nights when live [jazz] music plays."

Shepherd's ⊠ *British* | 18 | 17 | 21 | £44 |

Westminster | Marsham Ct., Marsham St., SW1 (Pimlico) | 020-7834 9552 | fax 7233 6047 | www.langansrestaurants.co.uk

Attracting a "high-wattage" Westminster crowd of "top cops and a smattering of politicians", this "charming", "clubby" haunt turns out Traditional British "comfort food" that's "good", if "not inventive", served by "cheery staff"; though "looking its age a little", it's still "comfortable" for a "quiet" meal.

Shogun ⊠ *Japanese* ▽ | 23 | 11 | 19 | £51 |

Mayfair | Millennium Hotel Mayfair | Adam's Row, W1 (Bond St.) | 020-7493 1255 | fax 7493 1255 | www.millenniumhotels.com

The "owner greets everyone as an old friend" at this "authentic Japanese experience" in a Mayfair basement, and whilst the "decor is rather depressing", it's a "consistent performer" when it comes to "excellent food"; but beware, "the bill can mount up alarmingly."

Signor Sassi ●⊠ *Italian* | 22 | 17 | 20 | £48 |

Knightsbridge | 14 Knightsbridge Green, SW1 (Knightsbridge) | 020-7584 2277 | fax 7225 3953

It's "fun to watch the waiters" "sing to the diners" at this "always full and noisy" Knightsbridge trattoria; whilst the "nothing-too-fancy" Italian *cucina* is "not cheap", it's "well executed"; P.S. "is what you want not on the menu? – no problem, they'll make it for you!"

Silks & Spice *Thai* | 16 | 13 | 15 | £23 |

City | Temple Ct. | 11 Queen Victoria St., EC4 (Bank/Mansion House) | 020-7248 7878 | fax 7248 9595 ⊠
Camden Town | 28 Chalk Farm Rd., NW10 (Camden Town/Chalk Farm) | 020-7482 2228 | fax 7482 3382
Chiswick | 95 Chiswick High Rd., W4 (Turnham Green) | 020-8995 7991 | fax 8994 7773
www.silksandspice.net

The Southeast Asian fare's only "average", but it's spiced by "generous portions" and "convenient locations" at this trio in Chiswick ("mind the sneaky [street] parking restrictions"), Chalk Farm and the City, an "overcrowded" outpost that turns into a nightclub on Thursdays–Fridays, "making conversation impossible."

	FOOD	DECOR	SERVICE	COST

Simpson's-in-the-Strand *British*

20 | 22 | 21 | £52

Covent Garden | 100 The Strand, WC2 (Charing Cross) | 020-7836 9112 |
fax 7836 1381 | www.fairmont.com/savoy

"As British as the changing of the guard", this "grand old icon" in
Covent Garden is a "throwback" to a "more genteel era", serving
from an "old-style carvery" trolley "full of meat" ("don't forget to tip
the carver") amidst "dark, panelled" "Hogwarts decor"; whilst some
"people put it down", claiming it has "lost its zing from eons past",
it's "still worth a visit for the tradition."

Singapore Garden *SE Asian*
21 | 17 | 19 | £32

Swiss Cottage | 83-83A Fairfax Rd., NW6 (Swiss Cottage) |
020-7328 5314 | fax 7624 0656 | www.singaporegarden.co.uk

A recent "refurb has given a new spark of life" – not to mention a
higher Decor score – to this "popular" Asian; though set in "out-of-
the-way" Swiss Cottage, it's "almost a destination" in its own right,
thanks to its "offbeat" but "lovely" Singaporean-Malay menu, proffered by "charming, pretty waitresses."

Singapura Ⓩ *SE Asian*
▽ 20 | 17 | 18 | £29

Blackfriars | 1-2 Limeburner Ln., EC4 (Blackfriars/St. Paul's) |
020-7329 1133 | fax 7236 1805
City | 31 Broadgate Circle, EC2 (Liverpool St.) | 020-7256 5045
City | 78-79 Leadenhall St., EC3 (Aldgate/Tower Hill) | 020-7929 0089 |
fax 7621 0366
www.singapuras.co.uk

"The takeaway queues can frustrate, but pay testament to the high
quality" of the fare at this Singaporean-Thai trio; their "dangerously
addictive" dishes make them a "favourite lunchtime destination" for
City folk (only the Blackfriars branch is open at night).

NEW Sitaaray ● *Indian*
- | - | - | M

Covent Garden | 167 Drury Ln., WC2 (Covent Garden/Holborn) |
020-7269 6422 | www.sitaaray.com

Housed in cramped digs above sister Tamarai, this Covent Garden
newcomer features a tongue-in-cheek cinematic theme (posters,
memorabilia, revolving lights, etc.) that pays homage to Hindi and
Bollywood movies (the name translates as 'stars'); the competitively priced Indian menu is biased towards the Northwest Frontier.

Six13 Ⓩ *Eclectic*
▽ 19 | 19 | 21 | £43

Marylebone | 19 Wigmore St., W1 (Bond St./Oxford Circus) |
020-7629 6133 | fax 7629 6135 | www.six13.com

"You don't leave feeling hungry" after sampling the Eclectic menu
running the gamut from sushi to steaks at this kosher venue (hence,
no dairy products) in Marylebone; despite a "nice" olive-and-tan,
art deco-ish setting, it is "too expensive" for some wallets.

Ⓩ Sketch – The Gallery Ⓩ *European*
19 | 26 | 18 | £61

Mayfair | 9 Conduit St., W1 (Oxford Circus) | 087-0777 4488 |
fax 7629 1684 | www.sketch.uk.com

"Eat among art and beautiful people" at this "funky" Mayfair spot
that morphs from art gallery to "dramatic" dining room at night,

with videos and music – oh, and you "must check out the [egglike] bathroom pods"; some suggest "if the decor were less 'out there', people would notice the wildly creative Modern European food" is "surprisingly good"; still, most "diners are there to be seen"; speaking of seeing, "where's the waiter?"

☑ Sketch – The Lecture Room & Library 🖪🅼 *European*

FOOD	DECOR	SERVICE	COST
21	27	23	£95

Mayfair | 9 Conduit St., W1 (Oxford Circus) | 087-0777 4488 | fax 7629 1684 | www.sketch.uk.com

"Big, comfortable armchairs envelop you as you talk in hushed tones" at this "magnificent" Mayfair dining room, "one of the most luxurious in London" ("the crystal bathrooms are a dream"); the "inspired, imaginative" Modern European menu is "really expensive", but it needs to be to "cover the costs of producing such complicated" – some say "fussy" – dishes; all's brought by "agreeable staff"; P.S. downstairs is The Parlour, "a great place for tea with a trendy crowd."

NEW Skylon *European*

FOOD	DECOR	SERVICE	COST
–	–	–	E

South Bank | Royal Festival Hall | Belvedere Rd., SE1 (Waterloo) | 020-7654 7800 | fax 7684 7801 | www.skylonrestaurant.co.uk

Named after an iconic attraction from the 1951 Festival of Britain, this confident newcomer in the newly revamped Royal Festival Hall offers a dramatic panoramic view across the Thames; a casual, hardwood-floored grill and smarter, retro-looking restaurant – both serving different incarnations of a Modern European menu from chef Helena Puolakka (ex Fifth Floor) – act as stylish bookends to an airy cocktail bar in the centre of the cavernous space.

Smiths of Smithfield – Dining Room 🖪 *British*

FOOD	DECOR	SERVICE	COST
20	18	17	£37

Smithfield | 67-77 Charterhouse St., 2nd fl., EC1 (Barbican/Farringdon) | 020-7251 7950 | fax 7236 0488 | www.smithsofsmithfield.co.uk

One of several dining options in the building opposite Smithfield Market, this Modern British "meat-lover's paradise" is a "huge room with great energy" and "the place to go" for "incredible cuts" and staples like a "perfect pork belly"; unlike the pricier upstairs, however, "here your steak costs £12 rather than £28, the difference being smaller portions and less choice."

Smiths of Smithfield – Top Floor *British/Chophouse*

FOOD	DECOR	SERVICE	COST
20	20	19	£52

Smithfield | 67-77 Charterhouse St., EC1 (Barbican/Farringdon) | 020-7251 7950 | fax 7236 0488 | www.smithsofsmithfield.co.uk

You "have to be a serious carnivore", since "superb steaks" star at this unashamedly meat-heavy Traditional Brit; but foes fume that the rest of the menu is "nothing out of the ordinary, given the price range" – in particular, "side dishes could be improved"; and whilst the "lovely terrace" offers "breathtaking views" "over the roofs of Smithfield", the "spartan" brick interior makes the place "vibrant or loud depending on your point of view."

	FOOD	DECOR	SERVICE	COST

Smollensky's
American Bar & Grill *Chophouse*
15 | 17 | 15 | £32

Covent Garden | 105 The Strand, WC2 (Charing Cross/Covent Garden) | 020-7497 2101 | fax 7836 3270
Canary Wharf | 1 Reuters Plaza, E14 (Canary Wharf) | 020-7719 0101 | fax 7719 0060
Tower Bridge | Hermitage Wharf | 22 Wapping High St., E1 (Tower Hill/Wapping) | 020-7680 1818 | fax 7680 1787 Ⓜ
Hammersmith | Bradmore House | Queen Caroline St., W6 (Hammersmith) | 020-8741 8124 | fax 8741 5695
www.smollenskys.co.uk

This imported chain seems to have an identity crisis: it pulls in office parties and "the after-work crowd" with "great cocktails" and disco or "live music", but it's also "suitable for all ages" with clowns at the Sunday kids' brunch; but diners have no doubts about the "standard American steaks and burgers" – "about as memorable as what your brother-in-law got you last Christmas" – and the "slapdash service."

Snows on the Green Ⓢ *British*
▽ 21 | 16 | 20 | £35

Shepherd's Bush | 166 Shepherd's Bush Rd., W6 (Hammersmith) | 020-7603 2142 | fax 7602 7553 | www.snowsonthegreen.co.uk

"Thank heaven for Snows" – "the oasis in our desert" sigh Brook Green locals of this "relaxed" bistro; the Modern British menu changes with the seasons but "signature dishes like foie gras and fried egg" are perennial favourites; one aspect gets an icy reception: the sometimes graphic black-and-white Bill Brandt photos ("not every diner's cup of tea").

Sofra ❶ *Turkish*
19 | 13 | 17 | £25

Covent Garden | 36 Tavistock St., WC2 (Covent Garden) | 020-7240 3773 | fax 7836 6633
Marylebone | 1 St. Christopher's Pl., W1 (Bond St.) | 020-7224 4080 | fax 7224 0022
Mayfair | 18 Shepherd St., W1 (Green Park) | 020-7493 3320 | fax 7499 8282
St. John's Wood | 11 Circus Rd., NW8 (St. John's Wood) | 020-7586 9889 | fax 7586 8778
www.sofra.co.uk

The signature "mezze is a riot of fresh tastes" at this "reliable Turkish chain" around town; purists pout the fare's "not as authentic as it should be", but it does "provide value for money that can't be beaten in central London"; alfresco options in some locations compensate for "rather cramped surroundings."

Soho House ❶ *British*
18 | 19 | 19 | £42

Private club; inquiries: 020-7734 5188

"It's members only", but once inside the "quirky Georgian townhouse", it's "star-spotting all the way" at this Soho scenester (indeed, the "volume level of the media folk can be irritating"); "courteous servers" offer up Modern British "food that's better than you'd expect", and whilst it's "quite expensive, you're paying for the chance to chat to a Hollywood A-lister over the toilet basins."

	FOOD	DECOR	SERVICE	COST

Soho Spice ● *Indian*

20 | 14 | 17 | £24

Soho | 124-126 Wardour St., W1 (Tottenham Court Rd.) |
020-7434 0808 | fax 7434 0799 | www.sohospice.co.uk

"Be prepared to wait in line for this spicy Indian eatery" that has "a
flair for [fare] with an edge" and a "Bollywood-meets–Austin Powers
vibe"; popular with Soho theatre-goers, an "edgy after-work crowd"
and those seeking "a post-pub bite", "it can be very noisy", but the
"low-cost" eats are worth it.

Solly's *Mideastern*

17 | 13 | 11 | £27

Golders Green | 148A Golders Green Rd., NW11 (Golders Green) |
020-8455 2121 | fax 8455 0061

"In a neighbourhood full of Kedassia stickers", this recently
enlarged "bit of Tel Aviv in Golders Green" draws both kosher fans
and an "appreciative non-Jewish clientele"; they come for the
"delicious Middle Eastern food" and stay for the "lively, almost
comical" atmosphere, but everybody kvetches about the
"consistently horrendous" service.

Song Que Café *SE Asian*

∇ 20 | 7 | 10 | £17

Shoreditch | 134 Kingsland Rd., E2 (Old St.) | 020-7613 3222

This Southeast Asian is "a popular place to name-check for many
Shoreditch residents" who can't get enough of the "amazing
Vietnamese food" – including "phantastic pho" – at "superb value";
small wonder "there's usually a queue late on Friday and Saturday."

Sonny's *European*

21 | 18 | 19 | £40

Barnes | 94 Church Rd., SW13 (Hammersmith) | 020-8748 0393 |
fax 8748 2698 | www.sonnys.co.uk

A "new chef has really improved things" at this Modern European, a
"favourite" of the "Barnes set"; in the main restaurant, "fresh ingredients" make for "well-executed", French-influenced meals, whilst
those on a budget can try the adjacent deli or the cafe, which is
"good for light lunches"; "nice venue, nice staff – all in all, very nice."

☑ Sophie's
Steakhouse & Bar ● *American/Chophouse*

23 | 18 | 19 | £33

Chelsea | 311-313 Fulham Rd., SW10 (South Kensington) |
020-7352 0088 | fax 7349 9776 | www.sophiessteakhouse.com

This "boisterous local hangout for the Fulham Road set" is "perpetually packed" with "young Sloanes" who rave about the British
"cracking bits of meat" ("great steaks" to you and me) and the "excellent desserts" ("ask for the banoffee pie"); the "no-booking policy means it's a no-no for big groups", but the waits make for a
"buzzing bar scene"; P.S. the "American-style weekend brunches"
are "more relaxed."

Sotheby's Cafe ☒ *British*

19 | 16 | 19 | £30

Mayfair | Sotheby's Auction House | 34 New Bond St., W1 (Bond St./
Oxford Circus) | 020-7293 5077 | fax 7293 6993 | www.sothebys.com

A good bid during the day (it serves breakfast, "lunch and tea only"),
this "upscale", "tiny spot" off the lobby in Sotheby's is "handy for

Bond Street shoppers and auction-goers" who peruse the catalogues over "rich" Modern British food; but what really ups its estimate is the "wonderful people-watching", with many "art movers-and-shakers to view."

Souk ◗ African
| | 18 | 22 | 16 | £24 |

Soho | 27 Litchfield St., WC2 (Leicester Sq.) | 020-7240 1796 | fax 7240 3382

Souk Medina ◗ African
Covent Garden | 1A Short's Gdns., WC2 (Covent Garden) | 020-7240 1796
www.soukrestaurant.co.uk

"Walking through caves makes you feel you are on an Indiana Jones-style mission to dine" at this North African duo, whose "kasbah setting" is a world away from the West End; "be prepared to sit on the floor" and balance "decently priced", "delightful food" on "woven mats", "with hookah and coffee afterward"; P.S. "belly dancers abound" Thursday–Saturday.

Spago ◗ Italian
| | 19 | 14 | 14 | £37 |

South Kensington | 6 Glendower Pl., SW7 (South Kensington) | 020-7225 2407

A real "find near the V&A and Natural History museums", this "lively neighbourhood Italian" is "where the pretty bankers go" to fuel up on "huge, well-prepared pizzas" and other "classic dishes"; also "very Italian is the hit-and-miss service", but that makes it "quite a fun place whenever there's a *calcio* (football) game on."

Spiga Italian
| | 15 | 13 | 16 | £29 |

Soho | 84-86 Wardour St., W1 (Leicester Sq./Piccadilly Circus) | 020-7734 3444 | fax 7734 3332 | www.vpmg.net

Supporters swear this "Soho standby" is a "reliable if unexciting Italian" that's "good for a business-type lunch", especially given the "gentle pricing"; but foes fume the food's "not what it used to be", and the "tacky" decor "needs freshening up."

NEW Spread Eagle French
| | ▽ 21 | 21 | 16 | £54 |

Greenwich | 1-2 Stockwell St., SE10 (Greenwich) | 020-8853 2333 | fax 8293 1024 | www.spreadeaglerestaurant.com

There's been a restaurant on this Greenwich site for over 350 years, and some say the "recent reinvention" has brought these "cranky old dining rooms" "up to West End standards" with exclusively prix fixe menus and local "artwork that's well worth a little look"; still, loyalists lament the fare "has lost its true French flair."

☒ Square, The French
| | 28 | 24 | 26 | £87 |

Mayfair | 6-10 Bruton St., W1 (Bond St./Green Park) | 020-7495 7100 | fax 7495 7150 | www.squarerestaurant.com

"Fantastic food", "faultless service", "my favourite" fawn fans of this "grown-up", "elegant eatery off Bond Street" that maintains its edge with an "inventive take on Classic French" food, a "gigantic wine list" and "understated" decor that has gotten "warmer after a make-over"; "though the set lunch is reasonable, it's very expensive for dinner" – better "bring your Black Amex" – but that doesn't stop it from being "simply the best all-rounder in London."

Sri Nam 🗷 *Thai*

| 18 | 16 | 14 | £28 |

Canary Wharf | 10 Cabot Sq., E14 (Canary Wharf) | 020-7715 9515 | fax 7715 9528 | www.orientalrestaurantgroup.co.uk

"Nicely positioned between the dives and the unaffordable of Canary Wharf", this "solid Thai" soldiers on, with staff who are "whizzed off their feet at lunchtime"; it's "a good place to catch a bite to eat and a beer after work", but be sure to "go upstairs for less noise."

NEW St. Alban ● *European*

| 21 | 18 | 23 | £51 |

Piccadilly | 4-12 Regent St., SW1 (Piccadilly Circus) | 020-7499 8558 | www.stalban.net

"Cool, sophisticated" and "celebrity-filled", this Modern European is "the latest Jeremy King/Chris Corbin outlet" (think The Wolseley); "charming, unobtrusive" staff serve up "robust" "culinary combinations" like "sublime slow-roasted pig"; and whilst the "grammar school cafeteria meets airport lounge" decor isn't to everyone's taste, most feel the "promise is high" at this Piccadilly premises.

NEW Stanza ●🗷 *British*

| – | – | – | M |

Soho | 93-107 Shaftesbury Ave., W1 (Leicester Sq.) | 020-7494 3240 | fax 7494 3050 | www.stanzalondon.com

Overlooking Shaftesbury Avenue, the former Teatro space is now a hip, laid-back eatery with competitively priced Modern British cuisine that plays up the provenance of its ingredients, supported by a succinct wine list; there's also a spacious bar with curved orange banquettes and a 3 AM license; P.S. the old private members' club adjacent has been reincarnated as a casual all-day venue.

Star of India ● *Indian*

| 24 | 18 | 20 | £33 |

South Kensington | 154 Old Brompton Rd., SW5 (Gloucester Rd./ South Kensington) | 020-7373 2901 | fax 7373 5664

Serving up "delicious" "Indian comfort food" (plus "some surprises") to the "denizens of Brompton", this "old faithful" is "up and running again" after a "long-overdue refit"; the now-"fresh interior" and "family-type service" keep fans flocking back.

NEW St. Germain ● *French*

| ▽ 21 | 18 | 20 | £34 |

Farringdon | 89-90 Turnmill St., EC1 (Farringdon) | 020-7336 0949 | fax 7336 0948 | www.stgermain.info

Set in a 19th-century print house, this spacious, "seriously nice" newcomer to the Farringdon foodie scene is already luring a "lively crowd in the evenings" with "French brasserie–style comfort food", served in a monochrome mod "open space" of black-and-white checkerboard floors, striped walls and hanging lamps.

Sticky Fingers *American*

| 14 | 18 | 14 | £24 |

Kensington | 1A Phillimore Gdns., W8 (High St. Kensington) | 020-7938 5338 | fax 7937 0145 | www.stickyfingers.co.uk

"The crowd seems younger than the Rolling Stones memorabilia that decorates" this "truly American", kid-friendly Kensington burger/ribs joint; but "without the Stones connection, it would be pretty ordinary" grouch grumps who counsel "consider it on half-price Mondays – otherwise stay away."

St. James's Restaurant 🛭 *British*　　　20 - 21 £38

St. James's | Fortnum & Mason | 181 Piccadilly, 4th fl., W1 (Picadilly Circus) | 020-7734 8040 | fax 7437 3278 | www.fortnumandmason.co.uk

"Check if renovations are complete" before entering this "establishment embedded in" Fortnum's, slated to reopen autumn 2007; the refurb includes decor by David Collins and a new but still Traditional British menu, including, one trusts, a "high tea fit for the queen."

🖬 St. John 🛭 *British*　　　25 16 20 £48

Smithfield | 26 St. John St., EC1 (Farringdon) | 020-7251 0848 | fax 7251 4090 | www.stjohnrestaurant.com

"Eating a pig's eyeball was never so much fun" swear supporters of this "snout-to-tail" Smithfield Modern Brit, "after 14 years still trendsetting" in its use of animal "innards in all their glory"; some beef that the "bare-white" "dreary decor" detracts, but the only moan of most is that "the best 'bits' often sell out quickly."

St. John Bread & Wine *British*　　　22 17 20 £34

Spitalfields | 94-96 Commercial St., E1 (Liverpool St.) | 020-7251 0848 | fax 7247 8924 | www.stjohnbreadandwine.com

The "less formal" ("still more art crowd than suits, thank God") Spitalfields "offshoot of St. John" has a smaller menu well-suited to "wine-soaked lunches"; expect "tasty English cuisine" in the same vein as its parent with lots of "funny animal bits" and "wonderful bread"; the "open kitchen and bakery add to the noise, but also the charm."

Strada *Italian*　　　18 15 17 £23

Holborn | 6 Great Queen St., WC2 (Holborn) | 020-7405 6293 | fax 7405 6284

Marylebone | 9-10 Market Pl., W1 (Oxford Circus) | 020-7580 4644 | fax 7580 7877

Mayfair | 15-16 New Burlington St., W1 (Oxford Circus) | 020-7287 5967 | fax 7287 6047

Clerkenwell | 8-10 Exmouth Mkt., EC1 (Farringdon) | 020-7278 0800 | fax 7278 6901

Islington | 105-106 Upper St., N1 (Angel) | 020-7226 9742 | fax 7226 9187

Clapham | 102-104 Clapham High St., SW4 (Clapham North) | 020-7627 4847 | fax 7720 2153

Clapham | 11-13 Battersea Rise, SW11 (Clapham Junction) | 020-7801 0794 | fax 7801 0754

Earl's Court | 237 Earl's Court Rd., SW5 (Earl's Ct.) | 020-7835 1180 | fax 7835 2093

Fulham | 175 New King's Rd., SW6 (Parsons Green) | 020-7731 6404 | fax 7731 1431

Wimbledon | 91 Wimbledon High St., SW19 (Wimbledon) | 020-8946 4363

www.strada.co.uk

Additional locations throughout London

"Easy and convenient", this "reasonably priced" Italian "chain that doesn't feel like a chain" is a "reliable solution" "if you don't want to cook" or are seeking "a safe bet with kids"; the "imaginative wood-fired oven pizzas" and "complimentary bottled water" place it "a cut above", "and the staff aren't too rude", either.

NEW Suka ◑ *Malaysian* — | — | — | VE

Fitzrovia | Sanderson Hotel | 50 Berners St., W1 (Oxford Circus/Goodge St.) | 020-7300 1444 | fax 7300 1488 | www.morganshotelgroup.com

Collaborating with acclaimed NYC chef Zak Pelaccio, Fitzrovia's Sanderson Hotel has replaced Spoon with this high-priced Malaysian, whose elevated tables are illuminated by a sea of low-slung ceiling lights; sharing and grazing is encouraged by the well-spiced menu with Western influences, which is also served on the calming, pond-filled terrace.

Sumosan ◑ *Japanese* 20 | 17 | 17 | £60

Mayfair | 26 Albemarle St., W1 (Green Park) | 020-7495 5999 | fax 7355 1247 | www.sumosan.com

"In the same style as Nobu and Zuma", this venue "has the makings of a top restaurant", with "neat, modern-style Japanese food" and a lower profile that means "you can always get a table"; "however, it lets itself down with space-cadet service", "lack of atmosphere" and cuisine that's "good, but not as great as it used to be"; "this being Mayfair, it's still very expensive", though.

☑ Sweetings ☒ *British/Seafood* 24 | 18 | 19 | £40

City | 39 Queen Victoria St., EC4 (Mansion House) | 020-7248 3062

It's weekday lunch only at this "noisy" City Traditional Brit that's served fish ("baked, frilled, poached" or battered) for more than a century; the "democratic 'no bookings' policy is as refreshing as the Guinness" and means you're likely to find yourself queuing "with all the jolly regulars who already know what they are going to order" from the predominantly piscatorial menu.

☑ Taman Gang ◑☒ *Pan-Asian* 22 | 27 | 17 | £56

Mayfair | 141 Park Ln., W1 (Marble Arch) | 020-7518 3160 | fax 7518 3161 | www.tamangang.co.uk

Under new management and, at time of writing, considering a renovation, this "beautiful Thai temple" complete with "carved stone, votives and orchids" "looks more like a spa than a restaurant"; Park Lane princesses and trendy gang members swing by for "amazing" cocktails and "somewhat overpriced" but "interesting Pan-Asian dishes."

NEW Tamarai ◑☒ *Pan-Asian* — | — | — | E

Covent Garden | 167 Drury Ln., WC2 (Covent Garden/Holborn) | 020-7831 9399 | www.tamarai.co.uk

"Dark", "chic and glossy", this "sexy Pan-Asian" that's just come to Covent Garden seems more like a "buzzy nightclub or bar" than "a proper restaurant"; "interesting fusions" pepper the menu, which can be too hot to handle ("the spice nearly required a fire extinguisher"), but fortunately an "extensive cocktail list" and "excellent wine" are on tap to douse any flames.

	FOOD	DECOR	SERVICE	COST
Z Tamarind ● *Indian*	25	21	23	£52

Mayfair | 20 Queen St., W1 (Green Park) | 020-7629 3561 |
fax 7499 5034 | www.tamarindrestaurant.com

"Deservedly popular" for over a decade, this "regal" Mayfair "milestone" "serves the Who's Who" with "nouvelle Indian" fare; highly "helpful waiters" will guide you through the "wonderfully spiced", simultaneously "earthy and ephemeral dal dishes"; but you better "not mind spending the rupees"– a typical "takeaway curry house this is not."

Tapas Brindisa ⊠ *Spanish*	22	14	16	£28

Borough | Borough Mkt. | 18-20 Southwark St., SE1 (London Bridge) |
020-7357 8880 | www.brindisa.com

It's "always busy" at this "Borough favourite" crammed with a "convivial after-work crowd" seeking Spanish delights like "distinctly delectable Tempranillo" to wash down the "amazing goat cheese with honey"; a few curse the casa for its "cramped interior" and no-booking policy, which means "wait times can be long."

Taqueria *Mexican*	18	10	16	£21

Notting Hill | 139-143 Westbourne Grove, W11 (Notting Hill Gate) |
020-7229 4734 | www.coolchiletaqueria.co.uk

"Finally, edible Mexican food in London" sigh surveyors enamoured by this Notting Hill outpost offering "authentic tapas-sized portions" and "interesting", "spicy" "Acapulco-style tacos"; *criticos* cry it's "completely overhyped", but most have only praise for this "pit stop."

Tartine *French*	18	18	17	£29

Chelsea | 114 Draycott Ave., SW3 (South Kensington) | 020-7589 4981 |
fax 7589 5048 | www.tartine.co.uk

This "modern", "social" sandwich bar is where Chelsea's "young, hip and rich go to show off the new bling"; although praised for its "*très* chic", "cool decor", most concur that the "simple French tartines" are "reasonable but not notable."

Tas ● *Turkish*	20	15	17	£23

NEW **Bloomsbury** | 22 Bloomsbury St., WC1 (Tottenham Crt. Rd.) |
020-7637 4555
NEW **Farringdon** | 37 Farringdon Rd., EC1 (Farringdon Rd.) |
020-7430 9721
South Bank | 20 New Globe Walk, SE1 (London Bridge) | 020-7928 3300 |
fax 7261 1166
South Bank | 72 Borough High St., SE1 (London Bridge) | 020-7403 7200 |
fax 7403 7022
Waterloo | 33 The Cut, SE1 (Southwark) | 020-7928 1444 |
fax 7633 9686
www.tasrestaurant.com

"Good value" set menus, "many mezze to pick from" and "lots of tasty vegetarian" options, all with "fantastically fresh" ingredients and "served at dervish speed", make this fast-expanding Turkish chain "great with a group", or perfect for "a quick pre/post-theatre meal."

	FOOD	DECOR	SERVICE	COST

Tate Britain Restaurant *British*

17 | 20 | 15 | £31

Westminster | Tate Britain | Millbank, SW1 (Pimlico) | 020-7887 8825 | fax 7887 8902 | www.tate.org.uk

"Go for the Whistler and the wine list" say fans of this **Modern Brit** on Millbank, where along with the "lovely mural-decorated room" and vino, Tate gallery-goers gaze upon "good English food prepared without too much fuss or sauces"; the only blot on the landscape? "pretty rough" service.

Tate Modern *European*

16 | 21 | 15 | £27

South Bank | Tate Modern | Bankside, SE1 (Blackfriars/London Bridge) | 020-7401 5020 | www.tate.org.uk/modern

"The view, the view, the view" exalt art lovers who make the trip to the "usually mobbed" Tate Modern's "top-floor restaurant for lunch or tea"; you go for the vista, "but the Modern European food's not bad", and that, combined with the rotating murals (currently by Beatriz Milhazes), furnishes "a feast for your eyes and stomach."

Tendido Cero ◑ *Spanish*

- | - | - | M

South Kensington | 174 Old Brompton Rd., SW5 (Gloucester St./South Kensington) | 020-7370 3685 | www.cambiodetercio.co.uk

Boasting "the same owner as the more upmarket Cambio de Tercio" across the street, this "laid-back" South Ken sibling "isn't playing second fiddle to the first-born" – in fact, some even find it "a better choice" (certainly, a cheaper one) for "fantastic quality" tapas and other Iberian eats; it "now has wine" too.

Tentazioni ☒ *Italian*

▽ 27 | 16 | 21 | £42

Tower Bridge | Lloyd's Wharf | 2 Mill St., SE1 (London Bridge/Tower Hill) | 020-7237 1100 | fax 7394 5248 | www.tentazioni.co.uk

"Why, oh why, are you so far away from me?" lament lovers of this "hard-to-find" modern Italian in Tower Bridge; the "sophisticated palates" that make the trek can expect "outstanding, creative" dishes, like foie gras lasagna, and "warm service" – "regulars are treated like royalty, newbies are treated with charm, you can't lose."

Ten Ten Tei ☒ *Japanese*

▽ 23 | 9 | 13 | £22

Soho | 58 Brewer St., W1 (Piccadilly Circus) | 020-7287 1738

In terms of amenities, this Japanese "hole-in-the-wall" can't compete with other swank Soho sites – frankly, "both decor and service are rather run-down"; but all agree the "fresh", "authentic" sushi and bento boxes at "low prices" are "great – so just ignore the rest."

Texas Embassy Cantina *Tex-Mex*

13 | 16 | 15 | £26

St. James's | 1 Cockspur St., SW1 (Charing Cross/Piccadilly Circus) | 020-7925 0077 | fax 7925 0444 | www.texasembassy.com

Those in "need of a burrito fix" mosey on over to this "funky faux Western" off Trafalgar Square; but once you get past the "nice atmosphere, the experience rapidly declines"; if the "slowest service" allows, start with the "good margaritas – after several, you might not notice" how "mediocre" the Tex-Mex fare is.

T.G.I. Friday's ◐ *American*

11 | 12 | 14 | £21

Covent Garden | 25-29 Coventry St., W1 (Piccadilly Circus) |
020-7839 6262 | fax 7839 6296
Covent Garden | 6 Bedford St., WC2 (Charing Cross/Covent Garden) |
020-7379 0585 | fax 7240 3239
Fulham | Fulham Broadway Ctr. | 472 Fulham Rd., SW6 (Fulham Broadway) |
020-7385 0470 | fax 7385 8230
Bayswater | 96-98 Bishop's Bridge Rd., W2 (Bayswater/Queensway) |
020-7229 8600 | fax 7727 4150
www.tgifridays.com

"You know what you're getting" at this American export that's "good
for a quick meal" or, cheerleaders chime, watching the "flair bar-
tenders toss their stuff"; but many more say skip the "bland burgers
and fried everything", wondering "why go here? even on Friday?"

Thai Pavilion *Thai*

▽ 18 | 17 | 19 | £23

Kennington | 82 Kennington Rd., SE11 (Lambeth North) |
020-7587 0455 | fax 7587 0484 | www.pavilioneast.com

Set "on a quiet Kennington corner", this tucked-away Thai ticks all the
boxes: "fair prices", "straightforward service" and "aromatic", "consistent" food; "don't leave without trying the divine mango mousse."

Thai Square *Thai*

19 | 16 | 16 | £26

Covent Garden | 148 The Strand, WC2 (Covent Garden) |
020-7497 0904 ◐ Ⓢ
Mayfair | 5 Princes St., W1 (Oxford Circus) | 020-7499 3333 Ⓢ
Soho | 27-28 St. Anne's Ct., W1 (Tottenham Court Rd.) |
020-7287 2000 ◐ Ⓢ
St. James's | 21-24 Cockspur St., SW1 (Charing Cross/Piccadilly Circus) |
020-7839 4000 ◐
City | 1 Great St. Thomas Apostle, EC4 (Mansion House) |
020-7329 0001 Ⓢ
City | 136-138 Minories, EC3 (Tower Hill) | 020-7680 1111 |
fax 7680 1112 Ⓢ
Islington | 347-349 Upper St., N1 (Angel) | 020-7704 2000
Putney | 2-4 Lower Richmond Rd., SW15 (Putney/Putney Bridge) |
020-8780 1811 | fax 8780 1211 ◐
NEW **Richmond** | 29 Kew Rd., Richmond (Richmond) | 020-8940 5253 |
fax 8940-4258
South Kensington | 19 Exhibition Rd., SW7 (South Kensington) |
020-7584 8359
www.thaisq.com

With many "convenient" branches, artefact-laden "artistic decor" and
"predictably good" cuisine, this chain is "becoming the Pizza Express
of Thai food"; true, "there are plenty more interesting" Asians around,
but this group's "consistency" "regardless of location" is "a real plus."

ⓏNEW Theo Randall
at The InterContinental *Italian*

26 | 21 | 24 | £57

Mayfair | InterContinental Park Ln. | 1 Hamilton Pl., W1 (Hyde Park Corner) |
020-7318 8747 | www.theorandall.com

Although it's still "unknown to many", this newly renovated hotel
restaurant is "a change for the positive at Hyde Park Corner"; the

"wonderful", "innovative Italian food" is "in the tradition of the River Café" (the ex-home of the eponymous chef), and is served by "genial" staff; only the room – "slick" but "somewhat sterile" – sets some back.

Thomas Cubitt, The British   21 20 19 £35

Belgravia | 44 Elizabeth St., SW1 (Victoria) | 020-7730 6060 | fax 7730 6055 | www.thethomascubitt.co.uk

"You'd be blessed to have this as your local" laud lovers of this bi-level place offering the best of Brit to "chic Belgravians"; snack on traditional treats in the "busy" ground-floor pub where "gorgeous floor-to-ceiling windows open up in summer", or have a "civilised", more modern meal in the "romantic" restaurant above; wherever you perch, expect "cheerful service" and "nice ambience."

Timo ⓢ Italian   22 17 18 £49

Kensington | 343 Kensington High St., W8 (High St. Kensington) | 020-7603 3888 | fax 7603 8111 | www.timorestaurant.net

Perhaps "the best-kept secret in Kensington" confide locals about this "rather modern Italian" with "absolutely delicous" "pasta, mains and wines", provided by charmingly "casual service"; "though you'd never be deluded you're in Tuscany, it delivers where it matters most – the belly."

Tokyo Diner ➊ Japanese   20 13 19 £17

Chinatown | 2 Newport Pl., WC2 (Leicester Sq.) | 020-7287 8777 | fax 7434 1415 | www.tokyodiner.com

"Near Leicester Square", this "cheap" "micro-cafe" offers "tasty, no-frills Japanese" fare to a "young, trendy" crowd that create a "casual, chattery atmosphere"; the "canteen-y feel", "closely packed tables and low ceilings" encourage swift turnover but, for a place with a "no-tipping policy", service is surprisingly "courteous."

Ⓩ Tom Aikens ⓢ French   26 22 24 £83

Chelsea | 43 Elystan St., SW3 (South Kensington) | 020-7584 2003 | fax 7584 2001 | www.tomaikens.co.uk

The "most imaginative food on the planet" enthuse "the shirt-sleeved expense-account crowd" enamoured by the "creative pairings" (both food and wine) offered in "huge portions" by "elegant servers" at this Chelsea New French; critics cavil it's "self-consciously clever" cooking "from the chemistry-set school of cuisine", and views on the monochrome decor range from "austere" to "smart"; either way, "eating here is a true experience"; P.S. the tasting menu is "the way to go."

Tom's Deli Eclectic   16 13 13 £18

Notting Hill | 226 Westbourne Grove, W11 (Notting Hill Gate) | 020-7221 8818 | fax 7221 7717

This "cute", crowded cafe is where the "moneyed" of Notting Hill "pretend to be ordinary Joes"; "if you can get a table", it's a "great spot for a weekend brunch" featuring "fantastic poached eggs" and other Eclectic delights; but better be quick, as "you'll feel the pressure to leave."

	FOOD	DECOR	SERVICE	COST

NEW Tom's Kitchen ❶ *British* — 19 | 17 | 14 | £40

Chelsea | 27 Cale St., SW3 (South Kensington) | 020-7349 0202 | fax 7823 2652 | www.tomskitchen.co.uk

"Brilliant" vs. "disappointing": commentators clash over what Chelsea-ites cheekily call Tom Aikens' new "ego pub venture", a "buzzing refectory-style" Modern Brit whose "cramped" "communal seating" means you "really get to know your fellow diners"; supporters salute the "über-quality", "simple food done very well" – "but not at these prices" snap sceptics, who also slam the "diffident staff"; even if "it's not as great as you'd expect from this great chef", "trying to get a table is [already] tricky."

Tootsies *American* — 16 | 14 | 16 | £20

Marylebone | 35 James St., W1 (Bond St.) | 020-7486 1611 | fax 7935 4957

Canary Wharf | Jubilee Pl. | 45 Bank St., E14 (Canary Wharf) | 020-7516 9110 | fax 7516 9877

Hampstead | 196-198 Haverstock Hill, NW3 (Belsize Park) | 020-7431 3812 | fax 7794 8478

Clapham | 36-38 Abbeville Rd., SW4 (Clapham South) | 020-8772 6646 | fax 8772 0672

NEW Putney | Putney Wharf | The Piazza, 30 Brewhouse Ln., SW15 (Putney Bridge) | 020-8788 8488 | fax 8788 6636

Wimbledon | 48 High St., SW19 (Wimbledon) | 020-8946 4135 | fax 8947 7936

Chiswick | 148 Chiswick High Rd., W4 (Turnham Green) | 020-8747 1869 | fax 8987 0486

Notting Hill | 120 Holland Park Ave., W11 (Holland Park) | 020-7229 8567

www.tootsiesrestaurants.co.uk

Ratings may not fully reflect that this veteran chain, long known for making "Americans feel right at home" with its hamburgers and "traditional breakfasts", is being overhauled by the owners of Gourmet Burger Kitchen; the "tired" decor's getting refreshed, and updated menus make it a place "where you can take kids" but now also get "interesting salads if you've promised yourself a detox."

Toto's *Italian* — 24 | 19 | 22 | £51

Chelsea | Walton House | Walton St. at Lennox Garden Mews, SW3 (Knightsbridge) | 020-7589 2062 | fax 7581 9668

Hellraisers should head elsewhere – this is "one of the quieter Italian restaurants" around – but for "elegant, classy" dining, this out-of-the-way Chelsea site remains a "favourite"; an "older crowd" "linger" by the 17th-century fireplace or "lovely" garden, deliberating over delicacies like "divine squid ink pasta" with "outgoing staff."

NEW Trinity *European* — ▽ 24 | 21 | 21 | £43

Clapham | 4 The Polygon, SW4 (Clapham Common) | 020-7622 1199 | fax 7622 1166 | www.trinityrestaurant.co.uk

"Clapham-based foodies can get a fix close to home" at this "fine-dining newcomer" from chef-owner Adam Byatt (fondly remembered for Thyme); within the beige-toned, "relaxed space", he serves an "imaginative and well-executed" Modern European menu paired with "great midrange wines"; but what's "absolutely brilliant" is the "absolute-bargain lunch – three courses for £18."

Troubadour, The ◐ *Eclectic*

14	21	16	£21

Earl's Court | 265 Old Brompton Rd., SW5 (Earl's Ct.) | 020-7370 1434 | fax 7341 6329 | www.troubadour.co.uk

"A slice of London and folk music history", this '50s Earl's Court coffeehouse is where the likes of Hendrix and Dylan jammed (there's still live music or poetry readings most nights); alas, "interesting characters", an "airy garden and trippy bathrooms" make for "great atmosphere" but not great dining – most kindly say the Eclectic eats "leave something to be desired."

Truc Vert *French*

22	15	16	£30

Mayfair | 42 N. Audley St., W1 (Bond St.) | 020-7491 9988 | fax 7491 7717

"If you can't get to the south of France straight away", this "quaint" Mayfair cafe is a "pleasant place for a simple breakfast"; at lunch it's "packed with embassy workers" tucking into "solid bistro fare" or grabbing something from the "spot-on", on-site deli.

Tsunami *Japanese*

24	18	16	£39

Clapham | 5-7 Voltaire Rd., SW4 (Clapham North) | 020-7978 1610 | fax 7978 1591

A wave of praise washes over this minimalist Japanese for its "fantastically fresh sushi" that's "reasonably priced" if you "go before 7 PM" (20 percent off); the "slightly odd nightclub-style decor" is due for a revamp as we write, and Claphamites hope the "variable service" will get a makeover too.

Tuttons Brasserie *British/French*

18	17	17	£29

Covent Garden | 11-12 Russell St., WC2 (Covent Garden) | 020-7836 4141 | fax 7379 9979 | www.tuttons.com

"In the thick of Covent Garden", this "bustling" British–French brasserie is "not worth a special trip"; but it offers a "reliable" pre-/post-theatre supper, or "comforting food for the weary shopper", plus an opportunity to "watch the world go by."

☑ Two Brothers Fish ⓈⓂ *Seafood*

24	12	16	£24

Finchley | 297-303 Regent's Park Rd., N3 (Finchley Central) | 020-8346 0469 | fax 8343 1978 | www.twobrothers.co.uk

You "might have to queue" at this "unpretentious" Finchley fish 'n' chippery that's been frying up a storm for over 15 years; it's "heavily patronised by regulars" who don't care that decor is "basic" but are reeled in by "fresh, clean-tasting" fish (fried, grilled or baked) "made with loving hands."

202 *European*

17	18	16	£27

Notting Hill | Nicole Farhi | 202 Westbourne Grove, W11 (Notting Hill Gate) | 020-7727 2722 | fax 7792 9217

"Watch out for well-known faces sitting behind outsized shades" at this "relaxed" cafe in the "fashionable" Nicole Farhi store; the "health-conscious" Modern European menu is "done with competence and some flourish, but is a little beside the point" to the "beau-

| | FOOD | DECOR | SERVICE | COST |

tiful people brunching, with the outside tables being the premium" place to be.

222 Veggie Vegan *Vegetarian*   - | - | - | M

Fulham | 222 North End Rd., W14 (West Kensington) | 020-7381 2322 | www.222veggievegan.com

"Possibly the best healthy restaurant in London" gush groupies of "genius" Ghanaian-born chef-owner Ben Asamani who "cuts no corners" and "elevates flavours beyond expectation" at his wallet-friendly vegetarian in simple Fulham premises; the eclectic eats come in "large portions" too.

NEW 2 Veneti ☒ *Italian*   - | - | - | E

Marylebone | 8-10 Wigmore St., W1 (Bond St./Oxford Circus) | 020-7637 0789

Owned by two Venetians (hence the name), this replacement for old-timer Eddalino makes "a good newcomer to Marylebone", with "friendly" staff serving a "well-executed" if "somewhat limited" menu of Northern Italian specialities and wines in a "quiet, relaxed" setting.

Ubon by Nobu ☒ *Japanese/Peruvian*   24 | 20 | 19 | £60

Canary Wharf | 34 Westferry Circus, E14 (Canary Wharf) | 020-7719 7800 | fax 7719 7801 | www.noburestaurants.com

This "Docklands take on Nobu" serves the signature "sophisticated, well-executed" Japanese-Peruvian fare, is quite "bookable" (unlike its "Mayfair cousins") and boasts "spectacular" river views; but cynics say a "Nobu by any other name" is a bit "like going out with David Beckham's sister" – in particular, the "brusque, impatient" "service is a real letdown" – and "it's surely expensive", not that the "wall-to-wall" "city-traders clientele" seem to care.

Uli *Pan-Asian*   ▽ 25 | 12 | 23 | £36

Notting Hill | 16 All Saints Rd., W11 (Ladbroke Grove) | 020-7727 7511

"Tucked away off Portobello" Road, this "tiny", "family-owned" Pan-Asian is a "great date place"; "popular with the Boho set", "it's hard to get a table" but, once seated, expect "superb" dishes like chile lobster tempura to be served by "attentive, friendly" staff.

☑ Umu ☒ *Japanese*   26 | 25 | 23 | £81

Mayfair | 14-16 Bruton Pl., W1 (Bond St.) | 020-7499 8881 | www.umurestaurant.com

"It always feels special" at this "stylish" Mayfair specialist in kaiseki (traditional Japanese tasting menus); devotees drool over the "delicate" dishes, especially the "exquisite experience" of "fish that still tastes of the sea", served with "finesse" "within a sombre, well-appointed room"; even the few who "don't get the hype", calling it "really overpriced", admit it's a "perfect" "place to impress."

Union Cafe *British/Mediterranean*   21 | 15 | 16 | £31

Marylebone | 96 Marylebone Ln., W1 (Bond St.) | 020-7486 4860 | fax 7935 1537 | www.brinkleys.com

"Like British cooking should be" claim converts of this cafe, which also offers some Med dishes; its "trendy" "comfort food" (think toffee cake, fillet burgers and seafood linguini) in happy union with a "sensibly priced wine list" "keeps you coming back" to this "Marylebone backstreet."

Upper Glas *Swedish* (fka Glas)

| 22 | 17 | 18 | £34 |

Islington | The Mall Bldg. | 359 Upper St., 1st fl., N1 (Angel) | 020-7359 1932 | fax 7359 2209 | www.glasrestaurant.co.uk

"Ikea without the arguments" is how Swedish-loving surveyors describe this "endearing" Scandinavian retreat "in the roof of Angel's antiques market"; "on advice of staff, you pick a series of small dishes, all of them amazing" – even if grazing on smoked reindeer amidst red-and-green "Christmassy surroundings" has a somewhat twisted appeal.

Upstairs Bar & Restaurant Ⓜ *French*

| - | - | - | M |

Brixton | 89B Acre Ln., SW2 (Brixton/Clapham North) | 020-7733 8855 | www.upstairslondon.com

"Once you've worked out where the entrance is" (just off Acre Lane), this "quintessentially French" venue offers welcome oasis in the culinary desert between Clapham and Brixton; the few who've found it rave about "relaxing in front of a roaring fire in the bar", before enjoying "exquisite" food, "enticing wines" and "charming" staff.

Vama ● *Indian*

| 24 | 16 | 19 | £40 |

Chelsea | 438 King's Rd., SW10 (Sloane Sq.) | 020-7565 8500 | fax 7565 8501 | www.vama.co.uk

A few feel it's being "outshone by newer haute Indians", but most still thrill to the "knock-your-socks-off renditions of Punjabi standards" – a "vibrant symphony of curry and spice" – at this "chic" subcontinental that's "expensive but worth it"; the outer Chelsea location is "a drag, but they offer" a delivery service.

Vasco & Piero's Pavilion Ⓢ *Italian*

| 21 | 13 | 20 | £40 |

Soho | 15 Poland St., W1 (Oxford Circus) | 020-7437 8774 | fax 7437 0467 | www.vascosfood.com

Those "serious" about Umbrian cuisine "pack into this place", politely ignoring "surroundings not meant to impress"; but the more blunt deem the "decor incredibly tired" – and declare that whilst this may be "one of the better Italians around Soho", it's still "nothing to write home about."

Veeraswamy *Indian*

| 22 | 20 | 21 | £43 |

Mayfair | Victory House | 99-101 Regent St., W1 (Piccadilly Circus) | 020-7734 1401 | fax 7439 8434 | www.realindianfood.com

For eight decades, this "granddaddy of Indian establishments" in Mayfair has been tickling taste buds with its "creative fare", "competently presented" in a vaguely Jazz Era "fantasyland of the Raj" environment ; however, unless you go for the "great value" set menu, remember it's "fancy schmancy" (lobster curry, anyone?) – and "priced accordingly."

	FOOD	DECOR	SERVICE	COST

NEW Via Condotti ✂ *Italian* ▽ 18 | 17 | 19 | £43

Mayfair | 23 Conduit St., W1 (Oxford Circus) | 020-7493 7050 |
fax 7409 7985 | www.viacondotti.co.uk

Opinion is split on this Italian "addition to the Mayfair scene"; some
reviewers reckon its "accomplished seasonal cooking" and "affordable set menus" make "you really think you're in Rome", whilst naysayers needle that it's "overpriced" for "nothing special."

Viet Hoa ● *Vietnamese* 23 | 9 | 15 | £18

Shoreditch | 70-72 Kingsland Rd., E2 (Old St.) | 020-7729 8293
After a morning spent "gallery-hopping 'round Hoxton Square,
those in need of a "cheap and cheerful" culinary experience make a
beeline for this "authentic Vietnamese cafe"; "you can't go wrong",
given the "marvellous flavours" at prices almost lower than you'd
find in Hanoi itself.

Villandry *French* 18 | 15 | 15 | £35

Bloomsbury | 170 Great Portland St., W1 (Great Portland St.) |
020-7631 3131 | fax 7631 3030 | www.villandry.com

There's definitely dissent over this "upscale" deli-meets-dining
room in Bloomsbury, recently "revamped" with "rustic" decor; disciples defend it as "efficient for a nice, simple French lunch" or brunch
"in a buzzy atmosphere"; "style over substance" scoff snubbers who
say the "embarrassing service" makes it "best for people filling picnic baskets for the park."

Vineyard at Stockcross *British/French* 24 | 21 | 24 | £70

Newbury | Vineyard at Stockcross | Stockcross, Berkshire | 01635 528770 |
fax 01635 528398 | www.the-vineyard.co.uk

With 2,000-odd labels on offer, "the wine has always been the star"
at this "intoxicating" venue in the Berkshire countryside; but some
imbibers insist the Classic French–Modern British "food has caught
up well", "reflecting seasonal specialties on the great-value" prix
fixes; all are adamant you should "stay at the adjacent hotel – so no
problem sampling the list!"

Vingt-Quatre ● *Eclectic* 15 | 11 | 14 | £26

Chelsea | 325 Fulham Rd., SW10 (South Kensington) | 020-7376 7224 |
fax 7352 2643 | www.vingtquatre.co.uk

"Not worth going to during daylight hours" but "great at 3 AM when
taste buds are dulled" is the general consensus on this 24/7 Chelsea
hangout; "a pleasant crowd" of late-nighters and early birds can expect Eclectic "hearty fare", served by "nonchalant staff."

Vivat Bacchus ✂ *European* 23 | 18 | 24 | £42

City | 47 Farringdon St., EC4 (Chancery Ln./Farringdon) |
020-7353 2648 | www.vivatbacchus.co.uk

From Modern European fine dining with an "exceptional" wine list to
South African bar snacks and beer, this "unpretentious, friendly"
City "power brokers'" "escape" is "well worth discovering"; for those
who like to get interactive with their ordering, the "walk-in wine cel-
lars and cheese rooms are a treat."

☑ Wagamama *Japanese*

FOOD	DECOR	SERVICE	COST
19	13	17	£17

Bloomsbury | 4 Streatham St., WC1 (Holborn/Tottenham Court Rd.) | 020-7323 9223 | fax 7323 9224

Covent Garden | 1 Tavistock St., WC2 (Covent Garden) | 020-7836 3330 | fax 7240 8846

Knightsbridge | Harvey Nichols | 109-125 Knightsbridge, SW1 (Knightsbridge) | 020-7201 8000 | fax 7201 8080

Marylebone | 101A Wigmore St., W1 (Bond St./Oxford Circus) | 020-7409 0111 | fax 7409 0088

Soho | 10A Lexington St., W1 (Oxford Circus/Piccadilly Circus) | 020-7292 0990

Blackfriars | 109 Fleet St., EC4 (Blackfriars/St. Paul's) | 020-7583 7889 Ⓢ

City | 1A Ropemaker St., EC2 (Moorgate) | 020-7588 2688 Ⓢ

Camden Town | 11 Jamestown Rd., NW1 (Camden Town) | 020-7428 0800 | fax 7482 4887

Islington | The N1 Centre | Parkfield St., N1 (Angel) | 020-7226 2664

Kensington | 26A Kensington High St., W8 (High St. Kensington) | 020-7376 1717

www.wagamama.com
Additional locations throughout London

Once again London's Most Popular, these Japanese "big space age cafeterias" continue to be "mobbed" with people slurping "bottomless bowls of fresh steaming noodles" and other "delicious, nutritious meals in minutes"; yes, the gizmo-holding "service is slipping towards the shambolic", and foes feel they've "outgrown" eating at long communal tables, surrounded by a "gaggle of screaming kids"; but "let's not be snobs about this" – the chain remains "the perfect antidote to an empty stomach and wallet."

☑ NEW Wallace, The *French*

20	25	16	£33

Marylebone | The Wallace Museum Collection | Hertford House, Manchester Sq., W1 (Baker St./Bond St.) | 020-7563 9505 | www.thewallacerestaurant.com

The "secretive location" of this "enclosed courtyard in a museum" "just off busy Oxford Street" creates a "lovely ambience" for "intimate dining"; as dinner is done "only Friday–Saturday", "lunch is the meal" here, though the "generous yet delicate" Classic French food is "wonderful for tea" too; sole downside: the "utterly disorganised service."

Wapping Food *European*

▽ 20	24	21	£39

Docklands | Wapping Hydraulic Power Station | Wapping Wall, E1 (Wapping) | 020-7680 2080 | www.thewappingproject.com

A former Docklands power station full of "pipes and old machinery parts" provides an "awe-inspiring" setting for this Modern European; if the "food's not as interesting as the surroundings", it still has its "imaginative" moments; besides, the building's "rotating art installations will add a little extra to your meal."

☑ Waterside Inn Ⓜ *French*

27	26	27	£96

Bray | Waterside Inn | Ferry Rd., Berkshire | 01628 620691 | fax 01628 784710 | www.waterside-inn.co.uk

"So very romantic" rave venturers to the "gastronomic hamlet" of Bray to visit the Roux *famille*'s "precious out-of-town offering, aka "Le

Gavroche on the Thames"; you're treated to "traditional" but "magnificent" French cuisine, "exemplary service", a "wine list to die for" and that "spectacular", "serene setting"; so "make the drive, spend the money" – it's "more than worth it" "for that really special occasion."

Waterway, The *European* ∇ | 18 | 21 | 14 | £28

St. John's Wood | 54 Formosa St., W9 (Warwick Ave.) | 020-7266 3557 | fax 7266 3579 | www.thewaterway.co.uk

"Beautiful, pretty things" are drawn to the "great canalside location" of this St. John's Wood "summer drinking hole" where a change of ownership has upped the food stakes with "generous portions" of Modern European favourites like "light, silky pumpkin soup"; still, sceptics sniff it's "overpriced for a place in the middle of a council estate."

Wells, The *European* 18 | 18 | 17 | £33

Hampstead | 30 Well Walk, NW3 (Hampstead) | 020-7794 3785 | fax 7266 3547 | www.thewellshampstead.co.uk

Reviewers divide over this Modern European, with converts calling it a "haven near the Heath" and dissenters deeming it "a true disappointment"; the secret lies in location – the "low-key", ground-floor gastropub is "more fun" than the "formal upstairs" – and in your order: "if you keep it simple, for the sake of the food and the service, you'll be fine."

Westbourne, The *Eclectic* 16 | 15 | 11 | £25

Notting Hill | 101 Westbourne Park Villas, W2 (Royal Oak/ Westbourne Park) | 020-7221 1332 | fax 7243 8081

"Definitely a destination gastropub", this Notting Hill boozer "is heaving" with "deafening hordes" who come for "great outdoor socializing almost any time of the year" on the "un-publike" heated terrace; the Eclectic grub is "decent", despite "the most obnoxious staff in London."

☒ Wilton's ☒ *British/Seafood* 24 | 22 | 24 | £66

St. James's | 55 Jermyn St., SW1 (Green Park/Piccadilly Circus) | 020-7629 9955 | fax 7495 6233 | www.wiltons.co.uk

"You can feel the gout seeping up your legs as you cross the threshold" of this "old haunt" in St. James's, where for over 200 years a jacket-clad clientele has consumed "classic" British fare ("remarkable" seafood, "particularly fine" game) under the "starched" gaze of the "superb" staff; some find it "terrifyingly traditional" but the greatest grouse is the cost, which even advocates agree is "expensive – but it keeps out the riffraff."

Wòdka ● *Polish* 20 | 14 | 19 | £38

Kensington | 12 St. Albans Grove, W8 (High St. Kensington) | 020-7937 6513 | fax 7937 8621 | www.wodka.co.uk

"When in London, do as the Polish do" at this Kensington kickback where "delicious waitresses" serve "delightful" traditional dishes and even better "untraditional flavoured vodkas", like cherry and horseradish; you "could drink here for hours" trying all the "great shots"; of course, "you may need a bit of help to get up . . ."

	FOOD	DECOR	SERVICE	COST

☑ Wolseley, The ☉ *European*
21 | 26 | 21 | £48

Piccadilly | 160 Piccadilly, W1 (Green Park) | 020-7499 6996 |
fax 7499 6888 | www.thewolseley.com

The "wow factor" of its setting – a marble-columned, "grand
mittel-Europe brasserie" – makes "everyone feel like the star in
the movie of his own life" at this "buzzy" Piccadilly playground;
although it's known as a place where the "elite meet to eat", it remains "surprisingly unstuffy", whether you swing by for a "baro-
nial" breakfast, "impressive" afternoon tea or "divine" dinner;
they serve continuously, so if you've neglected to book, try "stop-
ping by at odd hours."

Wong Kei ☉⊅ *Chinese*
16 | 6 | 9 | £13

Chinatown | 41-43 Wardour St., W1 (Leicester Sq./Piccadilly Circus) |
020-7437 8408

Things are changing at this Chinatown "standby": once "famous
for its rude waiters", staff are "positively polite" now, whilst the
Cantonese cuisine's "not as good as it used to be"; still, it's
"cheap" and "convenient for a quick plate of noodles"; as for the
"crummy" decor, "you want view, go to Buckingham Palace, you
want eat, sit here."

NEW XO *Pan-Asian*
16 | 18 | 16 | £40

Hampstead | 29 Belsize Ln., NW3 (Belsize Park) | 020-7433 0888 |
fax 7794 3474 | www.rickerrestaurants.com

Hampstead hipsters now have their own Will Ricker–backed "see-
and-be-seen" Pan-Asian, a green-tinged "carbon copy of e&o";
sceptics say this "pricey" place "doesn't compare to its sister – just
not as tasty and service not as good"; nonetheless, punters predict
lazy locals will make it "very successful."

Yakitoria *Japanese*
▽ 24 | 26 | 21 | £52

Paddington | 25 Sheldon Sq., W2 (Paddington) | 020-3214 3000 |
fax 3214 3001 | www.yakitoria.co.uk

"Don't want to wait to be put on the list at Nobu?" this "out-of-the-
way spot behind Paddington Station is exactly what the doctor
ordered" – a "spectacular" "Scando-Japanese" venue, all "cool vibe"
and "cosy alcoves", for "creative combinations" of yakitori and sushi
"conscientiously served"; though "difficult to find", it's "somewhere
to go back to."

☑ Yauatcha ☉ *Chinese*
25 | 22 | 17 | £40

Soho | 15 Broadwick St., W1 (Piccadilly Circus) | 020-7494 8888 |
fax 7287 6959

Owner "Alan Yau delivers" with this "sexy" split-level Soho
Chinese that attracts a "noisy" crowd of London's "most attractive yuppies"; "interesting" teas and "exquisite" pastries abound
in the ground-floor cafe, whilst down the "dark" staircase lies
"dim sum as theatre" with "innovative" delicacies like "melt-in-
the-mouth venison puffs" washed down with "standout cocktails"; the only "shame" is the "snippy servers'" "conveyor-belt
attitude to turning tables."

	FOOD	DECOR	SERVICE	COST

Ye Olde Cheshire Cheese *British*   15 | 23 | 16 | £21

Blackfriars | 145 Fleet St., EC4 (Blackfriars) | 020-7353 6170 |
fax 7353 0845

"History drips from the walls" of this 17th-century Fleet Street pub
(already old when Charles Dickens dropped in), a "touristy" but "superb place for a pint" or some "good ol' British" grub; and whilst
most "enjoy the setting more than the food", that's nothing that
some "awesome Samuel Smith brews" "can't fix."

Y Ming ●⊠ *Chinese*   - | - | - | M

Soho | 35-36 Greek St., W1 (Leicester Sq.) | 020-7734 2721 |
fax 7437 0292 | www.yminglondon.com

Y go anywhere else when the "excellent" northern specialities and
"friendly service" of this Soho veteran "put other Chinese restaurants to shame"; the downstairs room is ideal for groups, whilst an
early evening prix fixe and location "close to West End" theatres
make it good for show-goers too.

YO! Sushi *Japanese*   17 | 14 | 14 | £23

Bloomsbury | 11-13 Bayley St., WC1 (Tottenham Court Rd.) |
020-7636 0076

Knightsbridge | Harrods 102 | 102-104 Brompton Rd., SW3
(Knightsbridge) | 020-7893 8175

Knightsbridge | Harvey Nichols | 109-125 Knightsbridge, 5th fl., SW1
(Knightsbridge) | 020-7201 8641

Marylebone | Selfridges | 400 Oxford St., W1 (Bond St.) |
020-7318 3944

Soho | 52 Poland St., W1 (Oxford Circus) | 020-7287 0443

Westminster | County Hall | Belvedere Rd., SE1 (Westminster) |
020-7928 8871 | fax 7928 5619

Farringdon | 95 Farringdon Rd., EC1 (Farringdon) | 020-7841 0785 |
fax 7841 0798

Fulham | Fulham Broadway Ctr. | Fulham Rd., 1st fl., SW6
(Fulham Broadway) | 020-7385 6077

Bayswater | Whiteleys Shopping Ctr. | 151 Queensway, W2
(Bayswater) | 020-7727 9392 | fax 7727 9390

Paddington | Paddington Station, W2 (Paddington) |
020-7706 9550

www.yosushi.com

Additional locations throughout London

It's "the cute factor" ("conveyor belts full of fish, robots serving
drinks"), rather than the "unremarkable" Japanese eats, that draws
snackers to this "kitschy", "mother of all moving sushi" chain; "kids
love it", and adults agree that "in a pinch", "it's good, quick fun"; but
even addicts admit it "can get pricey if you're hungry."

Yoshino ⊠ *Japanese*   24 | 17 | 18 | £29

Piccadilly | 3 Piccadilly Pl., W1 (Piccadilly Circus) | 020-7287 6622 |
fax 7287 1733 | www.yoshino.net

"Tucked away off Piccadilly" "in a little alley", this Japanese is "hard
to find but worth the search" for super-"fresh", "beautiful sushi" "at
bargain prices" – there's a lunch menu for just £5.80 – especially for
"such a central location."

	FOOD	DECOR	SERVICE	COST

NEW Yumenoki *Japanese* — | — | — | M

Chelsea | 204 Fulham Rd., SW10 (Fulham Broadway/South Kensington) | 020-7351 2777 | fax 7351 4288 | www.yumenoki.co.uk

Though new, this "great Japanese" has already found favour with Fulham Road locals who can't get enough of the wide "variety of rolls and good-value Wagyu beef"; a small rear patio could make it an alfresco summer staple for scrummy sushi suppers.

☑ Zafferano *Italian* 26 | 20 | 22 | £59

Belgravia | 15 Lowndes St., SW1 (Knightsbridge) | 020-7235 5800 | fax 7235 1971 | www.zafferanorestaurant.com

"*Bellissima*" bellow believers in this Belgravia venue, for 18 years a "consistently high – very high, in fact" "standard-bearer" for The Boot's *cucina* ("go around truffle season" or try the "fantastic lobster linguini" anytime); true, tables are "tight" and the "tariffs be high", leading a few to wonder "is it worth it?", but the plethora of celebrities, "local hedge fund mangers and your friendly neighbourhood Russian tycoon dining" here seems to suggest *sì*.

Zaika *Indian* 25 | 24 | 21 | £47

Kensington | 1 Kensington High St., W8 (High St. Kensington) | 020-7795 6533 | fax 7937 8854 | www.zaika-restaurant.co.uk

In between its "creative" "fusion cuisine" (try a "divine chocolate samosa") and its vaulted-ceiling, "ethereal atmosphere, light years from the hustle of Kensington", this "modern" Indian "spoils you for the local" curry house; even so, hostiles huff its "high prices are hard to justify."

Zen Central ❶ *Chinese* 21 | 16 | 20 | £48

Mayfair | 20 Queen St., W1 (Green Park) | 020-7629 8089 | fax 7493 6181 | www.zencentralrestaurant.com

If you're craving "great crispy duck" and such, this "high-class" Chinese is a "reliable" choice; the Mayfair location may account for accusations that it's "overpriced", but doesn't explain the monochrome decor that makes some feel they're "sitting in a badly lit 1950s car showroom."

ZENW3 *Chinese* 16 | 17 | 16 | £33

Hampstead | 83-84 Hampstead High St., NW3 (Hampstead) | 020-7794 7863 | fax 7794 6956 | www.zenw3.com

This "warhorse" is "pretty much what you'd expect from Hampstead's favourite local Chinese": "ok for a culinary desert", but "a little past its sell-by date" compared to newer venues; and whilst the big windows afford "good people-watching", "up close the decor is dated."

Zetter
Restaurant & Rooms *Mediterranean* ▽ 19 | 23 | 21 | £35

Clerkenwell | The Zetter | 86-88 Clerkenwell Rd., EC1 (Farringdon) | 020-7324 4455 | fax 7324 4445 | www.thezetter.com

A "cool interior right out of *Wallpaper** magazine" characterises this "airy", all-day Clerkenwell hotel restaurant, whose "varied" Med menu "can be very good"; it's an "elegant" place to eat, provided "you're not intimidated by the 'anything as long as it's black and Prada', agency-and-meedjya crowd."

Ziani *Italian*   25 | 17 | 23 | £38

Chelsea | 45 Radnor Walk, SW3 (Sloane Sq.) | 020-7351 5297 | fax 7244 8387 | www.ziani.uk.com

Calf's liver cooked in onions and red wine vinegar and other "wonderful" Venetian specialities supplement the "warm Italian welcome" you get at this "nice little hideaway"; although it can be "cramped" and "rushed on busy nights", it remains "a perennial favourite", "always crowded" with Chelsea locals.

Zilli Fish ●⊠ *Italian/Seafood*   20 | 15 | 17 | £39

Soho | 36-40 Brewer St., W1 (Piccadilly Circus) | 020-7734 8649 | fax 7434 9807 | www.zillialdo.com

It's "not fancy" at this Soho Italian, but that "shouldn't detract" from the "emphasis on seafood", particularly the signature "spaghetti lobster (may be a cliché but it's delicious)"; "patchy service" displeases dissenters, but its late hours and location make it a perfect "pre/post-theatre" spot.

Zizzi ● *Pizza*   16 | 14 | 15 | £21

Covent Garden | 20 Bow St., WC2 (Covent Garden) | 020-7836 6101
Covent Garden | 73-75 The Strand, WC2 (Charing Cross) | 020-7240 1717
Marylebone | 110-116 Wigmore St., W1 (Bond St.) | 020-7935 2336
Marylebone | 35-38 Paddington St., W1 (Baker St.) | 020-7224 1450
Victoria | Unit 15, Cardinal Walk, SW1 (Victoria) | 020-7821 0402
Fitzrovia | 33-41 Charlotte St., W1 (Goodge St.) | 020-7436 9440
Finchley | 202-208 Regents Park Rd., N3 (Finchley Central) | 020-8371 6777
Highgate | 1-3 Hampstead Ln., N6 (Highgate) | 020-8347 0090
Earl's Court | 194-196 Earl's Court Rd., SW5 (Earl's Ct.) | 020-7370 1999
Chiswick | 231 Chiswick High Rd., W4 (Chiswick Park) | 020-8747 9400
www.zizzi.co.uk

Whilst there's "nothing to love, there's a lot to like" at this "consistent" chain specialising in "lovely" wood-fired pizzas; true, "service is a bit functional" and "it's often full of screaming kids", but "you know what you'll be getting" and "it won't break the bank."

ⓩ Zuma *Japanese*   26 | 24 | 21 | £64

Knightsbridge | 5 Raphael St., SW7 (Knightsbridge) | 020-7584 1010 | fax 7584 5005 | www.zumarestaurant.com

If you can breach the "obnoxious reservation system", you too can join the "ultrathin women, middle-aged bankers" "and expense-account types" at this "buzzy to the extreme" Knightsbridge "nouveau Japanese"; ranging from rave-worthy robata to "superb" sushi, the "food's mind-blowing" – and "it's easy to blow a fortune" on it as well; but despite that, and "staff not quite up to" handling the "hot, heaving" scene, this hipster still seems "sensational."

INDEXES

LOCATION MAPS

Cuisines

Includes restaurant names, locations and Food ratings. ☑ indicates places with the highest ratings, popularity and importance.

AMERICAN

All Star Lanes | multi. loc.	15
Automat | W1	17
Big Easy | SW3	16
Christopher's | WC2	19
Diner, The | multi. loc.	-
Eagle Bar Diner | W1	19
Ed's Easy Diner | multi. loc.	15
Hard Rock | W1	13
Harlem | W2	16
Joe Allen | WC2	17
NEW Kobe Jones | WC1	18
☑ Lucky 7 | W2	20
Maxwell's | WC2	17
Pizza on the Park | SW1	14
PJ's B&G | multi. loc.	16
Planet Hollywood | W1	11
Rainforest Cafe | W1	11
Smollensky's | multi. loc.	15
☑ Sophie's Steak | SW10	23
Sticky Fingers | W8	14
Texas Embassy | SW1	13
T.G.I. Friday's | multi. loc.	11
Tootsies | multi. loc.	16

ARGENTINEAN

Buen Ayre/Santa Maria | multi. loc.	23
El Gaucho | multi. loc.	21
☑ Gaucho Grill | multi. loc.	22

ASIAN FUSION

Aquasia | SW10	21
☑ Asia de Cuba | WC2	22
Blakes | SW7	19
Great Eastern | EC2	22
☑ L'Etranger | SW7	24

BAKERIES

Baker & Spice | multi. loc.	22
La Fromagerie | W1	24
Le Pain Quotidien | multi. loc.	19
☑ Ottolenghi | multi. loc.	24

BANGLADESHI

Ginger | W2	17

BARBECUE

Bodeans | multi. loc.	18
NEW Rhodes Bar-B-Q | E1	-

BELGIAN

☑ Belgo | multi. loc.	19
Bierodrome | multi. loc.	17
Le Pain Quotidien | multi. loc.	19

BRAZILIAN

NEW Mocotó | SW1	22
Rodizio Rico | multi. loc.	15

BRITISH (MODERN)

Academy | W1	13
NEW Acorn House | WC1	19
Adam St. | WC2	20
Admiral Codrington | SW3	18
Admiralty, The | WC2	19
Alastair Little | W1	24
Anchor & Hope | SE1	24
Anglesea Arms | W6	23
Annie's | multi. loc.	21
Aurora | EC2	19
Axis | WC2	20
Balans | multi. loc.	16
Balham Kitchen | SW12	16
Bankside | multi. loc.	19
Barnsbury, The | N1	21
Bedford & Strand | WC2	17
Belvedere, The | W8	20
Bevis Marks | EC3	-
Blandford St. | W1	18
Boxwood Café | SW1	21
Bradley's | NW3	15
NEW Bumpkin | W11	21
☑ Chez Bruce | SW17	28
☑ Clarke's | W8	25
Cow Dining Rm. | W2	21
Duke of Cambridge | N1	20
1802 | E14	16
NEW Empress of India | E9	-
Engineer | NW1	19
NEW Fat Badger | W10	15
Fifth Floor Cafe | SW1	18
Franklins | SE22	19
Frederick's | N1	20
Glasshouse, The | TW9	24
☑ Gravetye Manor | W. Sussex	24
NEW Great Queen St. | WC2	-
Greyhound, The | SW11	19
Groucho Club | W1	19
Gun, The | E14	19
Hand & Flowers | SL7	-
Hartwell House | HP17	19

☑ Home House | **W1**	20
Hush | **W1**	17
Island | **W2**	-
☑ Ivy, The | **WC2**	23
Joe's | **SW3**	19
Joe's Rest. Bar | **SW1**	21
Julie's | **W11**	18
Just St. James's | **SW1**	16
Kensington Place | **W8**	20
NEW Konstam | **WC1**	-
Lamberts | **SW12**	25
NEW Langtry's | **SW1**	-
Launceston Place | **W8**	21
☑ Le Caprice | **SW1**	24
Livebait | **multi. loc.**	18
Mash | **W1**	12
Medcalf | **EC1**	23
Menier Chocolate | **SE1**	14
NEW Mews of Mayfair | **W1**	22
NEW Narrow, The | **E14**	-
National Dining Rms. | **WC2**	18
Oratory, The | **SW3**	18
Palmerston, The | **SE22**	-
Paternoster Chop | **EC4**	18
Portrait | **WC2**	22
Potting Shed | **NW1**	-
Prism | **EC3**	18
Randall & Aubin | **W1**	19
Ransome's Dock | **SW11**	20
Rhodes W1 Brass. | **W1**	-
NEW Rhodes W1 Rest. | **W1**	-
Richard Corrigan | **W1**	23
Roast | **SE1**	19
R.S.J. | **SE1**	21
☑ Savoy Grill | **WC2**	24
Smiths/Dining Room | **EC1**	20
Snows on Green | **W6**	21
Soho House | **W1**	18
Sotheby's Cafe | **W1**	19
NEW Stanza | **W1**	-
☑ St. John | **EC1**	25
St. John Bread/Wine | **E1**	22
Tate Britain | **SW1**	17
Thomas Cubitt | **SW1**	21
NEW Tom's Kitchen | **SW3**	19
Tuttons Brass. | **WC2**	18
Union Cafe | **W1**	21
Vineyard/Stockcross | **Berks**	24

BRITISH (TRAD.)

Abbeville | **SW4**	15
NEW Albion, The | **N1**	-
Annabel's | **W1**	22
Bentley's | **W1**	24
Bistrot 190 | **SW7**	19
Bleeding Heart | **EC1**	22

Boisdale | **multi. loc.**	20
Brian Turner | **W1**	21
Browns | **multi. loc.**	16
Brown's/The Grill | **W1**	22
Builders Arms | **SW3**	17
NEW Butcher & Grill | **SW11**	15
Butlers Wharf | **SE1**	20
Café Fish | **W1**	20
Canteen | **multi. loc.**	22
Chelsea Bun | **SW10**	18
Coach & Horses | **EC1**	19
☑ Dorchester/The Grill | **W1**	24
☑ ffiona's | **W8**	24
Fortnum's Fountain | **W1**	20
Foxtrot Oscar | **SW3**	15
Frontline | **W2**	13
Goring Dining Rm. | **SW1**	23
Green's | **SW1**	22
Grenadier, The | **SW1**	16
Grumbles | **SW1**	17
Guinea Grill | **W1**	22
Hind's Head | **Berks**	23
Inn The Park | **SW1**	17
Kew Grill | **TW9**	18
Langan's Bistro | **W1**	19
Langan's Brass. | **W1**	18
Maggie Jones's | **W8**	21
Mark's Club | **W1**	24
Marquess Tavern | **N1**	-
Notting Grill | **W11**	21
Odin's | **W1**	20
Paternoster Chop | **EC4**	18
Pig's Ear | **SW3**	22
Porters | **WC2**	20
Quality Chop House | **EC1**	20
☑ Rhodes 24 | **EC2**	23
☑ Rib Rm. | **SW1**	24
Richoux | **multi. loc.**	15
☑ Ritz, The | **W1**	23
Rivington Grill | **multi. loc.**	20
Rowley's | **SW1**	19
☑ Rules | **WC2**	23
Salisbury, The | **SW6**	-
NEW 1707 Wine Bar | **W1**	22
Shepherd's | **SW1**	18
Simpson's/Strand | **WC2**	20
Smiths/Top Floor | **EC1**	20
☑ Sweetings | **EC4**	24
☑ Wilton's | **SW1**	24
Ye Olde Cheshire | **EC4**	15

BURMESE

Mandalay | **W2**	23

CARIBBEAN

Cottons | **multi. loc.**	19

CHINESE

(* dim sum specialist)

Bar Shu	**W1**	22
China Tang*	**W1**	21
Chinese Experience*	**W1**	21
Chuen Cheng Ku*	**W1**	19
dim t*	**multi. loc.**	16
Dragon Castle	**SE17**	-
ECapital	**W1**	22
Eight Over Eight*	**SW3**	23
Four Seasons	**W2**	22
Fung Shing	**WC2**	22
Golden Dragon*	**W1**	20
Good Earth	**multi. loc.**	20
Green Cottage	**NW3**	-
Gung-Ho	**NW6**	21
☑ Hakkasan*	**W1**	24
Harbour City*	**W1**	20
☑ Hunan	**SW1**	28
Imperial China*	**WC2**	21
Imperial City	**EC3**	17
Jade Garden*	**W1**	19
Jenny Lo's Tea	**SW1**	20
Joy King Lau*	**WC2**	20
☑ Kai Mayfair	**W1**	25
Lee Ho Fook*	**W1**	17
Mandarin Kitchen	**W2**	23
Mao Tai*	**SW6**	22
Memories of China	**multi. loc.**	21
Mr. Chow	**SW1**	21
Mr. Kong	**WC2**	21
New Culture Rev.	**multi. loc.**	17
New World*	**W1**	19
Phoenix Palace*	**NW1**	23
Ping Pong*	**multi. loc.**	18
Princess Garden*	**W1**	21
☑ Royal China*	**multi. loc.**	24
Royal China Club*	**W1**	24
Shanghai Blues*	**WC1**	21
Song Que Café	**E2**	20
Wong Kei	**W1**	16
☑ Yauatcha*	**W1**	25
Y Ming	**W1**	-
Zen Central	**W1**	21
ZENW3	**NW3**	16

CHOPHOUSE

Black & Blue	**multi. loc.**	17
Butlers Wharf	**SE1**	20
Christopher's	**WC2**	19
El Gaucho	**multi. loc.**	21
☑ Gaucho Grill	**multi. loc.**	22
Greig's	**W1**	21
Guinea Grill	**W1**	22
NEW Hawksmoor	**E1**	28
Kew Grill	**TW9**	18

Le Relais de Venise	**W1**	18
Notting Grill	**W11**	21
Paternoster Chop	**EC4**	18
Popeseye	**multi. loc.**	-
Quality Chop House	**EC1**	20
☑ Rib Rm.	**SW1**	24
☑ Rules	**WC2**	23
Smiths/Top Floor	**EC1**	20
Smollensky's	**multi. loc.**	15
☑ Sophie's Steak	**SW10**	23

CUBAN

☑ Asia de Cuba	**WC2**	22
Floridita	**W1**	16

DANISH

Lundum's	**SW7**	22

ECLECTIC

Annex 3	**W1**	16
☑ Archipelago	**W1**	21
Axis	**WC2**	20
NEW Bacchus	**N1**	21
Banquette	**WC2**	22
Blakes	**SW7**	19
☑ Books for Cooks	**W11**	24
Brinkley's	**SW10**	16
Brunello	**SW7**	20
Cafe Med	**NW8**	18
Cantina Vinopolis	**SE1**	19
NEW Club, The	**W1**	-
Collection	**SW3**	13
Court	**WC1**	16
Dans Le Noir	**EC1**	13
Delfina	**SE1**	-
Ebury Wine Bar	**SW1**	19
Electric Brass.	**W11**	19
Enterprise	**SW3**	20
Giraffe	**multi. loc.**	17
Hoxton Apprentice	**N1**	18
NEW Hoxton Grille	**EC2**	-
Kettners	**W1**	15
☑ Lanes	**W1**	24
☑ Lanesborough	**SW1**	21
Light House	**SW19**	17
Michael Moore	**W1**	22
☑ Mosimann's	**SW1**	26
Motcombs	**SW1**	17
Oscar	**W1**	-
PJ's B&G	**SW3**	16
Providores, The	**W1**	22
Ransome's Dock	**SW11**	20
Six13	**W1**	19
Sonny's	**SW13**	21
Tom's Deli	**W11**	16
Troubadour, The	**SW5**	14
222 Veggie Vegan	**W14**	-

Vingt-Quatre | **SW10**	15
Wapping Food | **E1**	20
Westbourne, The | **W2**	16

EUROPEAN (MODERN)

Abbeville | **SW4**	15
Abingdon, The | **W8**	22
About Thyme | **SW1**	-
Addendum | **EC3**	-
Admiral Codrington | **SW3**	18
Albannach | **WC2**	14
Ambassador, The | **EC1**	21
Andrew Edmunds | **W1**	22
Arbutus | **W1**	24
Auberge du Lac | **AL8**	23
Avenue, The | **SW1**	18
Babylon | **W8**	20
Bank Westminster | **SW1**	18
Blandford St. | **W1**	18
Bluebird | **SW3**	-
Blueprint Café | **SE1**	18
Brackenbury | **W6**	18
Bull, The | **N6**	19
Bush B&G | **W12**	17
Camden Brass. | **NW1**	21
Chancery | **EC4**	18
Chapter Two | **SE3**	24
Charlotte's Place | **W5**	-
City Café | **SW1**	19
Clerkenwell | **EC1**	23
🆕 Cookbook Cafe | **W1**	-
Cuckoo Club | **W1**	15
Don | **EC4**	22
Dover St. | **W1**	17
Draper's Arms | **N1**	18
Drones | **SW1**	18
Ebury Dining Rm. | **SW1**	20
1880 | **SW7**	21
11 Abingdon Rd. | **W8**	18
Embassy | **W1**	13
🗹 Fat Duck | **Berks**	27
Fifth Floor | **SW1**	20
Fig | **N1**	-
Flaneur | **EC1**	22
🗹 Foliage | **SW1**	26
🆕 Forge, The | **WC2**	-
Frederick's | **N1**	20
🗹 Gate, The | **W6**	25
George | **W1**	22
🗹 Gordon Ramsay/Claridge's | **W1**	25
Greyhound, The | **SW11**	19
🆕 Hat & Feathers | **EC1**	-
🆕 High Road Brass. | **W4**	20
🗹 Home House | **W1**	20
Indigo | **WC2**	22

Inside | **SE10**	24
🗹 Ivy, The | **WC2**	23
Ladbroke Arms | **W11**	20
La Fromagerie | **W1**	24
Lansdowne, The | **NW1**	20
🗹 La Trompette | **W4**	27
Le Café/Jardin | **WC2**	19
🗹 Le Caprice | **SW1**	24
Le Deuxième | **WC2**	20
Little Bay | **multi. loc.**	21
Living Rm. | **W1**	19
Lonsdale | **W11**	15
🆕 Magdalen | **SE1**	-
Mju | **SW1**	20
Nicole's | **W1**	19
Notting Hill Brass. | **W11**	24
Odette's | **NW1**	20
Old Bull & Bush | **NW3**	14
1 Lombard Brass. | **EC3**	20
Oriel | **SW1**	15
Oxo Tower | **SE1**	20
Patterson's | **W1**	22
Petersham, The | **TW10**	23
Petersham Nurseries | **Richmond**	25
Pigalle Club | **W1**	14
Quaglino's | **SW1**	18
Randall & Aubin | **SW10**	19
Refuel | **W1**	12
Royal Exchange | **EC3**	16
Salt Yard | **W1**	22
Sam's Brass. | **W4**	20
🗹 Sketch/Gallery | **W1**	19
🗹 Sketch/Lecture Rm. | **W1**	21
🆕 Skylon | **SE1**	-
Sonny's | **SW13**	21
🆕 St. Alban | **SW1**	21
Tate Modern | **SE1**	16
🆕 Trinity | **SW4**	24
202 | **W11**	17
Union Cafe | **W1**	21
Vivat Bacchus | **EC4**	23
Wapping Food | **E1**	20
Waterway, The | **W9**	18
Wells, The | **NW3**	18
🗹 Wolseley, The | **W1**	21

FISH 'N' CHIPS

Geales Fish | **W8**	-
Golden Hind | **W1**	-
Livebait | **multi. loc.**	18
Nautilus Fish | **NW6**	21
🗹 North Sea | **WC1**	23
Seashell | **NW1**	20
🗹 Sweetings | **EC4**	24
🗹 Two Brothers Fish | **N3**	24

FRENCH (BISTRO)

Aubaine	**multi. loc.**	20
Bedford & Strand	**WC2**	17
Bibendum Oyster	**SW3**	22
Bistrotheque	**E2**	19
Café des Amis	**WC2**	19
Café Rouge	**multi. loc.**	14
Circus	**W1**	14
Comptoir Gascon	**EC1**	21
French House	**W1**	17
🖼 Galvin Bistrot	**W1**	24
Grumbles	**SW1**	17
La Bouchée	**SW7**	20
Langan's Coq d'Or	**SW5**	22
La Poule au Pot	**SW1**	22
L'Artiste Muscle	**W1**	19
Le Boudin Blanc	**W1**	22
🖼 Le Café/Marché	**EC1**	23
Le Colombier	**SW3**	20
Patisserie Valerie	**multi. loc.**	20
🖼 Racine	**SW3**	22
Truc Vert	**W1**	22

FRENCH (BRASSERIE)

Bellamy's	**W1**	18
Brasserie Roux	**SW1**	20
Brasserie St. Quentin	**SW3**	18
Café Boheme	**W1**	16
NEW Chelsea Brass.	**SW1**	16
Cheyne Walk	**SW3**	23
Chez Gérard	**multi. loc.**	18
Incognico	**WC2**	21
La Brasserie	**SW3**	16
Langan's Brass.	**W1**	18
Mon Plaisir	**WC2**	18
Oriel	**SW1**	15
NEW St. Germain	**EC1**	21
Tartine	**SW3**	18
Tuttons Brass.	**WC2**	18

FRENCH (CLASSIC)

Almeida	**N1**	18
Annabel's	**W1**	22
Auberge du Lac	**AL8**	23
Aurora	**EC2**	19
Bradley's	**NW3**	15
Brasserie St. Quentin	**SW3**	18
Chez Gérard	**multi. loc.**	18
Chez Kristof	**W6**	22
NEW Chez Patrick	**W8**	21
Coq d'Argent	**EC2**	18
Ebury Wine Bar	**SW1**	19
Elena's l'Etoile	**W1**	20
Entrecote Café	**W1**	18
Farm	**SW6**	-
🖼 Foliage	**SW1**	26
French Horn	**Berks**	23

Hush	**W1**	17
La Bouchée	**SW7**	20
La Brasserie	**SW3**	16
Ladurée	**SW1**	23
Langan's Bistro	**W1**	19
Langan's Brass.	**W1**	18
La Poule au Pot	**SW1**	22
La Trouvaille	**W1**	20
L'Aventure	**NW8**	22
🖼 Le Café/Marché	**EC1**	23
Le Colombier	**SW3**	20
🖼 Le Gavroche	**W1**	27
Le Pont de la Tour	**SE1**	22
Le Relais de Venise	**W1**	18
L'Escargot	**W1**	22
🖼 Les Trois Garçons	**E1**	19
Le Suquet	**SW3**	23
Le Vacherin	**W4**	23
L'Oranger	**SW1**	24
Lou Pescadou	**SW5**	20
Mark's Club	**W1**	24
Mirabelle	**W1**	22
Mon Plaisir	**WC2**	18
Morel	**SW4**	-
Odin's	**W1**	20
Oslo Court	**NW8**	22
NEW Papillon	**SW3**	23
Pigalle Club	**W1**	14
Poissonnerie	**SW3**	21
🖼 Racine	**SW3**	22
🖼 Ritz, The	**W1**	23
Sauterelle	**EC3**	-
Villandry	**W1**	18
Vineyard/Stockcross	**Berks**	24
NEW 🖼 Wallace, The	**W1**	20
🖼 Waterside Inn	**Berks**	27

FRENCH (NEW)

🖼 Aubergine	**SW10**	26
Belvedere, The	**W8**	20
🖼 Bibendum	**SW3**	24
Bleeding Heart	**EC1**	22
Bonds	**EC2**	20
Café des Amis	**WC2**	19
🖼 Capital Rest.	**SW3**	27
Cellar Gascon	**EC1**	20
🖼 Cliveden House	**Berks**	24
Clos Maggiore	**WC2**	24
🖼 Club Gascon	**EC1**	26
Cross Keys	**SW3**	14
Dans Le Noir	**EC1**	13
1880	**SW7**	21
Food Rm.	**SW8**	-
Galvin/Windows	**W1**	22
🖼 Gordon Ramsay/68 Royal	**SW3**	28
Greenhouse, The	**W1**	25

Hand & Flowers | **SL7**	–
Incognico | **WC2**	21
Jaan | **WC2**	–
La Noisette | **SW1**	21
🆕 🗷 L'Atelier/Robuchon | **WC2**	26
🗷 La Trompette | **W4**	27
La Trouvaille | **W1**	20
Le Cercle | **SW1**	24
Ledbury | **W11**	25
🗷 Le Manoir/Quat | **Oxfordshire**	28
Le Mercury | **N1**	18
Le Palais Du Jardin | **WC2**	18
🗷 L'Etranger | **SW7**	24
🗷 Maze | **W1**	25
🗷 Morgan M | **N7**	27
Morton's | **W1**	24
1 Lombard St. | **EC3**	22
One-O-One | **SW1**	23
Orrery | **W1**	25
Pearl | **WC1**	24
🗷 Pétrus | **SW1**	28
🗷 Pied à Terre | **W1**	28
Pig's Ear | **SW3**	22
Plateau | **E14**	19
🗷 Roussillon | **SW1**	26
🆕 Spread Eagle | **SE10**	21
🗷 Square, The | **W1**	28
🗷 Tom Aikens | **SW3**	26
Upstairs | **SW2**	–
🗷 Waterside Inn | **Berks**	27

GASTROPUB

Admiral Codrington | British/Euro. | **SW3**	18
Anchor & Hope | British | **SE1**	24
Anglesea Arms | British | **W6**	23
🆕 Bacchus | Eclectic | **N1**	21
Barnsbury, The | British | **N1**	21
Builders Arms | British | **SW3**	17
Bull, The | Euro. | **N6**	19
🗷 Churchill Arms | Thai | **W8**	22
Coach & Horses | British/Med. | **EC1**	19
Cow Dining Rm. | British | **W2**	21
Draper's Arms | Euro. | **N1**	18
Duke of Cambridge | British | **N1**	20
Eagle, The | Med. | **EC1**	21
Ebury Dining Rm. | Euro. | **SW1**	20
Engineer | British | **NW1**	19
Enterprise | Eclectic | **SW3**	20
Farm | French | **SW6**	–
🆕 Great Queen St. | British | **WC2**	–
Grenadier, The | British | **SW1**	16
Greyhound, The | British/Euro. | **SW11**	19

Gun, The | British | **E14**	19
🆕 Hat & Feathers | Euro. | **EC1**	–
Ladbroke Arms | Euro. | **W11**	20
Lansdowne, The | Euro. | **NW1**	20
Marquess Tavern | British | **N1**	–
Mash | British | **W1**	12
🆕 Narrow, The | British | **E14**	–
1 Lombard Brass. | British/Euro. | **EC3**	20
Palmerston, The | British | **SE22**	–
Pig's Ear | British/French | **SW3**	22
Salusbury Pub | Italian/Med. | **NW6**	18
Thomas Cubitt | British | **SW1**	21
Wells, The | Euro. | **NW3**	18
Westbourne, The | Eclectic | **W2**	16
Ye Olde Cheshire | British | **EC4**	15

GREEK

Costas Grill | **W8**	18
Halepi | **W2**	24
Lemonia | **NW1**	20
Real Greak | **multi. loc.**	16

HAMBURGERS

Babes 'n' Burgers | **W11**	17
Diner, The | **EC2**	–
Eagle Bar Diner | **W1**	19
Ed's Easy Diner | **multi. loc.**	15
Gourmet Burger | **multi. loc.**	21
Hard Rock | **W1**	13
Joe Allen | **WC2**	17
Kettners | **W1**	15
🗷 Lucky 7 | **W2**	20
Maxwell's | **WC2**	17
Planet Hollywood | **W1**	11
Smollensky's | **multi. loc.**	15
🗷 Sophie's Steak | **SW10**	23
Sticky Fingers | **W8**	14
T.G.I. Friday's | **multi. loc.**	11
Tootsies | **multi. loc.**	16
Vingt-Quatre | **SW10**	15

HUNGARIAN

Gay Hussar | **W1**	16

INDIAN

🗷 Amaya | **SW1**	25
Benares | **W1**	23
Bengal Clipper | **SE1**	21
Bombay Bicycle | **multi. loc.**	18
Bombay Brass. | **SW7**	22
Café Spice Namasté | **E1**	23
Chor Bizarre | **W1**	21
Chowki | **W1**	21
Chutney Mary | **SW10**	23

Chutney's | **NW1**	23
🄩 Cinnamon Club | **SW1**	24
Deya | **W1**	23
Gopal's of Soho | **W1**	22
Imli | **W1**	20
Indian Zing | **W6**	-
Kastoori | **SW17**	-
Khan's | **W2**	20
Khan's of Kensington | **SW7**	22
🄩 La Porte des Indes | **W1**	21
Ma Goa | **multi. loc.**	23
Malabar | **W8**	20
Malabar Junction | **WC1**	23
Masala Zone | **multi. loc.**	19
Mela | **WC2**	23
Mint Leaf | **SW1**	20
Moti Mahal | **WC2**	19
Noor Jahan | **multi. loc.**	22
Painted Heron | **SW10**	22
🄩 Quilon | **SW1**	25
Rasa | **multi. loc.**	24
🄩 Rasoi Vineet Bhatia | **SW3**	27
Red Fort | **W1**	23
Sarkhel's | **SW18**	22
NEW Sitaaray | **WC2**	-
Soho Spice | **W1**	20
Star of India | **SW5**	24
🄩 Tamarind | **W1**	25
Vama | **SW10**	24
Veeraswamy | **W1**	22
Zaika | **W8**	25

INDONESIAN

Nancy Lam's Enak | **SW11**	-

IRISH

Richard Corrigan | **W1**	23

ITALIAN

Aglio e Olio | **SW10**	21
Al Duca | **SW1**	19
Alloro | **W1**	22
Amici Bar/Kitchen | **SW17**	15
Aperitivo | **W1**	20
Ark | **W8**	15
Armani Caffé | **SW3**	17
Artigiano | **NW3**	20
Ask Pizza | **multi. loc.**	16
🄩 Assaggi | **W2**	26
Bertorelli | **multi. loc.**	17
Brunello | **SW7**	20
Buona Sera | **multi. loc.**	23
Caldesi | **N** | **W1**	22
Camerino | **W1**	-
Cantina del Ponte | **SE1**	17
Caraffini | **SW1**	21
Caravaggio | **EC3**	19

🄩 Carluccio's | **multi. loc.**	17
Carpaccio | **SW3**	18
Casale Franco | **N1**	-
Cecconi's | **W1**	21
C Garden | **SW3**	18
🄩 Cipriani | **W1**	20
Ciro's Pizza | **multi. loc.**	17
Como Lario | **SW1**	18
Da Mario | **SW7**	22
Daphne's | **SW3**	21
🄩 Delfino | **W1**	23
Diverso | **W1**	21
Elena's l'Etoile | **W1**	20
Elistano | **SW3**	18
🄩 Enoteca Turi | **SW15**	27
Essenza | **W11**	18
Fiore | **SW1**	21
Franco's | **SW1**	15
Frankie's Italian | **multi. loc.**	15
Friends | **SW10**	18
Getti | **multi. loc.**	17
Giardinetto | **W1**	19
Giovanni's | **WC2**	21
Green Olive | **W9**	20
Harry's Bar | **W1**	24
🄩 Il Bordello | **E1**	23
Il Convivio | **SW1**	23
Il Falconiere | **SW7**	15
Il Portico | **W8**	22
L'Accento Italiano | **W2**	-
La Collina | **NW1**	-
La Famiglia | **SW10**	21
La Figa | **E14**	-
La Genova | **W1**	23
La Porchetta | **multi. loc.**	19
Latium | **W1**	25
L'Incontro | **SW1**	20
Little Italy | **W1**	16
🄩 Locanda Locatelli | **W1**	25
Locanda Ottoemezzo | **W8**	24
Luciano | **SW1**	20
Lucio | **SW3**	21
Made in Italy | **SW3**	21
Manicomio | **SW3**	18
Mediterraneo | **W11**	22
Metrogusto | **N1**	21
Mimmo d'Ischia | **SW1**	21
Montpeliano | **SW7**	18
Monza | **SW3**	20
Mosaico | **W1**	21
Oliveto | **SW1**	23
Olivo | **SW1**	21
NEW Olivomare | **SW1**	-
Orso | **WC2**	20
Osteria Antica | **SW11**	-
🄩 Osteria Basilico | **W11**	24
Osteria dell'Arancio | **SW10**	20

Pappagallo	W1	21
Passione	W1	23
Pellicano	SW3	20
Z Pizza Express	multi. loc.	17
Pizza Metro	SW11	-
Pizza on the Park	SW1	14
Quadrato	E14	24
Z Quirinale	SW1	25
Quo Vadis	W1	18
NEW Raviolo	SW12	-
Red Pepper	W9	19
Refettorio	EC4	20
Riccardo's	SW3	18
NEW Rist. Semplice	W1	-
Riva	SW13	20
Z River Café	W6	27
Rosmarino	NW8	17
Sale e Pepe	SW1	20
Salusbury Pub	NW6	18
San Lorenzo	multi. loc.	20
Santa Lucia	SW10	22
Santini	SW1	22
Sardo	W1	23
Sardo Canale	NW1	20
Sartoria	W1	20
Scalini	SW3	23
Signor Sassi	SW1	22
Spago	SW7	19
Spiga	W1	15
Strada	multi. loc.	18
Tentazioni	SE1	27
NEW Z Theo Randall	W1	26
Timo	W8	22
Toto's	SW3	24
NEW 2 Veneti	W1	-
Vasco & Piero's	W1	21
NEW Via Condotti	W1	18
Z Zafferano	SW1	26
Ziani	SW3	25
Zilli Fish	W1	20
Zizzi	multi. loc.	16

JAPANESE

(* sushi specialist)

Abeno	multi. loc.	21
Asakusa	NW1	-
NEW Atami	SW1	24
Benihana	multi. loc.	18
Z Café Japan*	NW11	26
City Miyama*	EC4	25
Z Defune*	W1	27
NEW Dinings*	W1	-
Feng Sushi*	multi. loc.	17
Ikeda*	W1	21
Ikkyu	W1	19
Inaho*	W2	21
itsu*	multi. loc.	18
Z Jin Kichi*	NW3	26
Kiku*	W1	24
NEW Kobe Jones	WC1	18
Koi*	W8	22
Kulu Kulu*	multi. loc.	20
Matsuri*	multi. loc.	21
Mitsukoshi*	SW1	19
Z Miyama*	W1	26
Moshi Moshi*	multi. loc.	20
Z Nobu Berkeley St*	W1	26
Z Nobu London*	W1	27
Nozomi	SW3	19
Roka*	W1	25
Saki Bar/Food Emp.*	EC1	-
Sakura*	W1	23
Satsuma	W1	20
Shogun*	W1	23
Sumosan	W1	20
Ten Ten Tei*	W1	23
Tokyo Diner	WC2	20
Tsunami	SW4	24
Ubon*	E14	24
Z Umu*	W1	26
Z Wagamama	multi. loc.	19
Yakitoria*	W2	24
YO! Sushi*	multi. loc.	17
Yoshino*	W1	24
NEW Yumenoki*	SW10	-
Z Zuma*	SW7	26

JEWISH

Bevis Marks	EC3	-
Bloom's	NW11	19
Gaby's	WC2	-
Harry Morgan's	multi. loc.	16
Reubens	W1	20

KOREAN

| Asadal | WC1 | - |

KOSHER

Bevis Marks	EC3	-
Bloom's	NW11	19
Met Su Yan	NW11	16
Reubens	W1	20
Six13	W1	19
Solly's	NW11	17

LEBANESE

Z Al Hamra	W1	22
Al Sultan	W1	22
Z Al Waha	W2	22
Beiteddine	SW1	22
Dish Dash	multi. loc.	18
Fairuz	multi. loc.	22
Fakhreldine	W1	21
Z Ishbilia	SW1	24

CUISINES

Levant | **W1** _19_
Levantine | **W2** _20_
Mamounia | **W1** _17_
Maroush | **multi. loc.** _20_
Noura | **multi. loc.** _21_

MALAYSIAN

Awana | **SW3** _17_
Champor | **SE1** _18_
Nyonya | **W11** _24_
Silks & Spice | **multi. loc.** _16_
Singapore Garden | **NW6** _21_
🆕 Suka | **W1** _-_

MEDITERRANEAN

About Thyme | **SW1** _-_
Aquasia | **SW10** _21_
Baker & Spice | **multi. loc.** _22_
Bistrot 190 | **SW7** _19_
Cafe Med | **NW8** _18_
Cantina Vinopolis | **SE1** _19_
Citrus | **W1** _20_
🄩 Cliveden House | **Berks** _24_
Coach & Horses | **EC1** _19_
Cru | **N1** _15_
Dover St. | **W1** _17_
Eagle, The | **EC1** _21_
Fifteen | **N1** _23_
Fifth Floor Cafe | **SW1** _18_
Food Rm. | **SW8** _-_
Franco's | **SW1** _15_
Leon | **multi. loc.** _19_
Little Bay | **multi. loc.** _21_
🆕 Mimosa | **SW1** _-_
Morel | **SW4** _-_
🄩 Moro | **EC1** _25_
Nicole's | **W1** _19_
🄩 Ottolenghi | **multi. loc.** _24_
Oxo Tower Brass. | **SE1** _20_
Pescatori | **W1** _22_
Portal | **EC1** _-_
Raoul's | **multi. loc.** _16_
Rocket | **multi. loc.** _17_
Salusbury Pub | **NW6** _18_
Sarastro | **WC2** _12_
Union Cafe | **W1** _21_
Zetter | **EC1** _19_

MEXICAN

Cafe Pacifico | **WC2** _18_
Crazy Homies | **W2** _20_
Green & Red Bar | **E1** _20_
La Perla | **multi. loc.** _15_
Mestizo | **NW1** _19_
Taqueria | **W11** _18_
Texas Embassy | **SW1** _13_

MIDDLE EASTERN

Gaby's | **WC2** _-_

MOROCCAN

Aziz | **SW6** _17_
Bouga | **N8** _-_
Mamounia | **W1** _17_
Original Tagine | **W1** _20_
Pasha | **SW7** _18_

NORTH AFRICAN

🄩 Momo | **W1** _19_
Souk | **WC2** _18_

PAKISTANI

New Tayyabs | **E1** _24_
Original Lahore | **multi. loc.** _24_
Salloos | **SW1** _23_

PAN-ASIAN

Cicada | **EC1** _15_
Cocoon | **W1** _21_
dim t | **multi. loc.** _16_
e&o | **W11** _22_
Eight Over Eight | **SW3** _23_
Gilgamesh | **NW1** _20_
🆕 Haiku | **W1** _-_
Mao Tai | **SW6** _22_
Met Su Yan | **NW11** _16_
Oxo Tower Brass. | **SE1** _20_
🄩 Park, The | **SW1** _24_
🄩 Taman gang | **W1** _22_
🆕 Tamarai | **WC2** _-_
Uli | **W11** _25_
🆕 XO | **NW3** _16_

PERSIAN

Alounak | **multi. loc.** _23_
Dish Dash | **multi. loc.** _18_
Kandoo | **W2** _-_

PIZZA

Ask Pizza | **multi. loc.** _16_
Basilico | **multi. loc.** _17_
Buona Sera | **multi. loc.** _23_
Cantina del Ponte | **SE1** _17_
Casale Franco | **N1** _-_
Ciro's Pizza | **multi. loc.** _17_
🄩 Delfino | **W1** _23_
Fire & Stone | **WC2** _18_
Firezza | **multi. loc.** _18_
Friends | **SW10** _18_
🄩 Il Bordello | **E1** _23_
Kettners | **W1** _15_
La Porchetta | **multi. loc.** _19_
Made in Italy | **SW3** _21_
Oliveto | **SW1** _23_

Orso	**WC2**	20
☑ Osteria Basilico	**W11**	24
☑ Pizza Express	**multi. loc.**	17
Pizza Metro	**SW11**	-
Pizza on the Park	**SW1**	14
Red Pepper	**W9**	19
Rocket	**multi. loc.**	17
Spago	**SW7**	19
Spiga	**W1**	15
Strada	**multi. loc.**	18
Zizzi	**multi. loc.**	16

POLISH

Baltic	**SE1**	21
Daquise	**SW7**	20
Wòdka	**W8**	20

PORTUGUESE

Eyre Brothers	**EC2**	22
Portal	**EC1**	-

RUSSIAN

Potemkin	**EC1**	-

SCOTTISH

Albannach	**WC2**	14
Boisdale	**multi. loc.**	20

SEAFOOD

☑ Belgo	**multi. loc.**	19
Bentley's	**W1**	24
Bibendum Oyster	**SW3**	22
Big Easy	**SW3**	16
Bluebird	**SW3**	-
Café Fish	**W1**	20
Cow Dining Rm.	**W2**	21
fish!	**SE1**	19
Fish Hook	**W4**	24
Fish Shop	**EC1**	19
FishWorks	**multi. loc.**	20
Geales Fish	**W8**	-
Green's	**SW1**	22
☑ J. Sheekey	**WC2**	25
Le Pont de la Tour	**SE1**	22
Le Suquet	**SW3**	23
Livebait	**multi. loc.**	18
Loch Fyne	**WC2**	18
Lou Pescadou	**SW5**	20
Nautilus Fish	**NW6**	21
☑ North Sea	**WC1**	23
NEW Olivomare	**SW1**	-
One-O-One	**SW1**	23
Pescatori	**W1**	22
Poissonnerie	**SW3**	21
Randall & Aubin	**multi. loc.**	19
Scott's	**W1**	22

Seashell	**NW1**	20
☑ Sweetings	**EC4**	24
☑ Two Brothers Fish	**N3**	24
☑ Wilton's	**SW1**	24
Zilli Fish	**W1**	20

SINGAPOREAN

Singapore Garden	**NW6**	21
Singapura	**multi. loc.**	20

SMALL PLATES

(See also Spanish tapas specialist)

☑ Amaya	Indian	**SW1**	25
Aperitivo	Italian	**W1**	20
NEW Burlington Club	French	**W1**	-
Cellar Gascon	French	**EC1**	20
☑ Club Gascon	French	**EC1**	26
NEW Dinings	Japanese	**W1**	-
☑ Hunan	Chinese	**SW1**	28
Il Convivio	Italian	**SW1**	23
La Perla	Mexican	**multi. loc.**	15
Le Cercle	French	**SW1**	24
Lonsdale	Pan-Asian	**W11**	15
☑ Maze	French	**W1**	25
Providores, The	Eclectic	**W1**	22
Real Greak	Greek	**N1**	16
NEW Trinity	Euro.	**SW4**	24
Upper Glas	Swedish	**N1**	22

SOUTH AMERICAN

El Rincon Latino	**SW4**	-
1492	**SW6**	21
La Piragua	**N1**	15
Sabor	**N1**	22

SPANISH

(* tapas specialist)

NEW Barrafina*	**W1**	24
NEW Burlington Club	**W1**	-
☑ Cambio de Tercio	**SW5**	24
Cigala*	**WC1**	22
El Blason*	**SW3**	18
☑ El Pirata*	**W1**	23
El Rincon Latino*	**SW4**	-
Eyre Brothers	**EC2**	22
☑ Fino*	**W1**	23
Galicia*	**W10**	22
Goya*	**SW1**	16
La Rueda*	**multi. loc.**	14
NEW L-Rest. & Bar*	**W8**	-
Meson Don Felipe*	**SE1**	18
Meza*	**W1**	17
Rebato's*	**SW8**	-
Salt Yard*	**W1**	22
Tapas Brindisa*	**SE1**	22
Tendido Cero*	**SW5**	-

SWEDISH

Garbo's | **W1**	15
Upper Glas | **N1**	22

THAI

Bangkok | **SW7**	19
NEW Benja | **W1**	-
Ben's Thai | **W9**	15
Blue Elephant | **SW6**	20
Z Busaba Eathai | **multi. loc.**	21
Chiang Mai | **W1**	21
Z Churchill Arms | **W8**	22
Crazy Bear | **W1**	21
Esarn Kheaw | **W12**	-
Isarn | **N1**	22
Jim Thompson's | **multi. loc.**	15
Mango Tree | **SW1**	20
Z Nahm | **SW1**	26
Z Patara | **multi. loc.**	23
Pepper Tree | **SW4**	19
Silks & Spice | **multi. loc.**	16
Singapura | **EC3**	20
Sri Nam | **E14**	18
Thai Pavilion | **SE11**	18
Thai Square | **multi. loc.**	19

TURKISH

Efes | **W1**	18
Gallipoli | **N1**	18
Haz | **E1**	25
Ishtar | **W1**	22
Ozer | **W1**	19
Pasha | **N1**	20
Sofra | **multi. loc.**	19
Tas | **multi. loc.**	20

VEGETARIAN
(* vegan)

Blah! Blah! Blah! | **W12**	18
Chutney's | **NW1**	23
Eat & Two Veg | **W1**	17
Z Food for Thought | **WC2**	24
Z Gate, The | **W6**	25
Kastoori | **SW17**	-
Z Lanesborough | **SW1**	21
Mildreds* | **W1**	22
Z Morgan M | **N7**	27
Rasa | **multi. loc.**	24
Z Roussillon | **SW1**	26
222 Veggie Vegan* | **W14**	-

VIETNAMESE

Bam-Bou | **W1**	21
Cay tre | **EC1**	24
Nam Long-Le Shaker | **SW5**	14
Viet Hoa | **E2**	23
Song Que Café | **E2**	20
Viet Hoa | **E2**	23

Locations

Includes restaurant names, cuisines, Food ratings and, for neighbourhoods that are mapped, top list and map coordinates. ⚡ indicates places with the highest ratings, popularity and importance.

Central London

BELGRAVIA
(See map on page 200)

TOP FOOD

Pétrus	*French*	**A9**	28
Zafferano	*Italian*	**B9**	26
Nahm	*Thai*	**B10**	26
Amaya	*Indian*	**B9**	25
Ishbilia	*Lebanese*	**A9**	24

LISTING

⚡ Amaya	*Indian*	**B9**	25
Baker & Spice	*Med.*	**E10**	22
Boxwood Café	*British*	**A9**	21
Drones	*Euro.*	**C9**	18
Ebury Wine Bar	*Eclectic*	**E11**	19
Goya	*Spanish*	**F11**	16
Grenadier, The	*British*	**B9**	16
Il Convivio	*Italian*	**E10**	23
⚡ Ishbilia	*Lebanese*	**A9**	24
Jenny Lo's Tea	*Chinese*	**E11**	20
⚡ Lanesborough	*Eclectic*	**A10**	21
La Noisette	*French*	**B8**	21
Memories of China	*Chinese*	**E11**	21
Mimmo d'Ischia	*Italian*	**E10**	21
NEW Mimosa	*Med.*	**C9**	–
⚡ Mosimann's	*Eclectic*	**C9**	26
Motcombs	*Eclectic*	**C9**	17
⚡ Nahm	*Thai*	**B10**	26
Oliveto	*Italian*	**E10**	23
NEW Olivomare	*Italian/Seafood*	**D11**	–
Patisserie Valerie	*French*	**B9**	20
⚡ Pétrus	*French*	**A9**	28
Pizza on the Park	*Pizza*	**A9**	14
⚡ Rib Rm.	*British/Chops*	**C9**	24
Salloos	*Pakistani*	**A9**	23
Santini	*Italian*	**D11**	22
Thomas Cubitt	*British*	**E10**	21
⚡ Zafferano	*Italian*	**B9**	26

BLOOMSBURY/
FITZROVIA

Abeno	*Jap.*	21
All Star Lanes	*Amer.*	15
Annex 3	*French*	16
⚡ Archipelago	*Eclectic*	21
Ask Pizza	*Pizza*	16
Bam-Bou	*SE Asian*	21

Bertorelli	*Italian*	17
⚡ Busaba Eathai	*Thai*	21
Camerino	*Italian*	–
⚡ Carluccio's	*Italian*	17
Chez Gérard	*French*	18
Cigala	*Spanish*	22
Court	*Eclectic*	16
Crazy Bear	*Thai*	21
dim t	*Chinese*	16
Eagle Bar Diner	*Amer.*	19
Efes	*Turkish*	18
Elena's l'Etoile	*French/Italian*	20
⚡ Fino	*Spanish*	23
⚡ Hakkasan	*Chinese*	24
Harry Morgan's	*Deli/Jewish*	16
Ikkyu	*Jap.*	19
NEW Kobe Jones	*Jap.*	18
La Perla	*Mex.*	15
Latium	*Italian*	25
Malabar Junction	*Indian*	23
Mash	*British*	12
⚡ North Sea	*Seafood*	23
Oscar	*Eclectic*	–
Passione	*Italian*	23
Pescatori	*Med.*	22
⚡ Pied à Terre	*French*	28
Ping Pong	*Chinese*	18
Rasa	*Indian*	24
Roka	*Jap.*	25
Salt Yard	*Euro.*	22
Sardo	*Italian*	23
NEW Suka	*Malaysian*	–
Tas	*Turkish*	20
Villandry	*French*	18
⚡ Wagamama	*Jap.*	19
YO! Sushi	*Jap.*	17
Zizzi	*Pizza*	16

CHINATOWN

Chinese Experience	*Chinese*	21
Chuen Cheng Ku	*Chinese*	19
ECapital	*Chinese*	22
Fung Shing	*Chinese*	22
Golden Dragon	*Chinese*	20
Harbour City	*Chinese*	20
Imperial China	*Chinese*	21
Jade Garden	*Chinese*	19
Joy King Lau	*Chinese*	20
Lee Ho Fook	*Chinese*	17
Mr. Kong	*Chinese*	21

New World | *Chinese* 19
Tokyo Diner | *Jap.* 20
Wong Kei | *Chinese* 16

COVENT GARDEN

(See map on page 202)

TOP FOOD

L'Atelier/Robuchon | *French* | **B8** 26
J. Sheekey | *Seafood* | **C8** 25
Food for Thought | *Veg.* | **B9** 24
Savoy Grill | *British* | **D10** 24
Clos Maggiore | *French* | **C9** 24

LISTING

Adam St. | *British* | **D10** 20
Admiralty, The | *British* | **D11** 19
☑ Asia de Cuba | *Asian/Cuban* | **C8** 22
Axis | *British/Eclectic* | **C10** 20
Banquette | *Eclectic* | **D10** 22
Bedford & Strand | *British/French* | **D9** 17
☑ Belgo | *Belgian* | **B9** 19
Bertorelli | *Italian* | **C9** | **D8** 17
Bierodrome | *Belgian* | **B11** 17
Browns | *British* | **C8** 16
Café des Amis | *French* | **C10** 19
Cafe Pacifico | *Mex.* | **C9** 18
Café Rouge | *French* | **C10** 14
Chez Gérard | *French* | **C10** 18
Christopher's | *Amer./Chops* | **C10** 19
Clos Maggiore | *French* | **C9** 24
Ed's Easy Diner | *Hamburgers* | **C8** 15
Fire & Stone | *Pizza* | **D9** 18
☑ Food for Thought | *Veg.* | **B9** 24
NEW Forge, The | *Euro.* | **C9** –
Gaby's | *Jewish/Mideast.* | **C8** –
Giovanni's | *Italian* | **C9** 21
Gourmet Burger | *Hamburgers* | **D9** 21
NEW Great Queen St. | *British* | **B10** –
Indigo | *Euro.* | **B10** 22
☑ Ivy, The | *British/Euro.* | **B8** 23
Jaan | *French* | **D11** –
Joe Allen | *Amer.* | **C10** 17
☑ J. Sheekey | *Seafood* | **C8** 25
Kulu Kulu | *Jap.* | **B9** 20
La Perla | *Mex.* | **D9** 15
NEW ☑ L'Atelier/Robuchon | *French* | **B8** 26
Le Café/Jardin | *Euro.* | **C10** 19
Le Deuxième | *Euro.* | **B10** 20
Leon | *Med.* | **D9** 19
Le Palais Du Jardin | *French* | **C9** 18
Livebait | *Seafood* | **D10** 18
Loch Fyne | *Seafood* | **C10** 18
Maxwell's | *Amer.* | **C9** 17

Mela | *Indian* | **B8** 23
Mon Plaisir | *French* | **B9** 18
Moti Mahal | *Indian* | **B10** 19
Orso | *Italian* | **C10** 20
Patisserie Valerie | *French* | **C10** 20
☑ Pizza Express | *Pizza* | **B10** 17
PJ's B&G | *Amer.* | **C10** 16
Porters | *British* | **D9** 20
Real Greak | *Greek* | **B9** 16
☑ Rules | *British/Chops* | **C9** 23
Sarastro | *Med.* | **C11** 12
☑ Savoy Grill | *British* | **D10** 24
Simpson's/Strand | *British* | **D10** 20
NEW Sitaaray | *Indian* | **B10** –
Smollensky's | *Chops* | **D10** 15
Sofra | *Turkish* | **C10** 19
Souk | *African* | **B9** 18
NEW Tamarai | *Pan-Asian* | **B10** –
T.G.I. Friday's | *Amer.* | **C7** | **D9** 11
Thai Square | *Thai* | **D10** 19
Tuttons Brass. | *British/French* | **C10** 18
☑ Wagamama | *Jap.* | **C10** 19
Zizzi | *Pizza* | **B10** | **D9** 16

HOLBORN

Asadal | *Korean* –
Bleeding Heart | *British/French* 22
Chancery | *Euro.* 18
Chez Gérard | *French* 18
☑ Gaucho Grill | *Argent./Chops* 22
La Porchetta | *Pizza* 19
Matsuri | *Jap.* 21
Pearl | *French* 24
Shanghai Blues | *Chinese* 21
Strada | *Italian* 18

KNIGHTSBRIDGE

(See map on page 200)

TOP FOOD

Capital Rest. | *French* | **B8** 27
Zuma | *Jap.* | **A7** 26
Foliage | *Euro./French* | **A8** 26
Ishbilia | *Lebanese* | **B7** 24
Park, The | *Pan-Asian* | **A8** 24

LISTING

Armani Caffé | *Italian* | **C6** 17
Beiteddine | *Lebanese* | **B8** 22
Brasserie St. Quentin | *French* | **C5** 18
Café Rouge | *French* | **C7** 14
☑ Capital Rest. | *French* | **B8** 27
Ciro's Pizza | *Pizza* | **C6** 17
Fifth Floor | *Euro.* | **A8** 20
Fifth Floor Cafe | *British/Med.* | **A8** 18
☑ Foliage | *Euro./French* | **A8** 26

Frankie's Italian | *Italian* | **C6**   15
Good Earth | *Chinese* | **C6**   20
Harry Morgan's | 16
  Deli/Jewish | **B7**
☑ Ishbilia | *Lebanese* | **B7**   24
Joe's Rest. Bar | *British* | **B8**   21
Ladurée | *French* | **B7**   23
Leon | *Med.* | **B7**   19
Maroush | *Lebanese* | **C7**   20
Mju | *Euro.* | **B8**   20
NEW Mocotó | *Brazilian* | **A7**   22
Montpeliano | *Italian* | **B6**   18
Monza | *Italian* | **C6**   20
Mr. Chow | *Chinese* | **A7**   21
Nozomi | *Jap.* | **C7**   19
One-O-One | 23
  French/Seafood | **A9**
Oratory, The | *British* | **D5**   18
☑ Park, The | *Pan-Asian* | **A8**   24
☑ Patara | *Thai* | **C7**   23
Patisserie Valerie | 20
  French | **B7** | **D5**
☑ Pizza Express | *Pizza* | **C7**   17
☑ Racine | *French* | **C5**   22
Richoux | *British* | **B7**   15
Sale e Pepe | *Italian* | **C8**   20
San Lorenzo | *Italian* | **C7**   20
Signor Sassi | *Italian* | **B7**   22
☑ Wagamama | *Jap.* | **A7**   19
YO! Sushi | *Jap.* | **B7** | **C10**   17
☑ Zuma | *Jap.* | **A7**   26

MARYLEBONE

Black & Blue | *Chops*   17
Blandford St. | *British/Euro.*   18
☑ Busaba Eathai | *Thai*   21
Caldesi | *Italian*   22
☑ Carluccio's | *Italian*   17
Chutney's | *Indian*   23
☑ Defune | *Jap.*   27
Deya | *Indian*   23
NEW Dinings | *Jap.*   -
Eat & Two Veg | *Veg.*   17
Entrecote Café | *French*   18
Fairuz | *Lebanese*   22
FishWorks | *Seafood*   20
Frankie's Italian | *Italian*   15
☑ Galvin Bistrot | *French*   24
Garbo's | *Swedish*   15
Getti | *Italian*   17
Giraffe | *Eclectic*   17
Golden Hind | *Seafood*   -
☑ Home House | *British/Euro.*   20
Ishtar | *Turkish*   22
Kandoo | *Persian*   -
La Fromagerie | *Euro.*   24
Langan's Bistro | *British/French*   19

☑ La Porte des Indes | *Indian*   21
La Rueda | *Spanish*   14
Leon | *Med.*   19
Le Pain Quotidien | 19
  Bakery/Belgian
Le Relais de Venise | *French*   18
Levant | *Lebanese*   19
☑ Locanda Locatelli | *Italian*   25
Mandalay | *Burmese*   23
Maroush | *Lebanese*   20
Michael Moore | *Eclectic*   22
Odin's | *British/French*   20
Original Tagine | *Moroccan*   20
Orrery | *French*   25
Ozer | *Turkish*   19
Patisserie Valerie | *French*   20
Phoenix Palace | *Chinese*   23
Ping Pong | *Chinese*   18
Potting Shed | *British*   -
Providores, The | *Eclectic*   22
Real Greak | *Greek*   16
Reubens | *Deli/Jewish*   20
Rhodes W1 Brass. | *British*   -
NEW Rhodes W1 Rest. | *British*   -
☑ Royal China | *Chinese*   24
Royal China Club | *Chinese*   24
Seashell | *Seafood*   20
Six13 | *Eclectic*   19
Sofra | *Turkish*   19
Strada | *Italian*   18
Tootsies | *Amer.*   16
NEW 2 Veneti | *Italian*   -
Union Cafe | *British/Med.*   21
☑ Wagamama | *Jap.*   19
NEW ☑ Wallace, The | *French*   20
YO! Sushi | *Jap.*   17
Zizzi | *Pizza*   16

MAYFAIR

(See map on page 202)

TOP FOOD

Square, The | *French* | **B4**   28
Le Gavroche | *French* | **B1**   27
Nobu London | *Jap./Peruvian* | **E2**   27
Theo Randall | *Italian* | **E2**   26
Miyama | *Jap.* | **D3**   26

LISTING

☑ Al Hamra | 22
  Lebanese | **D2** | **D3**
Alloro | *Italian* | **D4**   22
Al Sultan | *Lebanese* | **D3**   22
Annabel's | *British/French* | **C3**   22
Ask Pizza | *Pizza* | **A1**   16
Automat | *Amer.* | **C4**   17
Bellamy's | *French* | **B4**   18
Benares | *Indian* | **C4**   23

PICCADILLY

(See map on page 202)

TOP FOOD

LISTING

Noura | *Lebanese* | **D6** 21
Patisserie Valerie | *French* | **D4** 20
Pigalle Club | *Euro./French* | **D6** 14
Planet Hollywood | *Amer.* | **C6** 11
Rainforest Cafe | *Amer.* | **C6** 11
Richoux | *British* | **D5** 15
NEW 1707 Wine Bar | 22
   British | **D5**
NEW St. Alban | *Euro.* | **D6** 21
Z Wolseley, The | *Euro.* | **D4** 21
Yoshino | *Jap.* | **D6** 24

SOHO
(See map on page 202)

TOP FOOD
Yauatcha | *Chinese* | **B6** 25
Alastair Little | *British* | **B7** 24
Arbutus | *Euro.* | **A7** 24
Red Fort | *Indian* | **A7** 23
Richard Corrigan | 23
   British/Irish | **B7**

LISTING
Abeno | *Jap.* 21
Alastair Little | *British* | **B7** 24
Albannach | *Scottish* | **E8** 14
Andrew Edmunds | *Euro.* | **B6** 22
Aperitivo | *Italian* | **B6** 20
Arbutus | *Euro.* | **A7** 24
Balans | *British* | **B7** 16
NEW Barrafina | *Spanish* | **B7** 24
Bar Shu | *Chinese* | **B8** 22
NEW Benja | *Thai* | **B6** -
Bertorelli | *Italian* | **B7** 17
Bodeans | *BBQ* | **A6** 18
Z Busaba Eathai | *Thai* | **B7** 21
Café Boheme | *French* | **B8** 16
Café Fish | *British/Seafood* | **C7** 20
Chiang Mai | *Thai* | **B7** 21
Circus | *French* | **B6** 14
NEW Club, The | *Eclectic* | **B5** -
Diner, The | *Amer.* | **B6** -
Ed's Easy Diner | *Hamburgers* | **B8** 15
Floridita | *Cuban* | **B7** 16
French House | *French* | **A7** 17
Gay Hussar | *Hungarian* | **B8** 16
Gopal's of Soho | *Indian* | **B7** 22
Groucho Club | *British* | **A7** 19
Imli | *Indian* | **A7** 20
itsu | *Jap.* | **B7** 18
Kettners | *Eclectic* | **B8** 15
Kulu Kulu | *Jap.* | **C6** 20
La Trouvaille | *French* | **B6** 20
Leon | *Med.* | **A5** 19
Le Pain Quotidien | 19
   Bakery/Belgian | **A6**

L'Escargot | *French* | **B8** 22
Little Italy | *Italian* | **B7** 16
Meza | *Spanish* | **B7** 17
Mildreds | *Veg.* | **B6** 22
National Dining Rms. | 18
   British | **D8**
Z Patara | *Thai* | **B8** 23
Patisserie Valerie | *French* | **B7** 20
Ping Pong | *Chinese* | **A6** 18
Z Pizza Express | *Pizza* | **C7** 17
Portrait | *British* | **D8** 22
Quo Vadis | *Italian* | **B7** 18
Randall & Aubin | 19
   British/Euro. | **B7**
Red Fort | *Indian* | **A7** 23
Refuel | *Euro.* | **A7** 12
Richard Corrigan | 23
   British/Irish | **B7**
Satsuma | *Jap.* | **B7** 20
Soho House | *British* | **B8** 18
Soho Spice | *Indian* | **A7** 20
Souk | *African* | **C8** 18
Spiga | *Italian* | **B7** 15
NEW Stanza | *British* | **B8** -
Ten Ten Tei | *Jap.* | **C6** 23
Thai Square | *Thai* | **A7** 19
Vasco & Piero's | *Italian* | **A6** 21
Z Wagamama | *Jap.* | **B6** 19
Z Yauatcha | *Chinese* | **B6** 25
Y Ming | *Chinese* | **B8** -
YO! Sushi | *Jap.* | **A6** 17
Zilli Fish | *Italian/Seafood* | **C6** 20

ST. JAMES'S
(See map on page 202)

TOP FOOD
L'Oranger | *French* | **E5** 24
Wilton's | *British/Seafood* | **D5** 24
Le Caprice | *British/Euro.* | **D5** 24
Ritz, The | *British/French* | **D4** 23
Green's | *British/Seafood* | **D5** 22

LISTING
Al Duca | *Italian* | **D6** 19
Avenue, The | *Euro.* | **D5** 18
Brasserie Roux | *French* | **E7** 20
Fiore | *Italian* | **E5** 21
Fortnum's Fountain | *British* | **D5** 20
Franco's | *Italian/Med.* | **D5** 15
Getti | *Italian* | **D6** 17
Green's | *British/Seafood* | **D5** 22
Inn The Park | *British* | **E5** 17
Just St. James's | *British* | **E5** 16
Z Le Caprice | *British/Euro.* | **D5** 24
L'Oranger | *French* | **E5** 24
Luciano | *Italian* | **E5** 20
Matsuri | *Jap.* | **D5** 21

Mint Leaf	*Indian*	**D7**	20
Quaglino's	*Euro.*	**D5**	18
☑ Ritz, The	*British/French*	**D4**	23
Rowley's	*British*	**D6**	19
St. James's	*British*	**D5**	20
Texas Embassy	*Tex-Mex*	**E8**	13
Thai Square	*Thai*	**E7**	19
☑ Wilton's	*British/ Seafood*	**D5**	24

VICTORIA

Ask Pizza	*Pizza*	16
Bank Westminster	*Euro.*	18
Boisdale	*British/Scottish*	20
Chez Gérard	*French*	18
Goring Dining Rm.	*British*	23
Mango Tree	*Thai*	20
Noura	*Lebanese*	21
Olivo	*Italian*	21
☑ Quilon	*Indian*	25
Zizzi	*Pizza*	16

WESTMINSTER

NEW Atami	*Jap.*	24
☑ Cinnamon Club	*Indian*	24
City Café	*Euro.*	19
☑ Quirinale	*Italian*	25
Shepherd's	*British*	18
Tate Britain	*British*	17
YO! Sushi	*Jap.*	17

East/South East London

BLACKFRIARS/CITY

Aurora	*British/French*	19
Bankside	*British*	19
Bertorelli	*Italian*	17
Bevis Marks	*British/Jewish*	-
Boisdale	*British/Scottish*	20
Bonds	*French*	20
Browns	*British*	16
Café Spice Namasté	*Indian*	23
Caravaggio	*Italian*	19
Chez Gérard	*French*	18
Ciro's Pizza	*Pizza*	17
City Miyama	*Jap.*	25
Coq d'Argent	*French*	18
Don	*Euro.*	22
☑ Gaucho Grill	*Argent./Chops*	22
Haz	*Turkish*	25
Imperial City	*Chinese*	17
Leon	*Med.*	19
Moshi Moshi	*Jap.*	20
1 Lombard St.	*French*	22
1 Lombard Brass.	*Euro.*	20
Paternoster Chop	*British/Chops*	18

Patisserie Valerie	*French*	20
☑ Pizza Express	*Pizza*	17
Prism	*British*	18
Refettorio	*Italian*	20
☑ Rhodes 24	*British*	23
Rocket	*Med.*	17
Royal Exchange	*Euro.*	16
Sauterelle	*French*	-
Silks & Spice	*Thai*	16
Singapura	*SE Asian*	20
☑ Sweetings	*British/Seafood*	24
Thai Square	*Thai*	19
Vivat Bacchus	*Euro.*	23
☑ Wagamama	*Jap.*	19
Ye Olde Cheshire	*British*	15

BOW/MILE END/ HACKNEY/BETHNAL GREEN

Bistrotheque	*French*	19
Buen Ayre/Santa Maria	*Argent.*	23
NEW Empress of India	*British*	-
Green & Red Bar	*Mex.*	20

CANARY WHARF/ DOCKLANDS

Browns	*British*	16
Café Rouge	*French*	14
☑ Carluccio's	*Italian*	17
1802	*British*	16
☑ Gaucho Grill	*Argent./Chops*	22
Gun, The	*British*	19
itsu	*Jap.*	18
La Figa	*Italian*	-
Moshi Moshi	*Jap.*	20
Plateau	*French*	19
Quadrato	*Italian*	24
NEW Rhodes Bar-B-Q	*BBQ*	-
☑ Royal China	*Chinese*	24
Smollensky's	*Chops*	15
Sri Nam	*Thai*	18
Tootsies	*Amer.*	16
Ubon	*Jap./Peruvian*	24
Wapping Food	*Euro.*	20

CLERKENWELL/ SMITHFIELD/ FARRINGDON

Ambassador, The	*Euro.*	21
☑ Carluccio's	*Italian*	17
Cellar Gascon	*French*	20
Cicada	*Pan-Asian*	15
Clerkenwell	*Euro.*	23
☑ Club Gascon	*French*	26
Coach & Horses	*British/Med.*	19
Comptoir Gascon	*French*	21
Dans Le Noir	*French*	13

Eagle, The	*Med.*	21
Fish Shop	*Seafood*	19
Flaneur	*Euro.*	22
NEW Hat & Feathers	*Euro.*	-
La Porchetta	*Pizza*	19
☑ Le Café/Marché	*French*	23
Little Bay	*Euro./Med.*	21
Medcalf	*British*	23
☑ Moro	*Med.*	25
Mosaico	*Italian*	21
Portal	*Portug.*	-
Quality Chop House	*British/Chops*	20
Real Greak	*Greek*	16
Saki Bar/Food Emp.	*Jap.*	-
Smiths/Dining Room	*British*	20
Smiths/Top Floor	*British/Chops*	20
NEW St. Germain	*French*	21
☑ St. John	*British*	25
Strada	*Italian*	18
Tas	*Turkish*	20
YO! Sushi	*Jap.*	17
Zetter	*Med.*	19

GREENWICH/ BLACKHEATH

Chapter Two	*Euro.*	24
Inside	*Euro.*	24
Rivington Grill	*British*	20
NEW Spread Eagle	*French*	21

SHOREDITCH/ SPITALFIELDS/ HOXTON/WHITECHAPEL

NEW Bacchus	*Eclectic*	21
Canteen	*British*	22
Cay tre	*Vietnamese*	24
Cru	*Med.*	15
Diner, The	*Amer.*	-
Eyre Brothers	*Portug./Spanish*	22
Fifteen	*Med.*	23
Giraffe	*Eclectic*	17
Great Eastern	*Asian*	22
NEW Hawksmoor	*Chops*	28
Hoxton Apprentice	*Eclectic*	18
NEW Hoxton Grille	*Eclectic*	-
Leon	*Med.*	19
☑ Les Trois Garçons	*French*	19
New Tayyabs	*Pakistani*	24
Original Lahore	*Pakistani*	24
Real Greak	*Greek*	16
Rivington Grill	*British*	20
Song Que Café	*SE Asian*	20
St. John Bread/Wine	*British*	22
Viet Hoa	*Vietnamese*	23

SOUTH BANK/BOROUGH

Black & Blue	*Chops*	17
Canteen		22
Cantina Vinopolis	*Eclectic/Med.*	19
Delfina	*Eclectic*	-
Feng Sushi	*Jap.*	17
fish!	*Seafood*	19
Le Pain Quotidien	*Bakery/Belgian*	19
NEW Magdalen	*Euro.*	-
Oxo Tower	*Euro.*	20
Oxo Tower Brass.	*Asian/Med.*	20
Ping Pong		18
Real Greak	*Greek*	16
Roast	*British*	19
NEW Skylon	*Euro.*	-
Tapas Brindisa	*Spanish*	22
Tas	*Turkish*	20
Tate Modern	*Euro.*	16

TOWER BRIDGE/ LIMEHOUSE/WAPPING

Addendum	*Euro.*	-
Bengal Clipper	*Indian*	21
Blueprint Café	*Euro.*	18
Browns	*British*	16
Butlers Wharf	*British*	20
Cantina del Ponte	*Italian*	17
Champor	*Malaysian*	18
☑ Il Bordello	*Italian*	23
Le Pont de la Tour	*French/Seafood*	22
NEW Narrow, The	*British*	-
Smollensky's	*Chops*	15
Tentazioni	*Italian*	27

WATERLOO/ SOUTHWARK/ KENNINGTON

Anchor & Hope	*British*	24
Baltic	*Polish*	21
Bankside	*British*	19
Chez Gérard	*French*	18
Dragon Castle	*Chinese*	-
Franklins		19
Giraffe	*Eclectic*	17
Livebait	*Seafood*	18
Menier Chocolate	*British*	14
Meson Don Felipe	*Spanish*	18
Ping Pong	*Chinese*	18
Rebato's	*Spanish*	-
R.S.J.	*British*	21
Tas	*Turkish*	20
Thai Pavilion	*Thai*	18

CAMDEN TOWN/CHALK FARM/KENTISH TOWN/ PRIMROSE HILL

Asakusa	*Jap.*	–
🄩 Belgo	*Belgian*	19
Camden Brass.	*Euro.*	21
Cottons	*Caribbean*	19
Engineer	*British*	19
Feng Sushi	*Jap.*	17
FishWorks	*Seafood*	20
Gilgamesh	*Pan-Asian*	20
La Collina	*Italian*	–
Lansdowne, The	*Euro.*	20
Lemonia	*Greek*	20
Mestizo	*Mex.*	19
Odette's	*Euro.*	20
Sardo Canale	*Italian*	20
Silks & Spice	*Thai*	16
🄩 Wagamama	*Jap.*	19

GOLDERS GREEN/ FINCHLEY

Basilico	*Pizza*	17
Bloom's	*Deli/Jewish*	19
🄩 Café Japan	*Jap.*	26
Green Cottage	*Chinese*	–
Jim Thompson's	*Thai*	15
Met Su Yan	*Pan-Asian*	16
Solly's	*Mideastern*	17
🄩 Two Brothers Fish	*Seafood*	24
Zizzi	*Pizza*	16

HAMPSTEAD/KILBURN/ SWISS COTTAGE

Artigiano	*Italian*	20
Ask Pizza	*Pizza*	16
Baker & Spice	*Med.*	22
Benihana	*Jap.*	18
Black & Blue	*Chops*	17
Bombay Bicycle	*Indian*	18
Bradley's	*British/French*	15
dim t	*Chinese*	16
🄩 Gaucho Grill	*Argent./Chops*	22
Giraffe	*Eclectic*	17
Good Earth	*Chinese*	20
Gourmet Burger	*Hamburgers*	21
Gung-Ho	*Chinese*	21
🄩 Jin Kichi	*Jap.*	26
Little Bay	*Euro./Med.*	21
Nautilus Fish	*Seafood*	21
Old Bull & Bush	*Euro.*	14

Salusbury Pub	*Italian/Med.*	18
Singapore Garden	*SE Asian*	21
Tootsies	*Amer.*	16
Wells, The	*Euro.*	18
🆕 XO	*Pan-Asian*	16
ZENW3	*Chinese*	16

HIGHGATE/MUSWELL HILL/CROUCH END/ TUFNELL PARK

Bouga	*Moroccan*	–
Bull, The	*Euro.*	19
Café Rouge	*French*	14
dim t	*Chinese*	16
Giraffe	*Eclectic*	17
La Porchetta	*Pizza*	19
Original Lahore	*Pakistani*	24
Potemkin	*Russian*	–
Zizzi	*Pizza*	16

ISLINGTON

🆕 Albion, The	*British*	–
Almeida	*French*	18
Barnsbury, The	*British*	21
Basilico	*Pizza*	17
Bierodrome	*Belgian*	17
Browns	*British*	16
🄩 Carluccio's	*Italian*	17
Casale Franco	*Italian*	–
Cottons	*Caribbean*	19
Draper's Arms	*Euro.*	18
Duke of Cambridge	*British*	20
Fig	*Euro.*	–
Firezza	*Pizza*	18
FishWorks	*Seafood*	20
Frederick's	*British/Euro.*	20
Gallipoli	*Turkish*	18
Giraffe	*Eclectic*	17
Isarn	*Thai*	22
La Piragua	*S Amer.*	15
La Porchetta	*Pizza*	19
Le Mercury	*French*	18
Marquess Tavern	*British*	–
Masala Zone	*Indian*	19
Metrogusto	*Italian*	21
🄩 Morgan M	*French*	27
New Culture Rev.	*Chinese*	17
🄩 Ottolenghi	*Med.*	24
Pasha	*Moroccan*	20
Rasa	*Indian*	24
Rodizio Rico	*Brazilian*	15
Sabor	*S Amer.*	22
Strada	*Italian*	18
Thai Square	*Thai*	19
Upper Glas	*Swedish*	22
🄩 Wagamama	*Jap.*	19

KING'S CROSS

NEW Acorn House | *British*	19
NEW Konstam | *British*	-

ST. JOHN'S WOOD

Baker & Spice | *Med.*	22
Ben's Thai | *Thai*	15
Cafe Med | *Med.*	18
Café Rouge | *French*	14
Green Olive | *Italian*	20
Harry Morgan's | *Deli/Jewish*	16
L'Aventure | *French*	22
Oslo Court | *French*	22
Raoul's | *Med.*	16
Red Pepper | *Italian*	19
Richoux | *British*	15
Rosmarino | *Italian*	17
☑ Royal China | *Chinese*	24
Sofra | *Turkish*	19
Waterway, The | *Euro.*	18

STOKE NEWINGTON

La Porchetta | *Pizza*	19
Rasa | *Indian*	24

South/South West London

BARNES

Annie's | *British*	21
NEW Barnes Grill | *British*	-
Riva | *Italian*	20
Sonny's | *Euro.*	21

BATTERSEA

Buona Sera | *Italian*	23
NEW Butcher & Grill | *British*	15
Firezza | *Pizza*	18
FishWorks | *Seafood*	20
Food Rm. | *French/Med.*	-
Giraffe | *Eclectic*	17
Gourmet Burger | *Hamburgers*	21
Greyhound, The | *British/Euro.*	19
Little Bay | *Euro./Med.*	21
Nancy Lam's Enak | *Indonesian*	-
Osteria Antica | *Italian*	-
☑ Pizza Express | *Pizza*	17
Pizza Metro | *Pizza*	-
Ransome's Dock | *British/Eclectic*	20
Buen Ayre/Santa Maria | *Argent.*	23

BRIXTON/CLAPHAM

Abbeville | *British/Euro.*	15
Basilico | *Pizza*	17
Bierodrome | *Belgian*	17
Bodeans | *BBQ*	18
Bombay Bicycle | *Indian*	18
Café Rouge | *French*	14
El Rincon Latino | *S Amer./Spanish*	-
La Rueda | *Spanish*	14
Morel | *French/Med.*	-
Pepper Tree | *Thai*	19
Strada | *Italian*	18
Tootsies | *Amer.*	16
NEW Trinity | *Euro.*	24
Tsunami | *Jap.*	24
Upstairs | *French*	-

CAMBERWELL/DULWICH/HERNE HILL

Café Rouge | *French*	14
Firezza | *Pizza*	18
Franklins | *British*	19
Palmerston, The | *British*	-

CHELSEA

(See map on page 200)

TOP FOOD

Gordon Ramsay/68 Royal | *French* | **H7**	28
Rasoi Vineet Bhatia | *Indian* | **F8**	27
Tom Aikens | *French* | **E6**	26
Aubergine | *French* | **H2**	26
Ziani | *Italian* | **G6**	25

LISTING

Admiral Codrington | *British/Euro.* | **E6**	18
Aglio e Olio | *Italian* | **G2**	21
Aquasia | *Asian/Med.* | **I8**	21
Ask Pizza | *Pizza* | **H4**	16
☑ Aubergine | *French* | **H2**	26
Awana | *Malaysian* | **E6**	17
Baker & Spice | *Med.* | **E6**	22
Benihana | *Jap.* | **G6**	18
Big Easy | *Amer.* | **H4**	16
Bluebird | *Euro.* | **I3**	-
Brinkley's | *Eclectic* | **H1**	16
Builders Arms | *British* | **G6**	17
Buona Sera | *Italian* | **H4**	23
Caraffini | *Italian* | **F9**	21
Carpaccio | *Italian* | **F4**	18
C Garden | *Italian* | **G5**	18
NEW Chelsea Brass. | *French* | **E8**	16
Chelsea Bun | *British* | **I3**	18
Cheyne Walk | *French* | **I5**	23
Chutney Mary | *Indian* | **J1**	23
Cross Keys | *French* | **I5**	14
Daphne's | *Italian* | **E6**	21
Dish Dash | *Persian/Lebanese* | **H2**	18

Eight Over Eight	*Pan-Asian*	**I3**	23
El Blason	*Spanish*	**F8**	18
El Gaucho	*Argent./Chops*	**G5**	21
Elistano	*Italian*	**F6**	18
Enterprise	*Eclectic*	**D6**	20
Firezza	*Pizza*	**H1**	18
FishWorks	*Seafood*	**G2**	20
Foxtrot Oscar	*British*	**H7**	15
Friends	*Italian*	**H1**	18
☑ Gaucho Grill	*Argent./Chops*	**E6**	22
☑ Gordon Ramsay/68 Royal	*French*	**H7**	28
itsu	*Jap.*	**E6**	18
La Famiglia	*Italian*	**J2**	21
NEW Langtry's	*British*	**C8**	-
Le Cercle	*French*	**E8**	24
Le Colombier	*French*	**F4**	20
Le Suquet	*French/Seafood*	**E6**	23
Lucio	*Italian*	**G3**	21
Made in Italy	*Italian*	**I3**	21
Manicomio	*Italian*	**F8**	18
New Culture Rev.	*Chinese*	**I3**	17
Oriel	*Euro.*	**E9**	15
Osteria dell'Arancio	*Italian*	**I3**	20
Painted Heron	*Indian*	**J3**	22
Patisserie Valerie	*French*	**F8**	20
Pellicano	*Italian*	**F6**	20
Pig's Ear	*British/French*	**I4**	22
☑ Pizza Express	*Pizza*	**G6**	17
PJ's B&G	*Amer.*	**F4**	16
Poissonnerie	*French/Seafood*	**E6**	21
Randall & Aubin	*British/Euro.*	**H2**	19
☑ Rasoi Vineet Bhatia	*Indian*	**F8**	27
Riccardo's	*Italian*	**G3**	18
Santa Lucia	*Italian*	**H1**	22
Scalini	*Italian*	**D7**	23
☑ Sophie's Steak	*Amer./Chops*	**G2**	23
Tartine	*French*	**E6**	18
☑ Tom Aikens	*French*	**E6**	26
NEW Tom's Kitchen	*British*	**F5**	19
Toto's	*Italian*	**D7**	24
Vama	*Indian*	**I3**	24
Vingt-Quatre	*Eclectic*	**H2**	15
NEW Yumenoki	*Jap.*	**G2**	-
Ziani	*Italian*	**G6**	25

EARL'S COURT

Balans	*British*	16
Langan's Coq d'Or	*British/French*	22
Lou Pescadou	*French/Seafood*	20
Masala Zone	*Indian*	19

Strada	*Italian*	18
Troubadour, The	*Eclectic*	14
Zizzi	*Pizza*	16

FULHAM

Aziz	*Moroccan*	17
Basilico	*Pizza*	17
Blue Elephant	*Thai*	20
Bodeans	*BBQ*	18
☑ Carluccio's	*Italian*	17
Farm	*French*	-
Feng Sushi	*Jap.*	17
FishWorks	*Seafood*	20
1492	*S Amer.*	21
Gourmet Burger	*Hamburgers*	21
Jim Thompson's	*Thai*	15
La Rueda	*Spanish*	14
Little Bay	*Euro./Med.*	21
Ma Goa	*Indian*	23
Mao Tai	*Chinese*	22
☑ Pizza Express	*Pizza*	17
☑ Royal China	*Chinese*	24
Salisbury, The	*British*	-
Strada	*Italian*	18
T.G.I. Friday's	*Amer.*	11
222 Veggie Vegan	*Veg.*	-
YO! Sushi	*Jap.*	17

PIMLICO

About Thyme	*Euro.*	-
Como Lario	*Italian*	18
Ebury Dining Rm.	*Euro.*	20
Goya	*Spanish*	16
Grumbles	*British/French*	17
☑ Hunan	*Chinese*	28
La Poule au Pot	*French*	22
L'Incontro	*Italian*	20
☑ Roussillon	*French*	26

PUTNEY/RICHMOND

Ask Pizza	*Pizza*	16
Basilico	*Pizza*	17
Café Rouge	*French*	14
☑ Carluccio's	*Italian*	17
☑ Enoteca Turi	*Italian*	27
FishWorks	*Seafood*	20
Frankie's Italian	*Italian*	15
☑ Gaucho Grill	*Argent./Chops*	22
Giraffe	*Eclectic*	17
Glasshouse, The	*British*	24
Gourmet Burger	*Hamburgers*	21
Jim Thompson's	*Thai*	15
Kew Grill	*British*	18
Ma Goa	*Indian*	23
Petersham, The	*Euro.*	23
Petersham Nurseries	*Euro.*	25

Popeseye | *Chops* -
Real Greak | *Greek* 16
Rocket | *Med.* 17
Thai Square | *Thai* 19
Tootsies | *Amer.* 16

SOUTH KENSINGTON

(See map on page 200)

TOP FOOD

L'Etranger | *French* | **B1** 24
Star of India | *Indian* | **F1** 24
Cambio de Tercio | *Spanish* | **F1** 24
Bibendum | *French* | **E5** 24
Patara | *Thai* | **F4** 23

LISTING

Ask Pizza | *Pizza* | **C3** 16
Aubaine | *French* | **E5** 20
Bangkok | *Thai* | **E3** 19
Z Bibendum | *French* | **E5** 24
Bibendum Oyster | *French/Seafood* | **E5** 22
Bistrot 190 | *British/Med.* | **B3** 19
Black & Blue | *Chops* | **D2** 17
Blakes | *Eclectic* | **F2** 19
Bombay Brass. | *Indian* | **D1** 22
Z Cambio de Tercio | *Spanish* | **F1** 24
Collection | *Eclectic* | **E5** 13
Daquise | *Polish* | **D4** 20
dim t | *Chinese* | **E2** 16
1880 | *Euro./French* | **E3** 21
El Gaucho | *Argent./Chops* | **E4** 21
Il Falconiere | *Italian* | **E3** 15
Joe's | *British* | **D5** 19
Khan's of Kensington | *Indian* | **D4** 22
Kulu Kulu | *Jap.* | **D5** 20
La Bouchée | *French* | **E3** 20
La Brasserie | *French* | **E5** 16
Z L'Etranger | *French* | **B1** 24
Lundum's | *Danish* | **F2** 22
Nam Long-Le Shaker | *Vietnamese* | **F1** 14
Noor Jahan | *Indian* | **F1** 22
NEW Papillon | *French* | **E6** 23
Pasha | *Moroccan* | **B2** 18
Z Patara | *Thai* | **F4** 23
Spago | *Italian* | **D4** 19
Star of India | *Indian* | **F1** 24
Tendido Cero | *Spanish* | **F1** -
Thai Square | *Thai* | **D4** 19

WANDSWORTH/ BALHAM/WIMBLEDON

Amici Bar/Kitchen | *Italian* 15
Balham Kitchen | *British* 16
Z Chez Bruce | *British* 28

Dish Dash | *Persian/Lebanese* 18
Firezza | *Pizza* 18
Gourmet Burger | *Hamburgers* 21
Kastoori | *Indian* -
Lamberts | *British* 25
Light House | *Eclectic* 17
NEW Raviolo | *Italian* -
San Lorenzo | *Italian* 20
Sarkhel's | *Indian* 22
Strada | *Italian* 18
Tootsies | *Amer.* 16

West London

BAYSWATER

All Star Lanes | *Amer.* 15
Z Al Waha | *Lebanese* 22
Fairuz | *Lebanese* 22
Four Seasons | *Chinese* 22
Ginger | *Bangladeshi* 17
Gourmet Burger | *Hamburgers* 21
Halepi | *Greek* 24
Inaho | *Jap.* 21
Island | *Eclectic* -
Khan's | *Indian* 20
L'Accento Italiano | *Italian* -
Mandarin Kitchen | *Chinese* 23
Rodizio Rico | *Brazilian* 15
Z Royal China | *Chinese* 24
T.G.I. Friday's | *Amer.* 11
YO! Sushi | *Jap.* 17

CHISWICK

Annie's | *British* 21
Ask Pizza | *Pizza* 16
Balans | *British* 16
Café Rouge | *French* 14
Firezza | *Pizza* 18
Fish Hook | *Seafood* 24
FishWorks | *Seafood* 20
Frankie's Italian | *Italian* 15
Giraffe | *Eclectic* 17
Gourmet Burger | *Hamburgers* 21
NEW High Road Brass. | *Euro.* 20
Z La Trompette | *Euro./French* 27
Le Vacherin | *French* 23
Sam's Brass. | *Euro.* 20
Silks & Spice | *Thai* 16
Tootsies | *Amer.* 16
Zizzi | *Pizza* 16

EALING

Charlotte's Place | *Euro.* -

HAMMERSMITH

Brackenbury | *Euro.* 18
Z Carluccio's | *Italian* 17

Chez Kristof	*French*	22
🅙 Gate, The	*Veg.*	25
Indian Zing	*Indian*	-
🅙 River Café	*Italian*	27
Smollensky's	*Chops*	15

HOLLAND PARK/ WESTBOURNE GROVE

Alounak	*Persian*	23
Belvedere, The	*British/French*	20
Bombay Bicycle	*Indian*	18
Harlem	*Amer.*	16

KENSINGTON

(See map on page 198)

TOP FOOD

Clarke's	*British*	**G7**	25
Zaika	*Indian*	**I9**	25
ffiona's	*British*	**H8**	24
Locanda Ottoemezzo	*Italian*	**J9**	24
Koi	*Jap.*	**I10**	22

LISTING

Abingdon, The	*Euro.*	**K6**	22
Ask Pizza	*Pizza*	**K6**	16
Babylon	*Euro.*	**J7**	20
Balans	*British*	**J6**	16
Black & Blue	*Chops*	**F6**	17
Brunello	*Italian*	**I10**	20
🆕 Chez Patrick	*French*	**K7**	21
🅙 Clarke's	*British*	**G7**	25
Da Mario	*Italian*	**K10**	22
11 Abingdon Rd.	*Euro.*	**K6**	18
Feng Sushi	*Jap.*	**I7**	17
🅙 ffiona's	*British*	**H8**	24
Giraffe	*Eclectic*	**I8**	17
Il Portico	*Italian*	**K5**	22
Kensington Place	*British*	**F6**	20
Koi	*Jap.*	**I10**	22
Launceston Place	*British*	**K10**	21
Le Pain Quotidien	*Bakery/Belgian*	**J8**	19
Locanda Ottoemezzo	*Italian*	**J9**	24
🆕 L-Rest. & Bar	*Spanish*	**K6**	-
Maggie Jones's	*British*	**I8**	21
Memories of China	*Chinese*	**K5**	21
Patisserie Valerie	*French*	**I8**	20
🅙 Pizza Express	*Pizza*	**K6**	17
Sticky Fingers	*Amer.*	**J6**	14
Timo	*Italian*	**K4**	22
🅙 Wagamama	*Jap.*	**I8**	19
Wòdka	*Polish*	**K9**	20
Zaika	*Indian*	**I9**	25

NOTTING HILL

(See map on page 198)

TOP FOOD

Assaggi	*Italian*	**D7**	26
Ledbury	*French*	**B5**	25
Ottolenghi	*Med.*	**C5**	24
Notting Hill Brass.	*Euro.*	**D4**	24
Books for Cooks	*Eclectic*	**C4**	24

LISTING

Ark	*Italian*	**F7**	15
Ask Pizza	*Pizza*	**F5**	16
🅙 Assaggi	*Italian*	**D7**	26
Babes 'n' Burgers	*Hamburgers*	**B3**	17
🅙 Books for Cooks	*Eclectic*	**C4**	24
🆕 Bumpkin	*British*	**B5**	21
🅙 Churchill Arms	*Thai*	**G6**	22
Costas Grill	*Greek*	**F6**	18
Cow Dining Rm.	*British*	**A6**	21
Crazy Homies	*Mex.*	**A6**	20
e&o	*Pan-Asian*	**C3**	22
Electric Brass.	*Eclectic*	**C4**	19
Essenza	*Italian*	**C3**	18
🆕 Fat Badger	*British*	**A2**	15
Feng Sushi	*Jap.*	**F6**	17
Firezza	*Pizza*	**B4**	18
FishWorks	*Seafood*	**C5**	20
Galicia	*Spanish*	**A2**	22
Geales Fish	*Seafood*	**F6**	-
Julie's	*British*	**E2**	18
Ladbroke Arms	*Euro.*	**E3**	20
Ledbury	*French*	**B5**	25
Lonsdale	*Euro.*	**C5**	15
🅙 Lucky 7	*Hamburgers*	**C6**	20
Malabar	*Indian*	**F6**	20
Mediterraneo	*Italian*	**C3**	22
New Culture Rev.	*Chinese*	**F5**	17
Notting Grill	*British/Chops*	**D2**	21
Notting Hill Brass.	*Euro.*	**D4**	24
Nyonya	*Malaysian*	**E6**	24
🅙 Osteria Basilico	*Italian*	**C3**	24
🅙 Ottolenghi	*Med.*	**C5**	24
Ping Pong	*Chinese*	**C7**	18
🅙 Pizza Express	*Pizza*	**F5**	17
Raoul's	*Med.*	**B5**	16
Taqueria	*Mex.*	**C6**	18
Tom's Deli	*Eclectic*	**D5**	16
Tootsies	*Amer.*	**G3**	16
202	*Euro.*	**C5**	17
Uli	*Pan-Asian*	**B4**	25
Westbourne, The	*Eclectic*	**A6**	16

OLYMPIA

Alounak	*Persian*	23
Popeseye	*Chops*	-

PADDINGTON

Frontline | *British*	13
Levantine | *Lebanese*	20
Noor Jahan | *Indian*	22
Yakitoria | *Jap.*	24
YO! Sushi | *Jap.*	17

SHEPHERD'S BUSH

Anglesea Arms | *British*	23
Blah! Blah! Blah! | *Veg.*	18
Bush B&G | *Euro.*	17
Café Rouge | *French*	14
Esarn Kheaw | *Thai*	–
Snows on Green | *British*	21

In the Country

Auberge du Lac | *French*	23
☑ Cliveden House | *French/Med.*	24
☑ Fat Duck | *Euro.*	27
French Horn | *French*	23
☑ Gravetye Manor | *British*	24
Hand & Flowers | *British/French*	–
Hartwell House | *British*	19
Hind's Head | *British*	23
☑ Le Manoir/Quat | *French*	28
Vineyard/Stockcross | *British/French*	24
☑ Waterside Inn | *French*	27

LOCATIONS

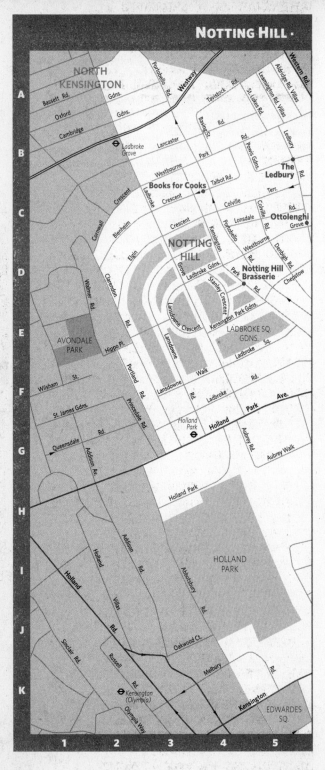

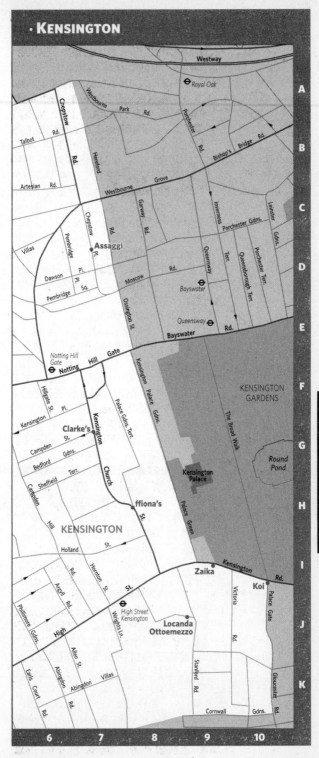

· KENSINGTON

Westway

⊖ *Royal Oak*

Westbourne Park Rd.

Porchester Rd.

Bishop's Bridge Rd.

Chepstow Rd.

Westbourne

Talbot Rd.

Hereford

Artesian Rd.

Westbourne Grove

Garway Rd.

Inverness Terr.

Porchester Gdns.

Leinster Gdns.

Chepstow Rd.

Pembridge Villas

Assaggi

Queensway

Porchester Terr.

Queensborough Terr.

Dawson Pl.

Pembridge Sq.

Moscow Rd.

Ossington St.

⊖ *Bayswater*

Queensway ⊖ Rd.

BAYSWATER

Notting Hill Gate

⊖ **Notting** Hill Gate

Kensington Palace Gdns.

KENSINGTON GARDENS

Hillgate St.

Pl.

Kensington

Clarke's

Palace Gdns. Terr.

Kensington Church St.

The Broad Walk

Round Pond

Campden Gdns.

Bedford

Sheffield Terr.

Camden

ffiona's

St.

Kensington Palace

Palace Green

KENSINGTON

Hill

Holland St.

Kensington Rd.

Horton St.

Zaika

Koi

Argyll Rd.

⊖ *High Street Kensington*

Victoria Rd.

Palace Gate

Phillimore Gdns.

Wrights Ln.

High St.

Locanda Ottoemezzo

Allen St.

Abingdon

Earl's Court Rd.

Abingdon Villas

Stanford Rd.

Gloucester Rd.

Cornwall Gdns.

MAPS

6   7   8   9   10

A B C D E F G H I J K

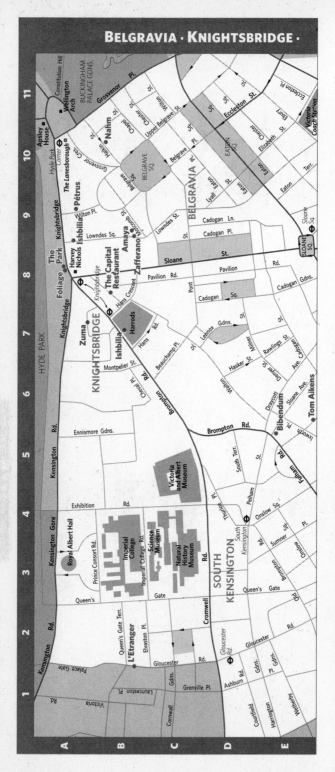

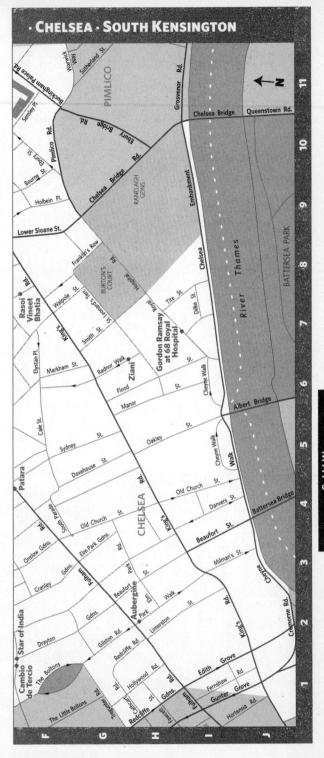

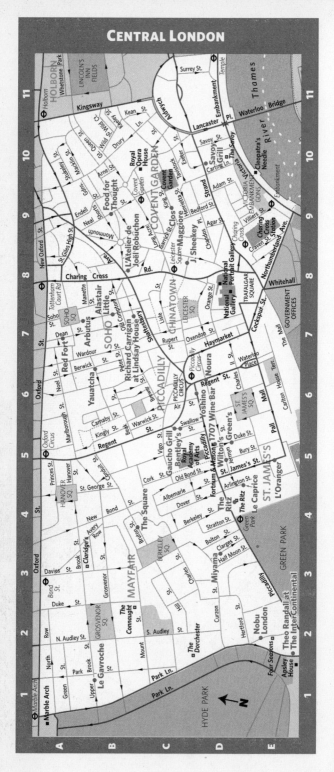

CENTRAL LONDON

Special Features

Listings cover the best in each category and include restaurant names, locations and Food ratings. Multi-location restaurants' features may vary by branch. ☑ indicates places with the highest ratings, popularity and importance.

ADDITIONS

(Properties added since the last edition of the book)

About Thyme | **SW1**	–
Academy | **W1**	13
Acorn House | **WC1**	19
Albion, The | **N1**	–
All Star Lanes | **W2**	15
Ambassador, The | **EC1**	21
Aquasia | **SW10**	21
Asadal | **WC1**	–
Asakusa | **NW1**	–
Atami | **SW1**	24
Aubaine | **W1**	20
Bacchus | **N1**	21
Baker & Spice | **W9**	22
Barnes Grill | **SW13**	–
Barrafina | **W1**	24
Basilico | **multi. loc.**	17
Bedford & Strand | **WC2**	17
Benja | **W1**	–
Bertorelli | **WC2**	17
Black & Blue | **SE1**	17
Bouga | **N8**	–
Buen Ayre/Santa Maria | **multi. loc.**	23
Bumpkin | **W11**	21
Burlington Club | **W1**	–
Butcher & Grill | **SW11**	15
Café Rouge | **SE21**	14
Canteen | **SE1**	22
Cay tre | **EC1**	24
C Garden | **SW3**	18
Charlotte's Place | **W5**	–
Chelsea Brass. | **SW1**	16
Chez Patrick | **W8**	21
Club, The | **W1**	–
Cookbook Cafe | **W1**	–
Cottons | **multi. loc.**	19
Court | **WC1**	16
Cross Keys | **SW3**	14
Cuckoo Club | **W1**	15
Da Mario | **SW7**	22
Delfina | **SE1**	–
Delfino | **W1**	23
dim t | **SW7**	16
Diner, The | **multi. loc.**	–
Dinings | **W1**	–
Dish Dash | **SW10**	18
Dover St. | **W1**	17

Dragon Castle | **SE17**	–
Eagle Bar Diner | **W1**	19
El Rincon Latino | **SW4**	–
Empress of India | **E9**	–
Fat Badger | **W10**	15
Feng Sushi | **multi. loc.**	17
Firezza | **multi. loc.**	18
FishWorks | **multi. loc.**	20
Flaneur | **EC1**	22
Forge, The | **WC2**	–
Foxtrot Oscar | **SW3**	15
Frankie's Italian | **W1**	15
Franklins | **multi. loc.**	19
Gaby's | **WC2**	–
Gaucho Grill | **Richmond**	22
Golden Hind | **W1**	–
Gourmet Burger | **WC2**	21
Goya | **SW1**	16
Great Queen St. | **WC2**	–
Greig's | **W1**	21
Haiku | **W1**	–
Hand & Flowers | **SL7**	–
Harry Morgan's | **multi. loc.**	16
Hat & Feathers | **EC1**	–
Hawksmoor | **E1**	28
High Road Brass. | **W4**	20
Hoxton Grille | **EC2**	–
Indian Zing | **W6**	–
Inside | **SE10**	24
Kobe Jones | **WC1**	18
Konstam | **WC1**	–
La Collina | **NW1**	–
La Figa | **E14**	–
Lamberts | **SW12**	25
Langtry's | **SW1**	–
L'Artiste Muscle | **W1**	19
L'Atelier/Robuchon | **WC2**	26
Leon | **multi. loc.**	19
Le Pain Quotidien | **multi. loc.**	19
Loch Fyne | **WC2**	18
Magdalen | **SE1**	–
Mamounia | **W1**	17
Marquess Tavern | **N1**	–
Menier Chocolate | **SE1**	14
Met Su Yan | **NW11**	16
Mews of Mayfair | **W1**	22
Mimosa | **SW1**	–
Mocotó | **SW1**	22
Mosaico | **W1**	21

SPECIAL FEATURES

Nancy Lam's Enak | **SW11**	-	Balans | **multi. loc.**	16
Narrow, The | **E14**	-	Balham Kitchen | **SW12**	16
New Tayyabs | **E1**	24	Banquette | **WC2**	22
Old Bull & Bush | **NW3**	14	Bar Shu | **W1**	22
Olivomare | **SW1**	-	Basilico | **multi. loc.**	17
Oratory, The | **SW3**	18	☑ Belgo | **WC2**	19
Oscar | **W1**	-	Bibendum Oyster | **SW3**	22
Ping Pong | **multi. loc.**	18	Big Easy | **SW3**	16
Potting Shed | **NW1**	-	Black & Blue | **multi. loc.**	17
Raviolo | **SW12**	-	Bloom's | **NW11**	19
Real Greak | **WC2**	16	☑ Al Hamra | **W1**	22
Rhodes Bar-B-Q | **E1**	-	Browns | **multi. loc.**	16
Rhodes W1 Rest. | **W1**	-	☑ Busaba Eathai | **multi. loc.**	21
Rist. Semplice | **W1**	-	Cafe Pacifico | **WC2**	18
Rocket | **EC2**	17	Café Rouge | **multi. loc.**	14
Royal China | **SW6**	24	Canteen | **multi. loc.**	22
Sarastro | **WC2**	12	☑ Carluccio's | **multi. loc.**	17
Scott's | **W1**	22	Cecconi's | **W1**	21
1707 Wine Bar | **W1**	22	**NEW** Chelsea Brass. | **SW1**	16
Silks & Spice | **NW10**	16	Chelsea Bun | **SW10**	18
Sitaaray | **WC2**	-	Chez Gérard | **multi. loc.**	18
Skylon | **SE1**	-	Chuen Cheng Ku | **W1**	19
Spread Eagle | **SE10**	21	**NEW** Cookbook Cafe | **W1**	-
St. Alban | **SW1**	21	Cross Keys | **SW3**	14
Stanza | **W1**	-	Daquise | **SW7**	20
St. Germain | **EC1**	21	Diner, The | **multi. loc.**	-
St. James's | **W1**	20	Ed's Easy Diner | **multi. loc.**	15
Suka | **W1**	-	Efes | **W1**	18
Tamarai | **WC2**	-	Feng Sushi | **multi. loc.**	17
Tas | **multi. loc.**	20	Fifth Floor Cafe | **SW1**	18
Tendido Cero | **SW5**	-	FishWorks | **SW11**	20
Ten Ten Tei | **W1**	23	Flaneur | **EC1**	22
Thai Square | **TW9**	19	☑ Food for Thought | **WC2**	24
Theo Randall | **W1**	26	Four Seasons | **W2**	22
Tom's Kitchen | **SW3**	19	☑ Gaucho Grill | **multi. loc.**	22
Tootsies | **SW15**	16	Giraffe | **multi. loc.**	17
Trinity | **SW4**	24	Gourmet Burger | **multi. loc.**	21
222 Veggie Vegan | **W14**	-	Grenadier, The | **SW1**	16
2 Veneti | **W1**	-	Gun, The | **E14**	19
Via Condotti | **W1**	18	Halepi | **W2**	24
Wallace, The | **W1**	20	Hard Rock | **W1**	13
XO | **NW3**	16	Harry Morgan's | **multi. loc.**	16
Y Ming | **W1**	-	Haz | **E1**	25
Yumenoki | **SW10**	-	**NEW** High Road Brass. | **W4**	20
Zizzi | **SW1**	16	Hind's Head | **Berks**	23
		Hoxton Apprentice | **N1**	18
ALL-DAY DINING		Hush | **W1**	17
		Inn The Park | **SW1**	17
Abeno | **multi. loc.**	21	Ishtar | **W1**	22
NEW Acorn House | **WC1**	19	itsu | **multi. loc.**	18
Albannach | **WC2**	14	Joe Allen | **WC2**	17
Ambassador, The | **EC1**	21	Joe's | **SW3**	19
Aperitivo | **W1**	20	Julie's | **W11**	18
Armani Caffé | **SW3**	17	Kettners | **W1**	15
Ask Pizza | **multi. loc.**	16	La Brasserie | **SW3**	16
Aubaine | **multi. loc.**	20	Ladurée | **SW1**	23
Automat | **W1**	17	La Fromagerie | **W1**	24
Baker & Spice | **multi. loc.**	22		

Leon	multi. loc.	19
Le Pain Quotidien	multi. loc.	19
Le Palais Du Jardin	WC2	18
Livebait	multi. loc.	18
Living Rm.	W1	19
Loch Fyne	WC2	18
☑ Lucky 7	W2	20
Meson Don Felipe	SE1	18
Mildreds	W1	22
Mon Plaisir	WC2	18
National Dining Rms.	WC2	18
Noura	multi. loc.	21
Old Bull & Bush	NW3	14
1 Lombard Brass.	EC3	20
Oriel	SW1	15
Original Lahore	NW4	24
Orso	WC2	20
☑ Ottolenghi	multi. loc.	24
Pasha	N1	20
Patisserie Valerie	multi. loc.	20
Ping Pong	multi. loc.	18
☑ Pizza Express	multi. loc.	17
Pizza Metro	SW11	-
PJ's B&G	multi. loc.	16
Planet Hollywood	W1	11
Porters	WC2	20
Portrait	WC2	22
Potting Shed	NW1	-
Rainforest Cafe	W1	11
Randall & Aubin	W1	19
Ransome's Dock	SW11	20
Raoul's	multi. loc.	16
Real Greak	multi. loc.	16
Riccardo's	SW3	18
Richoux	multi. loc.	15
☑ Royal China	multi. loc.	24
Royal China Club	W1	24
Royal Exchange	EC3	16
☑ Rules	WC2	23
Salt Yard	W1	22
Sam's Brass.	W4	20
Satsuma	W1	20
Shanghai Blues	WC1	21
Silks & Spice	NW10	16
Sofra	multi. loc.	19
Soho Spice	W1	20
Solly's	NW11	17
☑ Sophie's Steak	SW10	23
Sotheby's Cafe	W1	19
Sticky Fingers	W8	14
St. John Bread/Wine	E1	22
Strada	multi. loc.	18
Taqueria	W11	18
Tas	multi. loc.	20
Texas Embassy	SW1	13
T.G.I. Friday's	W1	11
Tom's Deli	W11	16

Tootsies	multi. loc.	16
Troubadour, The	SW5	14
Truc Vert	W1	22
202	W11	17
Villandry	W1	18
Vingt-Quatre	SW10	15
☑ Wagamama	multi. loc.	19
NEW ☑ Wallace, The	W1	20
☑ Wolseley, The	W1	21
Ye Olde Cheshire	EC4	15
YO! Sushi	multi. loc.	17
NEW Yumenoki	SW10	-
Zizzi	multi. loc.	16

BREAKFAST

(See also Hotel Dining)

Annie's	multi. loc.	21
Armani Caffé	SW3	17
Aubaine	multi. loc.	20
Automat	W1	17
Baker & Spice	multi. loc.	22
Balans	multi. loc.	16
Balham Kitchen	SW12	16
☑ Books for Cooks	W11	24
Café Boheme	W1	16
Café Rouge	multi. loc.	14
☑ Carluccio's	multi. loc.	17
Cecconi's	W1	21
☑ Cinnamon Club	SW1	24
Coq d'Argent	EC2	18
Eat & Two Veg	W1	17
Electric Brass.	W11	19
NEW Empress of India	E9	-
Engineer	NW1	19
Fifth Floor Cafe	SW1	18
Fortnum's Fountain	W1	20
Giraffe	multi. loc.	17
Hush	W1	17
Inn The Park	SW1	17
Joe's	SW3	19
Joe's Rest. Bar	SW1	21
Julie's	W11	18
La Brasserie	SW3	16
Ladurée	SW1	23
La Fromagerie	W1	24
☑ Lucky 7	W2	20
Lundum's	SW7	22
Nicole's	W1	19
1 Lombard Brass.	EC3	20
Oriel	SW1	15
☑ Ottolenghi	multi. loc.	24
Patisserie Valerie	multi. loc.	20
Portrait	WC2	22
Providores, The	W1	22
Raoul's	W9	16
Richoux	multi. loc.	15
Rivington Grill	EC2	20

Roast | **SE1**	_19_
Royal Exchange | **EC3**	_16_
Simpson's/Strand | **WC2**	_20_
Sotheby's Cafe | **W1**	_19_
St. John Bread/Wine | **E1**	_22_
Tate Britain | **SW1**	_17_
Tom's Deli | **W11**	_16_
Tootsies | **multi. loc.**	_16_
Troubadour, The | **SW5**	_14_
Tuttons Brass. | **WC2**	_18_
202 | **W11**	_17_
Villandry | **W1**	_18_
Vingt-Quatre | **SW10**	_15_
☑ Wolseley, The | **W1**	_21_

BRUNCH

Abingdon, The | **W8**	_22_
Admiral Codrington | **SW3**	_18_
Ambassador, The | **EC1**	_21_
Annie's | **multi. loc.**	_21_
Aubaine | **multi. loc.**	_20_
Automat | **W1**	_17_
Aziz | **SW6**	_17_
Balham Kitchen | **SW12**	_16_
Bistrot 190 | **SW7**	_19_
Bluebird | **SW3**	_–_
Blue Elephant | **SW6**	_20_
Cecconi's | **W1**	_21_
Christopher's | **WC2**	_19_
☑ Clarke's | **W8**	_25_
Cru | **N1**	_15_
1802 | **E14**	_16_
Fakhreldine | **W1**	_21_
Fifth Floor Cafe | **SW1**	_18_
Fish Shop | **EC1**	_19_
Garbo's | **W1**	_15_
Giraffe | **multi. loc.**	_17_
Harlem | **W2**	_16_
Joe Allen | **WC2**	_17_
Joe's Rest. Bar | **SW1**	_21_
La Brasserie | **SW3**	_16_
☑ Lanesborough | **SW1**	_21_
☑ Le Caprice | **SW1**	_24_
☑ Lucky 7 | **W2**	_20_
Lundum's | **SW7**	_22_
Motcombs | **SW1**	_17_
PJ's B&G | **multi. loc.**	_16_
Portrait | **WC2**	_22_
Providores, The | **W1**	_22_
Quadrato | **E14**	_24_
Ransome's Dock | **SW11**	_20_
Sam's Brass. | **W4**	_20_
☑ Sophie's Steak | **SW10**	_23_
NEW St. Germain | **EC1**	_21_
Tom's Deli | **W11**	_16_
NEW Tom's Kitchen | **SW3**	_19_
Troubadour, The | **SW5**	_14_

202 | **W11**	_17_
Vama | **SW10**	_24_
Villandry | **W1**	_18_
Vingt-Quatre | **SW10**	_15_
Wapping Food | **E1**	_20_
Zetter | **EC1**	_19_

BUSINESS DINING

Addendum | **EC3**	_–_
Al Duca | **SW1**	_19_
Alloro | **W1**	_22_
Almeida | **N1**	_18_
☑ Amaya | **SW1**	_25_
Arbutus | **W1**	_24_
NEW Atami | **SW1**	_24_
Auberge du Lac | **AL8**	_23_
☑ Aubergine | **SW10**	_26_
Aurora | **EC2**	_19_
Avenue, The | **SW1**	_18_
Awana | **SW3**	_17_
Axis | **WC2**	_20_
Bank Westminster | **SW1**	_18_
Bellamy's | **W1**	_20_
Belvedere, The | **W8**	_20_
Benares | **W1**	_23_
NEW Benja | **W1**	_–_
Bentley's | **W1**	_24_
☑ Bibendum | **SW3**	_24_
Blakes | **SW7**	_19_
Bleeding Heart | **EC1**	_22_
Bluebird | **SW3**	_–_
Blueprint Café | **SE1**	_18_
Bodeans | **W1**	_18_
Bonds | **EC2**	_20_
Boxwood Café | **SW1**	_21_
Brian Turner | **W1**	_21_
Brown's/The Grill | **W1**	_22_
Brunello | **SW7**	_20_
☑ Capital Rest. | **SW3**	_27_
Caravaggio | **EC3**	_19_
Cecconi's | **W1**	_21_
Chancery | **EC4**	_18_
NEW Chelsea Brass. | **SW1**	_16_
Chez Gérard | **multi. loc.**	_18_
China Tang | **W1**	_21_
Christopher's | **WC2**	_19_
☑ Cinnamon Club | **SW1**	_24_
☑ Cipriani | **W1**	_20_
Circus | **W1**	_14_
☑ Clarke's | **W8**	_25_
☑ Club Gascon | **EC1**	_26_
Deya | **W1**	_23_
☑ Dorchester/The Grill | **W1**	_24_
Drones | **SW1**	_18_
1880 | **SW7**	_21_
Elena's l'Etoile | **W1**	_20_
Embassy | **W1**	_13_

Fakhreldine | **W1**	21
Fifth Floor | **SW1**	20
☑ Fino | **W1**	23
Fiore | **SW1**	21
☑ Foliage | **SW1**	26
🆕 Forge, The | **WC2**	-
Franco's | **SW1**	15
Galvin/Windows | **W1**	22
☑ Galvin Bistrot | **W1**	24
Gilgamesh | **NW1**	20
Glasshouse, The | **TW9**	24
☑ Gordon Ramsay/Claridge's | **W1**	25
☑ Gordon Ramsay/68 Royal | **SW3**	28
Goring Dining Rm. | **SW1**	23
☑ Gravetye Manor | **W. Sussex**	24
Greenhouse, The | **W1**	25
Green's | **SW1**	22
🆕 Haiku | **W1**	-
Hartwell House | **HP17**	19
🆕 High Road Brass. | **W4**	20
🆕 Hoxton Grille | **EC2**	-
Il Convivio | **SW1**	23
Imperial City | **EC3**	17
Incognico | **WC2**	21
Indigo | **WC2**	22
☑ Ivy, The | **WC2**	23
Jaan | **WC2**	-
☑ J. Sheekey | **WC2**	25
Just St. James's | **SW1**	16
☑ Kai Mayfair | **W1**	25
La Genova | **W1**	23
☑ Lanes | **W1**	24
☑ Lanesborough | **SW1**	21
Langan's Bistro | **W1**	19
Langan's Brass. | **W1**	18
La Noisette | **SW1**	21
🆕☑ L'Atelier/Robuchon | **WC2**	26
☑ La Trompette | **W4**	27
Launceston Place | **W8**	21
☑ Le Café/Marché | **EC1**	23
☑ Le Caprice | **SW1**	24
Le Cercle | **SW1**	24
Ledbury | **W11**	25
☑ Le Gavroche | **W1**	27
☑ Le Manoir/Quat | **Oxfordshire**	28
Le Pont de la Tour | **SE1**	22
L'Escargot | **W1**	22
☑ L'Etranger | **SW7**	24
L'Incontro | **SW1**	20
☑ Locanda Locatelli | **W1**	25
L'Oranger | **SW1**	24
Luciano | **SW1**	20
🆕 Magdalen | **SE1**	-
Matsuri | **multi. loc.**	21

☑ Maze | **W1**	25
Memories of China | **multi. loc.**	21
🆕 Mews of Mayfair | **W1**	22
Mirabelle | **W1**	22
Mitsukoshi | **SW1**	19
☑ Miyama | **W1**	26
Mju | **SW1**	20
🆕 Mocotó | **SW1**	22
Mosaico | **W1**	21
Nahm | **SW1**	26
☑ Nobu Berkeley St | **W1**	26
☑ Nobu London | **W1**	27
Odin's | **W1**	20
🆕 Olivomare | **SW1**	-
One-O-One | **SW1**	23
Orrery | **W1**	25
Oxo Tower | **SE1**	20
🆕 Papillon | **SW3**	23
☑ Park, The | **SW1**	24
Paternoster Chop | **EC4**	18
☑ Pétrus | **SW1**	28
☑ Pied à Terre | **W1**	28
Plateau | **E14**	19
Poissonnerie | **SW3**	21
Princess Garden | **W1**	21
Prism | **EC3**	18
Providores, The | **W1**	22
Quadrato | **E14**	24
Quaglino's | **SW1**	18
☑ Quirinale | **SW1**	25
Quo Vadis | **W1**	18
Rasa | **multi. loc.**	24
☑ Rasoi Vineet Bhatia | **SW3**	27
Red Fort | **W1**	23
☑ Rhodes 24 | **EC2**	23
Rhodes W1 Brass. | **W1**	-
🆕 Rhodes W1 Rest. | **W1**	-
☑ Rib Rm. | **SW1**	24
Richard Corrigan | **W1**	23
🆕 Rist. Semplice | **W1**	-
☑ Ritz, The | **W1**	23
☑ River Café | **W6**	27
Roast | **SE1**	19
Roka | **W1**	25
☑ Rules | **WC2**	23
Santini | **SW1**	22
Sauterelle | **EC3**	-
☑ Savoy Grill | **WC2**	24
Scott's | **W1**	22
Shanghai Blues | **WC1**	21
Shepherd's | **SW1**	18
Shogun | **W1**	23
☑ Sketch/Lecture Rm. | **W1**	21
🆕 Skylon | **SE1**	-
Smiths/Dining Room | **EC1**	20
Smiths/Top Floor | **EC1**	20
☑ Square, The | **W1**	28

NEW St. Alban	**SW1**	21
NEW Stanza	**W1**	-
NEW Suka	**W1**	-
Z Tamarind	**W1**	25
NEW Z Theo Randall	**W1**	26
Z Tom Aikens	**SW3**	26
NEW Tom's Kitchen	**SW3**	19
NEW Trinity	**SW4**	24
Ubon	**E14**	24
Z Umu	**W1**	26
NEW Via Condotti	**W1**	18
Vineyard/Stockcross	**Berks**	24
NEW Z Wallace, The	**W1**	20
Z Waterside Inn	**Berks**	27
Z Wilton's	**SW1**	24
Z Zafferano	**SW1**	26
Zaika	**W8**	25
Zen Central	**W1**	21
ZENW3	**NW3**	16
Z Zuma	**SW7**	26

CELEBRITY CHEFS

Banquette	*Marcus Wareing*	**WC2**	22
NEW Barnes Grill	*Antony Worrall Thompson*	**SW13**	-
Belvedere, The	*Marco Pierre White*	**W8**	20
Benares	*Atul Kochhar*	**W1**	23
Bentley's	*Richard Corrigan*	**W1**	24
Boxwood Café	*Gordon Ramsay & Stuart Gillies*	**SW1**	21
Brasserie Roux	*Albert Roux*	**SW1**	20
Brian Turner	*Brian Turner*	**W1**	21
Café Spice Namasté	*Cyrus Todiwala*	**E1**	23
Z Capital Rest.	*Eric Chavot*	**SW3**	27
Z Carluccio's	*Antonio Carluccio*	**multi. loc.**	17
Cellar Gascon	*Pascal Aussignac*	**EC1**	20
Z Chez Bruce	*Bruce Poole*	**SW17**	28
Z Cinnamon Club	*Vivek Singh*	**SW1**	24
Z Clarke's	*Sally Clarke*	**W8**	25
Z Club Gascon	*Pascal Aussignac*	**EC1**	26
Comptoir Gascon	*Pascal Aussignac*	**EC1**	21
Drones	*Marco Pierre White*	**SW1**	18
Z Fat Duck	*Heston Blumenthal*	**Berks**	27
Fifteen	*Jamie Oliver*	**N1**	23
Frankie's Italian	*Marco Pierre White*	**multi. loc.**	15
Galvin/Windows	*Chris Galvin*	**W1**	22
Z Galvin Bistrot	*Chris Galvin*	**W1**	24

Gilgamesh	*Ian Pengelley*	**NW1**	20
Z Gordon Ramsay/Claridge's	*Gordon Ramsay & Mark Sargeant*	**W1**	25
Z Gordon Ramsay/68 Royal	*Gordon Ramsay & Mark Askew*	**SW3**	28
Hind's Head	*Heston Blumenthal*	**Berks**	23
Z Ivy, The	*Mark Hix*	**WC2**	23
Z J. Sheekey	*Mark Hix*	**WC2**	25
Kew Grill	*Antony Worrall Thompson*	**TW9**	18
La Noisette	*Bjorn van der Horst*	**SW1**	21
NEW Z L'Atelier/Robuchon	*Joël Robuchon*	**WC2**	26
Z Le Caprice	*Mark Hix*	**SW1**	24
Le Cercle	*Pascal Aussignac*	**SW1**	24
Z Le Gavroche	*Michel Roux Jr.*	**W1**	27
Z Le Manoir/Quat	*Raymond Blanc*	**Oxfordshire**	28
Z Locanda Locatelli	*Giorgio Locatelli*	**W1**	25
Luciano	*Marco Pierre White*	**SW1**	20
Z Maze	*Gordon Ramsay & Jason Atherton*	**W1**	25
Z Moro	*Sam & Sam Clark*	**EC1**	25
Z Nahm	*David Thompson*	**SW1**	26
NEW Narrow, The	*Gordon Ramsay*	**E14**	-
Z Nobu Berkeley St	*Nobu Matsuhisa & Mark Edwards*	**W1**	26
Z Nobu London	*Nobu Matsuhisa & Mark Edwards*	**W1**	27
Notting Grill	*Antony Worrall Thompson*	**W11**	21
Pearl	*Jun Tanaka*	**WC1**	24
Z Pétrus	*Marcus Wareing*	**SW1**	28
Providores, The	*Peter Gordon*	**W1**	22
Z Racine	*Henry Harris*	**SW3**	22
Randall & Aubin	*Ed Baines*	**multi. loc.**	19
Z Rasoi Vineet Bhatia	*Vineet Bhatia*	**SW3**	27
Refettorio	*Giorgio Locatelli*	**EC4**	20
Z Rhodes 24	*Gary Rhodes*	**EC2**	23
Rhodes W1 Brass.	*Gary Rhodes*	**W1**	-
NEW Rhodes W1 Rest.	*Gary Rhodes*	**W1**	-
Richard Corrigan	*Richard Corrigan*	**W1**	23
Z River Café	*Rose Gray & Ruth Rodgers*	**W6**	27
Roka	*Rainer Becker*	**W1**	25

Savoy Grill | *Marcus Wareing* | **WC2** — 24

Scott's | *Mark Hix* | **W1** — 22

Sketch/Gallery | *Pierre Gagnaire* | **W1** — 19

Sketch/Lecture Rm. | *Pierre Gagnaire* | **W1** — 21

Smiths/Dining Room | *John Torode* | **EC1** — 20

Smiths/Top Floor | *John Torode* | **EC1** — 20

Square, The | *Philip Howard* | **W1** — 28

St. John | *Fergus Henderson* | **EC1** — 25

St. John Bread/Wine | *Fergus Henderson* | **E1** — 22

Tamarind | *Cyrus Todiwala* | **W1** — 25

NEW Theo Randall | *Theo Randall* | **W1** — 26

Tom Aikens | *Tom Aikens* | **SW3** — 26

NEW Tom's Kitchen | *Tom Aikens* | **SW3** — 19

NEW Trinity | *Adam Byatt* | **SW4** — 24

Waterside Inn | *Michel Roux* | **Berks** — 27

Zilli Fish | *Aldo Zilli* | **W1** — 20

Zuma | *Rainer Becker* | **SW7** — 26

CHEESE BOARDS

Almeida | **N1** — 18

Ambassador, The | **EC1** — 21

Aquasia | **SW10** — 21

Auberge du Lac | **AL8** — 23

Aubergine | **SW10** — 26

Aurora | **EC2** — 19

Bedford & Strand | **WC2** — 17

Bibendum | **SW3** — 24

Bleeding Heart | **EC1** — 22

Bonds | **EC2** — 20

Caravaggio | **EC3** — 19

Cellar Gascon | **EC1** — 20

Charlotte's Place | **W5** — -

Cheyne Walk | **SW3** — 23

Chez Bruce | **SW17** — 28

Clarke's | **W8** — 25

Cliveden House | **Berks** — 24

NEW Cookbook Cafe | **W1** — -

Coq d'Argent | **EC2** — 18

Cross Keys | **SW3** — 14

Cru | **N1** — 15

Dorchester/The Grill | **W1** — 24

1802 | **E14** — 16

Elena's l'Etoile | **W1** — 20

Enoteca Turi | **SW15** — 27

Fat Duck | **Berks** — 27

Fifteen | **N1** — 23

Foliage | **SW1** — 26

French Horn | **Berks** — 23

Glasshouse, The | **TW9** — 24

Gordon Ramsay/Claridge's | **W1** — 25

Gordon Ramsay/68 Royal | **SW3** — 28

Goring Dining Rm. | **SW1** — 23

Gravetye Manor | **W. Sussex** — 24

Greenhouse, The | **W1** — 25

Green's | **SW1** — 22

Greig's | **W1** — 21

Hartwell House | **HP17** — 19

Julie's | **W11** — 18

La Fromagerie | **W1** — 24

Lanesborough | **SW1** — 21

La Noisette | **SW1** — 21

La Poule au Pot | **SW1** — 22

La Trompette | **W4** — 27

La Trouvaille | **W1** — 20

Launceston Place | **W8** — 21

Le Boudin Blanc | **W1** — 22

Le Café/Jardin | **WC2** — 19

Le Cercle | **SW1** — 24

Le Colombier | **SW3** — 20

Le Gavroche | **W1** — 27

Le Manoir/Quat | **Oxfordshire** — 28

Le Mercury | **N1** — 18

Le Pont de la Tour | **SE1** — 22

L'Escargot | **W1** — 22

Les Trois Garçons | **E1** — 19

L'Etranger | **SW7** — 24

L'Incontro | **SW1** — 20

Locanda Locatelli | **W1** — 25

L'Oranger | **SW1** — 24

Lou Pescadou | **SW5** — 20

Lucio | **SW3** — 21

Lundum's | **SW7** — 22

Manicomio | **SW3** — 18

Michael Moore | **W1** — 22

Mirabelle | **W1** — 22

Mju | **SW1** — 20

Mon Plaisir | **WC2** — 18

One-O-One | **SW1** — 23

Orrery | **W1** — 25

Oslo Court | **NW8** — 22

Osteria Basilico | **W11** — 24

Osteria dell'Arancio | **SW10** — 20

Oxo Tower | **SE1** — 20

Oxo Tower Brass. | **SE1** — 20

NEW Papillon | **SW3** — 23

Paternoster Chop | **EC4** — 18

Pearl | **WC1** — 24

Pellicano | **SW3** — 20

Petersham, The | **TW10** — 23

Pétrus | **SW1** — 28

Pied à Terre | **W1** — 28

Pig's Ear | **SW3** — 22

Plateau | **E14** — 19

Prism | **EC3** — 18

Quality Chop House | **EC1**	20
Refettorio | **EC4**	20
Refuel | **W1**	12
Z Rhodes 24 | **EC2**	23
NEW Rhodes W1 Rest. | **W1**	-
Z Rib Rm. | **SW1**	24
Richard Corrigan | **W1**	23
NEW Rist. Semplice | **W1**	-
Z Ritz, The | **W1**	23
Z River Café | **W6**	27
Roast | **SE1**	19
Z Roussillon | **SW1**	26
Royal Exchange | **EC3**	16
Salisbury, The | **SW6**	-
Salt Yard | **W1**	22
Salusbury Pub | **NW6**	18
San Lorenzo | **SW19**	20
Sarastro | **WC2**	12
Sartoria | **W1**	20
Sauterelle | **EC3**	-
Z Savoy Grill | **WC2**	24
Scott's | **W1**	22
Z Sketch/Gallery | **W1**	19
Z Sketch/Lecture Rm. | **W1**	21
Smiths/Dining Room | **EC1**	20
Smiths/Top Floor | **EC1**	20
NEW Spread Eagle | **SE10**	21
Z Square, The | **W1**	28
NEW Stanza | **W1**	-
Z St. John | **EC1**	25
St. John Bread/Wine | **E1**	22
Tate Britain | **SW1**	17
Tate Modern | **SE1**	16
Tentazioni | **SE1**	27
Thomas Cubitt | **SW1**	21
Z Tom Aikens | **SW3**	26
Toto's | **SW3**	24
Truc Vert | **W1**	22
Tuttons Brass. | **WC2**	18
Upstairs | **SW2**	-
Villandry | **W1**	18
Vineyard/Stockcross | **Berks**	24
Vivat Bacchus | **EC4**	23
Z Waterside Inn | **Berks**	27
Waterway, The | **W9**	18
Wells, The | **NW3**	18
Westbourne, The | **W2**	16
Z Wilton's | **SW1**	24
Z Zafferano | **SW1**	26
Zetter | **EC1**	19

CHILD-FRIENDLY

(Besides the normal fast-food places; * children's menu available)

Abbeville | **SW4**	15
Abingdon, The | **W8**	22
Al Duca | **SW1**	19
Almeida | **N1**	18

Aperitivo | **W1**	20
Z Archipelago | **W1**	21
Armani Caffè | **SW3**	17
Z Asia de Cuba* | **WC2**	22
Ask Pizza | **multi. loc.**	16
Z Assaggi | **W2**	26
Aubaine | **SW3**	20
Axis* | **WC2**	20
Babes 'n' Burgers* | **W11**	17
Babylon* | **W8**	20
Baker & Spice | **multi. loc.**	22
Balham Kitchen* | **SW12**	16
Baltic* | **SE1**	21
Banquette | **WC2**	22
Z Belgo* | **multi. loc.**	19
Benihana | **multi. loc.**	18
Z Bibendum | **SW3**	24
Bibendum Oyster | **SW3**	22
Big Easy* | **SW3**	16
Black & Blue | **multi. loc.**	17
Blandford St. | **W1**	18
Bloom's* | **NW11**	19
Bluebird* | **SW3**	-
Blue Elephant | **SW6**	20
Bodeans* | **multi. loc.**	18
Z Books for Cooks | **W11**	24
Boxwood Café* | **SW1**	21
Brasserie Roux* | **SW1**	20
Browns* | **multi. loc.**	16
Buona Sera | **multi. loc.**	23
Z Busaba Eathai | **multi. loc.**	21
Café Fish* | **W1**	20
Cafe Pacifico* | **WC2**	18
Café Rouge* | **multi. loc.**	14
Café Spice Namasté | **E1**	23
Cantina del Ponte | **SE1**	17
Caraffini | **SW1**	21
Caravaggio | **EC3**	19
Z Carluccio's* | **multi. loc.**	17
Carpaccio | **SW3**	18
Casale Franco | **N1**	-
Cecconi's | **W1**	21
Cheyne Walk | **SW3**	23
Z Chez Bruce | **SW17**	28
Chez Gérard* | **multi. loc.**	18
Chez Kristof* | **W6**	22
Christopher's* | **WC2**	19
Chuen Cheng Ku | **W1**	19
Z Churchill Arms | **W8**	22
Cigala | **WC1**	22
Z Cinnamon Club | **SW1**	24
Z Cipriani | **W1**	20
Circus | **W1**	14
Citrus* | **W1**	20
Coach & Horses | **EC1**	19
Daphne's | **SW3**	21
Drones | **SW1**	18

SPECIAL FEATURES

Six13* | **W1**	19
Smollensky's* | **multi. loc.**	15
Sofra* | **multi. loc.**	19
Sonny's* | **SW13**	21
☑ Sophie's Steak* | **SW10**	23
Spiga | **W1**	15
Sticky Fingers* | **W8**	14
Strada | **multi. loc.**	18
Tas | **SE1**	20
Texas Embassy* | **SW1**	13
T.G.I. Friday's* | **multi. loc.**	11
Tom's Deli | **W11**	16
NEW Tom's Kitchen | **SW3**	19
Tootsies* | **multi. loc.**	16
Truc Vert | **W1**	22
☑ Two Brothers Fish* | **N3**	24
202 | **W11**	17
Ubon | **E14**	24
Uli | **W11**	25
Vama | **SW10**	24
Villandry* | **W1**	18
Vingt-Quatre | **SW10**	15
☑ Wagamama* | **multi. loc.**	19
☑ Waterside Inn* | **Berks**	27
Wòdka | **W8**	20
☑ Wolseley, The | **W1**	21
☑ Yauatcha | **W1**	25
YO! Sushi* | **multi. loc.**	17
Yoshino | **W1**	24
☑ Zafferano | **SW1**	26
Zen Central | **W1**	21
ZENW3 | **NW3**	16
Zetter | **EC1**	19
Zizzi* | **multi. loc.**	16
☑ Zuma | **SW7**	26

DELIVERY/TAKEAWAY

(D=delivery, T=takeaway)

Alounak | D, T | **multi. loc.**	23
Baker & Spice | T | **multi. loc.**	22
Beiteddine | D, T | **SW1**	22
Big Easy | T | **SW3**	16
Bloom's | D, T | **NW11**	19
Blue Elephant | D, T | **SW6**	20
Café Spice Namasté | D, T | **E1**	23
Cantina del Ponte | T | **SE1**	17
☑ Carluccio's | T | **multi. loc.**	17
Chor Bizarre | T | **W1**	21
Chuen Cheng Ku | T | **W1**	19
☑ Churchill Arms | T | **W8**	22
Chutney Mary | T | **SW10**	23
Crazy Homies | T | **W2**	20
☑ Defune | T | **W1**	27
Eat & Two Veg | T | **W1**	17
Ed's Easy Diner | T | **W1**	15
Esarn Kheaw | T | **W12**	-
Fairuz | D, T | **multi. loc.**	22

Fakhreldine | D, T | **W1**	21
Frankie's Italian | T | **SW3**	15
Friends | T | **SW10**	18
Garbo's | T | **W1**	15
☑ Gaucho Grill | T | **multi. loc.**	22
Geales Fish | T | **W8**	-
Giraffe | T | **multi. loc.**	17
Golden Dragon | T | **W1**	20
Halepi | T | **W2**	24
Harbour City | T | **W1**	20
Harlem | T | **W2**	16
Ikeda | T | **W1**	21
Il Falconiere | T | **SW7**	15
Imperial City | T | **EC3**	17
Inn The Park | T | **SW1**	17
☑ Ishbilia | D, T | **SW1**	24
itsu | D, T | **multi. loc.**	18
Jenny Lo's Tea | D, T | **SW1**	20
☑ Jin Kichi | T | **NW3**	26
Khan's | T | **W2**	20
Khan's of Kensington | D, T | **SW7**	22
Kiku | T | **W1**	24
Koi | D, T | **W8**	22
Kulu Kulu | T | **multi. loc.**	20
La Fromagerie | D, T | **W1**	24
La Piragua | T | **N1**	15
La Porchetta | T | **multi. loc.**	19
☑ La Porte des Indes | T | **W1**	21
Levant | T | **W1**	19
Levantine | T | **W2**	20
☑ Lucky 7 | T | **W2**	20
Ma Goa | T | **SW15**	23
Mandalay | T | **W2**	23
Mango Tree | T | **SW1**	20
Mao Tai | D, T | **SW6**	22
Masala Zone | T | **multi. loc.**	19
Matsuri | T | **SW1**	21
Mela | T | **WC2**	23
Memories of China | T | **multi. loc.**	21
Moshi Moshi | D, T | **multi. loc.**	20
☑ North Sea | T | **WC1**	23
Noura | D, T | **multi. loc.**	21
Nyonya | T | **W11**	24
Oliveto | T | **SW1**	23
Original Lahore | T | **multi. loc.**	24
☑ Ottolenghi | T | **multi. loc.**	24
Ozer | T | **W1**	19
Painted Heron | T | **SW10**	22
☑ Patara | T | **multi. loc.**	23
☑ Pizza Express | T | **multi. loc.**	17
Pizza Metro | T | **SW11**	-
Rasa | T | **multi. loc.**	24
Red Pepper | T | **W9**	19
Reubens | T | **W1**	20
Riccardo's | T | **SW3**	18
Richoux | T | **multi. loc.**	15
☑ Royal China | T | **multi. loc.**	24

Salloos | T | **SW1**	23
Santa Lucia | T | **SW10**	22
Sarkhel's | D, T | **SW18**	22
Seashell | T | **NW1**	20
Singapore Garden | D, T | **NW6**	21
Singapura | T | **multi. loc.**	20
Six13 | D, T | **W1**	19
Solly's | T | **NW11**	17
Spago | T | **SW7**	19
Spiga | T | **W1**	15
Star of India | T | **SW5**	24
Sticky Fingers | T | **W8**	14
St. John Bread/Wine | T | **E1**	22
Strada | T | **multi. loc.**	18
☑ Tamarind | D, T | **W1**	25
Tas | D, T | **multi. loc.**	20
Thai Square | T | **multi. loc.**	19
Tom's Deli | T | **W11**	16
Truc Vert | D, T | **W1**	22
☑ Two Brothers Fish | T | **N3**	24
Ubon | T | **E14**	24
Vama | D, T | **SW10**	24
Veeraswamy | T | **W1**	22
Villandry | T | **W1**	18
YO! Sushi | D, T | **multi. loc.**	17
Yoshino | T | **W1**	24
Zen Central | D, T | **W1**	21
ZENW3 | D, T | **NW3**	16

DINING ALONE

(Other than hotels and places with counter service)

Academy | **W1**	13
☑ Amaya | **SW1**	25
Armani Caffé | **SW3**	17
Aubaine | **multi. loc.**	20
Baker & Spice | **multi. loc.**	22
NEW Barrafina | **W1**	24
Bibendum Oyster | **SW3**	22
☑ Books for Cooks | **W11**	24
☑ Busaba Eathai | **multi. loc.**	21
Café Rouge | **multi. loc.**	14
☑ Carluccio's | **multi. loc.**	17
Chowki | **W1**	21
Chuen Cheng Ku | **W1**	19
Coach & Horses | **EC1**	19
Comptoir Gascon | **EC1**	21
Eat & Two Veg | **W1**	17
Ed's Easy Diner | **W1**	15
Fifth Floor Cafe | **SW1**	18
☑ Fino | **W1**	23
Fortnum's Fountain | **W1**	20
☑ Hakkasan | **W1**	24
Inaho | **W2**	21
Inn The Park | **SW1**	17
Jenny Lo's Tea | **SW1**	20
Joe's Rest. Bar | **SW1**	21
Ladurée | **SW1**	23

La Fromagerie | **W1**	24
Le Colombier | **SW3**	20
Leon | **multi. loc.**	19
Manicomio | **SW3**	18
Matsuri | **multi. loc.**	21
☑ Maze | **W1**	25
Mildreds | **W1**	22
Mitsukoshi | **SW1**	19
Mon Plaisir | **WC2**	18
New Culture Rev. | **multi. loc.**	17
Nicole's | **W1**	19
Oriel | **SW1**	15
☑ Ottolenghi | **multi. loc.**	24
Patisserie Valerie | **multi. loc.**	20
Ping Pong | **multi. loc.**	18
Porters | **WC2**	20
Portrait | **WC2**	22
Providores, The | **W1**	22
Randall & Aubin | **multi. loc.**	19
Richoux | **multi. loc.**	15
NEW 1707 Wine Bar | **W1**	22
Sotheby's Cafe | **W1**	19
St. John Bread/Wine | **E1**	22
Tapas Brindisa | **SE1**	22
Taqueria | **W11**	18
Tate Modern | **SE1**	16
Tom's Deli | **W11**	16
NEW Tom's Kitchen | **SW3**	19
Truc Vert | **W1**	22
Villandry | **W1**	18
☑ Wagamama | **multi. loc.**	19
☑ Wolseley, The | **W1**	21
☑ Yauatcha | **W1**	25
YO! Sushi | **multi. loc.**	17

ENTERTAINMENT

(Call for days and times of performances)

Bengal Clipper | piano | **SE1**	21
Bentley's | Piano | **W1**	24
Big Easy | live bands | **SW3**	16
Boisdale | jazz | **SW1**	20
Cheyne Walk | jazz | **SW3**	23
Chutney Mary | jazz | **SW10**	23
Circus | DJ | **W1**	14
Coq d'Argent | jazz | **EC2**	18
Efes | belly dancing | **W1**	18
1802 | DJ | **E14**	16
Embassy | DJ | **W1**	13
Floridita | Cuban | **W1**	16
Gilgamesh | varies | **NW1**	20
☑ Hakkasan | DJ | **W1**	24
☑ Ishbilia | belly dancing | **SW1**	24
Joe Allen | jazz/piano | **WC2**	17
☑ Lanesborough | jazz | **SW1**	21
Langan's Brass. | jazz | **W1**	18
☑ Le Café/Marché | jazz | **EC1**	23

SPECIAL FEATURES

Le Caprice | piano | **SW1** 24
Le Pont de la Tour | piano | **SE1** 22
Levant | belly dancing | **W1** 19
Levantine | belly dancing | **W2** 20
Little Italy | DJ | **W1** 16
Maroush | varies | **W2** 20
Mash | DJ | **W1** 12
Meson Don Felipe | guitar | **SE1** 18
Mirabelle | piano | **W1** 22
Oxo Tower Brass. | jazz | **SE1** 20
Pigalle Club | cabaret | **W1** 14
Pizza on the Park | jazz | **SW1** 14
PJ's B&G | jazz | **WC2** 16
Planet Hollywood | DJ | **W1** 11
Quaglino's | jazz | **SW1** 18
☑ Rib Rm. | piano | **SW1** 24
☑ Ritz, The | piano | **W1** 23
Simpson's/Strand | piano | **WC2** 20
Smollensky's | varies | **multi. loc.** 15
Soho Spice | DJ | **W1** 20
Souk | belly dancing | **WC2** 18
Tas | guitar | **SE1** 20
Thai Square | varies | **multi. loc.** 19
Vineyard/Stockcross | jazz/piano | **Berks** 24

FIREPLACES

Abbeville | **SW4** 15
Admiral Codrington | **SW3** 18
Anglesea Arms | **W6** 23
Babylon | **W8** 20
Balham Kitchen | **SW12** 16
Bam-Bou | **W1** 21
Barnsbury, The | **N1** 21
☑ Belgo | **NW1** 19
Brackenbury | **W6** 18
☑ Al Hamra | **W1** 22
Brunello | **SW7** 20
Builders Arms | **SW3** 17
Bull, The | **N6** 19
☑ Cambio de Tercio | **SW5** 24
Cheyne Walk | **SW3** 23
Christopher's | **WC2** 19
☑ Churchill Arms | **W8** 22
Cicada | **EC1** 15
Clerkenwell | **EC1** 23
☑ Cliveden House | **Berks** 24
Clos Maggiore | **WC2** 24
Crazy Bear | **W1** 21
Daphne's | **SW3** 21
Draper's Arms | **N1** 18
Ebury Dining Rm. | **SW1** 20
Farm | **SW6** -
French Horn | **Berks** 23
Goring Dining Rm. | **SW1** 23
☑ Gravetye Manor | **W. Sussex** 24
Grenadier, The | **SW1** 16

NEW Hoxton Grille | **EC2** -
Julie's | **W11** 18
La Poule au Pot | **SW1** 22
Le Cercle | **SW1** 24
☑ Le Manoir/Quat | **Oxfordshire** 28
Lemonia | **NW1** 20
L'Escargot | **W1** 22
Living Rm. | **W1** 19
Lundum's | **SW7** 22
Old Bull & Bush | **NW3** 14
Oratory, The | **SW3** 18
Palmerston, The | **SE22** -
Raoul's | **W11** 16
Real Greak | **SW15** 16
Richard Corrigan | **W1** 23
☑ Rules | **WC2** 23
Salusbury Pub | **NW6** 18
San Lorenzo | **SW19** 20
Buen Ayre/Santa Maria | **SW8** 23
Sardo Canale | **NW1** 20
Sonny's | **SW13** 21
NEW Spread Eagle | **SE10** 21
Thomas Cubitt | **SW1** 21
Tsunami | **SW4** 24
Upstairs | **SW2** -
☑ Waterside Inn | **Berks** 27
Waterway, The | **W9** 18
Wells, The | **NW3** 18
Ye Olde Cheshire | **EC4** 15
Zilli Fish | **W1** 20

GAME IN SEASON

Abbeville | **SW4** 15
Adam St. | **WC2** 20
Addendum | **EC3** -
Admiralty, The | **WC2** 19
Albannach | **WC2** 14
NEW Albion, The | **N1** -
Almeida | **N1** 18
Anchor & Hope | **SE1** 24
Andrew Edmunds | **W1** 22
Arbutus | **W1** 24
Aurora | **EC2** 19
Axis | **WC2** 20
Belvedere, The | **W8** 20
☑ Bibendum | **SW3** 24
Bistrotheque | **E2** 19
Blandford St. | **W1** 18
Bleeding Heart | **EC1** 22
Bluebird | **SW3** -
Blueprint Café | **SE1** 18
Bonds | **EC2** 20
Boxwood Café | **SW1** 21
Brackenbury | **W6** 18
Brasserie Roux | **SW1** 20
Brasserie St. Quentin | **SW3** 18

Brian Turner	W1	21	Le Cercle	SW1	24
Brown's/The Grill	W1	22	Le Colombier	SW3	20
NEW Bumpkin	W11	21	Ledbury	W11	25
Butlers Wharf	SE1	20	Z Le Gavroche	W1	27
Z Capital Rest.	SW3	27	Z Le Manoir/Quat	Oxfordshire	28
Caraffini	SW1	21	Le Pont de la Tour	SE1	22
Caravaggio	EC3	19	L'Escargot	W1	22
Cellar Gascon	EC1	20	Z Les Trois Garçons	E1	19
Z Chez Bruce	SW17	28	Z L'Etranger	SW7	24
NEW Chez Patrick	W8	21	Z Locanda Locatelli	W1	25
Chutney Mary	SW10	23	Lucio	SW3	21
Z Cinnamon Club	SW1	24	Michael Moore	W1	22
Z Cipriani	W1	20	Mirabelle	W1	22
Z Cliveden House	Berks	24	Mon Plaisir	WC2	18
Clos Maggiore	WC2	24	Montpeliano	SW7	18
Z Club Gascon	EC1	26	Monza	SW3	20
Coach & Horses	EC1	19	Z Morgan M	N7	27
Comptoir Gascon	EC1	21	Z Moro	EC1	25
NEW Cookbook Cafe	W1	-	Mosaico	W1	21
Z Dorchester/The Grill	W1	24	Motcombs	SW1	17
11 Abingdon Rd.	W8	18	Notting Grill	W11	21
Z Enoteca Turi	SW15	27	Notting Hill Brass.	W11	24
Z Fat Duck	Berks	27	Odette's	NW1	20
Z ffiona's	W8	24	Olivo	SW1	21
Fifteen	N1	23	1 Lombard St.	EC3	22
Z Fino	W1	23	Orrery	W1	25
Z Foliage	SW1	26	Oxo Tower	SE1	20
NEW Forge, The	WC2	-	NEW Papillon	SW3	23
French Horn	Berks	23	Passione	W1	23
Glasshouse, The	TW9	24	Paternoster Chop	EC4	18
Z Gordon Ramsay/Claridge's	W1	25	Pearl	WC1	24
Z Gordon Ramsay/68 Royal	SW3	28	Z Pétrus	SW1	28
Goring Dining Rm.	SW1	23	Pig's Ear	SW3	22
Z Gravetye Manor	W. Sussex	24	Prism	EC3	18
NEW Great Queen St.	WC2	-	Providores, The	W1	22
Greenhouse, The	W1	25	Quadrato	E14	24
Green's	SW1	22	Quaglino's	SW1	18
Grenadier, The	SW1	16	Z Quirinale	SW1	25
Hand & Flowers	SL7	-	Z Racine	SW3	22
Hartwell House	HP17	19	Randall & Aubin	SW10	19
NEW Hat & Feathers	EC1	-	Refettorio	EC4	20
Il Convivio	SW1	23	NEW Rhodes Bar-B-Q	E1	-
Julie's	W11	18	Z Rhodes 24	EC2	23
Kensington Place	W8	20	Rhodes W1 Brass.	W1	-
Kew Grill	TW9	18	NEW Rhodes W1 Rest.	W1	-
La Famiglia	SW10	21	Z Rib Rm.	SW1	24
Z Lanesborough	SW1	21	Riccardo's	SW3	18
Langan's Bistro	W1	19	Richard Corrigan	W1	23
La Noisette	SW1	21	NEW Rist. Semplice	W1	-
La Poule au Pot	SW1	22	Z Ritz, The	W1	23
Z La Trompette	W4	27	Riva	SW13	20
La Trouvaille	W1	20	Z River Café	W6	27
Launceston Place	W8	21	Rivington Grill	multi. loc.	20
L'Aventure	NW8	22	Roast	SE1	19
Z Le Caprice	SW1	24	Rodizio Rico	multi. loc.	15
			Z Roussillon	SW1	26
			Z Rules	WC2	23

SPECIAL FEATURES

Restaurant	Location	Score
San Lorenzo	multi. loc.	20
Santini	SW1	22
Sardo	W1	23
Sardo Canale	NW1	20
Sartoria	W1	20
🆉 Savoy Grill	WC2	24
Simpson's/Strand	WC2	20
🆉 Sketch/Gallery	W1	19
🆉 Sketch/Lecture Rm.	W1	21
Smiths/Dining Room	EC1	20
Smiths/Top Floor	EC1	20
Snows on Green	W6	21
Sonny's	SW13	21
NEW Spread Eagle	SE10	21
🆉 Square, The	W1	28
NEW St. Alban	SW1	21
NEW Stanza	W1	–
🆉 St. John	EC1	25
St. John Bread/Wine	E1	22
Tate Britain	SW1	17
Tentazioni	SE1	27
NEW🆉 Theo Randall	W1	26
Thomas Cubitt	SW1	21
Timo	W8	22
🆉 Tom Aikens	SW3	26
NEW Tom's Kitchen	SW3	19
NEW Trinity	SW4	24
Upper Glas	N1	22
Veeraswamy	W1	22
Villandry	W1	18
Vineyard/Stockcross	Berks	24
Vivat Bacchus	EC4	23
Wapping Food	E1	20
🆉 Waterside Inn	Berks	27
🆉 Wilton's	SW1	24
Wòdka	W8	20
🆉 Wolseley, The	W1	21
🆉 Zafferano	SW1	26
Zaika	W8	25

HISTORIC PLACES

(Year opened; * building)

Year	Restaurant	Location	Score
1300	Hand & Flowers*	SL7	–
1520	Just St. James's*	SW1	16
1550	Fat Duck*	Berks	27
1571	Royal Exchange*	EC3	16
1598	Gravetye Manor*	W. Sussex	24
1662	Bleeding Heart*	EC1	22
1667	Ye Olde Cheshire*	EC4	15
1680	French Horn*	Berks	23
1690	Hind's Head	Berks	23
1692	Giovanni's*	WC2	21
1700	Admiralty, The*	WC2	19
1700	Bellamy's*	W1	18
1700	Cru*	N1	15
1700	Lanesborough*	SW1	21

Year	Restaurant	Location	Score
1700	Ransome's Dock*	SW11	20
1721	Old Bull & Bush	NW3	14
1725	Patisserie Valerie*	WC2	20
1740	Richard Corrigan*	W1	23
1742	Grenadier, The*	SW1	16
1742	Wilton's	SW1	24
1750	Food for Thought*	WC2	24
1750	Gun, The*	E14	19
1755	Blandford St.*	W1	18
1755	Randall & Aubin*	W1	19
1760	Auberge du Lac*	AL8	23
1760	Sotheby's Cafe*	W1	19
1780	Andrew Edmunds*	W1	22
1790	Carluccio's*	EC1	17
1790	Chez Gérard*	EC2	18
1790	Rowley's*	SW1	19
1798	Don*	EC4	22
1798	Rules*	WC2	23
1800	Anglesea Arms*	W6	23
1800	Axis*	WC2	20
1800	Churchill Arms*	W8	22
1800	Cuckoo Club*	W1	15
1800	Hoxton Apprentice*	N1	18
1800	Ladbroke Arms*	W11	20
1800	Oratory, The*	SW3	18
1800	Snows on Green*	W6	21
1802	1802*	E14	16
1810	Pig's Ear*	SW3	22
1820	Builders Arms*	SW3	17
1828	Simpson's/Strand*	WC2	20
1834	Albion, The*	N1	–
1837	Brown's/The Grill*	W1	22
1849	Harry Morgan's*	SW1	16
1850	Coach & Horses*	EC1	19
1850	El Blason*	SW3	18
1850	Marquess Tavern*	N1	–
1855	Baltic*	SE1	21
1860	Pepper Tree*	SW4	19
1865	Petersham, The*	TW10	23
1867	Kettners*	W1	15
1872	Bistrot 190*	SW7	19
1875	Quality Chop House*	EC1	20
1880	Bombay Brass.*	SW7	22
1881	Duke of Cambridge*	N1	20
1889	Foliage*	SW1	26
1889	Savoy Grill	WC2	24
1889	Sweetings	EC4	24
1890	Aurora*	EC2	19
1890	Bradley's*	NW3	15
1890	La Fromagerie*	W1	24
1890	Maggie Jones's*	W8	21
1890	Potemkin*	EC1	–
1890	R.S.J.*	SE1	21
1894	Ciro's Pizza*	EC2	17
1896	Elena's l'Etoile*	W1	20
1898	J. Sheekey*	WC2	25
1900	Annie's*	W4	21

SPECIAL FEATURES

Hyatt Regency - The Churchill
  ☑ Locanda Locatelli | **W1** 25
InterContinental Park Ln.
  NEW Cookbook Cafe | **W1** –
  NEW ☑ Theo Randall | **W1** 26
Jumeirah Carlton Tower Hotel
  La Noisette | **SW1** 21
  ☑ Rib Rm. | **SW1** 24
Jumeirah Lowndes Hotel
  NEW Mimosa | **SW1** –
Lanesborough
  ☑ Lanesborough | **SW1** 21
Le Manoir aux
  Quat'Saisons Hotel
  ☑ Le Manoir/Quat | 28
  Oxfordshire
London Hilton on Park Ln.
  Galvin/Windows | **W1** 22
Mandarin Oriental Hyde Park
  ☑ Foliage | **SW1** 26
  ☑ Park, The | **SW1** 24
Metropolitan Hotel
  ☑ Nobu London | **W1** 27
Millennium Hotel Mayfair
  Brian Turner | **W1** 21
  Shogun | **W1** 23
Millennium Knightsbridge Hotel
  Mju | **SW1** 20
One Aldwych Hotel
  Axis | **WC2** 20
  Indigo | **WC2** 22
Park Lane Hotel
  Citrus | **W1** 20
Petersham Hotel
  Petersham, The | **TW10** 23
Renaissance Chancery Court
  Pearl | **WC1** 24
Ritz Hotel
  ☑ Ritz, The | **W1** 23
Royal Lancaster Hotel
  Island | **W2** –
Sanderson Hotel
  NEW Suka | **W1** –
Savoy Hotel
  Banquette | **WC2** 22
  ☑ Savoy Grill | **WC2** 24
Sheraton Park Tower
  One-O-One | **SW1** 23
Sloane Square Hotel
  NEW Chelsea Brass. | **SW1** 16
Sofitel St. James London
  Brasserie Roux | **SW1** 20
Soho Hotel
  Refuel | **W1** 17
St. Giles Hotel
  NEW Kobe Jones | **WC1** 18

St. Martin's Lane Hotel
  ☑ Asia de Cuba | **WC2** 22
Swissôtel - The Howard
  Jaan | **WC2** –
Thistle Hotel
  Chez Gérard | **SW1** 18
Threadneedles Hotel
  Bonds | **EC2** 20
Vineyard at Stockcross
  Vineyard/Stockcross | **Berks** 24
Waterside Inn
  ☑ Waterside Inn | **Berks** 27
Wyndham Hotel
  Aquasia | **SW10** 21
Zetter
  Zetter | **EC1** 19

LATE DINING

(Weekday closing hour)

Alounak | varies | **W14** 23
Annex 3 | 12 AM | **W1** 16
☑ Asia de Cuba | varies | **WC2** 22
Automat | 1 AM | **W1** 17
Avenue, The | 12 AM | **SW1** 18
Balans | varies | **multi. loc.** 16
Basilico | 12 AM | **multi. loc.** 17
Beiteddine | 12 AM | **SW1** 22
Blakes | 12 AM | **SW7** 19
Blue Elephant | 12 AM | **SW6** 20
Boxwood Café | 12 AM | **SW1** 21
NEW Bumpkin | varies | **W11** 21
Buona Sera | 12 AM | **multi. loc.** 23
Cecconi's | 12 AM | **W1** 21
Chelsea Bun | 12 AM | **SW10** 18
Chuen Cheng Ku | 12 AM | **W1** 19
Circus | 12 AM | **W1** 14
Ciro's Pizza | varies | **SW3** 17
Cocoon | varies | **W1** 21
Cross Keys | 12 AM | **SW3** 14
Diner, The | varies | **W1** –
Efes | 12 AM | **W1** 18
Electric Brass. | 1 AM | **W11** 19
Fakhreldine | 12 AM | **W1** 21
Floridita | 1 AM | **W1** 16
NEW Forge, The | 12 AM | **WC2** –
1492 | 12 AM | **SW6** 21
Friends | 12 AM | **SW10** 18
☑ Gaucho Grill | 12 AM | **NW3** 22
Gilgamesh | 12 AM | **NW1** 20
Greig's | 12 AM | **W1** 21
☑ Hakkasan | 12 AM | **W1** 24
Halepi | 12 AM | **W2** 24
Hard Rock | 12:30 AM | **W1** 13
Harlem | 1 AM | **W2** 16
Haz | 12 AM | **E1** 25
Imperial China | 12 AM | **WC2** 21
☑ Ishbilia | 12 AM | **SW1** 24

Ishtar	12 AM	**W1**	22

Ishtar | 12 AM | **W1** — 22
Ⓩ Ivy, The | 12 AM | **WC2** — 23
Joe Allen | 12:45 AM | **WC2** — 17
Ⓩ J. Sheekey | 12 AM | **WC2** — 25
Julie's | varies | **W11** — 18
Kandoo | 12 AM | **W2** — -
Kettners | 1 AM | **W1** — 15
La Porchetta | 12 AM | **multi. loc.** — 19
NEW Ⓩ L'Atelier/Robuchon | varies | **WC2** — 26
Le Café/Jardin | 12 AM | **WC2** — 19
Ⓩ Le Caprice | 12 AM | **SW1** — 24
Le Deuxième | 12 AM | **WC2** — 20
Lee Ho Fook | 12 AM | **W1** — 17
Le Mercury | 1 AM | **N1** — 18
Levant | 1 AM | **W1** — 19
Little Bay | 12 AM | **multi. loc.** — 21
Little Italy | 4 AM | **W1** — 16
Living Rm. | 12 AM | **W1** — 19
Lou Pescadou | 12 AM | **SW5** — 20
Mamounia | varies | **W1** — 17
Maroush | varies | **multi. loc.** — 20
Maxwell's | 12 AM | **WC2** — 17
Mestizo | varies | **NW1** — 19
Meza | varies | **W1** — 17
Montpeliano | 12 AM | **SW7** — 18
Mr. Chow | 12 AM | **SW1** — 21
Mr. Kong | 2:45 AM | **WC2** — 21
New World | 12 AM | **W1** — 19
Noura | varies | **multi. loc.** — 21
Original Lahore | 12 AM | **multi. loc.** — 24
Orso | 12 AM | **WC2** — 20
Ozer | 12 AM | **W1** — 19
Pasha | 12 AM | **SW7** — 18
Ping Pong | varies | **multi. loc.** — 18
Ⓩ Pizza Express | varies | **multi. loc.** — 17
PJ's B&G | varies | **WC2** — 16
Planet Hollywood | 1 AM | **W1** — 11
Quaglino's | 12 AM | **SW1** — 18
Sabor | varies | **N1** — 22
Saki Bar/Food Emp. | 12 AM | **EC1** — -
Sam's Brass. | 12:30 AM | **W4** — 20
Sofra | 12 AM | **multi. loc.** — 19
Souk | 12 AM | **WC2** — 18
Spago | 12 AM | **SW7** — 19
NEW St. Alban | 12 AM | **SW1** — 21
NEW St. Germain | varies | **EC1** — 21
NEW Suka | varies | **W1** — -
Thai Square | varies | **multi. loc.** — 19
Tokyo Diner | 12 AM | **WC2** — 20
NEW Tom's Kitchen | 12 AM | **SW3** — 19
Troubadour, The | 12 AM | **SW5** — 14
Vingt-Quatre | 24 hrs. | **SW10** — 15
Ⓩ Wolseley, The | 12 AM | **W1** — 21

OFFBEAT

NEW Acorn House | **WC1** — 19
Albannach | **WC2** — 14
All Star Lanes | **WC1** — 15
Alounak | **multi. loc.** — 23
Annex 3 | **W1** — 16
Annie's | **multi. loc.** — 21
Aperitivo | **W1** — 20
Ⓩ Archipelago | **W1** — 21
Ⓩ Asia de Cuba | **WC2** — 22
Baker & Spice | **multi. loc.** — 22
Ⓩ Belgo | **multi. loc.** — 19
Benihana | **multi. loc.** — 18
Bierodrome | **multi. loc.** — 17
Blah! Blah! Blah! | **W12** — 18
Bloom's | **NW11** — 19
Blue Elephant | **SW6** — 20
Boisdale | **multi. loc.** — 20
Ⓩ Books for Cooks | **W11** — 24
Ⓩ Cambio de Tercio | **SW5** — 24
Cellar Gascon | **EC1** — 20
Chor Bizarre | **W1** — 21
Chowki | **W1** — 21
Ⓩ Club Gascon | **EC1** — 26
Cocoon | **W1** — 21
Costas Grill | **W8** — 18
Crazy Bear | **W1** — 21
Crazy Homies | **W2** — 20
Cru | **N1** — 15
Dans Le Noir | **EC1** — 13
Daquise | **SW7** — 20
NEW Dinings | **W1** — -
Dish Dash | **SW12** — 18
Ⓩ Fat Duck | **Berks** — 27
Ⓩ ffiona's | **W8** — 24
Fifteen | **N1** — 23
FishWorks | **W4** — 20
Flaneur | **EC1** — 22
Ⓩ Food for Thought | **WC2** — 24
Gilgamesh | **NW1** — 20
Hoxton Apprentice | **N1** — 18
Inaho | **W2** — 21
itsu | **multi. loc.** — 18
Jenny Lo's Tea | **SW1** — 20
Jim Thompson's | **multi. loc.** — 15
Kulu Kulu | **multi. loc.** — 20
La Fromagerie | **W1** — 24
Ⓩ La Porte des Indes | **W1** — 21
Le Cercle | **SW1** — 24
Ⓩ Les Trois Garçons | **E1** — 19
Levant | **W1** — 19
Levantine | **W2** — 20
Ⓩ Lucky 7 | **W2** — 20
Maggie Jones's | **W8** — 21
Menier Chocolate | **SE1** — 14
Mju | **SW1** — 20
Ⓩ Momo | **W1** — 19

SPECIAL FEATURES

☑ Moro | **EC1**	25
Moshi Moshi | **EC2**	20
☑ Nahm | **SW1**	26
Nautilus Fish | **NW6**	21
☑ Ottolenghi | **multi. loc.**	24
Petersham Nurseries | **Richmond**	25
Pizza Metro | **SW11**	-
Providores, The | **W1**	22
Quality Chop House | **EC1**	20
Rainforest Cafe | **W1**	11
Randall & Aubin | **W1**	19
Ransome's Dock | **SW11**	20
☑ Rasoi Vineet Bhatia | **SW3**	27
Real Greak | **EC1**	16
Richard Corrigan | **W1**	23
Rivington Grill | **EC2**	20
Sabor | **N1**	22
Sale e Pepe | **SW1**	20
☑ Sketch/Gallery | **W1**	19
Solly's | **NW11**	17
Souk | **WC2**	18
☑ St. John | **EC1**	25
St. John Bread/Wine | **E1**	22
Tapas Brindisa | **SE1**	22
Taqueria | **W11**	18
Tate Britain | **SW1**	17
Tom's Deli | **W11**	16
Troubadour, The | **SW5**	14
Truc Vert | **W1**	22
Tsunami | **SW4**	24
☑ Wagamama | **multi. loc.**	19
Wapping Food | **E1**	20
YO! Sushi | **multi. loc.**	17

OUTDOOR DINING

(G=garden; P=patio; PV=pavement;
T=terrace; W=waterside)

Abbeville | PV | **SW4**	15
Abingdon, The | PV | **W8**	22
Admiral Codrington | P | **SW3**	18
🆕 Albion, The | G | **N1**	-
☑ Al Hamra | P | **W1**	22
Anglesea Arms | P | **W6**	23
☑ Archipelago | P | **W1**	21
Ark | T | **W8**	15
Artigiano | PV | **NW3**	20
Aubaine | PV | **SW3**	20
Babylon | T | **W8**	20
Balham Kitchen | PV | **SW12**	16
Bam-Bou | T | **W1**	21
Bank Westminster | T | **SW1**	18
🆕 Barrafina | PV | **W1**	24
Belvedere, The | T | **W8**	20
Blandford St. | T | **W1**	18
Blueprint Café | T, W | **SE1**	18
Brackenbury | P | **W6**	18
Brunello | T | **SW7**	20

Builders Arms | PV | **SW3**	17
Butlers Wharf | P, W | **SE1**	20
Cantina del Ponte | P, W | **SE1**	17
Caraffini | PV | **SW1**	21
Casale Franco | P | **N1**	-
C Garden | P | **SW3**	18
Chez Kristof | T | **W6**	22
Coq d'Argent | G, T | **EC2**	18
Eagle, The | PV | **EC1**	21
e&o | PV | **W11**	22
1802 | T, W | **E14**	16
Elistano | PV | **SW3**	18
Embassy | P | **W1**	13
Engineer | G | **NW1**	19
Fifth Floor Cafe | T | **SW1**	18
fish! | T | **SE1**	19
FishWorks | G | **W4**	20
Hard Rock | T | **W1**	13
Hoxton Apprentice | T | **N1**	18
Hush | P | **W1**	17
Inn The Park | T | **SW1**	17
☑ Ishbilia | PV | **SW1**	24
Joe's | PV | **SW3**	19
Julie's | P, PV | **W11**	18
Kandoo | G | **W2**	-
La Famiglia | G | **SW10**	21
La Poule au Pot | P | **SW1**	22
☑ La Trompette | T | **W4**	27
L'Aventure | T | **NW8**	22
Le Colombier | T | **SW3**	20
Ledbury | P | **W11**	25
Le Pont de la Tour | P, W | **SE1**	22
Locanda Ottoemezzo | PV | **W8**	24
L'Oranger | P | **SW1**	24
Lundum's | T | **SW7**	22
Made in Italy | T | **SW3**	21
Manicomio | P | **SW3**	18
Mediterraneo | PV | **W11**	22
Mildreds | PV | **W1**	22
Mirabelle | P | **W1**	22
☑ Momo | T | **W1**	19
Monza | PV | **SW3**	20
☑ Moro | PV | **EC1**	25
Motcombs | PV | **SW1**	17
Notting Grill | T | **W11**	21
🆕 Olivomare | PV | **SW1**	-
Oriel | PV | **SW1**	15
Orrery | T | **W1**	25
Osteria Antica | PV | **SW11**	-
☑ Osteria Basilico | P | **W11**	24
Oxo Tower | T, W | **SE1**	20
Oxo Tower Brass. | T, W | **SE1**	20
Ozer | PV | **W1**	19
Painted Heron | G | **SW10**	22
Passione | P | **W1**	23
Pellicano | PV | **SW3**	20
Plateau | T | **E14**	19

Porters | PV | **WC2**	20
Quadrato | T | **E14**	24
Ransome's Dock | T | **SW11**	20
Riccardo's | T | **SW3**	18
☑ Ritz, The | T | **W1**	23
☑ River Café | P, W | **W6**	27
Rocket | PV, T, W | **multi. loc.**	17
Roka | PV | **W1**	25
Rosmarino | T | **NW8**	17
Santini | T | **SW1**	22
Smiths/Top Floor | T | **EC1**	20
NEW Suka | G, T | **W1**	–
Texas Embassy | PV | **SW1**	13
Tom's Deli | G | **W11**	16
Toto's | G | **SW3**	24
202 | G, PV | **W11**	17
Uli | P | **W11**	25
Vama | P | **SW10**	24
Villandry | PV | **W1**	18
Vineyard/Stockcross | T, W | **Berks**	24
Wapping Food | G, P | **E1**	20
Westbourne, The | T | **W2**	16

PEOPLE-WATCHING

Admiral Codrington | **SW3**	18
NEW Albion, The | **N1**	–
All Star Lanes | **WC1**	15
☑ Amaya | **SW1**	25
Armani Caffè | **SW3**	17
☑ Asia de Cuba | **WC2**	22
NEW Atami | **SW1**	24
Aubaine | **multi. loc.**	20
Avenue, The | **SW1**	18
Bam-Bou | **W1**	21
Bangkok | **SW7**	19
NEW Barrafina | **W1**	24
Bar Shu | **W1**	22
Bellamy's | **W1**	18
Belvedere, The | **W8**	20
☑ Bibendum | **SW3**	24
Bibendum Oyster | **SW3**	22
Blakes | **SW7**	19
Boxwood Café | **SW1**	21
Brown's/The Grill | **W1**	22
NEW Bumpkin | **W11**	21
NEW Butcher & Grill | **SW11**	15
Caraffini | **SW1**	21
Carpaccio | **SW3**	18
Cecconi's | **W1**	21
C Garden | **SW3**	18
China Tang | **W1**	21
Christopher's | **WC2**	19
☑ Cinnamon Club | **SW1**	24
☑ Cipriani | **W1**	20
Circus | **W1**	14
NEW Club, The | **W1**	–

☑ Club Gascon | **EC1**	26
Daphne's | **SW3**	21
Drones | **SW1**	18
e&o | **W11**	22
Eight Over Eight | **SW3**	23
Electric Brass. | **W11**	19
Fifteen | **N1**	23
☑ Fino | **W1**	23
Frankie's Italian | **multi. loc.**	15
Galvin/Windows | **W1**	22
☑ Galvin Bistrot | **W1**	24
Gilgamesh | **NW1**	20
☑ Gordon Ramsay/Claridge's | **W1**	25
☑ Gordon Ramsay/68 Royal | **SW3**	28
NEW Great Queen St. | **WC2**	–
☑ Hakkasan | **W1**	24
NEW High Road Brass. | **W4**	20
Hush | **W1**	17
☑ Ivy, The | **WC2**	23
Joe's | **SW3**	19
☑ J. Sheekey | **WC2**	25
Kensington Place | **W8**	20
La Famiglia | **SW10**	21
Langan's Bistro | **W1**	19
Langan's Brass. | **W1**	18
NEW ☑ L'Atelier/Robuchon | **WC2**	26
☑ La Trompette | **W4**	27
☑ Le Caprice | **SW1**	24
Le Cercle | **SW1**	24
Ledbury | **W11**	25
☑ Locanda Locatelli | **W1**	25
Luciano | **SW1**	20
Lucio | **SW3**	21
Manicomio | **SW3**	18
☑ Maze | **W1**	25
NEW Mews of Mayfair | **W1**	22
Mirabelle | **W1**	22
NEW Mocotó | **SW1**	22
☑ Momo | **W1**	19
NEW Narrow, The | **E14**	–
Nicole's | **W1**	19
☑ Nobu Berkeley St | **W1**	26
☑ Nobu London | **W1**	27
Olivo | **SW1**	21
NEW Olivomare | **SW1**	–
Orso | **WC2**	20
NEW Papillon | **SW3**	23
☑ Pétrus | **SW1**	28
Pigalle Club | **W1**	14
PJ's B&G | **SW3**	16
☑ Racine | **SW3**	22
Riccardo's | **SW3**	18
NEW Rist. Semplice | **W1**	–
☑ River Café | **W6**	27

Roka | **W1**	25
San Lorenzo | **SW3**	20
Santini | **SW1**	22
Z Savoy Grill | **WC2**	24
Scott's | **W1**	22
Z Sketch/Gallery | **W1**	19
Z Sketch/Lecture Rm. | **W1**	21
Smiths/Dining Room | **EC1**	20
Z Sophie's Steak | **SW10**	23
Sotheby's Cafe | **W1**	19
NEW St. Alban | **SW1**	21
NEW Stanza | **W1**	-
NEW Suka | **W1**	-
Sumosan | **W1**	20
Tartine | **SW3**	18
NEW Z Theo Randall | **W1**	26
Z Tom Aikens | **SW3**	26
Tom's Deli | **W11**	16
NEW Tom's Kitchen | **SW3**	19
202 | **W11**	17
Ubon | **E14**	24
Vingt-Quatre | **SW10**	15
Z Waterside Inn | **Berks**	27
Z Wilton's | **SW1**	24
Z Wolseley, The | **W1**	21
NEW XO | **NW3**	16
Z Yauatcha | **W1**	25
Z Zafferano | **SW1**	26
Zetter | **EC1**	19
Z Zuma | **SW7**	26

POWER SCENES

NEW Acorn House | **WC1**	19
Aurora | **EC2**	19
Avenue, The | **SW1**	18
Belvedere, The | **W8**	20
Bentley's | **W1**	24
Blueprint Café | **SE1**	18
Boxwood Café | **SW1**	21
Brown's/The Grill | **W1**	22
Caravaggio | **EC3**	19
China Tang | **W1**	21
Z Cinnamon Club | **SW1**	24
Z Cipriani | **W1**	20
Circus | **W1**	14
Z Club Gascon | **EC1**	26
Daphne's | **SW3**	21
Drones | **SW1**	18
Z Gordon Ramsay/Claridge's | **W1**	25
Z Gordon Ramsay/68 Royal | **SW3**	28
Goring Dining Rm. | **SW1**	23
Greenhouse, The | **W1**	25
Green's | **SW1**	22
NEW Hat & Feathers | **EC1**	-
Z Ivy, The | **WC2**	23

Z J. Sheekey | **WC2**	25
Z Lanes | **W1**	24
Langan's Brass. | **W1**	18
La Noisette | **SW1**	21
NEW Z L'Atelier/Robuchon | **WC2**	26
Launceston Place | **W8**	21
Z Le Caprice | **SW1**	24
Ledbury | **W11**	25
Z Le Gavroche | **W1**	27
Z Le Manoir/Quat | **Oxfordshire**	28
Le Pont de la Tour | **SE1**	22
L'Incontro | **SW1**	20
Luciano | **SW1**	20
Z Maze | **W1**	25
Mirabelle | **W1**	22
Z Nahm | **SW1**	26
Z Nobu Berkeley St | **W1**	26
Z Nobu London | **W1**	27
1 Lombard St. | **EC3**	22
Z Pétrus | **SW1**	28
Prism | **EC3**	18
Z Quirinale | **SW1**	25
Z Rhodes 24 | **EC2**	23
Z Ritz, The | **W1**	23
San Lorenzo | **SW3**	20
Z Savoy Grill | **WC2**	24
Shepherd's | **SW1**	18
Z Sketch/Lecture Rm. | **W1**	21
Z Square, The | **W1**	28
NEW St. Alban | **SW1**	21
NEW St. Germain | **EC1**	21
Z Tom Aikens | **SW3**	26
Z Umu | **W1**	26
NEW Via Condotti | **W1**	18
Z Waterside Inn | **Berks**	27
Z Wilton's | **SW1**	24
Z Wolseley, The | **W1**	21
Z Zafferano | **SW1**	26
Z Zuma | **SW7**	26

PRE-THEATRE MENUS

(Call for prices and times)

Al Duca | **SW1**	19
Almeida | **N1**	18
Arbutus | **W1**	24
Z Asia de Cuba | **WC2**	22
Axis | **WC2**	20
Baltic | **SE1**	21
Bank Westminster | **SW1**	18
Benares | **W1**	23
Brasserie Roux | **SW1**	20
Brasserie St. Quentin | **SW3**	18
Brown's/The Grill | **W1**	22
Christopher's | **WC2**	19
Z Cinnamon Club | **SW1**	24
NEW Empress of India | **E9**	-

subscribe to zagat.com

☑ Gordon Ramsay/Claridge's | **W1**	25
Goring Dining Rm. | **SW1**	23
Indigo | **WC1**	22
Joe Allen | **WC2**	17
La Bouchée | **SW7**	20
La Trouvaille | **W1**	20
Le Café/Jardin | **WC2**	19
Le Deuxième | **WC2**	20
L'Escargot | **W1**	22
Matsuri | **SW1**	21
Mint Leaf | **SW1**	20
Mon Plaisir | **WC2**	18
Orso | **WC2**	20
Oxo Tower Brass. | **SE1**	20
Porters | **WC2**	20
Quaglino's | **SW1**	18
Quo Vadis | **W1**	18
☑ Racine | **SW3**	22
Red Fort | **W1**	23
Richard Corrigan | **W1**	23
☑ Ritz, The | **W1**	23
☑ Savoy Grill | **WC2**	24
Veeraswamy | **W1**	22
Zaika | **W8**	25

PRIVATE ROOMS

(Call for capacity)

Admiral Codrington | **SW3**	18
Admiralty, The | **WC2**	19
Alastair Little | **W1**	24
Albannach | **WC2**	14
Alloro | **W1**	22
All Star Lanes | **WC1**	15
Almeida | **N1**	18
☑ Amaya | **SW1**	25
☑ Asia de Cuba | **WC2**	22
Auberge du Lac | **AL8**	23
Babylon | **W8**	20
Baltic | **SE1**	21
Bam-Bou | **W1**	21
☑ Belgo | **WC2**	19
Belvedere, The | **W8**	20
Benares | **W1**	23
Benihana | **multi. loc.**	18
Bentley's | **W1**	24
Blakes | **SW7**	19
Blue Elephant | **SW6**	20
Bombay Bicycle | **SW12**	18
Boxwood Café | **SW1**	21
Brasserie Roux | **SW1**	20
Brian Turner | **W1**	21
Brunello | **SW7**	20
☑ Cambio de Tercio | **SW5**	24
☑ Capital Rest. | **SW3**	27
☑ Chez Bruce | **SW17**	28
Chez Kristof | **W6**	22
China Tang | **W1**	21

Christopher's | **WC2**	19
Chuen Cheng Ku | **W1**	19
Chutney Mary | **SW10**	23
Chutney's | **NW1**	23
☑ Cinnamon Club | **SW1**	24
☑ Cipriani | **W1**	20
Circus | **W1**	14
Clerkenwell | **EC1**	23
Cocoon | **W1**	21
Cru | **N1**	15
Daphne's | **SW3**	21
Drones | **SW1**	18
e&o | **W11**	22
1802 | **E14**	16
Eight Over Eight | **SW3**	23
Embassy | **W1**	13
Fairuz | **W1**	22
Farm | **SW6**	-
Floridita | **W1**	16
Franco's | **SW1**	15
French Horn | **Berks**	23
Gilgamesh | **NW1**	20
☑ Gordon Ramsay/Claridge's | **W1**	25
☑ Gravetye Manor | **W. Sussex**	24
Greenhouse, The | **W1**	25
Green's | **SW1**	22
Greyhound, The | **SW11**	19
Guinea Grill | **W1**	22
☑ Hakkasan | **W1**	24
Hard Rock | **W1**	13
NEW Hawksmoor | **E1**	28
Hush | **W1**	17
Il Convivio | **SW1**	23
☑ Ishbilia | **SW1**	24
itsu | **multi. loc.**	18
☑ Ivy, The | **WC2**	23
Julie's | **W11**	18
Just St. James's | **SW1**	16
☑ Kai Mayfair | **W1**	25
Kensington Place | **W8**	20
☑ La Porte des Indes | **W1**	21
La Poule au Pot | **SW1**	22
La Trouvaille | **W1**	20
Launceston Place | **W8**	21
Le Cercle | **SW1**	24
Le Colombier | **SW3**	20
☑ Le Manoir/Quat | **Oxfordshire**	28
Le Pont de la Tour | **SE1**	22
L'Escargot | **W1**	22
☑ Les Trois Garçons | **E1**	19
Le Suquet | **SW3**	23
☑ L'Etranger | **SW7**	24
L'Incontro | **SW1**	20
L'Oranger | **SW1**	24
Lundum's | **SW7**	22

Made in Italy | **SW3**	21
Manicomio | **SW3**	18
Mao Tai | **SW6**	22
Masala Zone | **multi. loc.**	19
Matsuri | **multi. loc.**	21
Memories of China | **SW1**	21
Metrogusto | **N1**	21
Mimmo d'Ischia | **SW1**	21
Mint Leaf | **SW1**	20
Mirabelle | **W1**	22
Mitsukoshi | **SW1**	19
☑ Momo | **W1**	19
Mon Plaisir | **WC2**	18
☑ Morgan M | **N7**	27
Motcombs | **SW1**	17
Mr. Chow | **SW1**	21
☑ Nahm | **SW1**	26
☑ Nobu London | **W1**	27
Notting Grill | **W11**	21
Notting Hill Brass. | **W11**	24
Noura | **W1**	21
Nyonya | **W11**	24
1 Lombard St. | **EC3**	22
1 Lombard Brass. | **EC3**	20
One-O-One | **SW1**	23
NEW Papillon | **SW3**	23
Pasha | **SW7**	18
☑ Patara | **SW3**	23
Patterson's | **W1**	22
Pearl | **WC1**	24
Pellicano | **SW3**	20
☑ Pétrus | **SW1**	28
☑ Pied à Terre | **W1**	28
Plateau | **E14**	19
Poissonnerie | **SW3**	21
Prism | **EC3**	18
Quaglino's | **SW1**	18
Quo Vadis | **W1**	18
Rainforest Cafe | **W1**	11
Rasa | **multi. loc.**	24
☑ Rasoi Vineet Bhatia | **SW3**	27
Real Greak | **multi. loc.**	16
☑ Rib Rm. | **SW1**	24
Richard Corrigan | **W1**	23
☑ Ritz, The | **W1**	23
Rivington Grill | **EC2**	20
Rocket | **multi. loc.**	17
☑ Roussillon | **SW1**	26
☑ Royal China | **multi. loc.**	24
Royal Exchange | **EC3**	16
☑ Rules | **WC2**	23
San Lorenzo | **SW19**	20
Santini | **SW1**	22
Sarkhel's | **SW18**	22
Sartoria | **W1**	20
☑ Savoy Grill | **WC2**	24
Shepherd's | **SW1**	18

Six13 | **W1**	19
☑ Sketch/Lecture Rm. | **W1**	21
Smiths/Dining Room | **EC1**	20
☑ Square, The | **W1**	28
Star of India | **SW5**	24
☑ St. John | **EC1**	25
Sumosan | **W1**	20
Tentazioni | **SE1**	27
Texas Embassy | **SW1**	13
Thai Square | **multi. loc.**	19
Thomas Cubitt | **SW1**	21
Timo | **W8**	22
☑ Tom Aikens | **SW3**	26
NEW Tom's Kitchen | **SW3**	19
Vasco & Piero's | **W1**	21
Veeraswamy | **W1**	22
Villandry | **W1**	18
Vineyard/Stockcross | **Berks**	24
Vivat Bacchus | **EC4**	23
☑ Waterside Inn | **Berks**	27
Wells, The | **NW3**	18
☑ Wilton's | **SW1**	24
Wòdka | **W8**	20
Ye Olde Cheshire | **EC4**	15
☑ Zafferano | **SW1**	26
Zetter | **EC1**	19
☑ Zuma | **SW7**	26

PUDDING SPECIALISTS

Alastair Little | **W1**	24
Almeida | **N1**	18
☑ Amaya | **SW1**	25
☑ Asia de Cuba | **WC2**	22
Aubaine | **multi. loc.**	20
Auberge du Lac | **AL8**	23
☑ Aubergine | **SW10**	26
Aurora | **EC2**	19
Baker & Spice | **multi. loc.**	22
Belvedere, The | **W8**	20
Bibendum Oyster | **SW3**	22
Blakes | **SW7**	19
Boxwood Café | **SW1**	21
☑ Capital Rest. | **SW3**	27
☑ Chez Bruce | **SW17**	28
☑ Cipriani | **W1**	20
☑ Clarke's | **W8**	25
☑ Club Gascon | **EC1**	26
Embassy | **W1**	13
☑ Fat Duck | **Berks**	27
Fifth Floor | **SW1**	20
☑ Foliage | **SW1**	26
Fortnum's Fountain | **W1**	20
Galvin/Windows | **W1**	22
☑ Galvin Bistrot | **W1**	24
Glasshouse, The | **TW9**	24
☑ Gordon Ramsay/Claridge's | **W1**	25

☑ Gordon Ramsay/68 Royal | **SW3**	28
Greenhouse, The | **W1**	25
Ladurée | **SW1**	23
☑ Lanes | **W1**	24
Lanesborough | **SW1**	21
NEW ☑ L'Atelier/Robuchon | **WC2**	26
☑ La Trompette | **W4**	27
Le Cercle | **SW1**	24
Ledbury | **W11**	25
☑ Le Gavroche | **W1**	27
☑ Le Manoir/Quat | **Oxfordshire**	28
☑ Locanda Locatelli | **W1**	25
L'Oranger | **SW1**	24
☑ Maze | **W1**	25
Mirabelle | **W1**	22
☑ Nobu Berkeley St | **W1**	26
☑ Nobu London | **W1**	27
Orrery | **W1**	25
☑ Ottolenghi | **multi. loc.**	24
Patisserie Valerie | **multi. loc.**	20
☑ Pétrus | **SW1**	28
☑ Pied à Terre | **W1**	28
Plateau | **E14**	19
Providores, The | **W1**	22
☑ Rasoi Vineet Bhatia | **SW3**	27
NEW Rhodes W1 Rest. | **W1**	-
Richard Corrigan | **W1**	23
Richoux | **multi. loc.**	15
NEW Rist. Semplice | **W1**	-
☑ Ritz, The | **W1**	23
☑ River Café | **W6**	27
☑ Savoy Grill | **WC2**	24
☑ Sketch/Gallery | **W1**	19
☑ Sketch/Lecture Rm. | **W1**	21
☑ Square, The | **W1**	28
NEW St. Alban | **W1**	21
NEW ☑ Theo Randall | **W1**	26
☑ Tom Aikens | **SW3**	26
Ubon | **E14**	24
☑ Waterside Inn | **Berks**	27
☑ Wolseley, The | **W1**	21
☑ Yauatcha | **W1**	25
☑ Zafferano | **SW1**	26
☑ Zuma | **SW7**	26

QUIET CONVERSATION

Addendum | **EC3**	-
Al Sultan | **W1**	22
Arbutus | **W1**	24
☑ Aubergine | **SW10**	26
Aurora | **EC2**	19
Axis | **WC2**	20
Banquette | **WC2**	22
Benares | **W1**	23
Bengal Clipper | **SE1**	21

NEW Benja | **W1**	-
Blakes | **SW7**	19
Brian Turner | **W1**	21
☑ Capital Rest. | **SW3**	27
C Garden | **SW3**	18
NEW Chelsea Brass. | **SW1**	16
NEW Cookbook Cafe | **W1**	-
1880 | **SW7**	21
Embassy | **W1**	13
☑ Foliage | **SW1**	26
Goring Dining Rm. | **SW1**	23
Green's | **SW1**	22
Hartwell House | **HP17**	19
Il Convivio | **SW1**	23
Indigo | **WC2**	22
Jaan | **WC2**	-
La Genova | **W1**	23
☑ Lanes | **W1**	24
☑ Lanesborough | **SW1**	21
Launceston Place | **W8**	21
☑ Le Gavroche | **W1**	27
☑ Le Manoir/Quat | **Oxfordshire**	28
L'Oranger | **SW1**	24
NEW L-Rest. & Bar | **W8**	-
Lundum's | **SW7**	22
NEW Magdalen | **SE1**	-
Mitsukoshi | **SW1**	19
Mju | **SW1**	20
Morel | **SW4**	-
Mosaico | **W1**	21
☑ Nahm | **SW1**	26
Odin's | **W1**	20
One-O-One | **SW1**	23
Orrery | **W1**	25
☑ Park, The | **SW1**	24
☑ Pied à Terre | **W1**	28
Quadrato | **E14**	24
☑ Quirinale | **SW1**	25
☑ Rasoi Vineet Bhatia | **SW3**	27
Rhodes W1 Brass. | **W1**	-
NEW Rhodes W1 Rest. | **W1**	-
☑ Ritz, The | **W1**	23
☑ Roussillon | **SW1**	26
Saki Bar/Food Emp. | **EC1**	-
Salloos | **SW1**	23
☑ Sketch/Lecture Rm. | **W1**	21
NEW ☑ Theo Randall | **W1**	26
NEW Via Condotti | **W1**	18
☑ Waterside Inn | **Berks**	27
☑ Wilton's | **SW1**	24

ROMANTIC PLACES

NEW Albion, The | **N1**	-
☑ Amaya | **SW1**	25
Andrew Edmunds | **W1**	22
☑ Archipelago | **W1**	21

SPECIAL FEATURES

Galvin/Windows | **W1**	22
Ⓩ Galvin Bistrot | **W1**	24
Glasshouse, The | **TW9**	24
Ⓩ Gordon Ramsay/Claridge's | **W1**	25
Ⓩ Gordon Ramsay/68 Royal | **SW3**	28
Goring Dining Rm. | **SW1**	23
Ⓩ Gravetye Manor | **W. Sussex**	24
Greenhouse, The | **W1**	25
Green's | **SW1**	22
Hartwell House | **HP17**	19
Ⓩ Ivy, The | **WC2**	23
Jaan | **WC2**	-
Ⓩ J. Sheekey | **WC2**	25
Ⓩ Kai Mayfair | **W1**	25
Ladurée | **SW1**	23
La Genova | **W1**	23
Ⓩ Lanes | **W1**	24
Ⓩ Lanesborough | **SW1**	21
Langan's Bistro | **W1**	19
La Noisette | **SW1**	21
La Poule au Pot | **SW1**	22
NEW Ⓩ L'Atelier/Robuchon | **WC2**	26
Launceston Place | **W8**	21
Ⓩ Le Caprice | **SW1**	24
Le Colombier | **SW3**	20
Ledbury | **W11**	25
Ⓩ Le Gavroche | **W1**	27
Ⓩ Le Manoir/Quat | **Oxfordshire**	28
Le Suquet | **SW3**	23
Ⓩ L'Etranger | **SW7**	24
L'Incontro | **SW1**	20
Ⓩ Locanda Locatelli | **W1**	25
L'Oranger | **SW1**	24
Luciano | **SW1**	20
Lundum's | **SW7**	22
NEW Magdalen | **SE1**	-
Mimmo d'Ischia | **SW1**	21
Mirabelle | **W1**	22
Montpeliano | **SW7**	18
Morel | **SW4**	-
Motcombs | **SW1**	17
Noura | **multi. loc.**	21
Odin's | **W1**	20
NEW Olivomare | **SW1**	-
One-O-One | **SW1**	23
Orrery | **W1**	25
NEW Papillon | **SW3**	23
Ⓩ Park, The | **SW1**	24
Patisserie Valerie | **multi. loc.**	20
Ⓩ Pétrus | **SW1**	28
Poissonnerie | **SW3**	21
Quadrato | **E14**	24
Ⓩ Quirinale | **SW1**	25
Ⓩ Racine | **SW3**	22

Red Fort | **W1**	23
Reubens | **W1**	20
NEW Rhodes W1 Rest. | **W1**	-
Ⓩ Rib Rm. | **SW1**	24
Richoux | **multi. loc.**	15
NEW Rist. Semplice | **W1**	-
Ⓩ Ritz, The | **W1**	23
Riva | **SW13**	20
Roast | **SE1**	19
Rosmarino | **NW8**	17
Rowley's | **SW1**	19
Ⓩ Rules | **WC2**	23
Santini | **SW1**	22
Sartoria | **W1**	20
Ⓩ Savoy Grill | **WC2**	24
Scalini | **SW3**	23
Scott's | **W1**	22
Shepherd's | **SW1**	18
Shogun | **W1**	23
Simpson's/Strand | **WC2**	20
Ⓩ Sketch/Lecture Rm. | **W1**	21
Sotheby's Cafe | **W1**	19
Ⓩ Square, The | **W1**	28
NEW St. Alban | **SW1**	21
St. James's | **W1**	20
Tate Britain | **SW1**	17
NEW Ⓩ Theo Randall | **W1**	26
Ⓩ Tom Aikens | **SW3**	26
Toto's | **SW3**	24
NEW Via Condotti | **W1**	18
NEW Ⓩ Wallace, The | **W1**	20
Ⓩ Waterside Inn | **Berks**	27
Ⓩ Wilton's | **SW1**	24
Ⓩ Wolseley, The | **W1**	21
Ⓩ Zafferano | **SW1**	26
Zen Central | **W1**	21

SET-PRICE MENUS

(Call for prices and times)

Abeno | **multi. loc.**	21
Abingdon, The | **W8**	22
Alastair Little | **W1**	24
Albannach | **WC2**	14
Al Duca | **SW1**	19
Alloro | **W1**	22
Almeida | **N1**	18
Ⓩ Amaya | **SW1**	25
Arbutus | **W1**	24
Ⓩ Asia de Cuba | **WC2**	22
Ⓩ Aubergine | **SW10**	26
Aurora | **EC2**	19
Avenue, The | **SW1**	18
Axis | **WC2**	20
NEW Bacchus | **N1**	21
Baltic | **SE1**	21
Bellamy's | **W1**	18
Benares | **W1**	23

Bengal Clipper | **SE1**	21
🄩 Bibendum | **SW3**	24
Blue Elephant | **SW6**	20
Boxwood Café | **SW1**	21
Brasserie Roux | **SW1**	20
Brasserie St. Quentin | **SW3**	18
Brian Turner | **W1**	21
Brown's/The Grill | **W1**	22
Brunello | **SW7**	20
Butlers Wharf | **SE1**	20
🄩 Café Japan | **NW11**	26
Café Spice Namasté | **E1**	23
🄩 Capital Rest. | **SW3**	27
Caravaggio | **EC3**	19
Champor | **SE1**	18
🄩 Chez Bruce | **SW17**	28
Chez Kristof | **W6**	22
Chor Bizarre | **W1**	21
Christopher's | **WC2**	19
Chutney Mary | **SW10**	23
Cigala | **WC1**	22
🄩 Cinnamon Club | **SW1**	24
🄩 Cipriani | **W1**	20
🄩 Clarke's | **W8**	25
Clerkenwell | **EC1**	23
Clos Maggiore | **WC2**	24
🄩 Club Gascon | **EC1**	26
Coq d'Argent | **EC2**	18
Crazy Bear | **W1**	21
🄩 Defune | **W1**	27
Deya | **W1**	23
🄩 Dorchester/The Grill | **W1**	24
Drones | **SW1**	18
ECapital | **W1**	22
1880 | **SW7**	21
Eight Over Eight | **SW3**	23
🄩 El Pirata | **W1**	23
🄩 Enoteca Turi | **SW15**	27
Essenza | **W11**	18
Fakhreldine | **W1**	21
🄩 Fat Duck | **Berks**	27
Fifteen | **N1**	23
Fiore | **SW1**	21
Fish Shop | **EC1**	19
🄩 Foliage | **SW1**	26
🄩 Galvin Bistrot | **W1**	24
Glasshouse, The | **TW9**	24
🄩 Gordon Ramsay/Claridge's | **W1**	25
🄩 Gordon Ramsay/68 Royal | **SW3**	28
Goring Dining Rm. | **SW1**	23
🄩 Gravetye Manor | **W. Sussex**	24
Greenhouse, The | **W1**	25
NEW High Road Brass. | **W4**	20
🄩 Hunan | **SW1**	28
Ikeda | **W1**	21
Il Convivio | **SW1**	23
Indigo | **WC2**	22
🄩 Ivy, The | **WC2**	23
Joy King Lau | **WC2**	20
🄩 J. Sheekey | **WC2**	25
🄩 Kai Mayfair | **W1**	25
Kensington Place | **W8**	20
Kiku | **W1**	24
🄩 Lanes | **W1**	24
🄩 Lanesborough | **SW1**	21
Langan's Bistro | **W1**	19
La Noisette | **SW1**	21
La Poule au Pot | **SW1**	22
NEW🄩 L'Atelier/Robuchon | **WC2**	26
Latium | **W1**	25
🄩 La Trompette | **W4**	27
Launceston Place | **W8**	21
L'Aventure | **NW8**	22
🄩 Le Café/Marché | **EC1**	23
Le Cercle | **SW1**	24
Le Colombier | **SW3**	20
Ledbury | **W11**	25
🄩 Le Gavroche | **W1**	27
🄩 Le Manoir/Quat | **Oxfordshire**	28
L'Escargot | **W1**	22
🄩 Les Trois Garçons | **E1**	19
Le Suquet | **SW3**	23
🄩 L'Etranger | **SW7**	24
L'Incontro | **SW1**	20
Livebait | **multi. loc.**	18
Locanda Ottoemezzo | **W8**	24
L'Oranger | **SW1**	24
Lucio | **SW3**	21
Lundum's | **SW7**	22
Matsuri | **multi. loc.**	21
🄩 Maze | **W1**	25
Mela | **WC2**	23
Memories of China | **multi. loc.**	21
Mint Leaf | **SW1**	20
Mirabelle | **W1**	22
Mitsukoshi | **SW1**	19
🄩 Morgan M | **N7**	27
Motcombs | **SW1**	17
Mr. Chow | **SW1**	21
🄩 Nobu Berkeley St | **W1**	26
🄩 Nobu London | **W1**	27
Noura | **multi. loc.**	21
Olivo | **SW1**	21
1 Lombard St. | **EC3**	22
One-O-One | **SW1**	23
Orrery | **W1**	25
Oslo Court | **NW8**	22
Oxo Tower | **SE1**	20
Ozer | **W1**	19
🄩 Patara | **multi. loc.**	23

Patterson's | **W1**	22
Pellicano | **SW3**	20
☑ Pétrus | **SW1**	28
☑ Pied à Terre | **W1**	28
Plateau | **E14**	19
Poissonnerie | **SW3**	21
Porters | **WC2**	20
Princess Garden | **W1**	21
Quaglino's | **SW1**	18
☑ Quilon | **SW1**	25
☑ Racine | **SW3**	22
Rasa | **multi. loc.**	24
☑ Rasoi Vineet Bhatia | **SW3**	27
☑ Rib Rm. | **SW1**	24
Richard Corrigan | **W1**	23
NEW Rist. Semplice | **W1**	-
☑ Ritz, The | **W1**	23
Roka | **W1**	25
☑ Roussillon | **SW1**	26
☑ Royal China | **multi. loc.**	24
Sardo Canale | **NW1**	20
Sarkhel's | **SW18**	22
Sartoria | **W1**	20
☑ Savoy Grill | **WC2**	24
Shogun | **W1**	23
Six13 | **W1**	19
☑ Sketch/Lecture Rm. | **W1**	21
Snows on Green | **W6**	21
Sonny's | **SW13**	21
☑ Sophie's Steak | **SW10**	23
☑ Square, The | **W1**	28
☑ Taman gang | **W1**	22
☑ Tamarind | **W1**	25
Tentazioni | **SE1**	27
☑ Tom Aikens | **SW3**	26
Toto's | **SW3**	24
NEW Trinity | **SW4**	24
Vama | **SW10**	24
Vasco & Piero's | **W1**	21
Veeraswamy | **W1**	22
NEW Via Condotti | **W1**	18
Vineyard/Stockcross | **Berks**	24
☑ Waterside Inn | **Berks**	27
NEW XO | **NW3**	16
Yoshino | **W1**	24
☑ Zafferano | **SW1**	26
Zaika | **W8**	25
Zen Central | **W1**	21
Ziani | **SW3**	25
☑ Zuma | **SW7**	26

SINGLES SCENES

Admiral Codrington | **SW3**	18
Albannach | **WC2**	14
☑ Amaya | **SW1**	25
Annex 3 | **W1**	16
☑ Asia de Cuba | **WC2**	22

Avenue, The | **SW1**	18
Balans | **multi. loc.**	16
Bank Westminster | **SW1**	18
☑ Belgo | **multi. loc.**	19
Bierodrome | **multi. loc.**	17
Big Easy | **SW3**	16
Bistrot 190 | **SW7**	19
Bluebird | **SW3**	-
Brinkley's | **SW10**	16
Browns | **multi. loc.**	16
Buona Sera | **SW3**	23
Cafe Pacifico | **WC2**	18
Cecconi's | **W1**	21
Cellar Gascon | **EC1**	20
Christopher's | **WC2**	19
Circus | **W1**	14
Cocoon | **W1**	21
Collection | **SW3**	13
Dish Dash | **SW12**	18
Draper's Arms | **N1**	18
e&o | **W11**	22
Ebury Wine Bar | **SW1**	19
Eight Over Eight | **SW3**	23
Engineer | **NW1**	19
Enterprise | **SW3**	20
Fifteen | **N1**	23
Fifth Floor Cafe | **SW1**	18
☑ Fino | **W1**	23
Floridita | **W1**	16
Gilgamesh | **NW1**	20
☑ Hakkasan | **W1**	24
Hush | **W1**	17
Just St. James's | **SW1**	16
Kettners | **W1**	15
La Perla | **WC2**	15
La Rueda | **multi. loc.**	14
Le Cercle | **SW1**	24
Living Rm. | **W1**	19
Maroush | **multi. loc.**	20
☑ Maze | **W1**	25
Medcalf | **EC1**	23
NEW Mews of Mayfair | **W1**	22
NEW Mocotó | **SW1**	22
☑ Momo | **W1**	19
☑ Moro | **EC1**	25
Motcombs | **SW1**	17
Nam Long-Le Shaker | **SW5**	14
☑ Nobu Berkeley St | **W1**	26
☑ Nobu London | **W1**	27
Nozomi | **SW3**	19
Oriel | **SW1**	15
Oxo Tower | **SE1**	20
Oxo Tower Brass. | **SE1**	20
Ping Pong | **multi. loc.**	18
Pizza on the Park | **SW1**	14
PJ's B&G | **SW3**	16
Quaglino's | **SW1**	18

SPECIAL FEATURES

Real Greak | **multi. loc.** 16
Roka | **W1** 25
Sabor | **N1** 22
🛂 Sketch/Gallery | **W1** 19
Smiths/Dining Room | **EC1** 20
🛂 Sophie's Steak | **SW10** 23
Spiga | **W1** 15
Sticky Fingers | **W8** 14
NEW Suka | **W1** -
Sumosan | **W1** 20
Tartine | **SW3** 18
Texas Embassy | **SW1** 13
Waterway, The | **W9** 18
NEW XO | **NW3** 16
🛂 Zuma | **SW7** 26

SLEEPERS

(Good to excellent food,
but little known)

🛂 Books for Cooks | **W11** 24
🛂 Café Japan | **NW11** 26
Cay tre | **EC1** 24
Chapter Two | **SE3** 24
City Miyama | **EC4** 25
🛂 Cliveden House | **Berks** 24
Clos Maggiore | **WC2** 24
🛂 Defune | **W1** 27
🛂 Enoteca Turi | **SW15** 27
🛂 ffiona's | **W8** 24
Fish Hook | **W4** 24
🛂 Gate, The | **W6** 25
🛂 Graveye Manor | **W. Sussex** 24
Halepi | **W2** 24
NEW Hawksmoor | **E1** 28
Haz | **E1** 25
Inside | **SE10** 24
🛂 Jin Kichi | **NW3** 26
Kiku | **W1** 24
Lamberts | **SW12** 25
🛂 Lanes | **W1** 24
Latium | **W1** 25
Le Cercle | **SW1** 24
🛂 L'Etranger | **SW7** 24
Locanda Ottoemezzo | **W8** 24
🛂 Miyama | **W1** 26
🛂 Morgan M | **N7** 27
New Tayyabs | **E1** 24
Nyonya | **W11** 24
Original Lahore | **multi. loc.** 24
🛂 Park, The | **SW1** 24
Pearl | **WC1** 24
Petersham Nurseries | **Richmond** 25
Quadrato | **E14** 24
🛂 Quilon | **SW1** 25
🛂 Quirinale | **SW1** 25
Royal China Club | **W1** 24

Star of India | **SW5** 24
🛂 Sweetings | **EC4** 24
Tentazioni | **SE1** 27
NEW 🛂 Theo Randall | **W1** 26
NEW Trinity | **SW4** 24
Tsunami | **SW4** 24
🛂 Two Brothers Fish | **N3** 24
Uli | **W11** 25
🛂 Umu | **W1** 26
Vineyard/Stockcross | **Berks** 24
Yakitoria | **W2** 24
Yoshino | **W1** 24
Ziani | **SW3** 25

SPECIAL OCCASIONS

Almeida | **N1** 18
🛂 Amaya | **SW1** 25
🛂 Asia de Cuba | **WC2** 22
Auberge du Lac | **AL8** 23
🛂 Aubergine | **SW10** 26
Belvedere, The | **W8** 20
NEW Benja | **W1** -
Bentley's | **W1** 24
🛂 Bibendum | **SW3** 24
Blakes | **SW7** 19
Bluebird | **SW3** -
Blue Elephant | **SW6** 20
Boxwood Café | **SW1** 21
Brown's/The Grill | **W1** 22
Brunello | **SW7** 20
🛂 Capital Rest. | **SW3** 27
Cecconi's | **W1** 21
🛂 Chez Bruce | **SW17** 28
China Tang | **W1** 21
Chutney Mary | **SW10** 23
🛂 Cinnamon Club | **SW1** 24
🛂 Cipriani | **W1** 20
🛂 Clarke's | **W8** 25
🛂 Club Gascon | **EC1** 26
Crazy Bear | **W1** 21
Daphne's | **SW3** 21
🛂 Dorchester/The Grill | **W1** 24
Drones | **SW1** 18
🛂 Fat Duck | **Berks** 27
Fifteen | **N1** 23
🛂 Fino | **W1** 23
Floridita | **W1** 16
🛂 Foliage | **SW1** 26
French Horn | **Berks** 23
Galvin/Windows | **W1** 22
🛂 Galvin Bistrot | **W1** 24
Glasshouse, The | **TW9** 24
🛂 Gordon Ramsay/Claridge's | **W1** 25
🛂 Gordon Ramsay/68 Royal | **SW3** 28
Goring Dining Rm. | **SW1** 23

☑ Gravetye Manor | **W. Sussex**	24
Greenhouse, The | **W1**	25
NEW Haiku | **W1**	–
☑ Hakkasan | **W1**	24
Hartwell House | **HP17**	19
☑ Ivy, The | **WC2**	23
☑ J. Sheekey | **WC2**	25
☑ Lanesborough | **SW1**	21
La Noisette | **SW1**	21
NEW ☑ L'Atelier/Robuchon | **WC2**	26
☑ La Trompette | **W4**	27
Launceston Place | **W8**	21
☑ Le Caprice | **SW1**	24
Le Cercle | **SW1**	24
Ledbury | **W11**	25
☑ Le Gavroche | **W1**	27
☑ Le Manoir/Quat | **Oxfordshire**	28
Le Pont de la Tour | **SE1**	22
☑ Locanda Locatelli | **W1**	25
L'Oranger | **SW1**	24
Luciano | **SW1**	20
Lundum's | **SW7**	22
☑ Maze | **W1**	25
Mirabelle | **W1**	22
NEW Mocotó | **SW1**	22
☑ Momo | **W1**	19
☑ Morgan M | **N7**	27
☑ Nahm | **SW1**	26
☑ Nobu Berkeley St | **W1**	26
☑ Nobu London | **W1**	27
Orrery | **W1**	25
☑ Pétrus | **SW1**	28
☑ Pied à Terre | **W1**	28
Plateau | **E14**	19
Providores, The | **W1**	22
Quaglino's | **SW1**	18
☑ Rasoi Vineet Bhatia | **SW3**	27
NEW Rhodes W1 Rest. | **W1**	–
Richard Corrigan | **W1**	23
NEW Rist. Semplice | **W1**	–
☑ Ritz, The | **W1**	23
☑ River Café | **W6**	27
Roast | **SE1**	19
San Lorenzo | **SW3**	20
Santini | **SW1**	22
☑ Savoy Grill | **WC2**	24
Scott's | **W1**	22
☑ Sketch/Lecture Rm. | **W1**	21
NEW Skylon | **SE1**	–
Smiths/Dining Room | **EC1**	20
Smiths/Top Floor | **EC1**	20
☑ Square, The | **W1**	28
NEW St. Alban | **SW1**	21
NEW ☑ Theo Randall | **W1**	26
☑ Tom Aikens | **SW3**	26

NEW Trinity | **SW4**	24
Ubon | **E14**	24
☑ Umu | **W1**	26
Vineyard/Stockcross | **Berks**	24
☑ Waterside Inn | **Berks**	27
☑ Wilton's | **SW1**	24
☑ Wolseley, The | **W1**	21
☑ Zafferano | **SW1**	26
Zaika | **W8**	25
☑ Zuma | **SW7**	26

TEA SERVICE

(See also Hotel Dining)

Armani Caffé | **SW3**	17
☑ Asia de Cuba | **WC2**	22
Aubaine | **W1**	20
Café Rouge | **multi. loc.**	14
Chor Bizarre | **W1**	21
☑ Cipriani | **W1**	20
Court | **WC1**	16
NEW Empress of India | **E9**	–
Fifth Floor Cafe | **SW1**	18
☑ Food for Thought | **WC2**	24
Fortnum's Fountain | **W1**	20
Frontline | **W2**	13
Inn The Park | **SW1**	17
Joe's Rest. Bar | **SW1**	21
Julie's | **W11**	18
La Brasserie | **SW3**	16
Ladurée | **SW1**	23
La Fromagerie | **W1**	24
☑ Momo | **W1**	19
National Dining Rms. | **WC2**	18
Nicole's | **W1**	19
Patisserie Valerie | **multi. loc.**	20
Porters | **WC2**	20
Portrait | **WC2**	22
Richoux | **multi. loc.**	15
Roast | **SE1**	19
Sotheby's Cafe | **W1**	19
NEW Stanza | **W1**	–
St. James's | **W1**	20
Tate Britain | **SW1**	17
Tate Modern | **SE1**	16
Truc Vert | **W1**	22
202 | **W11**	17
NEW ☑ Wallace, The | **W1**	20
☑ Wolseley, The | **W1**	21
☑ Yauatcha | **W1**	25

TRENDY

Admiral Codrington | **SW3**	18
NEW Albion, The | **N1**	–
Alloro | **W1**	22
All Star Lanes | **WC1**	15
☑ Amaya | **SW1**	25
Anchor & Hope | **SE1**	24

Ⓩ River Café | **W6**	27
Roka | **W1**	25
Salt Yard | **W1**	22
San Lorenzo | **SW3**	20
Scott's | **W1**	22
Ⓩ Sketch/Gallery | **W1**	19
Smiths/Dining Room | **EC1**	20
Ⓩ Sophie's Steak | **SW10**	23
Sotheby's Cafe | **W1**	19
NEW St. Alban | **SW1**	21
NEW Stanza | **W1**	-
NEW St. Germain | **EC1**	21
Ⓩ St. John | **EC1**	25
St. John Bread/Wine | **E1**	22
NEW Suka | **W1**	-
NEW Tamarai | **WC2**	-
Tapas Brindisa | **SE1**	22
Taqueria | **W11**	18
Tartine | **SW3**	18
Thomas Cubitt | **SW1**	21
Ⓩ Tom Aikens | **SW3**	26
Tom's Deli | **W11**	16
NEW Tom's Kitchen | **SW3**	19
Tsunami | **SW4**	24
202 | **W11**	17
Ubon | **E14**	24
Vama | **SW10**	24
Vingt-Quatre | **SW10**	15
Ⓩ Wagamama | **multi. loc.**	19
Wapping Food | **E1**	20
Wells, The | **NW3**	18
Ⓩ Wolseley, The | **W1**	21
NEW XO | **NW3**	16
Ⓩ Yauatcha | **W1**	25
YO! Sushi | **multi. loc.**	17
Ⓩ Zafferano | **SW1**	26
Zetter | **EC1**	19
Ziani | **SW3**	25
Zilli Fish | **W1**	20
Ⓩ Zuma | **SW7**	26

VIEWS

Addendum | **EC3**	-
Amici Bar/Kitchen | **SW17**	15
Aquasia | **SW10**	21
Auberge du Lac | **AL8**	23
Babylon | **W8**	20
Belvedere, The | **W8**	20
Blueprint Café | **SE1**	18
NEW Butcher & Grill | **SW11**	15
Butlers Wharf | **SE1**	20
Café Spice Namasté | **E1**	23
Cantina del Ponte | **SE1**	17
Cheyne Walk | **SW3**	23
Cocoon | **W1**	21
Coq d'Argent | **EC2**	18
1802 | **E14**	16

Fakhreldine | **W1**	21
Fifth Floor | **SW1**	20
Ⓩ Foliage | **SW1**	26
French Horn | **Berks**	23
Galvin/Windows | **W1**	22
Ⓩ Gaucho Grill | **E14**	22
Ⓩ Gravetye Manor | **W. Sussex**	24
Greenhouse, The | **W1**	25
Gun, The | **E14**	19
Hartwell House | **HP17**	19
Inn The Park | **SW1**	17
Ⓩ Lanes | **W1**	24
Ⓩ Le Manoir/Quat | **Oxfordshire**	28
Le Pont de la Tour | **SE1**	22
Ⓩ Maze | **W1**	25
NEW Narrow, The | **E14**	-
Ⓩ Nobu Berkeley St | **W1**	26
Ⓩ Nobu London | **W1**	27
Orrery | **W1**	25
Oslo Court | **NW8**	22
Oxo Tower | **SE1**	20
Oxo Tower Brass. | **SE1**	20
Ⓩ Park, The | **SW1**	24
Petersham, The | **TW10**	23
Pizza on the Park | **SW1**	14
Plateau | **E14**	19
Portrait | **WC2**	22
Ransome's Dock | **SW11**	20
Ⓩ Rhodes 24 | **EC2**	23
Ⓩ River Café | **W6**	27
Roast | **SE1**	19
Rocket | **SW15**	17
Ⓩ Royal China | **E14**	24
NEW Skylon | **SE1**	-
Smiths/Top Floor | **EC1**	20
Smollensky's | **E1**	15
Tate Modern | **SE1**	16
Thai Square | **SW15**	19
Tootsies | **SW15**	16
Ubon | **E14**	24
Ⓩ Waterside Inn | **Berks**	27
Waterway, The | **W9**	18
Yakitoria | **W2**	24

VISITORS ON EXPENSE ACCOUNT

Addendum | **EC3**	-
Almeida | **N1**	18
Ⓩ Amaya | **SW1**	25
Arbutus | **W1**	24
Ⓩ Asia de Cuba | **WC2**	22
Auberge du Lac | **AL8**	23
Ⓩ Aubergine | **SW10**	26
Aurora | **EC2**	19
Bank Westminster | **SW1**	18
Belvedere, The | **W8**	20

SPECIAL FEATURES

NEW Trinity | SW4	24
Ubon | E14	24
Z Umu | W1	26
NEW Via Condotti | W1	18
Vineyard/Stockcross | Berks	24
Z Waterside Inn | Berks	27
Z Wilton's | SW1	24
Z Zafferano | SW1	26
Zaika | W8	25
Zen Central | W1	21
Z Zuma | SW7	26

WINNING WINE LISTS

Andrew Edmunds | W1	22
Auberge du Lac | AL8	23
Z Aubergine | SW10	26
Aurora | EC2	19
Belvedere, The | W8	20
Z Bibendum | SW3	24
Bleeding Heart | EC1	22
Boisdale | multi. loc.	20
Brown's/The Grill | W1	22
Cantina Vinopolis | SE1	19
Z Capital Rest. | SW3	27
Caravaggio | EC3	19
Cellar Gascon | EC1	20
Z Chez Bruce | SW17	28
Christopher's | WC2	19
Chutney Mary | SW10	23
Z Cinnamon Club | SW1	24
Z Cipriani | W1	20
Z Clarke's | W8	25
Z Cliveden House | Berks	24
Z Club Gascon | EC1	26
Coq d'Argent | EC2	18
Cru | N1	15
Z Dorchester/The Grill | W1	24
Drones | SW1	18
Ebury Wine Bar | SW1	19
ECapital | W1	22
1880 | SW7	21
Embassy | W1	13
Z Enoteca Turi | SW15	27
Z Fat Duck | Berks	27
Fifteen | N1	23
Fifth Floor | SW1	20
Z Fino | W1	23
Z Foliage | SW1	26
NEW Forge, The | WC2	-
Glasshouse, The | TW9	24
Z Gordon Ramsay/Claridge's | W1	25
Z Gordon Ramsay/68 Royal | SW3	28
Z Gravetye Manor | W. Sussex	24
Greenhouse, The | W1	25

Greyhound, The | SW11	19
Z Hakkasan | W1	24
Il Convivio | SW1	23
Z Lanes | W1	24
Z Lanesborough | SW1	21
Langan's Bistro | W1	19
La Noisette | SW1	21
Latium | W1	25
Z La Trompette | W4	27
Le Cercle | SW1	24
Ledbury | W11	25
Z Le Gavroche | W1	27
Z Le Manoir/Quat | Oxfordshire	28
Le Pont de la Tour | SE1	22
L'Escargot | W1	22
Z L'Etranger | SW7	24
L'Incontro | W1	20
Z Locanda Locatelli | W1	25
L'Oranger | SW1	24
NEW Magdalen | SE1	-
Z Maze | W1	25
Mirabelle | W1	22
Mju | SW1	20
Z Morgan M | N7	27
Z Nahm | SW1	26
Odette's | NW1	20
1 Lombard St. | EC3	22
Orrery | W1	25
NEW Papillon | SW3	23
Z Pétrus | SW1	28
Z Pied à Terre | W1	28
Plateau | E14	19
Prism | EC3	18
Ransome's Dock | SW11	20
Refettorio | EC4	20
Z Rib Rm. | SW1	24
Richard Corrigan | W1	23
Z Ritz, The | W1	23
R.S.J. | SE1	21
Sartoria | W1	20
Z Savoy Grill | WC2	24
Z Sketch/Lecture Rm. | W1	21
Sotheby's Cafe | W1	19
Z Square, The | W1	28
Tate Britain | SW1	17
NEW Z Theo Randall | W1	26
Z Tom Aikens | SW3	26
Z Umu | W1	26
Vineyard/Stockcross | Berks	24
Vivat Bacchus | EC4	23
Z Waterside Inn | Berks	27
Z Wilton's | SW1	24
Z Zafferano | SW1	26
Z Zuma | SW7	26

SPECIAL FEATURES

Wine Vintage Chart

This chart, based on our 0 to 30 scale, is designed to help you select wine. The ratings (by **Howard Stravitz,** a law professor at the University of South Carolina) reflect the vintage quality and the wine's readiness to drink. We exclude the 1987, 1991–1993 vintages because they are not that good. A dash indicates the wine is either past its peak or too young to rate.

Whites	86	88	89	90	94	95	96	97	98	99	00	01	02	03	04	05
French:																
Alsace	-	-	26	26	25	24	24	23	26	24	26	27	25	22	24	25
Burgundy	25	-	23	22	-	28	27	24	23	26	25	24	27	23	25	26
Loire Valley	-	-	-	-	-	-	-	-	-	-	24	25	26	23	24	25
Champagne	25	24	26	29	-	26	27	24	23	24	24	22	26	-	-	-
Sauternes	28	29	25	28	-	21	23	25	23	24	24	28	25	26	21	26
California:																
Chardonnay	-	-	-	-	-	-	-	-	-	24	23	26	26	27	28	29
Sauvignon Blanc	-	-	-	-	-	-	-	-	-	-	27	28	26	27	26	
Austrian:																
Grüner Velt./Riesling	-	-	-	-	-	25	21	28	28	27	22	23	24	26	26	26
German:	-	25	26	27	24	23	26	25	26	23	21	29	27	25	26	26

Reds	86	88	89	90	94	95	96	97	98	99	00	01	02	03	04	05
French:																
Bordeaux	25	23	25	29	22	26	25	23	25	24	29	26	24	25	23	27
Burgundy	-	-	24	26	-	26	27	26	22	27	22	24	27	24	24	25
Rhône	-	26	28	28	24	26	22	24	27	26	27	26	-	25	24	-
Beaujolais	-	-	-	-	-	-	-	-	-	-	24	-	23	27	23	28
California:																
Cab./Merlot	-	-	-	28	29	27	25	28	23	26	22	27	26	25	24	24
Pinot Noir	-	-	-	-	-	-	-	24	23	24	23	27	28	26	23	-
Zinfandel	-	-	-	-	-	-	-	-	-	-	25	23	27	22	-	
Oregon:																
Pinot Noir	-	-	-	-	-	-	-	-	-	-	-	26	27	24	25	-
Italian:																
Tuscany	-	-	-	25	22	24	20	29	24	27	24	26	20	-	-	-
Piedmont	-	-	27	27	-	23	26	27	26	25	28	27	20	-	-	-
Spanish:																
Rioja	-	-	-	-	26	26	24	25	22	25	24	27	20	24	25	-
Ribera del Duero/Priorat	-	-	-	-	26	26	27	25	24	25	24	27	20	24	26	-
Australian:																
Shiraz/Cab.	-	-	-	-	24	26	23	26	28	24	24	27	27	25	26	-

ON THE GO.
IN THE KNOW.

ZAGAT TO GO℠

Unlimited access
to Zagat dining &
travel content
in 65 major cities.

Search and browse
by ratings, cuisines,
special features
and Top Lists.

For BlackBerry,® Palm,®
Windows Mobile®
and mobile phones.

Get it now at **mobile.zagat.com**
or text* **ZAGAT** to **78247**